W9-CAM-895

"If your idea of a vacation includes avoiding large cities and bumper-to-bumper traffic, pick up a copy of *Hidden Oregon*."

—*The Nashville Tennessean*

"This is a book with some things to offer both visitors and permanent Oregonians. It lists quite a few attractions you might not otherwise find out about."

—*The Oregon Statesman Journal*

HIDDEN® Oregon

Including Portland, the Coast, Cascades and Columbia River Gorge

Maria Lenhart

SIXTH EDITION

Ulysses Press®
BERKELEY, CALIFORNIA

Copyright © 1995, 1997, 1999, 2001, 2003, 2005 Ulysses Press. All rights reserved, including the right to reproduce this book or portions thereof in any form whatsoever, except for use by a reviewer in connection with a review.

Published by:
Ulysses Press
P.O. Box 3440
Berkeley, CA 94703
www.ulyssespress.com

ISSN 1524-1300
ISBN 1-56975-496-9

Printed in Canada by Transcontinental Printing

10 9

Managing Editor: Claire Chun
Copy Editors: Steven Zah Schwartz, Lily Chou
Editorial Associates: Kate Allen, Leona Benten, Laura Brancella Amy Hough, Alice Riegert, Barbara Schultz
Typesetters: Lisa Kester, Tamara Kowalski, Matt Orendorff
Cartography: Pease Press
Cover Design: Sarah Levin, Leslie Henriques
Indexer: Sayre Van Young
Cover Photography: John Wang/gettyimages.com (Japanese Garden Society of Oregon, Portland)
Illustrator: Mittie Cuetara

Distributed by Publishers Group West

Hidden is a federally registered trademark of BookPack, Inc.

Ulysses Press is a federally registered trademark of BookPack, Inc.

The author and publisher have made every effort to ensure the accuracy of information contained in *Hidden Oregon*, but can accept no liability for any loss, injury or inconvenience sustained by any traveler as a result of information or advice contained in this guide.

Write to us!

If in your travels you discover a spot that captures the spirit of Oregon, or if you live in the region and have a favorite place to share, or if you just feel like expressing your views, write to us and we'll pass your note along to the author.

We can't guarantee that the author will add your personal find to the next edition, but if the writer does use the suggestion, we'll acknowledge you in the credits and send you a free copy of the new edition.

ULYSSES PRESS
3286 Adeline Street, Suite 1
Berkeley, CA 94703
E-mail: readermail@ulyssespress.com

What's Hidden?

At different points throughout this book, you'll find special listings marked with this symbol:

◄ HIDDEN

This means that you have come upon a place off the beaten tourist track, a spot that will carry you a step closer to the local people and natural environment of Oregon.

The goal of this guide is to lead you beyond the realm of everyday tourist facilities. While we include traditional sightseeing listings and popular attractions, we also offer alternative sights and adventure activities. Instead of filling this guide with reviews of standard hotels and chain restaurants, we concentrate on one-of-a-kind places and locally owned establishments.

Our authors seek out locales that are popular with residents but usually overlooked by visitors. Some are more hidden than others (and are marked accordingly), but all the listings in this book are intended to help you discover the true nature of Oregon and put you on the path of adventure.

Contents

Maps

OUTDOOR ADVENTURE SYMBOLS

The following symbols accompany national, state and regional park listings, as well as beach descriptions throughout the text.

- Camping
- Hiking
- Biking
- Horseback Riding
- Downhill Skiing
- Cross-country Skiing
- Swimming
- Snorkeling or Scuba Diving
- Surfing
- Waterskiing
- Windsurfing
- Canoeing or Kayaking
- Boating
- Boat Ramps
- Fishing

ONE

Oregon Wandering

With its abundance of natural riches, Oregon has long been a magnet for explorers, fortune seekers and those simply desiring a saner way of life. Nicknamed "The Beaver State," Oregon first attracted white settlers with its bountiful population of furry, dam-building creatures dwelling in rivers and lakes throughout the state. Later, the fur trade gave way to such enticements as timber, gold and fertile farmland.

Today, Oregon's natural resources remain a powerful draw for visitors who, fortunately, more often come to sightsee and relax than to exploit. Bordered by California and Nevada to the south, Washington to the north and Idaho to the east, Oregon is in many ways a microcosm of the grand scenic diversity the West is known for. Within its borders can be found redwood forests, volcanic craters, marine tidepools, river gorges, fossil beds, snow-capped mountains, sagebrush desert and fern-carpeted forests. Here, too, are pleasures of a more civilized sort: nationally renowned theater, innovative museums, performing-arts festivals, American Indian cultural centers and restored historic monuments honoring the proud and fiercely independent pioneer spirit that is still alive and well in Oregon today.

The heavy rainfall for which Oregon is famous helps keep its vegetation lush. The drizzle and clouds that blanket the coastal region during much of the winter and spring nourish the incredibly green landscape that grows thick and fast and softens the sharp edges of alpine peaks and jagged sea cliffs. But there's a flip side: over half the state (meaning points east of the Cascade Range) is actually warm and dry throughout much of the year.

Much of Oregon—particularly in the eastern region—remains undeveloped, and there are vast expanses of wilderness close to all metropolitan centers. Almost without exception, each of its cities is surrounded by countless recreational opportunities, with mountains, lakes, streams and an ocean within easy reach. It's no surprise that residents and visitors tend to have a hardy, outdoorsy glow. After all, it is the proximity to nature that draws people here.

Hidden Oregon will help you explore this wonderful area, tell of its history, introduce you to its flora and fauna. Besides taking you to countless popular spots, it will lead you to off-the-beaten-path locales. Each chapter will suggest places to eat, to stay, to sightsee, to shop and to enjoy the outdoors and nightlife, covering a range of tastes and budgets.

The book begins in Portland, Oregon's thriving cultural and metropolitan center. From there it's a short trip east to the Columbia River Gorge, subject of Chapter Three. Next we go on one of the nation's most scenic drives along the Oregon Coast in Chapter Four and on to the cultural, learning and political centers lining the Heart of Oregon in Chapter Five. Mt. Hood, Mt. Bachelor, Crater Lake and the other majestic peaks of the Oregon Cascades are covered in Chapter Six. The arid, sparsely populated plateau and desert region of Eastern Oregon is in Chapter Seven.

What you choose to see and do is up to you, but don't delay; things are changing here. Oregon is no longer the quiet backwater of a decade ago. Growth and expansion continue in the major population centers strung along the long, black ribbon of Route 5. While many Oregonians are vociferous advocates for preserving nature, rapidly increasing population and growing economic demands are taking a toll.

Sadly, it's becoming difficult to miss the horrid clear-cut swaths through the evergreen background, evidence of the logging industry that feeds the local economies. Salmon that once choked the many streams and rivers have dwindled in number, as have numerous forest creatures such as the spotted owl.

Tourism has also had an impact. As the beauty of the area has been "discovered" by travelers who've taken home tales of this don't-spread-it-around secret vacationland, it's become a hot destination, especially among international visitors. It's getting harder and harder to find those special hidden spots—go soon before "hidden" no longer applies.

The Oregon Story

GEOLOGY

In terms of geology, the Pacific Northwest is a relatively young land mass formed at the junction of the Juan de Fuca and North American plates. About 200 million years ago, the Klamath-Siskiyou Mountains in southwestern Oregon were created during the Triassic uplift. These mountains, grouped perpendicularly to the Coast Range rising up from California, are rugged and considered tall for a range near the Pacific; Mt. Ashland rises over 7500 feet.

The Cascade Range, which includes such Oregon peaks as Mt. Hood and Mt. Jefferson, began to rise only 20 million years ago, about the time of the massive Columbia lava flow, second-largest in the world, that formed the Columbia Plateau spreading across Oregon and Washington. Volcanic eruptions reached a peak about two million years ago with the formation of the Northwest's long chain of "fire mountains" that are part of the Pacific Rim Ring of Fire. Copious precipitation on the western side of the range has eroded many of the mountains and formed lovely streams and river basins to provide water runoff. The eastern flank faces Oregon's high desert, and maintains much more of a dry volcanic look.

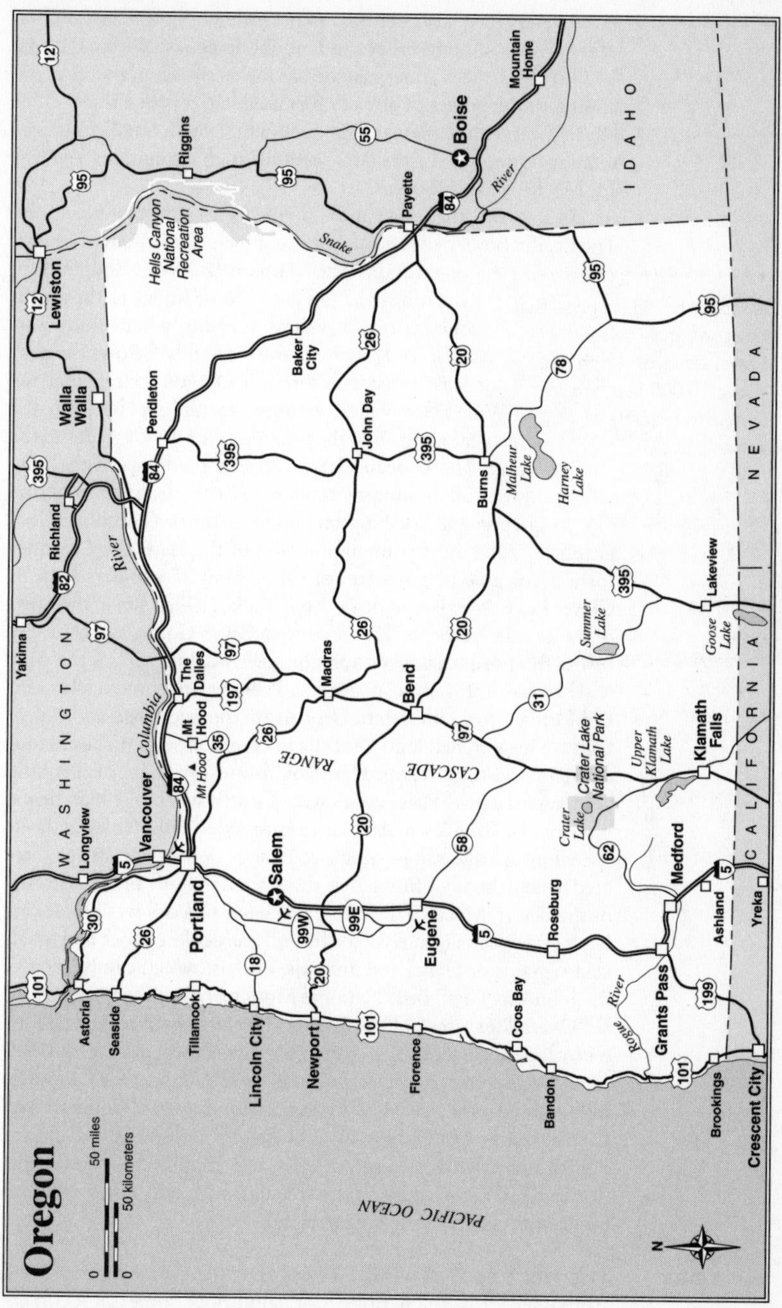

Oregon
0
50 miles
0
50 kilometers
PACIFIC OCEAN
N
WASHINGTON
IDAHO
NEVADA
CALIFORNIA
Yakima
Richland
Walla Walla
Lewiston
Riggins
Hells Canyon National Recreation Area
Snake
River
Payette
Boise
Mountain Home
Longview
Vancouver
Columbia
River
The Dalles
Mt Hood
Portland
Salem
Pendleton
Baker City
John Day
Madras
Bend
CASCADE
RANGE
Burns
Malheur Lake
Harney Lake
Summer Lake
Goose Lake
Lakeview
Crater Lake National Park
Crater Lake
Upper Klamath Lake
Klamath Falls
Eugene
Roseburg
Medford
Ashland
Yreka
Grants Pass
Rogue
River
Astoria
Seaside
Tillamook
Lincoln City
Newport
Florence
Coos Bay
Bandon
Brookings
Crescent City

Glaciers have also played a major role within the last million years or so, sculpting valleys and mountain peaks. Within the past 10,000 years, the warmer climate has melted much of the ice mass, adding to the power of already formidable rivers like the Columbia that carved the plateau and continental shelf. Smaller glaciers remain, especially in the area around high mountains such as 11,235-foot Mt. Hood.

As a whole, the area can be divided into four distinct zones. The Pacific Border zone along the coast includes a chain of coastal mountains (the Klamath-Siskiyou Mountains in the south and Oregon's Coast Range to the north) and a series of valleys forming what's known as the Great Trough. Route 5 roughly follows the path of least resistance through Oregon, paralleling the Willamette Valley, a moist, fertile gap between the coastal ranges and the behemoths of the Cascades to the east. The Cascade Sierra zone is made up of the long range of mountains stretching from California across Oregon and Washington and into British Columbia. Geographically the most stunning portion of the state, the Cascades form a volcanic phalanx full of topographical wonders such as Crater Lake, North America's deepest lake, which sits in the bowl of a one-time volcano. The Columbia River Gorge, which today forms the border between Oregon and Washington, is the only wide break in this imposing range. Pushing up from Nevada and California into southeastern Oregon are the arid Basin and Range zones. This parched land has little in common with the lush landscape of coastal Oregon. Here you'll find dry sagebrush rolling across hard earth. These zones were formed where the high desert west of the Rockies meets the eastern side of the volatile, lava-spewing Cascade range. Small volcanoes dot the landscape, created when the lava flows met the irregular fault-block patterns of the desert. Much of the area has the feel of a dry western desert, but it is occasionally interrupted by brilliantly colored rock and fossilized remains of plants and animals, both of which can be seen at the John Day Fossil Beds National Monument (see Chapter Seven).

It should be no surprise that Oregon's truly awesome peaks, some of which rise above 10,000 feet, are comprised mostly of volcanic rock.

Overall features of Oregon that travelers are likely to encounter include spectacular sea cliffs, a narrow coastal plain with small estuaries and bays, and a major range of mountains, the Cascades, miles inland as is typical of a young coastal region. Compared to the coastlines of Washington and British Columbia, which are highly varied with strong currents and headlands, islands and fjords, the Oregon coast is fairly regular, with only a few offshore monoliths cut from the jagged cliffs.

HISTORY

THE FIRST PEOPLE It is believed that the first migrants came from Asia across the Bering Strait land bridge some 25,000 years ago. From the diverse background of those earliest inhabitants descended the many American Indian tribes that populated the North American continent. Kwakiutl, Haida, Bella Coola, Tlingit, Salish, Yakima, Nez Perce, Paiutes, Shoshone, Umpqua and Rogue are but a few of the Northwest tribes.

The verdant land both provided for and dictated the lifestyles of the various tribes. Those that lived inland east of the mountain ranges were forced to live nomadic lifestyles, depending primarily on foraging and hunting game for survival, moving along as the climate and animal migrations demanded. They generally lived in caves during hunting migration and constructed large pit houses for winter camp.

The mild climate and abundant resources of the valley and coast led to a fairly sedentary life for the tribes that lived west of the mountain ranges. They constructed permanent villages of longhouses from the readily available wood, fished the rich waters of the coast, foraged in lush forests and had enough free time to develop ritualized arts, ceremonies and other cultural pursuits along with an elaborate social structure. The potlatch, a complex ceremony of gaining honor by giving away lavish gifts to the point of bankruptcy, is one of the more renowned ritualized traditions of the Northwest tribes.

Arrival of the white man brought many changes to the generally peaceful natives. Introduction of the horse made life easier for a period, facilitating hunting and travel for the nomadic tribes. However, disease, drugs (namely alcohol) and distrust accompanied the newcomers and eventually added to the decline of the Indian population. Land grabbing by European settlers forced the tribes onto ever-shrinking reservations.

EARLY EXPLORATION While 16th-century explorers such as Spain's Juan Cabrillo and England's Sir Francis Drake are believed to have sailed their ships at least partway up the Oregon coast, real exploration of the area did not begin until the late 1700s, when the search began for the mythical Northwest Passage, a supposed trade route connecting the Atlantic and Pacific oceans. Seafarers such as Captain James Cook, who went on to discover Hawaii, were among those who scoured the Oregon coast in vain for the elusive passage.

Most early European settlement in Oregon was prompted by the region's rich supply of otter and beaver pelts, drawing such enterprises as John Jacob Astor's Pacific Fur Company, which founded a settlement called Astoria at the mouth of the Columbia River. England's Hudson Bay Company established several outposts in Oregon as well, prompting a struggle for supremacy in the region between British and Americans that was not fully resolved until the U.S. government mandated the creation of the Oregon Territory in 1848 and began closely regulating the land.

Helping secure an American foothold in Oregon was the famous Lewis and Clark expedition dispatched by Thomas Jefferson in 1804 to map and explore the vast lands of the Louisiana Purchase and beyond. Meriwether Lewis and William Clark, aided by Sacajawea, a 15-year old Shoshone girl, eventually arrived in Oregon, making their way through mountain passes before sailing in canoes down the Columbia River to the Pacific Ocean.

SETTLEMENT AND STATEHOOD In the 1830s, Methodist missionaries created settlements along the Columbia River, sometimes facing violent clashes with the local American Indian tribes. But the real onslaught of settlement came a decade later when the U.S. government established the Organic Act, which granted 640 free acres of Oregon land to any white male who could make the trip to claim them. Well over 50,000 pioneers made the tortuous journey west from Missouri over the 2000-mile-long Oregon Trail, traversing endless plains, pulling wagons up mountain slopes and then piling their animals and possessions onto rafts heading down the Columbia River.

The advent of the California Gold Rush in 1849 proved a boon for the new Oregon Territory, creating a market for lumber, wheat and other goods required by a booming population too infused with gold fever to meet its own essential needs. In 1859, partly as a political move to add another nonslave state to the Union, Oregon was made the nation's 33rd state.

With natural resources in abundance, Oregon's economy grew by leaps and bounds in the late 19th century. Vast cattle ranches and wheat farms covered eastern Oregon, while railroad and lumber barons combined forces to make fortunes from the state's virgin forests. Portland, with its strategic location on the Willamette and Columbia waterways, quickly emerged as the state's major city and an international shipping hub.

INTO THE 21ST CENTURY In the early years of the century, Oregon's economy continued to boom due to its own natural resources—with wheat, timber and salmon in seemingly endless supply. The state prospered even during the Great Depression when enormous public-works projects such as the Bonneville Dam supplied thousands of jobs and tapped natural resources even further. During World War II, Portland became an important center for shipbuilding.

In today's era of environmental regulations, Oregon has been forced to reexamine its reliance on natural resources. While timber and agriculture are still the state's leading moneymakers, tourism and high-tech industries continue to grow in importance. Corporations like Nike, Teletronix and Intel now rival timber-based Weyerhaeuser and Georgia-Pacific. And even agriculture has taken a different turn, increasingly characterized by organic and specialty products such as fine wines, gourmet cheeses and designer produce. "Made in Oregon" products from marionberry jam to handcrafted furniture can be found in stores throughout the state.

The state motto—"She Flies With Her Own Wings"—has proved to be an apt one for Oregon, which has a reputation as a maverick state on political and social issues. Despite its economic dependence on the land, Oregon was one of the first states to pass measures such as bottle recycling. Oregon was also an early proponent of such once-radical ideas as women's suffrage and compulsory education.

Land use, especially the protection of rural areas, remains one of the most important issues to many Oregonians. The state fears sprawl—the glut of subdivisions and malls that has devoured the outskirts of many cities in neighboring California and Washington—and has taken steps to keep rural land protected. Each of Oregon's 241 cities is hemmed by an "urban growth boundary," a zone beyond which land cannot be developed. The boundary takes into account the estimated growth of a community, but ensures that development stays close to a city's core area. Many residents agree that the statewide regulations have kept the cities thriving and the rural areas peaceful. A perfect example is how Portland's sleek downtown is a mere 30 minutes from the awesome, untouched Columbia River Gorge. Oregonians wouldn't have it any other way.

Oregon has a number of American Indian–owned and –operated resorts such as Ka-Nee-Ta, a hot spring and golf retreat in central Oregon.

Resurgence in American Indian arts and crafts is evident in galleries and museums throughout the region. While most natives no longer live on the reservations but have integrated into white society, many have banded together to fight for change. Tribal organizations are now reclaiming lands and fishing rights.

While tourism continues to grow in importance to Oregon, many in the state cast a wary eye on outsiders, particularly urban refugees from California who come in search of lower housing costs and elbow room. "Don't Californicate Oregon" was a frequently sighted bumper sticker during the 1980s. Now the attitude is clearly "Come for a visit, just don't move here." Still, Oregon is a largely hospitable state for travelers and offers such innovations as roadside "Welcome Centers" offering tourist information and coffee to the road-weary. And, once acquainted with Oregon's natural, relatively unspoiled beauty, most visitors can't blame Oregonians for wanting to keep things just the way they are.

FLORA

While it's generally the coniferous and myrtlewood trees that everyone equates with Oregon, there is much more to the flora of the region than its abundance of Douglas fir, Western hemlock and white pine, red cedar and other evergreens. Each of the distinct geologic zones hosts its own particular ecosystem.

In the moist woodlands of the coastline, glossy madrone and immense Coast redwoods tower over Pacific trilliums and delicate lady's slippers. Bogs full of skunk cabbage thrive alongside fields of yellow Scotch broom and hardy rhododendrons in a riot of color.

In the lowland valleys, alders, oaks, maples and other deciduous trees provide brilliant displays of color against an evergreen backdrop each spring and fall. Wild berry bushes run rampant in this clime, bringing blackberries, huckleberries, currants and strawberries for the picking. Indian paintbrush, columbines, foxglove, buttercups and numerous other wildflowers are also abundant.

The lush parks and forests of the mountain chains contain some of the biggest trees in the world, holding records in height and circumference, with fir, pine, hemlock and cedar generally topping the charts. Thick groves filter the sunlight, providing the perfect environment for mushrooms, lichens, ferns and mosses. The elegant tiger lily, beargrass, asters, fawnlily, phlox, columbine, valerian and a breathtaking array of alpine wildflowers thrive in high meadows and on sunny slopes.

With the dramatic decrease in rainfall in the plateau and desert zones comes a paralleling drop in the amount of plantlife, though it is still rich in pine, juniper, cottonwood and sagebrush. Flowers of the area include wild iris, foxglove, camas, balsam root and pearly everlasting.

FAUNA

It was actually the proliferation of wildlife that brought about white colonization of Oregon, beginning with the trappers who came in droves in search of fur. It turns out that beaver and otter pelts were highly valued in China during the 1800s, so these creatures were heavily hunted. Nearly decimated colonies, now protected by law, are coming back strong. Playful otters are often spotted floating tummy up in coastal waters, while the shy beaver is harder to spot, living in secluded mountain retreats and coming out to feed at night.

Fish, especially salmon, were also a major factor in the economic development of the region, and remain so to this day, though numbers of spawning salmon are dropping drastically. Nonetheless, fishing fanatics are still drawn here in search of the five varieties of Pacific salmon along with flounder, lingcod, rockfish, trout, bass and many other varieties of sportfish. Those who don't fish will still be fascinated by the seasonal spawning frenzy of salmon, easily observed at fish ladders in the Columbia River region.

Among the more readily recognized creatures that reside in Oregon are the orca (killer whales), porpoises, dolphins, seals and sea lions often spotted cavorting in the waters just offshore. Twice-yearly migrations of gray whales on the trip between Alaska and

California are much anticipated all along the coastline. Minke whales are more numerous, as are Dall's porpoises, often mistaken for baby orca because of their similar coloration and markings.

Of the varieties of bear living in Oregon's remote forests, black bear are the most common. Weighing upwards of 300 pounds and reaching six feet tall, they usually feed on berries, nuts and fish and avoid humans unless provoked by offers of food or danger to a cub. Grizzly and brown bear are more prevalent farther north. Big-game herds of deer, elk, antelope along with moose, cougar and mountain goats range the more remote mountainous areas. Scavengers such as chipmunks, squirrels, raccoons, opossums and skunks are abundant as well.

Watch for the Pacific giant salamander in fallen, rotting logs: it is the largest of its kind in the world, growing up to a foot in length and capable of eating small mice.

Over 300 species of birds live in the Pacific Northwest for at least a portion of the year. Easily accessible mud flats and estuaries throughout the region provide refuge for tufted puffins, egrets, cormorants, loons and other migratory waterfowl making their way along the Pacific Flyway. Hundreds of pairs of bald eagles winter along the Oregon coast, along with great blue herons and cormorants. You might also see red-tailed hawks and spotted owls if you venture quietly into the region's old-growth zones.

On a smaller scale is the slimy slug that thrives in the moist climate. Not quite large enough to be mistaken for a speed bump, they leave telltale viscous trails. While the slug is the bane of gardeners, it is still regarded as a sort of mascot for the region; souvenir shops stock plush toy replicas and gag cans of slug soup.

Where to Go

The number of tourists visiting Oregon continues to grow as the secrets of its beauty and sunny summer and fall weather get out. The landscape is widely varied, and each of the six geographic areas of the state has its own appeal. We start in Oregon's populous metropolis, detour through the spectacular river gorge beside it, and then follow an eastward progression from the Pacific to the Snake, in the process crossing the verdant Willamette Valley, scaling the mammoth face of the Cascades and retracing the pioneers' path across Eastern Oregon.

Bounded by an evergreen forest, productive greenbelt and the mighty Columbia River, **Portland** remains as close to nature as a growing metropolis can be. Portland, the "City of Roses," reflects a pleasant mix of historic buildings decorated in glazed terra cotta and modern structures combining smoked glass and brushed steel. These buildings lie in the downtown core, an area intersected by the Willamette River and numerous parks. With the most culturally diverse population found in the state, Portland is very much a city on the Pacific Rim, a vital product of both Asian and European influences.

From Portland, it's an easy drive to the **Columbia River Gorge,** which dramatically defines the Oregon–Washington border with towering cliffs and cascading waterfalls. The heritage of the region can be enjoyably discovered in such places as Fort Vancouver, The Dalles, Hood River and the Columbia Gorge Interpretive Center in Stevenson.

The awe-inspiring beauty of the **Oregon Coast** includes 400 miles of rugged coastline dotted by small, artsy communities such as Yachats and Bandon and larger fishing villages like Astoria, Newport and Coos Bay, all connected by Route 101, one of the most beautiful drives in the nation. Foresight on the part of the state legislature preserved the coast from crass commercial corruption, so great stretches remain untouched and entirely natural.

Cradled between the Coastal and Cascade mountain ranges is the **Heart of Oregon,** a pastoral valley of historic stage stops, gold-mining boomtowns and small farming communities. Sheep-covered meadows, cloud-shrouded bluffs and striped pastures line Route 5, the primary artery traversing the valley. Salem (the state capital), Eugene (home of the University of Oregon) and Ashland (site of the celebrated Shakespeare Festival) are included in this section.

The **Oregon Cascades** hold a bevy of treasures including world-famous rivers like the Rogue and the Umpqua (fishing haunt of Zane Grey), the Mt. Hood and Mt. Bachelor ski resorts and the sapphire splendor of Crater Lake, the country's deepest lake. This is a region of national forests and wildernesses.

Eastern Oregon, encompassing over half the state, is a world in itself. This is cowboy country, reflected by a high-desert landscape, vast ranches and such annual events as the Pendleton

SO, WHO GIVES A HOOT?

The spotted owl has been the center of controversy in recent years, the focus of the recurring nature-versus-commerce debate. As logging companies cut deeper into the old-growth forests, which have taken 150 years or more to grow, the habitat for this endangered owl—only about 700 pairs survive in Washington today—grows smaller. (These nocturnal birds need thousands of acres per pair to support their indulgent eating habits.) The old-growth forests of the Pacific Northwest provide adequate nesting spots in the protected snags and broken branches of tall trees that shelter their flightless young. Some environmentalists predict the owl's impending extinction if logging continues at its present rate.

Roundup, a pioneer celebration and rodeo. But it also offers such diversity as the alpine wilderness of the Wallowa Mountains, the geologic wonders of the John Day Fossil Beds and the surging whitewater of Hells Canyon and the Owyhee River.

When to Go

SEASONS

Oregon isn't the rain-soaked, snow-covered tundra many imagine it to be. Summer and fall days (June–September) are generally warm, dry and sunny. Overall temperatures range from the mid-30s in winter to the upper 80s in summer, except in Eastern Oregon, where summer temperatures average in the mid-90s. There are distinct seasons in each of the primary zones, and the climate varies greatly with local topography.

The enormous mountain ranges play a major role in the weather, protecting most areas from the heavy rains generated over the Pacific and dumped on the coastline. Mountaintops are often covered in snow year-round at higher elevations, while the valleys, home to most of the cities, remain snow-free but wet during the winter months. East of the mountain ranges are temperature extremes and a distinct lack of rain. Travelers spend time at the rivers, lakes and streams during the hot, dry summers and frolic in the snow during the winter.

The mountainous zones are a bit rainy in spring but warm and dry during the summer, when crowds file in for camping, hiking and other outdoor delights. Fall brings auto traffic attracted by the changing seasonal colors, while winter means snow at higher elevations, providing the perfect playground for cold-weather sports.

The coastal region is generally soggy and overcast during the mild winter and early spring, making this the low season for tourism. However, winter is high season among Northwesterners drawn to the coast to watch the fantastic storms that blow in across the Pacific. Summer is typically warm and dry in the coastal valleys and along the crisp, windy coast, making it the prime season for travelers. And visitors *do* show up in droves, clogging smaller highways with recreational vehicles.

CALENDAR OF EVENTS

Festivals and events are a big part of life in Oregon, especially when the rains disappear and everyone is ready to spend time outdoors enjoying the sunshine. Below is a sampling of some of the biggest attractions. Check with local chambers of commerce (listed in the regional chapters of this book) to see what will be going on when you are in the area.

JANUARY

Portland The Northwest Film Center at the Portland Art Museum celebrates music from film classics with screenings and live performances during the **Reel Music** festival.

Eastern Oregon Ice sculptures, sled-dog racing, ski competitions and snowmobiling events are among the winter enchantments at the **Hells Canyon Sno Fest** in Halfway.

FEBRUARY

Portland The **Portland International Film Festival** presents new films from around the world at the Portland Art Museum's Northwest Film Center.

Coast **The Oregon Dixieland Jubilee** presents a weekend of musical performances in Seaside. The **Seafood and Wine Fest** in Newport, the oldest and largest wine festival in the Northwest, promises plenty of seafood and wine. Munch crustaceans to your heart's content at the annual **Crab Feed** in Charleston.

MARCH

Portland Collectors flock to the Portland Expo Center for **America's Largest Antique & Collectible Show,** where over seven acres of goods are on display.

Coast Events in Lincoln City and all along the coast celebrate the northward migration of gray whales during **Spring Whale Watch Week.**

Cascades Alpine and nordic ski competitions highlight the **Annual Winter Games of Oregon** at Mount Hood Ski Bowl.

Eastern Oregon The **Walleye Spring Classic** draws participants from around the region for a major fishing tournament on the Columbia River near Irrigon.

APRIL

Columbia River Gorge Delicate pink-and-white apple blossoms of the area orchards steal the show during the **Hood River Blossom Festival.**

Coast The **Great Astoria Crab & Seafood Festival** features food, winetasting, arts and crafts and live entertainment.

Heart of Oregon Downtown Medford is the scene of a street fair with arts and crafts, food and entertainment, as well as a parade and footrace during the **Pear Blossom Parade and Run.**

Eastern Oregon Birding, historical tours, arts-and-crafts exhibits and Western barbecue highlight the **John Scharff Migratory Bird Festival** in Burns.

MAY

Portland The **Cinco de Mayo Festival** celebrates Portland's sister-city relationship with Guadalajara and features Mexican foods, dancing, arts and crafts and entertainment.

Columbia River Gorge Cowboys from all over the country demonstrate their roping and riding skills at the **Salem Rodeo.**

Coast When rhododendrons burst into bloom, Florence celebrates with its **Rhododendron Festival,** which includes a floral parade, carnival and arts-and-crafts fair. During the **Wild Rivers Coast Seafood, Art and Wine Festival** in Gold Beach, you can sample a glass of Oregon wine or join a 10k run that includes a jet boat ride.

Heart of Oregon A hydroplane boat race, waterskiing show, parade and skydiving competition are part of the fun at **Boatnik** in Grants Pass.

Eastern Oregon Actors portraying cowboys, dancehall girls and other colorful characters from Pendleton's early days provide lively entertainment during **Pendleton Underground Comes to Life.**

JUNE

Portland Portland's biggest festival of the year, the **Rose Festival** is a month-long celebration with parties, pageants and a "Grand Floral Parade" second only to California's Rose Parade.

Columbia River Gorge **Fort Vancouver Days**, a citywide celebration with rodeo, chili cook-off and jazz concert takes place in Vancouver, Washington. **Sternwheeler Days** marks the return of the sternwheeler *Columbia Gorge* to Cascade Locks for the summer season with wine- and cheese-tasting, a salmon barbecue, street dance and run.

Coast The **Spring Kite Festival** takes off in Lincoln City, the "Kite Capital of the World." Participants from around the globe come to create a world of perishable marvels at the **Cannon Beach Sandcastle Contest**, ranked one of the top competitions in the world. The **Astoria Scandinavian Festival** celebrates the area's heritage.

Heart of Oregon The region celebrates the harvest with annual **Strawberry Festivals** throughout June, including one in Lebanon in which all the bakers in town turn out to build an enormous strawberry shortcake. Outstanding jazz, bluegrass and gospel, as well as classical concerts, mark the month-long **Oregon Bach Festival** at the University of Oregon in Eugene. A similarly outstanding event is the **Peter Britt Music Festival** near Medford, which features an array of music, dance and theatrical performances and runs through early September.

Cascades The High Cascades play host to the **Sisters Rodeo** in Sisters.

Eastern Oregon Fiddlers, banjo players and other musicians from around the region converge in Burns for the **Old Time Country Music Jamboree.**

JULY

Portland Featuring food, entertainment and more than 130 beers, the **Oregon Brewers' Festival** is the largest gathering of independent brewers in North America. Major recording stars and local talent takes the stage at the **Waterfront Blues Festival.** The **Robin Hood Festival** in Sherwood hosts a parade, live music and—what else?—an archery competition.

Coast Coos Bay and other coast towns join forces to present the **Oregon Coast Music Festival.**

Heart of Oregon The **International Pinot Noir Celebration**, attracts top winemakers to McMinnville. Salem's Bush Pasture

Park comes alive with fine arts and crafts, food and live entertainment during the **Salem Art Fair and Festival.** Corvallis celebrates art, science and technology during **da Vinci Days,** which features interactive exhibits and presentations on subjects such as computer-generated art, animation and kinetic sculpture.

Eastern Oregon Cowboys and Indians turn out in force to take part in the rodeo and American Indian exhibition that are the centerpieces of the **Chief Joseph Days** in Joseph. Gliders come from the world over to take part in the **Hang Gliding Festival** in Lakeview.

AUGUST

Portland The city's most delicious annual event is **The Bite . . . A Taste of Portland,** where participants can sample specialties from more than 20 local restaurants, enjoy live music from 80 bands and wash it all down with local wines or beers.

Columbia River Gorge The renowned **Mt. Hood Festival of Jazz** in Gresham is an eagerly awaited weekend of big-name musicians performing in the great outdoors. The **Dufur Threshing Bee,** ten miles south of The Dalles, recalls pioneer life with demonstrations of soap-making, spinning, horse-shoeing, wheelwrighting and horse-drawn wheat harvesting.

Coast Fresh blackberries and quality arts and crafts draw large crowds to the **Annual Blackberry Arts Festival** in Coos Bay.

Heart of Oregon A carnival, agriculture and craft exhibits, lots of entertainment and plenty of junk food await at the **Oregon State Fair** in Salem. Junction City's Danish roots are celebrated during the **Scandinavian Festival** with folk dancing, food and crafts.

Cascades Classical music is performed in the Sunriver Resorts' magnificent Great Hall during the **Sunriver Music Festival.**

Eastern Oregon **The Steens Mountain Ten-Kilometer Run** is followed by sagebrush roping, a barbecue and beer garden at the **Frenchglen Jamboree,** both in Frenchglen.

SEPTEMBER

Portland **Art in the Pearl** shakes up the city with dance, music, theater performances and visual-art displays.

Columbia River Gorge At the **Roy Webster Columbia River Cross Channel Swim** in Hood River, hundreds of swimmers make the 1.1-mile course across the Columbia.

Coast Vast quantities of salmon are slow-baked over an open alderwood fire at the **Indian Style Salmon Bake** in Depoe Bay. The **Bandon Cranberry Festival** in Bandon celebrates the autumn harvest with a cranberry foods fair, crafts and a parade.

Heart of Oregon Continuous live entertainment, juried arts-and-crafts booths, a Saturday-night street dance and special children's activities mark the end of summer at the **Corvallis Fall Festival.** A citywide block party swings into action with music, a parade and Kidzone children's area at the **Eugene Celebration.**

Eastern Oregon The main event is the **Pendleton Roundup**, a major rodeo along with a historical parade of covered wagons and buggies and a pageant of American Indian culture.

OCTOBER

Portland The **Portland Marathon** draws thousands of participants for a marathon, five-mile run, major's run, kid's run, live entertainment and a sports-medicine and fitness fair.

Columbia River Gorge Pie-eating, pumpkin-carving, apple-peeling and other fruit-related contests highlight the **Hood River Valley Harvest Fest.** Celebrate two Northwest natives at the Mt. Hood **Salmon & Mushroom Festival** in Welches.

Heart of Oregon Top jazz bands play in venues throughout the city during the **Medford Jazz Jubilee.** Celebrate fungi and all their uses at the **Falls City Mushroom Festival** in Falls City.

NOVEMBER

Coast Artists, musicians, writers and craftspeople gather for the **Stormy Weather Arts Festival** in Cannon Beach.

DECEMBER

Portland The annual **Festival of Lights at The Grotto** is illuminated by some 50,000 lights and features such diversions as a petting zoo, puppet shows, pony rides, a calligraphy-art display and holiday foods. Portland's most elegant Victorian home gets decked out for the holidays during **Christmas at Pittock Mansion.** Elaborately decorated and lighted ships sail the Willamette and Columbia rivers nightly during the **Holiday Parade of Ships.**

Coast Arts and crafts, lamplighting ceremonies and theatrical productions are part of Cannon Beach's **Haystack Holidays.** Some 125,000 lights sparkle at Shores Acres State Park in Coos Bay at the **Holiday Festival of Lights.**

Heart of Oregon The works of regional artists are on display at the **Douglass County Christmas Fair**, a good place to pick up those last-minute gifts. Roseburg celebrates the holiday season with its **Festival of Lights**, which features Christmas lights formed into a variety of shapes, from Santa Claus to Mickey Mouse. Jacksonville's **Victorian Christmas** gets into the holiday spirit with wagon rides, carolers, hot cider, roasted chestnuts, home tours and children's activities.

Eastern Oregon The historic homes of Baker City are decorated in Christmas finery and open for inspection during the **Historic Homes Parlor Tour.**

Before You Go

VISITORS CENTERS

Before you come to Oregon, you may want to arm yourself with the 100-page *Oregon: The Official Travel Guide.* Contact **Travel Oregon** for a copy. ~ 670 Hawthorne Avenue Southeast, 240, Salem, OR 97301; 800-547-7842; www.traveloregon.com.

Large cities and small towns throughout the state have chambers of commerce or visitor information centers; a number of them are listed in the appropriate chapter.

For folks arriving by automobile, Oregon provides numerous **Welcome Centers** at key points along the major highways where you can pull off for a stretch, grab a cup of coffee or juice and receive plenty of advice on what to see and do in the area. The centers are clearly marked and are usually open during daylight hours throughout the spring, summer and fall.

PACKING

Comfortable and casual are the norm for dress in Oregon. You will want something dressier if you plan to catch a show, indulge in high tea or spend your evenings in posh restaurants and clubs, but for the most part your topsiders and slacks are acceptable garb everywhere else.

Layers of clothing are your best bet since the weather changes so drastically depending on which part of the state you are visiting; shorts will be perfectly comfortable during the daytime in the hot, arid interior, but once you pass over the mountains and head for the coastline, you'll appreciate having packed a jacket to protect you from the nippy ocean breezes, even on the warmest of days.

Wherever you're headed, during the summer bring some long-sleeve shirts, pants and lightweight sweaters and jackets along with your shorts, T-shirts and bathing suit; the evenings can be quite crisp. Bring along those warmer clothes—pants, sweaters, jackets, hats and gloves—in spring and fall, too, since days may be warm but it's rather chilly after sundown. Winter calls for thick sweaters, knitted hats, down jackets and, in the mountains, snug ski clothes.

It's not a bad idea to call ahead to check on weather conditions. Sturdy, comfortable walking shoes are a must for sightseeing. If you plan to explore tidal pools or go for long walks on the beach, bring a pair of lightweight canvas shoes that you don't mind getting wet.

Scuba divers will probably want to bring their own gear, though rentals are generally available in all popular dive areas. Many places also rent tubes for river floats and sailboards for windsurfing. Fishing gear is often available for rent as well. Campers will need to bring their own basic equipment.

Don't forget your camera for capturing Oregon's glorious scenery and a pair of binoculars for watching the abundant wildlife that live here. And pack an umbrella and raincoat, just in case.

LODGING

Lodging in Oregon runs the gamut, from rustic cabins in the woods to sprawling resorts on the coastline. Chain motels line most major thoroughfares and mom-and-pop enterprises still vie successfully for lodgers in every region. Large hotels with names you'd know anywhere appear in most centers of any size.

Bed and breakfasts, small inns and cozy lodges where you can have breakfast with the handful of other guests are appearing throughout the region as these more personable forms of accommodation continue to grow in popularity. In fact, in areas like Ashland they outnumber hotels and motels.

Special museums and exhibits throughout the coastal zone attest to the importance of whales, dolphins and other marine animals in the region.

Whatever your preference and budget, you can probably find something to suit your taste with the help of the regional chapters in this book. Remember, rooms are scarce and prices rise in the high season, which is generally summer along the coastline and winter in the mountain ranges. Off-season rates are often drastically reduced in many places. Whatever you do, plan ahead and make reservations, especially in the prime tourist seasons.

Accommodations in this book are organized by region and classified according to price. Rates referred to are for two people during high season, so if you are looking for low-season bargains, it's good to inquire. *Budget* lodgings are generally less than \$60 per night and are satisfactory and clean but modest. *Moderate*-priced lodgings run from \$60 to \$110; what they have to offer in the way of luxury will depend on where they are located, but they often offer larger rooms and more attractive surroundings. At *deluxe*-priced accommodations, you can expect to spend between \$110 and \$150 for a homey bed and breakfast or a double in a hotel or resort. You'll usually find spacious rooms, a fashionable lobby, a restaurant and a group of shops. *Ultra-deluxe* properties, priced above \$150, are a region's finest, offering all the amenities of a deluxe hotel plus plenty of extras.

Whether you crave a room facing the surf or one looking out on the ski slopes, be sure to specify when making reservations. If you are trying to save money, keep in mind that lodgings a block or so from the waterfront or a mile or so from the ski lift are going to offer lower rates than those right in the midst of the area's major attractions.

DINING

Seafood is a staple, especially along the coast, where salmon is king. Whether it's poached in herbs or grilled on a stake Indian-style, plan to treat yourself to this regional specialty often. While each area has its own favorite dishes, ethnic influences and gourmet spots, Oregon's cuisine as a whole tends to be hearty and is often crafted around organically grown local produce.

Within a particular chapter, restaurants are categorized geographically, with each entry describing the type of cuisine, general decor and price range. Restaurants offer lunch and dinner unless noted otherwise. Dinner entrées at *budget* restaurants usually cost under $8. The ambience is informal, service usually speedy and the crowd a local one. *Moderate*-priced restaurants range between $8 and $16 at dinner; surroundings are casual but pleasant, the menu offers more variety and the pace is usually slower. *Deluxe* establishments tab their entrées from $16 to $25; cuisines may be simple or sophisticated, depending on the location, but the decor is plusher and the service more personalized. *Ultra-deluxe* dining rooms, where entrées begin at $25, are often gourmet places where the cooking and service have become an art form.

The Oregon flag bears two different images on each side—the only state flag in the Union to do so.

Some restaurants change hands often; others are closed in low seasons. Efforts have been made to include places with established reputations for good eating. Breakfast and lunch menus vary less in price from restaurant to restaurant than evening dinners. If you are on a budget and still hope to experience the best of the bunch, visit at lunch when portions and prices are likely to be reduced.

TRAVELING WITH CHILDREN

Oregon is a wonderful place to bring the kids. Besides the many museums and festivals, the region also has hundreds of beaches and parks, and many nature sanctuaries sponsor children's activities, especially during the summer months. A few guidelines will help make travel with children a pleasure.

Many bed and breakfasts do not accept children, so be sure of the policy when you make reservations. If you need a crib or cot, arrange for it ahead of time. A travel agent can be of help here, as well as with most other travel plans.

If you're traveling by air, try to reserve bulkhead seats where there is plenty of room. Take along extras you may need, such as diapers, changes of clothing, snacks, toys and books. When traveling by car, be sure to carry the extras, along with plenty of juice and water. And always allow extra time for getting places, especially on rural roads.

A first-aid kit is a must for any trip. Along with adhesive bandages, antiseptic cream and something to stop itching, include any medicines your pediatrician might recommend to treat allergies, colds, diarrhea or any chronic problems your child may have.

When spending time at the beach or in the snow, take extra care the first few days. Children's skin is especially sensitive to sun, and severe sunburn can happen before you realize it, even on overcast days. Hats for the kids are a good idea, along with liberal applications of sunblock. Be sure to keep a constant eye on children who are near the water or on the slopes, and never leave children unattended in a car on a hot day.

Even the smallest towns usually have stores that carry diapers, baby food, snacks and other essentials, but these may close early in the evening. Larger urban areas usually have all-night grocery or convenience stores that stock them.

Many towns, parks and attractions offer special activities designed just for children. Consult local newspapers and/or the chambers of commerce listed in this guide to see what's happening where you're going.

WOMEN TRAVELING ALONE

Traveling solo grants an independence and freedom different from that of traveling with a partner, but single travelers are more vulnerable to crime and must take additional precautions.

It's unwise to hitchhike and probably best to avoid inexpensive accommodations on the outskirts of town; the money saved does not outweigh the risk. Bed and breakfasts, youth hostels and YWCAs are generally your safest bet for lodging, and they also foster an environment ideal for bonding with fellow travelers.

Keep all valuables well-hidden and clutch cameras and purses tightly. Avoid late-night treks or strolls through undesirable parts of town, but if you find yourself in this situation, continue walking with a confident air until you reach a safe haven. A fierce scowl never hurts.

These hints should by no means deter you from seeking out adventure. Wherever you go, stay alert, use your common sense and trust your instincts. If you are hassled or threatened in some way, never be afraid to yell for assistance. It's a good idea to carry change for a phone call and to know the number to call in case of emergency. For helpful hints, get a copy of *Safety and Security for Women Who Travel* (Travelers Tales, 2004).

Most major cities have hotlines for victims of rape and violent crime. In Portland contact the **Portland Women's Crisis Line.** ~ 503-235-5333, 888-235-5333. The **Sexual Assault Support Services** offers assistance in Eugene. ~ 541-343-7277, 800-788-4727.

GAY & LESBIAN TRAVELERS

While gay and lesbian communities thrive in some of Oregon's cities, there are many conservative groups working to strip them of their civil rights. Especially pesky is the Oregon Citizens Alliance, an organization that has thrice failed (with Ballot Measure 9 in 1992, Ballot Measure 13 in 1994 and Ballot Measure 9 in 2000) to pass statewide ordinances eliminating all special rights for gays and lesbians. The measures were both defeated by very narrow margins, and, unfortunately, the Citizen's Alliance continues to gather signatures for similar initiatives in upcoming elections. The best news is that gay and lesbian organizations have been successful in fighting them off and at the same time educating and mobilizing forces both within and outside their communities.

Text continued on page 22.

High Adventure in Oregon

Whether you're an expert or a novice, a fanatic or simply curious, there's a sport here with your name written on it. Remember, Oregon and the Pacific Northwest are known as the "Evergreen Playground," not "Evergreen Couch Potato Land." So if what turns you on is shooting the rapids or climbing a towering peak, do it!

For heart-stopping thrills, Oregon offers dramatic locations for *bungee jumping*. Jumpers strapped into a full-body harness with three to five connecting bungee cords swan dive off a 191-foot-high bridge, the highest commercial bungee bridge in the Western Hemisphere. If this sounds great until you actually eyeball the 20-story drop, **Bungee.com** will refund the jump fee. Those who make the plunge are awarded membership in the Dangerous Sports Club. ~ P.O. Box 121, Fairview, OR 97024; 503-520-0303.

With so many majestic ranges, *mountaineering* abounds. Rock and ice climbing are big draws in the Cascades. Climbers should be familiar with cold-weather survival techniques before tackling Northwest heights, which are tricky at best. For climbers' guidelines and further information, turn to the **Outdoor Recreation Information Center.** ~ 222 Yale Avenue North, Seattle, WA 98109; 206-470-4060. Mountaineering clubs like the **Mazamas** conduct classes and lead trips to Oregon peaks. ~ 909 Northwest 19th Avenue, Portland, OR 97209; 503-227-2345; www.mazamas.org.

Every September, the Beaver State welcomes one of the most popular bicycle tours in the country, **Cycle Oregon**. This seven-day tour visits a different part of rural Oregon each year, attracting over 2000 cyclists who cover 40 to 80 miles per day. Riders camp in tents in small towns along the way, and the tour provides meals and a shuttle for cyclists' bags during the day. The fee for this spirited, fast-growing event varies from year to year. ~ 2125 North Flint Avenue, Portland, OR, 97227, 503-287-0405, 800-292-5367; www.cycleoregon.com.

Rest assured: There are tamer outdoor adventures here. In fact, many swear that the best way to soak in the region's beauty is to travel slowly by bike or foot. Extensive guided *bicycling* and *walking* tours of the mountains, forests and coastline last anywhere from two days to weeks. **The Sierra Club**. ~ Outing Department, 85 2nd Street, Second Floor, San Francisco, CA 94105; 415-977-5522.

In this realm of lakes, streams, rivers and ocean, it's no surprise that many of the top adventure sports are water related. *Whitewater rafting* is one of the best-known adventure activities in the state, with challenging rapids on the Rogue, Deschutes and McKenzie rivers. If you aren't acquainted with these rivers, join a guided trip or chat with outfitters who know the treacherous spots to look out for. **The North West Rafters Association** is a good source for further information. ~ 10117 Southeast Sunnyside Road F1234, Clackamas, OR 97015; www.nwrafters.org.

Kayaking and *canoeing* are also popular ways to shoot the rapids. Placid bodies of water suitable for kayak and canoe exploration include the Willamette and Columbia rivers. Ocean kayaking is most popular in Oregon's protected bays, such as Tillamook Bay and Nehalem Bay. The folks at **Portland River Company** can tell you more about the waters and outfitters of the area. ~ 6315 Southwest Montgomery Street, Suite 330, Portland, OR 97201; 503-229-0551.

Squeezed between the border of Washington and Oregon, the breezy Columbia Gorge is reputed to be the *windsurfing* capital of the continent, with championship competitions held annually. Numerous outfits in Hood River are set up to teach would-be windsurfers and rent the sailboards and wetsuits. **The Columbia Gorge Windsurfing Association** can put you in touch with top schools in the region. ~ P.O. Box 182, Hood River, OR 97031; 541-386-9225; www.cgwa.net. Or you can try the **United States Windsurfing Association**. ~ P.O. Box 320629, Cocoa Beach, FL 32932; 877-386-8708.

Information hotlines and social and support groups for gay and lesbians exist in several of Oregon's larger cities and towns. In Portland, there is the **Lesbian Community Project.** ~ 503-227-0605; www.lesbiancommunityproject.org. Roseburg offers the **Gay & Lesbian Switchboard.** ~ 541-672-4126. **AIDS Hotlines** are in Portland (503-223-2437), Corvallis (541-752-6322, 800-588-2437) and Eugene (541-342-5088).

Just Out (503-236-1252) serves as a forum and resource for gays and lesbians in Oregon and can be picked up at many locations.

SENIOR TRAVELERS

Oregon is a hospitable place for senior citizens to visit, especially west of the Cascades during the cool, sunny summer months that offer respite from hotter climes elsewhere in the country. Countless museums, historic sights and even restaurants and hotels offer senior discounts that can cut a substantial chunk off vacation costs. The national park system's Golden Age Passport, which must be applied for in person, allows free admission for anyone 62 and older to the numerous national monuments in the region, as well as to Crater Lake National Park, Oregon's only national park. Passports are available at any national park, ranger station or park office.

Be aware that the 503 and 971 area codes now require 10-digit local dialing—just dial the area code and phone number, no "1" or "0" needed.

The **American Association of Retired Persons** (AARP) offers membership to anyone age 50 or over. AARP's benefits include travel discounts with a number of firms and escorted tours with Gray Line buses. ~ 601 E Street Northwest, Washington, DC 20049; 888-687-2277; www.aarp.org.

Elderhostel offers reasonably priced, all-inclusive educational programs in a variety of Oregon locations throughout the year. ~ 11 Avenue de Lafayette, Boston, MA 02111; 877-426-8056; www.elderhostel.org, e-mail registration@elderhostel.org.

Be extra careful about health matters. In addition to the medications you ordinarily use, it's a good idea to bring along the prescriptions for obtaining more. Consider carrying a medical record with you—including your medical history and current medical status, as well as your doctor's name, phone number and address. Make sure your insurance covers you while you are away from home.

DISABLED TRAVELERS

Oregon is striving to make more destinations accessible for travelers with disabilities. For information on the areas you will be visiting, contact **Center for Independent Living.** ~ 2410 Southeast 11th Avenue, Portland, OR 97214; 503-232-7411.

The **Society for Accessible Travel & Hospitality** (SATH) has general information regarding traveling with disabilities. ~ 347

5th Avenue, Suite 610, New York, NY 10016; 212-447-7284, fax 212-725-8253; www.sath.org. **MossRehab ResourceNet** provides more information and services. ~ MossRehab Hospital, 1200 West Tabor Road, Philadelphia, PA 19141; 215-456-9900, 800-225-5667; www.mossresourcenet.org. **Flying Wheels Travel** is a travel agency specifically for disabled people. ~ P.O. Box 382, Owatonna, MN 55060; 507-451-5005, fax 507-451-1685; www.flyingwheelstravel.com. **Travelin' Talk**, a network of people and organizations, also provides assistance. ~ P.O. Box 1796, Wheat Ridge, CO 80034; 303-232-2979; www.travelintalk.net, e-mail travelin@travelintalk.net. **Access-Able Travel Source** has worldwide information online. ~ 303-232-2979; www.access-able.com, e-mail bill@access-able.com.

FOREIGN TRAVELERS

Passports and Visas Most foreign visitors need a passport and tourist visa to enter the United States. Contact your nearest U.S. Embassy or Consulate well in advance to obtain a visa and to check on any other entry requirements.

Customs Requirements Foreign travelers are allowed to carry in the following: 200 cigarettes (1 carton), 50 cigars or 2 kilograms (4.4 pounds) of smoking tobacco; one liter of alcohol for personal use only (you must be 21 years of age to bring in alcohol); and US$100 worth of duty-free gifts that may include an additional 100 cigars. You may bring in any amount of currency, but must fill out a form if you bring in over US$10,000. Carry any prescription drugs in clearly marked containers. (You may have to produce a written prescription or doctor's statement for the customs officers.) Meat or meat products, seeds, plants, fruits, and narcotics may not be brought into the United States. Contact the **United States Customs Service** for further information. ~ 1300 Pennsylvania Avenue NW, Washington, DC 20229; 202-354-1000; www.cbp.gov.

Driving If you plan to rent a car, an international driver's license should be obtained before arriving in the United States. Some car rental agencies require both a foreign license and an international driver's license. Many also require a lessee to be at least 25 years of age; all require a major credit card. Seat belts are mandatory for the driver and all passengers. Children under the age of six or under 60 pounds should be in the back seat in approved child-safety restraints.

Currency United States money is based on the dollar. Bills come in denominations of $1, $5, $10, $20, $50 and $100. Every dollar is divided into 100 cents. Coins are the penny (1 cent), nickel (5 cents), dime (10 cents) and quarter (25 cents). Half-dollar and dollar coins are rarely used. You may not use foreign currency to purchase goods and services in the United States. Consider buying traveler's checks in dollar amounts. You may also use credit cards affiliated with an American company such as Visa, Interbank, Barclay Card and American Express.

Electricity and Electronics Electric outlets use currents of 110 volts, 60 cycles. For appliances made for other electrical systems, you need a transformer or other adapter. Travelers who use laptop computers for telecommunication should be aware that modem configurations for U.S. telephone systems may be different from their European counterparts. Similarly, the U.S. format for videotapes is different from that in Europe; U.S. Park Service visitors centers and other stores that sell souvenir videos often have them available in European format.

Weights and Measures The United States uses the English system of weights and measures. American units and their metric equivalents are: 1 inch = 2.5 centimeters; 1 foot (12 inches) = 0.3 meter; 1 yard (3 feet) = 0.9 meter; 1 mile (5280 feet) = 1.6 kilometers; 1 ounce = 28 grams; 1 pound (16 ounces) = 0.45 kilograms; 1 quart (liquid) = 0.9 liter.

Outdoor Adventures

CAMPING

Parks in the state of Oregon rank among the top in North America as far as attendance goes, so plan ahead if you hope to do any camping during the busy summer months. Late spring and early fall present fewer crowds to deal with and the weather is still fine.

You'll find a multitude of marvelous campsites along Oregon's protected coast and in its green mountain ranges. Twenty-two of the 50 state parks with campgrounds are open year-round. Reservations are accepted at 16 parks and are essential if you hope to get a spot during July and August. The **Oregon Parks and Recreation Department** maintains a reservation line (800-452-5687) to provide updated campsite availability. ~ 725 Summer Street Northeast, Suite C, Salem, OR 97301; 503-986-0707, 800-551-6949; www.oregonstateparks.org.

For information on camping in Oregon's national forests, parks and recreation areas, contact the **Nature of the Northwest Information Center**. ~ 800 Northeast Oregon Street, Suite 177, Portland, OR 97232; 503-872-2750; www.naturenw.org.

PERMITS

Wilderness camping is not permitted in Oregon's state parks, but there are primitive sites available in most parks. In other words, you must pitch your tent at a designated campsite, although many basic sites without facilities are free. Permits are required for wilderness camping in parts of the Mt. Jefferson, Mt. Washington and Three Sisters wilderness areas; permits are available at the ranger stations. Campers should check with all other parks individually to see if permits are required.

Follow low-impact camping practices in wilderness areas; "leave only footprints, take only pictures." When backpacking and hiking, stick to marked trails or tread lightly in areas where no trail exists. Be prepared with map and compass since signs are limited to directional information and don't include mileage. Guidelines on wilderness camping are available from the **Nature of the Northwest Information Center.** ~ 800 Northeast Oregon Street, Suite 177, Portland, OR 97232; 503-872-2750; www.naturenw.org.

WATER SAFETY

Oregon offers an incredible array of water sports to choose from, be it on the ocean, a quiet lake or stream or tumbling rapids. Swimming, scuba diving, walking the shoreline in search of clams or just basking in the sun are options when you get to the shore, lake or river.

Be careful though. People have drowned in Oregon waters, but drownings are easily avoided when you respect the power of the water, heed appropriate warnings and use good common sense.

Whitewater rafting is particularly popular, especially on the Rogue and Deschutes rivers, where you will find outfitters renting equipment and running tours throughout the summer months. *The White Water River Book* (Pacific Research, 1982) is a good guide to techniques, equipment and safety. When you're going rafting or canoeing, always scout the river from land before the first trip, and check available literature. Rivers may have danger areas such as falls, boulders, rapids and dams.

Oregon grows 99 percent of the entire U.S. commercial crop of hazelnuts. (That's why the hazelnut coffee is so delicious here!)

Shallow lakes, rivers and bays tend to be the most populated spots since they warm up during the height of summer; otherwise, the waters of the Northwest are generally chilly. Always swim in designated areas, preferably where there are lifeguards. On the ocean, always face the incoming waves. Respect signs warning of dangerous currents and undertows. Whenever you swim, never do so alone, and never take your eyes off of children in or near the water.

FISHING

With its multitude of rivers, streams, lakes and miles of protected coastline, Oregon affords some of the best fishing in the world. Salmon is the main draw, but each area features special treats for the fishing enthusiast that are described in the individual chapters of *Hidden Oregon*.

Fees and regulations vary, but licenses are required for salt- and freshwater fishing throughout Oregon and can be purchased at sporting-goods stores, bait-and-tackle shops and fishing lodges. You can also find leads on guides and charter services in these locations if you are interested in trying a type of fishing that's new to you. Charter fishing is the most expensive way to go out to sea; party boats take a crowd and are less expensive but usually great fun. On rivers, lakes and streams, guides can show you the best place to throw a hook or skim a fly. Whatever your pleasure, in saltwater or fresh, a good guide will save you time and grief and will increase the likelihood of a full string.

The **Oregon Department of Fish and Wildlife** can supply information on fishing in the state. ~ P.O. Box 59, Portland, OR 97207; 503-947-6000, 800-720-6339; www.dfw.state.or.us.

SKIING

As winter blankets the Cascades, ski season heats up at numerous resorts. The largest alpine ski areas are found at (surprise) the largest mountains: Mt. Hood and Mt. Bachelor, where skiing often continues into the early summer. Throughout the Cascades and the eastern part of the state are scattered a number of downhill mountains and cross-country areas, the latter especially concentrated around Bend. Crater Lake National Park offers some of the best nordic trails in the state, many overlooking the lake's deep-blue waters. Specifics on the top resorts are listed in each regional chapter.

For more skiing information in Oregon, contact the **Pacific Northwest Ski Areas Association.** ~ P.O. Box 1720, Hood River, OR 97031; 541-386-9600; www.pnsaa.org.

TWO

Portland

But for the flip of a coin, Portland could have been called Boston. Our story begins with two pioneers, Asa Lovejoy of Massachusetts and Francis Pettygrove of Maine, hitting the Oregon Trail in search of the American Dream. On a fall 1843 canoe journey up the Willamette River from Fort Vancouver to Oregon City, Tennessee drifter William Overton (traveling with Lovejoy) thought the land was perfect for a settlement. Lacking the 25-cent filing fee, he split the claim with Lovejoy in return for the money. Overton soon grew tired of working the land, and sold his half to Francis W. Pettygrove.

Soon, Lovejoy found himself partners with Pettygrove at "The Clearing," what native guides called the area. Lovejoy wanted to call the new town Boston, but Pettygrove preferred to appropriate the name of Maine's Portland. True gentlemen, they settled the matter with a coin toss at Oregon City's Francis Ermatinger House.

Pettygrove won, but it was years before Portland began to rival Oregon City, the immigrant hub at the end of the overland trail. Even today, with a metropolitan population of more than 1.5 million, many visitors wonder how this city emerged as Oregon's centerpiece. Unlike the largest cities of the Pacific Northwest or California, it is not located on a major coast or sound. Although it is midway between the equator and the North Pole, Portland is not central to the geography of its own state. Yet from the arts and winter recreation to architecture and vineyards, this city is an admirable metropolis, one that merits inclusion on any Northwest itinerary.

The community boasts a rich cultural life, has a popular National Basketball Association franchise, is blessed with some of the prettiest urban streets in the Northwest, is a veritable haven for antique lovers, runners, cyclists and garden aficionados and has an impressive array of jazz clubs, bistros and offbeat museums.

And yet the legacy of "The Clearing" is very much intact as the city remains intimately connected to the great outdoors. Near the entrance to the fabled Columbia River Gorge, Portland is just 65 miles from the nearest glacier and 110 miles from the ocean. Riverfront greenspace, the 5000-acre Forest Park and the wonderful wetlands of Sauvie Island all demonstrate why this city has been named "best" on the Green Index, a study of pollution, public health and environmental policy.

When the weather turns very wet, as it does in the winter months, residents head for the powder-packed slopes of Mt. Hood or start gearing up for a bit of steelheading on the nearby coastal rivers. Winter is also the height of the cultural season, enjoyed at the Portland Center for the Performing Arts and dozens of other venues around town.

Portland's emergence as a major city owes much to emigrant New England ship captains who decided, in the mid-19th century, that the town's deep riverfront harbor was preferable to the shallows of Oregon City. Easy ocean access via the Columbia made the new port a convenient link to the emerging agrarian economy of the Willamette Valley, as well as the region's up-and-coming lumber mills. Like San Francisco, Portland flourished as an international shipping hub and as a gateway for the 1852 gold rush that began in the Jacksonville region.

As the Northwest's leading port and economic center, the town soon attracted the state's new gentry, the lumber barons, shipping titans, traders, mercantilists and agribusiness pioneers. They drew heavily on the architectural legacy of the Northeast and Europe, erecting Cape Cod–style homes, Victorian mansions, villas and French Renaissance–style mini-châteaus complete with Italian marble and virgin-redwood interiors.

A city that started out in life as a kind of New England–style village crafted out of native fir was made over with brick office blocks sporting cast-iron facades. Florentine, Italianate, gothic, even Baroque architecture began to emerge along the main drags. City fathers worked hard to upgrade the town's agrarian image, often with mixed results.

To unify the community, planners added a 25-block-long promenade through the heart of town. Lined with churches, office blocks, apartments and homes, these "Park Blocks" offered a grassy median ideal for contemplating the passing scene. Like a Parisian boulevard, this was the place where one might come for the hour and stay for the day. Brass water fountains, known as Benson Bubblers and left on 24 hours a day, brought the pure waters of the Cascades to street level.

While the city's New England quality made Bostonians feel right at home, Portland also attracted a significant Chinese community that labored long and hard on railroad lines and in salmon factories. Badly persecuted, they were just one of many victims of intolerance in this city that became a Ku Klux Klan center. Blacks, Jews and Catholics were also victimized at various times. But as Portland grew, this deplorable bigotry was replaced by a new egalitarianism. The city's intellectual life flourished thanks to the arrival of several major universities and prestigious liberal arts colleges.

As Portland modernized, it developed into a manufacturing center famous for everything from swimsuits to footwear. But as the city flourished as a center for high-tech industry, it did not forget its roots. Visitors eager to discover the Northwest flock here and to the Columbia River Gorge in pursuit of outdoor activities from windsurfing to birding. An ideal home base, this city has also drawn many famous artists, musicians and writers from larger, more congested and expensive communities like New York and Los Angeles.

Although much of Portland's best is within easy walking distance of downtown, the city's outer reaches are also well worth your time. The touchstones of

Text continued on page 32.

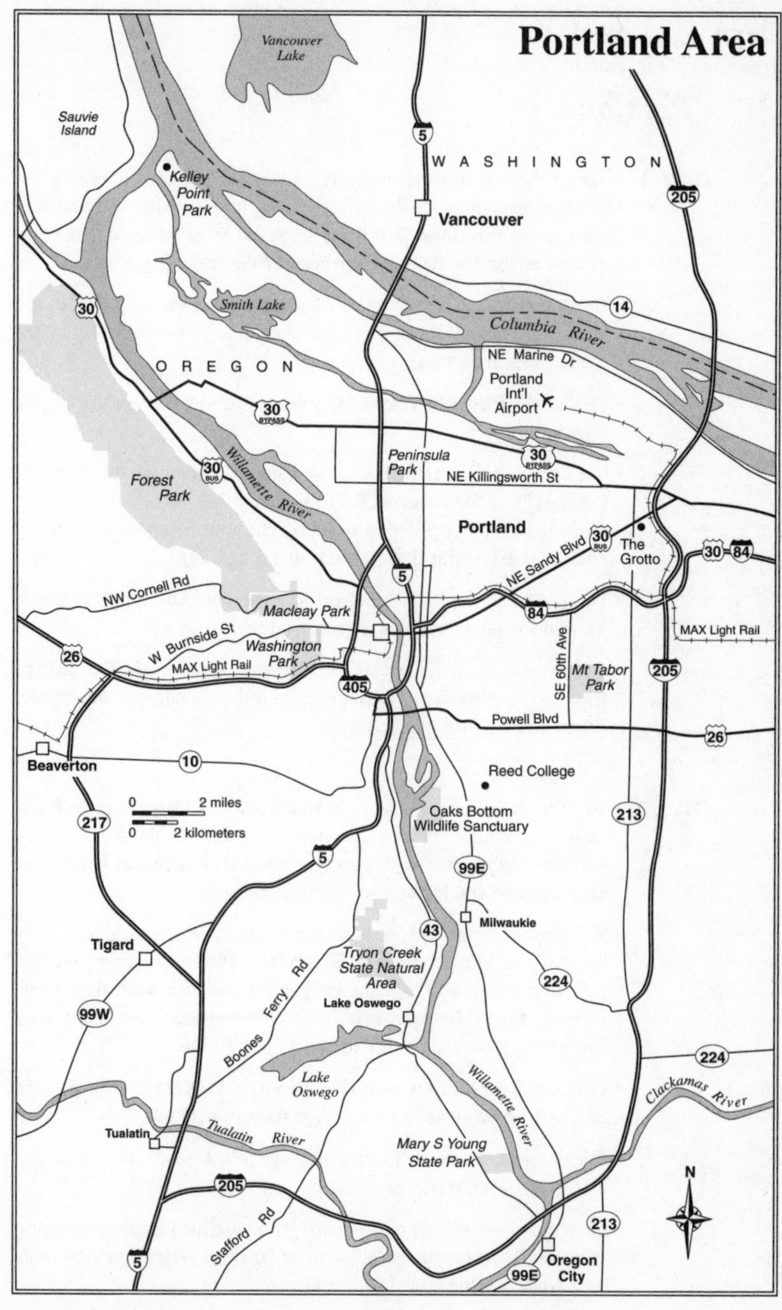
Portland Area
Vancouver Lake
Sauvie Island
Kelley Point Park
WASHINGTON
Vancouver
Smith Lake
Columbia River
NE Marine Dr
Portland Int'l Airport
OREGON
Forest Park
Willamette River
Peninsula Park
NE Killingsworth St
Portland
NE Sandy Blvd
The Grotto
NW Cornell Rd
Macleay Park
W Burnside St
Washington Park
MAX Light Rail
MAX Light Rail
SE 60th Ave
Mt Tabor Park
Powell Blvd
Beaverton
Reed College
0 2 miles
0 2 kilometers
Oaks Bottom Wildlife Sanctuary
Milwaukie
Tigard
Tryon Creek State Natural Area
Boones Ferry Rd
Lake Oswego
Lake Oswego
Willamette River
Clackamas River
Tualatin
Tualatin River
Mary S Young State Park
Stafford Rd
N
Oregon City

Three-day Weekend

Portland

DAY 1

- Spend the day downtown. Start with a walking tour, admiring (or at least chuckling at) Portland's quirky architecture and statuary such as the **Portland Building** (page 35) and *Portlandia* (page 42), as well as the **Ira Keller Memorial Fountain** (page 35).
- Try **Alexis** (page 39) or **Jake's Famous Crawfish** (page 40) for lunch. Eat well before or after the noon hour, when both landmark restaurants are packed.
- Don't miss **Powell's City of Books** (page 41), the world's largest bookstore.
- If it's not raining, continue your walking tour through the **Yamhill** (page 36) and **Skidmore/Old Town** (page 36) historic districts and **Chinatown** (page 36). If it *is* raining, get your intercultural experience at the **Portland Art Museum** (page 34).
- The place for dinner is **Harborside Restaurant** (page 40), with its wildly eclectic menu and great waterfront view.
- Afterwards, head to the Echo Theater and watch **Do Jump! Extremely Physical Theater** (page 49) combine comedy, music, dance and high-flying acrobatics.

DAY 2

- Stroll or drive through the Nob Hill district to **Washington Park** (page 52), where it's easy to while away the whole day. Begin by surrounding yourself with beauty at the **International Rose Test Garden** and the **Japanese Garden Society**.
- You may (or may not) wish to learn about Oregon's logging heritage at the **World Forest Discovery Museum** (page 54). Or, rejecting the notion that the only good tree is a dead tree, stroll through **Hoyt Arboretum** (page 54) for proof that absolutely everything grows tall in Portland's misty climate.
- Give equal time to the animal kingdom at the **Oregon Zoo** (page 53), with its wonderful open-space African habitats.
- For dinner, check out **Bluehour** (page 58), where Northwest cuisine gets a Mediterranean kick.
- Later on, one nightlife option is to go to the movies at the historic **Mission Theater** (page 60), where you can watch from a comfy sofa while sipping your favorite libation.

DAY 3

- Today's the day to take in two great sightseeing experiences just past the city's outskirts. Head east on Route 84 to Troutdale and turn off to drive the **Historic Columbia River Highway** (page 74). Take your time—you can easily visit every scenic stop and wish there were more. (Actually, there is, but you have to hike to the upper rim to see it.)
- Finish your visit with lunch at **Multnomah Falls Lodge** (page 82).
- Driving back toward Portland via Route 84, veer south on Route 205 to **Oregon City** (pages 62–63). Starting at the **End of the Oregon Trail Interpretive Center and Historic Site**, tour the 19th-century museum houses of the historic district.
- Take a sunset ride on the **Oregon City Municipal Elevator.**
- Heading back to downtown Portland, put the crowning touch on your visit with an elegant dinner at **Typhoon! on Broadway** (page 39), arguably the city's best Thai restaurant.

great urban centers—science museums, zoos, children's museums and craft centers—are all found here. Amid its multiple museums and theater companies, as well as countless other amenities, Portland also offers many pleasant surprises such as a strong used book–seller community, the sole extinct volcano within the limits of a continental U.S. city and the world's smallest park.

Careful restoration of the downtown core and historic old town, a beautiful riverfront area and thriving nightlife make Portland a winner. Neighborhoods such as Nob Hill, Hawthorne and Sellwood all invite leisurely exploration. And when it comes to parks you can choose from more than 80 spanning 37,000 acres.

In this chapter we have divided the city into three geographic regions. The Central Portland region encompasses downtown, the Skidmore Old Town District and the Yamhill Historic District. Portland West covers the balance of the city and metropolitan region west of the Willamette River. Portland East explores the metro area east of the Willamette River including Lloyd Center, Burnside, Sellwood and southerly destinations like Oregon City.

Central Portland

The urban renaissance is clearly a success in Portland. A walkable city with perpetually flowing drinking fountains, this riverfront town is a place where commerce, history, classic architecture and the arts flourish side by side. Even when the weather is foul, Portland is an inviting place.

Downtown Portland *does* have its sleek towers, but it also contains plenty of low-lying delights as well. It's easy to tell that the city has spent a lot of time and money on parks and public art projects—Portland, after all, is the city whose mayor dreamed up the "Expose Yourself to Art" campaign in the 1970s (and that was mayor Bud Clark himself clad in an open trench coat on the famous poster).

A city that focuses so much on user-friendly public spaces certainly is welcoming to visitors. Whether you're taking a slow stroll along Park Avenue or shopping the markets of Portland's Chinatown (once the West Coast's largest Chinese community), Central Portland will impress you as much more than just the place where the populace clocks in from 9 to 5.

SIGHTS

A good place to orient yourself is the **Portland Oregon Information Center**. Here you can pick up helpful maps and brochures. ~ Pioneer Courthouse Square; 503-275-8355, 800-962-3700; www.travelportland.com.

Pioneer Courthouse Square is a popular gathering point. A waterfall and 64,000 red bricks inscribed with the names of local residents who donated money for the square's construction are all here. Named for adjacent **Pioneer Courthouse**, the oldest public building in Oregon (completed in 1873), which you may want to explore, the square offers a variety of special events including

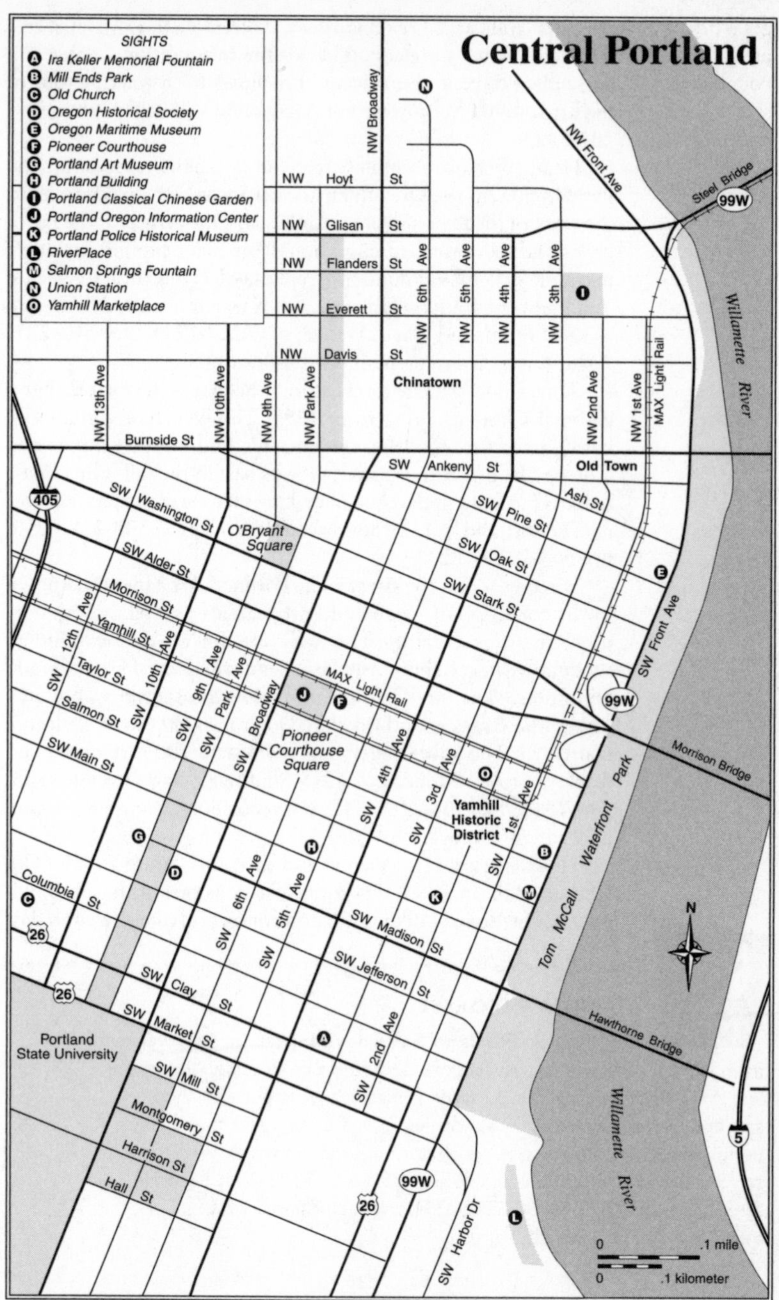
Central Portland
SIGHTS
A Ira Keller Memorial Fountain
B Mill Ends Park
C Old Church
D Oregon Historical Society
E Oregon Maritime Museum
F Pioneer Courthouse
G Portland Art Museum
H Portland Building
I Portland Classical Chinese Garden
J Portland Oregon Information Center
K Portland Police Historical Museum
L RiverPlace
M Salmon Springs Fountain
N Union Station
O Yamhill Marketplace
NW Broadway
NW Front Ave
Steel Bridge
99W
NW Hoyt St
NW Glisan St
NW Flanders St
NW Everett St
NW Davis St
NW 6th Ave
NW 5th Ave
NW 4th Ave
NW 3th Ave
Chinatown
NW 13th Ave
NW 10th Ave
NW 9th Ave
NW Park Ave
NW 2nd Ave
NW 1st Ave
MAX Light Rail
Willamette River
Burnside St
SW Ankeny St
Old Town
Ash St
405
SW Washington St
O'Bryant Square
SW Pine St
SW Oak St
SW Alder St
SW Stark St
Morrison St
Yamhill St
Taylor St
Salmon St
SW Main St
SW 12th Ave
SW 10th Ave
SW 9th Ave
SW Park Ave
SW Broadway
MAX Light Rail
SW Front Ave
Pioneer Courthouse Square
SW 4th Ave
SW 3rd Ave
SW 1st Ave
Yamhill Historic District
Morrison Bridge
Tom McCall Waterfront Park
Columbia St
26
SW 6th Ave
SW 5th Ave
SW Madison St
SW Jefferson St
SW Clay St
SW Market St
SW 2nd Ave
Hawthorne Bridge
Portland State University
SW Mill St
Montgomery St
Harrison St
Hall St
SW Harbor Dr
5
0 .1 mile
0 .1 kilometer
N

concerts and, at Christmas time, a ceremonial Christmas-tree lighting and tuba concert. The **Visitor Information Center** is a great place to pick up maps and brochures for a walking tour of the area. ~ 701 Southwest 6th Avenue; 503-223-1613, fax 503-222-7425.

Head west on Yamhill Street for one block then south on Park Avenue to the **Oregon Historical Society,** the place to learn the story of the region's American Indians, the arrival of the Europeans and the westward migration. Permanent exhibits include a maritime gallery and miniature replicas of 19th-century vehicles. You'll also find a museum store and research library. Admission. ~ 1200 Southwest Park Avenue; 503-222-1741, fax 503-221-2035; www.ohs.org, e-mail orhist@ohs.org.

Adjacent to the Oregon Historical Society is the **First Congregational Church**, dating from 1895. This Venetian gothic–style basalt structure, modeled on Boston's Old South Church and crowned by a 175-foot tower, is at its best in the fall. Elms shade the street in front of the church, making this one of the prettiest corners in Portland. ~ 1126 Southwest Park Avenue; 503-228-7219, fax 503-228-6522.

Directly across the street is the **Portland Art Museum**, known for its collection of Asian and European art as well as 20th-century American sculpture. The vast collection of American Indian art and artifacts showcases excellent tribal masks and wood sculptures. The pre-Columbian pieces, box drums, potlatch dishes and cones are all notable. Don't miss the skylit sculpture courtyard. The Silver gallery has more than 100 rare objects on display. Closed Monday. ~ 1219 Southwest Park Avenue; 503-226-2811, fax 503-226-4842; www.portlandartmuseum.org, e-mail info@pam.org.

Head east to 11th Avenue and then turn south to **The Old Church.** Built in 1883, this gothic classic is one of the city's oldest and best-loved buildings. Noon concerts are held Wednesday.

sights

AUTHOR FAVORITE

The open-air **Portland Saturday Market**, held on weekends from March to Christmas, offers a wonderful slice of local life. Ankeny Park and the district beneath the Burnside Bridge is a great place to shop for arts and crafts, sample savory specialties served up by vendors and enjoy performances by musicians, street performers and clowns. A permanent store showcases arts and crafts during the week. ~ 108 West Burnside Street; 503-222-6072, fax 503-222-0254; www.saturdaymarket.org, e-mail info@saturdaymarket.org.

Closed weekends. ~ 1422 Southwest 11th Avenue; 503-222-2031, fax 503-222-2981; www.oldchurch.org, e-mail staff@oldchurch.org.

Head east on Columbia Street to Southwest 5th Avenue. Take 5th Avenue north to the **Portland Building**, a postmodern office landmark opened in 1982. Designed by Michael Graves, this whimsical skyscraper represents the Northwest with an American Indian motif, making extensive use of turquoise and earth tones. ~ 1120 Southwest 5th Avenue; 503-823-4000, fax 503-823-3050.

On the Portland Building's second floor is the **Metropolitan Center for Public Art.** Here you'll find a portion of the *Portlandia* mold and renderings of the building, as well as pieces from the *Visual Chronicle of Portland*, a continually evolving series of works on paper meant to represent how the city views itself. The center is unstaffed—it's more an exhibition space than a museum—but it has assembled a walking-tour book that is available at the information desk on the first floor of the Portland Building. Open during regular business hours (when the building is open). ~ 1120 Southwest 5th Avenue; 503-823-5111, fax 503-823-5432; www.racc.org, e-mail info@racc.org.

Walk east on Main Street to Justice Center and learn about the history of local law enforcement at the **Portland Police Historical Museum**. Closed Saturday through Monday. ~ Room 1682, 1111 Southwest 2nd Avenue; 503-823-0019.

When you're ready to take a break, head south to the **Ira Keller Memorial Fountain**, located across from the Civic Auditorium. Situated in a pretty little park, this is a lovely spot to rest your weary feet. ~ Clay Street between 3rd and 4th avenues.

Farther south, past the Hawthorne Bridge on Harbor Way, you'll come to the sloped-roof buildings of **RiverPlace**, a popular shopping, hotel, restaurant and nightclub complex on the water. A promenade overlooks the Willamette River and the marina's many plush yachts.

Then return north to **Salmon Springs Fountain**, a synchronized fountain that is a favorite meeting place. Kids and dogs love to play in its cool water on hot days. ~ Salmon Street at Front Avenue.

A block away is **Mill Ends Park**, located in the median at Southwest Front Avenue and Taylor Street. Just two feet wide, this is the smallest official city park in the world, according to the *Guinness Book of World Records*.

Proceed northward to **Tom McCall Waterfront Park**, which is notable for being the green river frontage that in the 1970s replaced a busy, ugly stretch of freeway blocking the Willamette. You'll get a great view of Portland's skyline here. ~ Front Avenue.

Bounded by the Willamette River, Southwest 2nd Avenue, and Morrison and Taylor streets is the **Yamhill Historic District**. This area, on the National Register of Historic Places, boasts 19th-century cast-iron architecture favoring the Italianate style.

Walk west on Yamhill to the shops and cafés of **Yamhill Marketplace**. ~ 110 Southwest Yamhill Street; 503-224-3450, fax 503-224-3450.

Then stroll back to the waterfront and walk north on Front to the **Oregon Maritime Museum**. Here's your chance to learn Northwestern maritime history and see models of early ships, historical photographs and interpretive displays, all aboard the steam sternwheeler *Portland*. Closed Monday through Thursday in winter, Monday and Tuesday the rest of the year. Admission. ~ River Wall, between Morrison and Burnside bridges at the foot of Pine Street; 503-224-7724, fax 503-224-7767; www.oregonmaritimemuseum.org, e-mail info@oregonmaritimemuseum.org.

To fully experience the Portland waterfront consider boarding an excursion boat. **Sternwheeler Rose** departs from the Oregon Museum of Science and Industry and offers scenic Willamette River cruises. ~ 503-286-7673, fax 503-286-9661; www.sternwheelerrose.com. Another possibility is Portland's cruise ship **Portland Spirit**, which has year-round lunch, brunch, and Saturday-night dinner cruises. The *Portland Spirit* leaves from Salmon Street Springs Fountain in Tom McCall Waterfront Park. ~ 503-224-3900, fax 503-231-9089; www.portlandspirit.com.

The **Skidmore/Old Town** area illustrates Portland's commitment to adaptive reuse. This area between Front and 3rd streets both north and south of Burnside Street boomed in the later 19th century when the harbor was bustling. The look of the buildings from that era derives from Florentine civic palaces: broad, strong, imposing facades constructed of brick and cast iron. Eventually this became the rowdy part of town where sailors caroused, and polite society began to keep away as the buildings fell into disrepair. But interest has grown in the waterfront over the past 30 years, and historic commercial buildings and warehouses have been reborn as trendy shops, galleries, restaurants and nightclubs.

Next, head north through **Chinatown** on 4th Avenue. Not as large as it was at the turn of the 20th century, it is still packed with Chinese restaurants and markets. The ornate entry gate to Chinatown at the corner of Burnside Street and 4th Avenue looks a bit out of place among the neighboring adult bookstores.

Continue north on 4th to Northwest Everett Street and turn right. In one block you'll arrive at the **Portland Classical Chinese Garden**, a walled oasis of plants, ponds, stone sculptures and pavilions linked by winding pathways. The traditional teahouse here provides a serene setting for a light snack after strolling the premises. Admission. ~ Corner of Northwest 3rd Avenue and

Northwest Everett Street; 503-228-8131; www.portlandchinesegarden.org.

Walk north on Northwest 3rd Avenue; at Glisan Street head west to 6th Avenue. Then walk north to **Union Station**, Portland's marble-walled Amtrak Station. ~ 800 Northwest 6th Avenue; 503-273-4865.

LODGING

Lodgings in tightly packed downtown Portland are concentrated in large, historic hotels similar to those you'll find in cosmopolitan eastern cities like New York or Boston. As a result of the hustle for space, the majority of quality hotels in Central Portland are priced in the deluxe or ultra-deluxe range. If you're looking to save money, you may want to stay outside the downtown area (see "Lodging" in the "Portland East" and "Portland West" sections below).

A grand hotel and a registered historic landmark, **The Benson Hotel** offers casual fireside elegance in the lobby and 287 comfortably large guest rooms with understated gray decor, oak furniture, armoires and Early American prints. Like a good English club, the walnut-paneled lobby court contains easy chairs, comfortable sofas and a mirrored bar. Marbled halls, chandeliers, brass fixtures, a grand staircase and grandfather clock add an elegant touch. The stamped-tin ceiling, a common architectural feature in the late 19th and early 20th centuries, is one of the finest we've seen. Amenities include a health club and two restaurants. ~ 309 Southwest Broadway; 503-228-2000, 888-523-6766, fax 503-471-3920; www.bensonhotel.com, e-mail reservations@bensonhotel.com. ULTRA-DELUXE.

A good value is the 127-room **Hotel Lucia**, conveniently located to shops, cafés and clubs. Contemporary in feel, the cozy

AUTHOR FAVORITE

When the inevitable Portland rain begins to fall, I like to sneak off to the library at **The Heathman Hotel**, where many of the books are signed by authors who've stayed here. Later I'll mosey down to the lounge for an evening of soft jazz or have dinner in the lively restaurant. These are just the everyday delights offered by this landmark hotel. How far does The Heathman go to make its guests happy? When Luciano Pavarotti wanted to sleep in after a late arrival, the hotel manager asked a contractor across the street to postpone the start of noisy construction from 7 to 10 a.m. They agreed and the tenor slept soundly. ~ 1001 Southwest Broadway at Salmon Street; 503-241-4100, 800-551-0011, fax 503-790-7110; www.heathmanhotel.com, e-mail info@heathmanhotel.com. ULTRA-DELUXE.

guest rooms have mostly king- or queen-sized beds covered with down comforters and plush bathrooms for guests' use. A lounge, restaurant and fitness center round out the amenities. ~ 400 South west Broadway; 503-225-1717, 877-225-1717, fax 503-205-2051; www.hotellucia.com. DELUXE.

Boutique hotels are one of the fastest-growing trends in the lodging industry and Portland has one of its own, **Hotel Vintage Plaza**. A remake of the historic Wells Building, this hotel features a ten-story atrium. Each of the 107 guest rooms and expansive suites is named for a local winery. Rooms with burgundy and green color schemes come with cherry-wood armoires, neoclassical furniture, columned headboards, black-granite nightstands and Empire-style column bedside lamps. On the top floor are some "Starlight" rooms, with light-sand beach motifs and one-way solarium windows for stargazers. Local fine wines can be sampled at the complimentary tasting held each evening in front of the fireplace in the lobby. ~ 422 Southwest Broadway; 503-228-1212, 800-243-0555, fax 503-228-3598; www.vintageplaza.com, e-mail reservations@vintageplaza.com. ULTRA-DELUXE.

An excellent value, **Four Points Sheraton Hotel** is the place to enjoy views of boat traffic on the Willamette. The rooms have a contemporary feel, with oak furniture and earth-toned decor. Enjoy the sunset from the comfort of your deck. The 140-room inn is within walking distance of Portland's business and shopping district. A café and bar are also here. ~ 50 Southwest Morrison Street; 503-221-0711, fax 503-484-1417; www.fourpointsportland.com. MODERATE.

Enjoying one of the best locations in town, **RiverPlace Hotel** offers 84 rooms, suites and condos, many with views of the Willamette. In the midst of the Esplanade area featuring bookstores, antique shops and restaurants, this establishment is a short walk from the downtown business district. Wing-back chairs, teak tables, writing desks, fireplaces and pastel decor make the rooms inviting. A sauna, whirlpool baths and 24-hour room service are all available. ~ 1510 Southwest Harbor Way; 503-228-3233, 800-227-1333, fax 503-295-6161; www.riverplacehotel.com, e-mail sales@riverplacehotel.com. ULTRA-DELUXE.

For reasonably priced rooms and suites head for the **Hotel Mallory**. This 130-unit establishment built in 1912 has a mirrored lobby, leaded skylights and a chandelier. The eclectic rooms here come with down bedding, oak furniture, contemporary couches and, in some cases, small chandeliers. There is also a classy dining room with marble pillars supporting the embossed gold-leaf ceiling. ~ 729 Southwest 15th Avenue; 503-223-6311, 800-228-8657, fax 503-223-0522; www.malloryhotel.com, e-mail reservations@malloryhotel.com. MODERATE TO DELUXE.

Thai native Bo Kline re-invents the complex flavors of her home country at **Typhoon! on Broadway**, a downtown restaurant crowded with satisfied diners. Artfully presented dishes include wild shrimp in red curry, pineapple fried rice and stir-fry ginger beef. If you have room for dessert, there's homemade coconut ice cream or espresso crème brûlée. ~ Hotel Lucia, 410 Southwest Broadway; 503-224-8285, fax 503-224-3468; www.typhoonrestaurants.com. MODERATE.

The interior of **Saucebox** is mesmerizing, with glowing lanterns, a gleaming bar and two huge original paintings. The food is equally stunning, a pan-Asian and regional Hawaiian menu featuring Javanese salmon, Korean-style baby back ribs and seared ahi. The bar is known for its expansive repertoire of fabulous drinks—try a coconut-lime Rickey, a ginger cosmopolitan or wild ginseng martini. Dinner only. Closed Sunday and Monday. ~ 214 Southwest Broadway; 503-241-3393, fax 503-243-3251; www.saucebox.com, e-mail info@saucebox.com. MODERATE.

The brick pizza oven, trattoria ambience, dark-wood booths and gleaming bar make **Pazzo Ristorante** a valuable member of the Portland restaurant scene. Dip a little of the fresh-baked bread in the special-press extra virgin olive oil, hoist a glass of the red and survey the Mediterranean menu. Wood oven–baked pizza, housemade pastas, line-caught fish, and Piedmontese beef are some of the popular entrées. ~ 627 Southwest Washington Street; 503-228-1515, fax 503-228-5935; www.pazzoristorante.com, e-mail pazzoristorante@pazzo.com. MODERATE TO DELUXE.

Pass the retsina and toast **Alexis**. This family-style taverna brings the Aegean to the Columbia in the time-honored manner. Belly dancing on the weekend, wallhangings and long tables upstairs with checkered blue-and-white tablecloths add to the ambience. Lamb souvlaki, moussaka, charbroiled shrimp and vege-

AUTHOR FAVORITE

A favorite in Portland is **The Heathman Restaurant**. The menu, which changes seasonally, transforms traditional French dishes with Northwest ingredients, seafood and game meats. Some specialties include grilled lightly smoked salmon, seared ahi tuna wrapped in prosciutto, and roast rack of lamb. This spacious dining room and adjacent brass and marble bar is a great place to watch the passing scene on Broadway. The walls are graced with a classy collection of contemporary art. The Heathman also has an extensive breakfast menu. ~ 1001 Southwest Broadway at Salmon Street; 503-790-7752, fax 503-790-7112; www.heathmanhotel.com, e-mail info@heathmanhotel.com. MODERATE TO DELUXE.

tarian specialties are all on the menu. Be sure to try the dolmas and share an order of hummus and homemade pita. No lunch on Saturday. Closed Sunday. ~ 215 West Burnside Street; 503-224-8577, fax 503-224-9354. MODERATE.

A memorable dining room is **Jake's Famous Crawfish**. This mahogany-paneled, late-19th-century landmark has a grand bar, big tables and a seafood menu that seems to stretch from here to Seattle. Inevitably packed, the restaurant offers tasty chowder, smoked and fresh salmon, halibut, oysters and a good bouillabaisse. For the non-seafood lover, they also offer pasta and steak dishes. ~ 401 Southwest 12th Avenue; 503-226-1419, fax 503-220-1856; www.jakesfamouscrawfish.com. MODERATE TO DELUXE.

With a vast menu of Northwest cuisine, the **Harborside Restaurant** is a kind of culinary United Nations. Window tables on the river and paneled booths on the upper levels provide great views of the harbor traffic. Excellent seafood salads, pasta dishes, stir frys, steaks, hamburgers and pizza are served. ~ 0309 Southwest Montgomery Street; 503-220-1865, fax 503-220-1855. MODERATE TO DELUXE.

The setting alone justifies a trip to **Old Town Pizza Company**. A landmark commercial building with stained glass, wicker furniture, enough antiques to furnish a store and old root beer advertising signs make this two-level establishment a genuine period piece. Over two dozen toppings from goat cheese to roasted garlic give you plenty of options. Focaccia, antipasti, lasagna and salads are also available. ~ 226 Northwest Davis Street; 503-222-9999. BUDGET.

For a light but satisfying meal, stop by **Pearl Bakery** for a sandwich on classic focaccia or sourdough, or an original offering like fig or walnut bread. Seasonal sandwich fillings such as tuna salad, eggplant and peanut and jelly are always fresh. There are also plenty of tempting coffee cakes, croissants, danishes and cakes. ~ 102 Northwest 9th Avenue; 503-827-0910, fax 503-827-0912; www.pearlbakery.com. BUDGET.

Traditional yet chic, **Fratelli** exudes warmth from its open kitchen and tabletop candlelight. The layout is reminiscent of alley-side cafés in southern Italy, long and narrow with stucco walls. The menu, though not extensive, is authentic and changes seasonally. You'll find mouth-watering entrées such as Dungeness crab and fennel-broth ravioli, polenta with wild mushrooms, and risotto with scallops and fresh spinach. The wine list has a great Italian selection. ~ 1230 Northwest Hoyt Street; 503-241-8800; www.fratellicucina.com.

With fresh flowers and big red chairs, **Wilf's Restaurant and Bar** is one of the most elaborate dining rooms in Portland. In this elegant setting along the tracks you can enjoy a menu emphasizing organic and sustainably produced ingredients in dishes like

Northwest salmon filet with an apricot glaze, veal lafayette or rack of lamb. Since they specialize in tableside cooking, entrées such as steak Diane and prawns flambé, and desserts like bananas Foster or crêpes Suzette are works of performance and culinary art. No lunch on Saturday. Closed Sunday. ~ 800 Northwest 6th Avenue; 503-223-0070, fax 503-223-1386. DELUXE.

Obi is the place for sushi, *yaki soba*, shrimp tempura, salmon teriyaki and dozens of other Japanese specialties. The dark dining room has modest plastic tables and displays silk-screen art, watercolors and traditional costumes. No lunch Saturday and Sunday. ~ 101 Northwest 2nd Avenue; 503-226-3826. MODERATE.

SHOPPING

The **Oregon Historical Society Museum Store** has an outstanding collection of local and regional history titles. From American Indian culture to walking tours of Portland, this admirable shop is definitely worth a look. Souvenir books, guides, children's literature, and historical toys as well as regional gifts are all found in abundance. ~ Corner of Broadway and Madison; 503-306-5230, fax 503-306-5230; www.ohs.org.

Classic newsstands are rare these days. Fortunately, **Rich's Cigar Store**, dating to the late 1800s, continues this grand tradition. Browse for your favorite magazine or out-of-town newspaper in this beautiful wood-paneled shop. ~ 820 Southwest Alder Street; 503-228-1700, fax 503-227-4247.

Whether you're on the lookout for hard-to-find vintage vinyl or the newest indie releases, look no farther than **2nd Avenue Records**. Punk music is well-represented here, as is metal, hip hop, electronica, ska, reggae and rock. The sheer volume of merchandise can be daunting, but the knowledgeable sales staff can point you in the right direction. There's also a wide selection of T-shirts, buttons, patches and stickers. ~ 400 Southwest 2nd Avenue; 503-222-3783.

BOOKTOPIA

Bigger than many libraries, **Powell's City of Books** is only one of Portland's many fine bookstores. What makes it unique is its size—it would be hard to dispute its claim of being the world's largest bookstore. With over a million new and used titles, this Goliath encourages customers to pick up a large map, indexed into hundreds of categories ranging from abortion to Zen. Somewhere in between you're likely to find the title you want. Powell's also hosts guest readings by well-known authors. Along the way, stop by the Coffee Room for a snack and a leisurely read. ~ 1005 West Burnside Street; 503-228-4651, 800-878-7323, fax 503-228-4631; www.powells.com. Powell's also has six other locations in the Portland area.

The **Attic Gallery** features paintings, sculpture, prints and ceramics by major Northwest artists. Closed Sunday. ~ 205 Southwest 1st Avenue; 503-228-7830.

Several major malls are in the downtown area. **Pioneer Place** boasts 80 stores spread across a three-block area. ~ Southwest 5th Avenue and Morrison Street.

One of the region's best-known apparel makers offers its line at **The Portland Pendleton Shop**. Skirts, shirts, slacks, jackets and blankets are sold at this popular store. While its reputation was built on woolens, it also sells high-quality apparel in silk, rayon and other fabrics. ~ 4th Avenue between Salmon and Taylor streets; 503-242-0037; www.pendleton-usa.com.

Above the entrance to the Portland Building is *Portlandia*, the world's second-largest hammered-bronze sculpture.

Elizabeth Leach Gallery presents an array of regional and national painters, sculptors, photographers and print makers. Closed Sunday and Monday. ~ 417 Northwest 9th Street; 503-224-0521; www.elizabethleach.com.

Quintana Galleries houses a fine collection of both antique and contemporary American Indian art from Alaska and the Pacific Northwest. You can browse through (and purchase) an array of authentic objects, from totems to whalebone carvings to hand-painted drums. Closed Sunday and Monday. ~ 120 Northwest 9th Avenue; 503-223-1729, 800-321-1729; www.quintanagalleries.com.

Nearly 300 artisans display handcrafted glass, jewelry, hats, sweaters, furniture, rugs, music boxes and folk and fine art at the **Portland Saturday Market**. There's also live entertainment and food. Open Saturday and Sunday; closed January and February. ~ Between Front and 1st streets underneath the Burnside Bridge; 503-222-6072, fax 503-222-0254; www.portlandsaturdaymarket.com.

NIGHTLIFE

The city's cultural hub is the **Portland Center for the Performing Arts**. Included are the Arlene Schnitzer Concert Hall and the Newmark and Winningstad theaters. The center is home of the **Oregon Symphony Orchestra** (503-228-1353), the **Keller Auditorium** and **Portland Center Stage** (503-274-6588). ~ 1111 Southwest Broadway; 503-248-4335; www.pcpa.com.

Artists Repertory Theater is the place for off-Broadway productions with a focus on current contemporary playwrights and modern-day issues. ~ 1516 Southwest Alder Street; 503-241-1278 (box office); www.artistsrep.org.

Both the **Oregon Ballet Theatre** (503-222-5538) and **Portland Opera** (503-241-1802) perform at the Keller Auditorium, located at 222 Southwest Clay Street.

At **The Heathman Lobby Lounge**, musicians like Dave Firshberg play jazz on the Steinway. ~ 1001 Southwest Broadway at Salmon Street; 503-241-4100.

Enjoy a cocktail to the strains of live pop and jazz piano at **The Benson Hotel's Lobby Court.** This elegant setting includes plush sofas and wing chairs and walnut paneling. The lounge is a great place to impress your friends—or yourself. ~ 309 Southwest Broadway; 503-228-2000.

Brasserie Montmartre is another good jazz venue. This art-deco establishment, where patrons are encouraged to draw on their paper tablecloths, even has a strolling magician. Contemporary drawings, comfortable banquettes, chandeliers and a checkered black-and-white floor all add to the café's charm. ~ 626 Southwest Park Avenue; 503-224-5552.

The **Portland Art Museum—After Hours** is the perfect way to spend a spring or fall Wednesday evening. Take a seat or explore the collection while the halls resonate to jazz or blues. Beer, wine and hors d'oeuvres are served. Admission. ~ 1219 Southwest Park Avenue; 503-226-2811.

With male strippers six nights a week, neon bar signs and a swinging dancefloor, **Silverado** has plenty of action. In addition, you'll encounter deejay music, a long bar and dining room. Cover Friday and Saturday. ~ 1217 Southwest Stark Street; 503-224-4493.

The Pilsner Room is an upscale bar attached to a microbrewery, serving fish-and-chips, hamburgers and the like. ~ 0309 Southwest Montgomery Street; 503-220-1865.

Billiards, darts and beer on tap create a relaxed atmosphere at **Scandal's Restaurant and Lounge,** which has a loyal gay following. ~ 1038 Southwest Stark Street; 503-227-5887; www.scandalspdx.com.

Female impersonators perform Wednesday through Saturday nights at **Darcelle XV,** a small theater where dinner is available by reservation. Closed Sunday. Cover. ~ 208 Northwest 3rd Avenue; 503-222-5338.

Embers on the Avenue features drag shows Wednesday through Saturday. The rear of this brick building houses Portland's largest dancefloor, hosting a mixed crowd of gay and straight partygoers. With neon-lit walls, two bars and deejay music, this room is always jumping. Cover Friday and Saturday. ~ 110 Northwest Broadway; 503-222-3082.

Regarded as one of the top places in the world for jazz music, **Jimmy Mak's Bar & Grill** features soulful live acts almost every night. Intimate and often crowded, you can ensure a comfortable seat by arriving early for dinner. A basement lounge with two pool tables and a full bar provides a casual alternative to the main stage. Closed Sunday. ~ 300 Northwest 10th Avenue; 503-295-6542; www.jimmymaks.com.

Portland East

Just across the Willamette from the frenzied downtown core are some of Portland's most inviting neighborhoods. The city planners have emphasized good public transportation throughout the entire metropolitan area, keeping the neighborhoods east of the river unified with the downtown core. But only here can you glimpse Portland's lower-key charms: a shopping area devoted exclusively to antiques, a city park featuring an extinct volcano and a religious retreat doubling as a peaceful garden. Portland East is also home to a rare heirloom—a classic old-time amusement park.

This section of Portland also includes such suburbs as Oregon City and Milwaukie, the former of which once welcomed settlers who had made the arduous trek overland on the Oregon Trail. Today, Portland East is a network of streets and parks designed, like much of Portland, for maximum use by its residents.

SIGHTS

Cross the Willamette via MAX Light Rail and disembark at the beautiful **Oregon Convention Center** plaza, landscaped with terraced planters. Stroll over for a look at the 18-acre campus of the center crowned by a matching pair of glass-and-steel spires soaring 250 feet above the hall. The center's interior contains art, dragon boats, a bronze pendulum and inspirational quotes about the state. Everywhere you go, even in the restrooms, you'll find talented artists and craftspeople have left their decorative touch. ~ 777 Northeast Martin Luther King Jr. Boulevard; 503-235-7575, fax 503-235-7712; www.oregoncc.org.

A mile south of the convention center, the **Oregon Museum of Science and Industry** (OMSI) is a 220,000-square-foot science education center. Four exhibition halls offer displays on the physical, earth, life and information sciences, while another has traveling exhibits. In addition, you'll find an OMNIMAX theater and the Harry C. Kendall Planetarium presenting astronomy and laser light shows (additional admission). Special exhibits focus on biotechnology, computers, engineering for kids, communications and chemistry. Closed Monday from September through May. Admission. ~ 1945 Southeast Water Avenue; 503-797-4000, fax 503-797-4500; www.omsi.edu.

To the south are two popular Portland shopping districts. **Hawthorne Boulevard** from 30th to 40th avenues has become one of the city's more intriguing commercial districts. A great place to browse, shop and eat, this district is known for its used bookstores and offbeat boutiques. Another popular neighborhood is **Sellwood,** an antique center extending along 13th Avenue from Clatsop to Malden streets.

While cities across the land have scrapped these period pieces, Portland has held on to the **Oaks Amusement Park**, located just west of the Sellwood district. In addition to vintage thrill rides, you can enjoy roller skating to the strains of the last Wurlitzer organ playing at a rink in the United States. This pretty park is next to the **Oaks Bottom Wildlife Sanctuary**, a major Portland marsh habitat. Rides are closed mid-October to mid-March. ~ Oaks Park, east end of the Sellwood Bridge; 503-233-5777, fax 503-236-9143; www.oakspark.com.

One of the nation's most progressive liberal arts institutions, **Reed College** has a wooded, 98-acre campus cloaked in ivy. Reed's gothic buildings and old dorms are close to Crystal Springs Rhododendron Garden at 28th Avenue and Woodstock Boulevard (see "Parks" below for more information). Pick up a visitors guide in Eliot Hall or the Greywood Community Service Building. ~

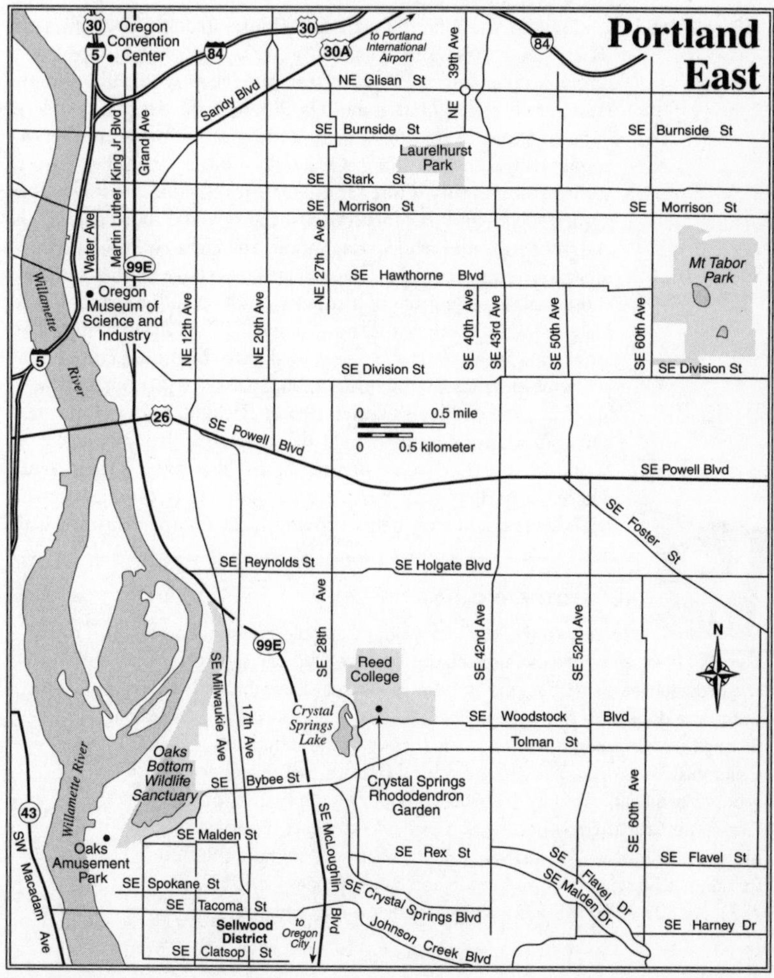

3203 Southeast Woodstock Boulevard; 503-771-1112, 800-547-4750, fax 503-777-7553; www.reed.edu.

LODGING In northeast Portland's Irvington District, **The Lion and the Rose Victorian Bed and Breakfast** is a historical Queen Anne–style mansion with six guest rooms furnished in period antiques. The decor is warm with rich shades of plum and ivy green, and natural light makes the rooms bright and airy. Amenities range from jacuzzi and clawfoot tubs to wrought-iron and four-poster beds. Enjoy tea in the outdoor gazebo and English gardens. ~ 1810 Northeast 15th Avenue; 503-287-9245, 800-955-1647, fax 503-287-9247; www.lionrose.com, e-mail innkeeper@lionrose.com. MODERATE TO DELUXE.

HIDDEN ► Hail to the Chief! **Portland's House** strongly resembles the other White House in Washington, D.C. The stately Greek columns, circular driveway and crystal chandeliers would all make the First Family feel right at home. The difference here is that you don't have to stand in line for a tour, and there are no Secret Service agents to hustle you along. Originally built as a lumber baron's summer home, this White House features handpainted murals of garden scenes and oak-inlaid floors. Canopy and four-poster beds, clawfoot tubs and leaded glass adorn the eight rooms. Three additional rooms in an adjacent carriage house have feather beds and stained glass. The price of a room includes a full gourmet breakfast. ~ 1914 Northeast 22nd Avenue; 503-287-7131, 800-272-7131, fax 503-249-1641; www.portlandswhitehouse.com, e-mail pdxwhi@portlandswhitehouse.com. MODERATE TO DELUXE.

The 1908 **Sullivan's Gulch Bed & Breakfast** offers four guest accommodations with themed decor ranging from Bangkok to Scotland; the two with private baths also have sitting areas. There's a garden with two decks and a stately dining room. A friendly resident dog helps provide furry companionship. Gay-

sights

AUTHOR FAVORITE

No visit to the city's east side is complete without a stop at **The Grotto**. Near the Portland airport, this 62-acre Catholic sanctuary and garden is a peaceful refuge that seems to have as much in common with a Zen retreat as it does with the Vatican. Beautiful ponds and shrines, paths leading through flower gardens and expansive views of the mountains and the Columbia River make The Grotto a local favorite. In December, the grounds are illuminated by 200,000 lights during the Festival of Lights. Choral performances, a petting zoo and refreshments round out the experience. Admission for festival. ~ 8840 Northeast Skidmore Street (parking at Northeast 85th Avenue and Sandy Boulevard); 503-254-7371, fax 503-254-7948; www.thegrotto.org, e-mail gifts@thegrotto.org.

friendly. ~ 1744 Northeast Clackamas Street; 503-331-1104, fax 815-327-1794; www.sullivansgulch.com, e-mail atlantisplace@yahoo.com. MODERATE TO DELUXE.

In the Hawthorne neighborhood, **Hostelling International—Portland Hawthorne** offers dorm accommodations for men and women, a family room and a couples room. This older home also has a self-serve kitchen and all-you-can-eat pancakes in the morning. Internet kiosks and free internet connections for laptops are available. Check-in begins at noon. Quiet time starts at 10 p.m. Complimentary bread and pastries are included. ~ 3031 Southeast Hawthorne Boulevard; 503-236-3380, 866-447-3031, fax 503-236-7940; www.portlandhostel.org, e-mail hip@portlandhostel.org. BUDGET.

In Oregon City, south of Portland and on the banks of the Willamette, the **Rivershore Hotel** is pretty much the only remaining lodging option. Each of the 120 rooms has a balcony with a view and a queen- or king-size bed—clean and comfortable, but nothing to write home about. There is, however, an indoor spa and an outdoor heated pool. ~ 1900 Clackamette Drive, Oregon City; 503-655-7141, 800-443-7777, fax 503-655-1927; www.rivershorehotel.com, e-mail info@rivershorehotel.com. MODERATE.

DINING

The Tin Shed Garden Café offers delicious breakfast choices like grits, buttermilk biscuits, latkes and scrambled eggs, all made with the freshest ingredients. There is a kids' menu as well. In nice weather, ask to sit on the patio by the open-hearth fireplace. No dinner Monday or Tuesday. ~ 1438 Northeast Alberta Street; 503-288-6966. BUDGET.

Laughing Planet Café serves wholesome pastries, soups, juices and espresso, plus the build-your-own burrito bar, in a hip, fun setting. This eco-friendly café offers many vegetarian and vegan options. ~ 3320 Southeast Belmont Street; 503-235-6472, fax 503-235-0146. BUDGET.

Inventive Mexican food and an extensive cocktail menu distinguish **Dingo's Mexican Grill** from your run-of-the-mill burrito place. Entrées include lime chicken enchiladas, rock shrimp tacos and ahi burritos. Happy hour (4 p.m. to 6 p.m.) features $3-a-plate specials. Thursday is Girl's Night Out, popular with local lesbians. ~ 4612 Southeast Hawthorne Boulevard; 503-233-3996, fax 503-233-0778; www.dingosonline.com, e-mail webmaster@dingosonline.com. BUDGET.

One of Portland's better breakfasts is found at **Tabor Hill Café** in the Hawthorne neighborhood. This small, red-brick establishment with eclectic decor features modern art, gray carpet and red tables. The seasonal fruit pancake (that's singular, not plural) is large enough to blanket your entire plate. Other choices are chicken omelettes and a fresh fruit cup. Lunch specialties include avocado-and-bacon sandwich, burgers, marinated chicken breast and blackened-snapper salad. ~ 3766 Southeast Hawthorne Boulevard; 503-230-1231. BUDGET.

HIDDEN ►

Yes, there really is a free dinner at **Sayler's Old Country Kitchen.** All you have to do is eat one of the 72-ounce top-sirloin steaks along with a salad, a slice of french bread, ten fries or a baked potato, two carrot sticks, two celery sticks, two olives, a beverage and ice cream—and the house will pick up the tab. You only get one hour to finish, and it is a one-time-only offer. Over 500 customers have won the bet. If you're not that hungry try the tenderloin, prime rib, chicken, scallops, prawns or halibut steaks. Dinner only. ~ 10519 Southeast Stark Street, Portland; 503-252-4171, fax 503-257-0088. BUDGET TO MODERATE.

Located in the Sellwood district known for its antique stores, **Papa Haydn** is a yummy storefront café where fans twirl from the ceilings, watercolors grace the gray walls and wicker furniture accommodates guests who don't come to count calories. Weekend brunch features French toast stuffed with pears, hazelnuts and cranberries or a smoked salmon omelette. Dinner entrées include herb-crusted steak and organic chicken with hazelnut *spaetzle*. An extensive wine list and espresso drinks are found here along with one of the longest dessert menus in the Pacific Northwest. ~ 5829 Southeast Milwaukie Avenue; 503-232-9440, fax 503-236-5815; www.papahaydn.com, e-mail jobarhaydn@aol.com. MODERATE.

SHOPPING

Vestiges has two floors of funky and eclectic antique and new items, all artfully displayed. ~ 4743 Northeast Fremont Avenue; 503-331-3920.

Take home a piece of art for your kitchen table—the **Guardino Gallery** gift shop has handcrafted clay and glass vases, sculptures, plates and bowls, as well as jewelry and paintings. ~ 2939 Northeast Alberta Street; 503-281-9048; www.guardinogallery.com.

Oregon Mountain Community is the ultimate shop for recreational equipment and supplies. In addition to a full line of outdoor

BRUNCH AND MORE

It's not easy to find a hearty Sunday brunch these days, but we did it at **Bread and Ink Café**. The coffee is strong, the lox is beautiful and the children are kept content with crayons and paper. In addition to bagels and cream cheese, challah and a variety of omelettes, you'll enjoy the family-style atmosphere. Set in an elegant commercial building adorned with terra cotta, this weekly happening is a Portland original. The restaurant is also famous for its burgers. Breakfast, lunch and dinner. ~ 3610 Southeast Hawthorne Boulevard; 503-239-4756. MODERATE.

wear, there's skiing, backpacking and climbing gear. ~ 2975 Northeast Sandy Boulevard; 503-227-1038.

The **Lloyd Center Mall** is the largest mall in the state, with over 125 stores. ~ 13th and Multnomah Street; 503-282-2511; www.lloydcentermall.com.

Along Hawthorne Boulevard are many small, independent shops with interesting selections. Stop by **Artichoke Music** for acoustic and folk instruments, guitar sheet music and lesson books. On a weekend you can catch live acoustic music or join the song circle; on the first Friday of every month check out the highly acclaimed variety revue. Closed Sunday and Monday. ~ 3130 Southeast Hawthorne Boulevard; 503-232-8845; www.artichokemusic.com, e-mail folks@artichokemusic.com.

The Goddess Gallery features statues and museum replicas of gods and goddesses art from around the world. ~ 3574 Southeast Hawthorne Boulevard; 503-239-7458, 866-334-7458; www.goddess-gallery.com.

Death can be proud at **Murder by the Book**. Mystery addicts will get their fix here and also become acquainted with many well-known Northwest authors. In addition to new and used books, you can buy accessories, games and puzzles. ~ 3210 Southeast Hawthorne Boulevard; 503-232-9995, fax 503-232-2554; www.mbtb.com, e-mail books@mbtb.com.

NIGHTLIFE

Atmosphere is the key word at **Crush**. Low lighting and art-plastered walls make this fairly large space seem intimate, while creative touches such as a multicolored beer-bottle chandelier and movie-playing TV screens in the bathrooms provide unique charm. An arched doorway leads to three separate rooms—the lounge, with a long curved bar, plush couches and granite coffee tables; the blue room, for live music and dancing; and a smokers' lounge. It's a great place for a casual cocktail or dancing on the weekends. ~ 1400 Southeast Morrison Street; 503-235-8150; www.crushbar.com, e-mail crush@crushbar.com.

The Moorish **Baghdad Theater and Pub** has a fairy-tale decor with painted walls and a fountain in the lobby. Every other row of theater seating has been removed to accommodate tables where patrons can order food and drinks and enjoy second-run films. Customers under 21 years of age are welcome for the Saturday and Sunday matinees only when accompanied by a parent. ~ 3702 Southeast Hawthorne Boulevard; 503-236-9234, 503-225-5555 ext. 8830 (movie line).

The **Echo Theater** is the home of **Do Jump! Extremely Physical Theater**. Shows include acrobatic and trapeze acts. Visiting dance troupes also use the theater's stage. ~ 1515 Southeast 37th Avenue; 503-231-1232, fax 503-231-2937; www.dojump.org, e-mail dojump@dojump.org.

One of the city's finest classical programs is **Chamber Music Northwest.** Nationally known groups perform year-round in the beautiful settings at Reed College and Catlin Gabel School, with a five-week festival in June and July. ~ 503-223-3202, fax 503-294-1690; for tickets, call 503-294-6400; www.cmnw.org, e-mail info@cmnw.org.

The 9000-square-foot **Egyptian Club**, located in a former milk plant, features three different rooms. There's a dancefloor in the Tomb and a retro bar room with pool tables and video games. A third bar, the Room, features open-mic night and karaoke. Occasional Wednesday nights there is belly dancing in the Tomb. The crowd is primarily lesbian. Cover Friday and Saturday. ~ 3701 Southeast Division Street; 503-236-8689; e-mail egykim@aol.com.

For a listing of current shows and popular venues in the area, pick up a copy of *Willamette Week*, a free alternative newspaper available at groceries and newsstands. ~ www.wweek.com.

PARKS

HIDDEN ►

KELLEY POINT PARK At the confluence of the Willamette and Columbia rivers, this forested site is popular for biking and hiking. The park, largely undeveloped, is busy during the summer months but wide open the rest of the year. There are picnic tables and restrooms. ~ Located in northernmost Portland at the west end of Suttle Road off Northeast Marine Drive; 503-823-2223, fax 503-823-5297.

PENINSULA PARK This 16-acre park features beautiful sunken rose gardens highlighted with fountains and a charming gazebo. Extensive recreational facilities, a formal rose garden and a small pond make Peninsula popular with families. Facilities include picnic tables, a basketball court, horseshoe pits, a pool, a soccer field, tennis courts and restrooms. ~ North Albina Street and Portland Boulevard; 503-823-2223, fax 503-823-5297.

POWELL BUTTE NATURE PARK This rustic, 600-acre park centers around a 630-foot-high volcanic mound that offers great views of the city and the Cascades. If you can, circle this volcanic butte via a two-mile loop route at day's end and take advantage of the sunset. Facilities are limited to restrooms and picnic tables. ~ Northeast 162nd Avenue and Powell Boulevard; 503-823-2223, fax 503-823-5297.

LAURELHURST PARK Bordered by rhododendron, a pretty lake is the heart of this 34-acre park in a historic residential district. Along the way you're likely to spot geese, ducks, swans and turtles. Forested with fir and oak, the park also features glens, gardens and contemporary sculpture. You'll find restrooms, picnic tables, a playground, a soccer field and tennis, volleyball and basketball courts. ~ Northeast 39th Avenue and Stark Street; 503-823-2223, fax 503-823-5297.

MT. TABOR PARK The only extinct volcano within the limits of an American city, Mt. Tabor was discovered during excavations in 1912. While the cinder cone is the park's star attraction, it also offers an extensive network of trails for hiking and jogging. This forested setting affords smashing views of the city. There are picnic tables, restrooms, horseshoe pits, a playground, tennis courts, basketball courts, a volleyball court and an amphitheater. ~ Southeast Salmon Street and 60th Avenue; 503-823-2223, fax 503-823-5297.

LEACH BOTANICAL GARDEN These 15 acres are home to over 2000 flowers and plants, including many native species. Johnson Creek meanders through the original Leach Property. You can explore the grounds of this one-time estate on your own or via a guided tour. You'll find a manor house, stone cabin and carriage house, a library, a gift shop and plant table, restrooms and self-guiding brochures. Closed Monday. ~ 6704 Southeast 122nd Avenue; 503-761-9503, fax 503-823-9504.

When it comes to parks, Portland offers more than 80, covering 37,000 acres.

CRYSTAL SPRINGS RHODODENDRON GARDEN Boasting seven acres of flora and fauna, this park is at its best in April and May. The colorful panorama of more than 2000 rhododendron and azalea is enhanced by three waterfalls and two bridges spanning a creek that flows into Crystal Springs Lake. Ducks and other waterfowl are found year-round at this refuge near Reed College. Call ahead to arrange a guided tour. There are restrooms. Admission during the summer months. ~ Southeast 28th Avenue north of Woodstock Boulevard; 503-771-8386.

CLACKAMETTE PARK A haven for ducks and geese, Clackamette's 22 acres border the Willamette River in the Oregon City area. It's also a prime spot to see blue herons nesting on Goat Island. Restrooms are available. ~ Take Exit 9 from Route 205 toward Oregon City and Gladstone. Go west on Clackamette two-tenths of a mile; 503-657-8299, fax 503-656-7488.

▲ There are 38 RV hookup sites; $15 to $18 per night, ten-day maximum stay. No reservations taken.

Portland West

From vineyards to Japanese gardens, Portland's west side has many of the city's best parks, major museums and wildlife preserves. Charming Victorians line many streets and the city's fabled Pittock Mansion reminds visitors of Portland's glamorous past. Washington Park, the city's beloved green oasis, presides over Portland West in much the same way that Central Park does in New York. Most of the other worthwhile attractions here also involve the outdoors: just half an hour from downtown, you can enjoy wilderness areas or cycle along placid sloughs, in addition to other delights.

Heading south from downtown along the western side of the Willamette, you'll pass residential 'burbs like Tigard and Beaverton before encountering the vineyards that comprise Oregon's wine country. The original settlers believed the Willamette Valley to have some of the best soil in the world, and the area just beyond the city limits does maintain a rural flavor. But Portland's populace has also worked hard not to overdevelop all of its own land, and this section of the city definitely benefits as a result. Still, the area closest to downtown does maintain a cosmopolitan air.

SIGHTS

We begin our tour in one of the trendiest areas in Portland, **Nob Hill**. The district was given its name by a 19th-century San Franciscan who saw a similarity to his old neighborhood. At the **Portland Oregon Information Center** downtown (Pioneer Courthouse Square, 701 Southwest 6th Avenue; 503-275-8355), you can pick up the walking guide to this district focused around Northwest 23rd Avenue, north of Burnside Street. Home of many of the city's finest restaurants, bookstores and antique and art shops, Nob Hill also has noteworthy early-20th-century Victorian and Georgian homes, as well as churches and commercial buildings. Among them are the **Charles F. Adams House** (2363 Northwest Flanders Street) and the **Ayer-Shea House** (1809 Northwest Johnson Street).

When the roses are in bloom (from late June to early September), it's hard to find a better vantage point for the city than the International Rose Test Garden.

This tree-lined district is also convenient to **Washington Park**, a 130-acre refuge created by the Olmsted brothers, from the family of landscape architects who gave the world Central Park in New York and Golden Gate Park in San Francisco. Home to several gardens and the zoo, this park is one of Portland's most worthy destinations. ~ Southwest Park Place, two blocks west of Vista Avenue; 503-823-3635, fax 503-823-1667.

Begin your visit at the **International Rose Test Garden**. Consisting of three terraces, this four-and-a-half-acre gem has over 8700 bushes, enough to make this park a true mecca for rose aficionados worldwide. In addition to the test area, visitors are welcome to see the Shakespearean Garden and Gold Medal Award Garden. ~ 400 Southwest Kingston Avenue; 503-823-3636, fax 503-823-1667.

Directly west of the Rose Garden is the **Japanese Garden Society of Oregon**. Five traditional gardens spread across five and a half acres make this tranquil spot a great place for a quiet walk. The Flat Garden is a sea of raked sand. The Sand and Stone Garden is abstract and inspired by Zen Buddhism. The Tea Garden contains a Japanese teahouse, while the Natural Garden is filled with foliage growing in its natural state. Don't miss the Strolling Pond Garden with its Heavenly Falls, koi pools and beautiful moon bridge. There's also a pavilion overlooking Mt. Hood, Oregon's answer to Mt. Fuji. Admission. ~ 611 Southwest Kingston Avenue; 503-223-1321, fax 503-223-8303; www.japanesegarden.com.

Follow Kingston Avenue until you see signs leading to 64-acre **Oregon Zoo**. Also accessible by a steam train from the Japanese and International Rose Test gardens during the summer months, the zoo features an African rainforest as well as a savannah roamed by giraffes, zebras, rhinos and hippos. Stellar Cove is a marine environment with sea lions, sea otters, a kelp forest and a coastal tide pool display. Other points of interest are the zoo's Humboldt penguins, Arctic polar bears and orangutans. The staff is proud of the fact that it has one of the world's most successful Asian elephant–breeding programs. You'll also find an extensive collection of Pacific Northwest animals, including beavers and

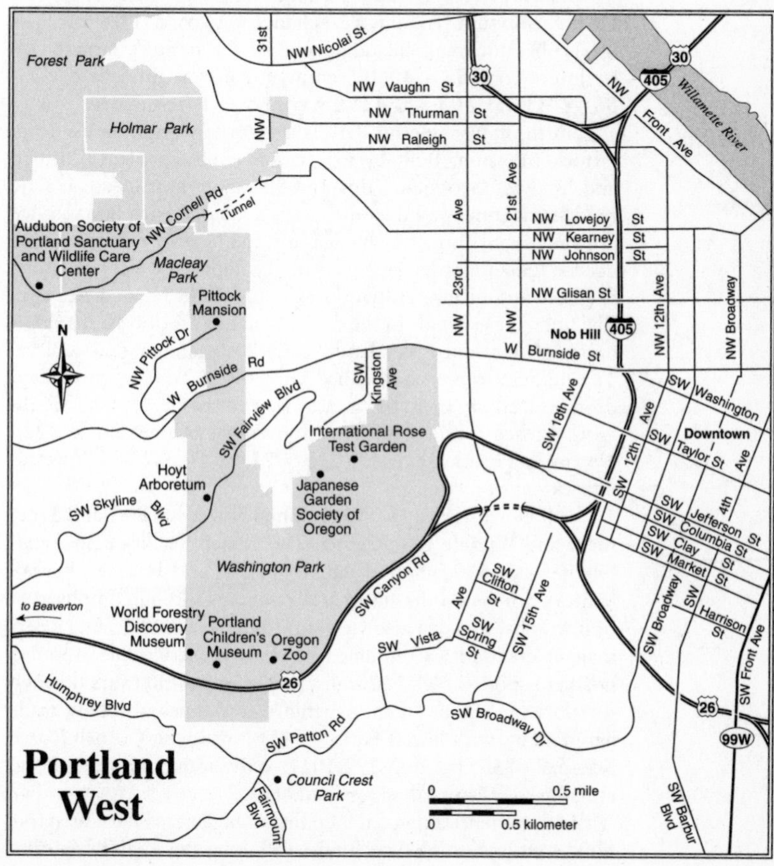

otters. Admission. ~ 4001 Southwest Canyon Road; 503-226-1561, fax 503-226-6836; www.oregonzoo.org.

Portland Children's Museum is a must for families with small children (infant through ten years of age). Fun-filled exhibits here include a pint-sized grocery complete with a bar-code scanner and a medical center where kids can "operate" on parents and friends. Closed Monday during the school year. Admission. ~ 4015 Southwest Canyon Road; 503-223-6500, fax 503-223-6600; www.portlandchildrensmuseum.org.

Nearby is the **World Forestry Discovery Museum.** Here's your chance to learn about tree nomenclature, logging history and subterranean forest life. While this center has a pro-logging slant, it does offer a useful perspective on the state's lumber industry. Admission. ~ 4033 Southwest Canyon Road; 503-228-1367, fax 503-228-4608; www.worldforestry.org.

One way to tell the trees from the forest is to visit the 185-acre **Hoyt Arboretum**. You'll have a chance to see over 1100 varieties of shrubs and trees, including one of the nation's largest collection of conifers. ~ 4000 Southwest Fairview Boulevard; 503-865-8733, fax 503-823-4213; www.hoytarboretum.org.

North of Washington Park is a favorite Oregon house tour, **Pittock Mansion**. Built by *Oregonian* publisher Henry Pittock and his wife Georgiana, this 16,000-square-foot, château-style residence features an Edwardian dining room, French Renaissance drawing room, Turkish smoking room and Jacobean library. Chandeliers, Italian marquetry, friezes on the doorways, a carved-stone fireplace and bronze grillwork make this 1914 home a treasure. The finest craftspeople of the day used native Northwest materials to make this house Portland's early-20th-century masterpiece. The 46-acre estate, landscaped with roses, azaleas, rhododendrons and cherry trees, has a great view of the city and the mountains. Closed the last weeks of November. Admission. ~ 3229 Northwest Pittock Drive; 503-823-3624, fax 503-823-3619; www.pittockmansion.com.

Well worth visiting is the **Audubon Society of Portland Sanctuary and Wildlife Care Center**. The 90-acre facility helps rehabilitate over 3500 injured native animals and birds each year. Visitors can watch the staff handle animals through an observation window and can also view up close a few of the center's permanent creatures: a red-tailed hawk, a peregrine falcon and a northern spotted owl. Naturalist guides often lead tours through the flora and fauna of the sanctuary, and miles of hiking trails here link up with Forest Park. ~ 5151 Northwest Cornell Road; 503-292-6855, fax 503-292-1021; www.audubonportland.org, e-mail general@audubonportland.org.

To experience one of the country's biggest wilderness parks fully, continue on Skyline Boulevard along the Tualatin Mountains. Overlooking the Willamette River, Forest Park extends west for eight miles. Turn right at Germantown Road and drive north through Forest Park's woodlands to Route 30. Continue west to the Sauvie Island Bridge. Cross the bridge and proceed one mile to **James F. Bybee House and Howell Territorial Park**. Open only on summer weekends, the Bybee House is a restored 1858 Classical Revival reflecting the island's culture and development during the 1850–75 period. ~ 13901 Northwest Howell Park Road; 503-621-3344, 503-222-1741.

On the grounds of the James F. Bybee House is the **Agricultural Museum** displaying pioneer equipment, shops and hands-on exhibits. In addition you'll want to explore the **Pioneer Orchard**, containing over 120 varieties of apple trees, as well as pears and plums.

Washington County west of Portland has a number of excellent wineries. **Oak Knoll Winery,** known for pinot noirs and pinot gris, produces more than a dozen wines. This small vineyard has a white-tiled tasting room and a charming picnic area. ~ 29700 Southwest Burkhalter Road, Hillsboro; 503-648-8198, 800-625-5665, fax 503-648-3377; www.oakknollwinery.com.

Traveling south, the **Willamette Shore Trolley** offers a 105-minute, 14-mile roundtrip scenic tour along the Willamette River that takes you through two parks, stately mansions and a tunnel. Your trip aboard a vintage trolley runs along a section of the Jefferson Street Line built in the late 19th century. ~ 311 North State Street, Lake Oswego; 503-697-7436; oregonelectricrailway.org.

LODGING

◄ HIDDEN

The **Park Lane Suites** offers 44 contemporary rooms. Within walking distance of the popular shops and restaurants in the Nob Hill district, this five-story motel building is tucked into a residential neighborhood. Nondescript from the outside, the inn has attrac-

AUTHOR FAVORITE

After a busy afternoon perusing Nob Hill's trendy boutiques, I doubly appreciate the quiet, secluded garden at **Heron Haus**. What's more, this beautifully renovated English Tudor provides pleasant views of the city, the Cascades, Mt. Hood and Mt. St. Helens. The blend of country casual and contemporary furniture, oak-parquet flooring, mahogany library, sun room and patio make the establishment a delight. Fireplaces, private baths and quilts add to the comfort of the six spacious rooms. Continental breakfast includes delicious pastries and fresh fruit. ~ 2545 Northwest Westover Road; 503-274-1846, fax 503-248-4055; www.heronhaus.com. DELUXE TO ULTRA-DELUXE.

Text continued on page 58.

Portland's Microbreweries & Brewpubs

Portland, with more microbreweries and brewpubs than any other city in the United States, is a beer connoisseur's paradise. Partly responsible for this phenomenon is Oregon's abundance of the natural ingredients needed to produce fine beers: two-row malting barley, pure mountain water and the renowned Cascade Hop developed by Oregon State University.

Most of the city's microbreweries specialize in small-batch designer ales, stouts, porters and lagers available only on draft. While some are bottled for regional consumption, most are best enjoyed in one of the city's numerous brewpubs, convivial establishments which usually also feature hearty "pub grub" fare such as burgers and pizza. Some are also good places to hear live blues, jazz or folk music on weekend nights.

Oregon's oldest serving microbrewery is the **Bridgeport Brewery and Brew Pub**, located in an 1895 rope factory in northwest Portland's Pearl District. Patrons can gather inside or, in fair weather, outside on the loading dock and imbibe such creations as Blue Heron, Bridgeport India Pale Ale, Bridgeport ESB and Bridgeport Porter. Pub grub includes focaccia-bread sandwiches and pizzas with sourdough crust. ~ 1313 Northwest Marshall Street, Portland; 503-241-7179, fax 503-241-0625.

Housed in an old creamery, **Pyramid Brewing Co.**, with its Honduras mahogany interior and large windows providing a view of the brewing process, is pretty elegant for a brewpub. On-tap specialities like Highland Pale Ale, MacTarnahan's Amber Ale and Black Watch Cream Porter (gold medalists at the Great American Beer Festival) can be accompanied by rotisserie chicken and ribs, or pasta, salads and specialty sandwiches. Tours of the microbrewery are available (call for an appointment). ~ 2730 Northwest 31st Avenue, Portland; 503-226-7623, fax 503-226-2702; www.macsbeer.com, e-mail info@macbeers.com.

Over a dozen draft beers, ales and cider are on tap at the **Fulton Pub & Brewery**, a neighborhood pub located across from Willamette Park in an old house with colorful murals on the walls. The choicest spot, however, is the outside garden where tables are shaded by a canopy of hop vines. The menu offers burgers, salads, soups, sandwiches and nightly specials. ~ 0618 Southwest Nebraska Street, Portland; 503-246-9530; e-mail fulton@mcmenamins.com.

The **Widmer Brewing Co.** serves up the freshest traditional German-style beers you can imagine at its restaurant/pub. Sip a pint of hefeweizen or bock and peer through the big windows to see how the bräumeisters work their magic. The extensive menu at the Gasthaus features several German specialties. Brewery tours are on Friday and Saturday. ~ 955 North Russell Street, Portland; 503-281-3333, fax 503-281-1496; www.widmer.com.

One of the city's larger, more sophisticated brewpubs is **The Pilsner Room**, which is located in the McCormick & Schmick Restaurant at the RiverPlace Marina and has large picture windows facing the Willamette River. Inside the two-story establishment are a large horseshoe-shaped bar downstairs, three dining areas and a brewery visible behind windows. Full Sail ales are among the brews on tap and the usual pub fare is augmented by a wide selection of appetizers that include crab cakes and baked brie, as well as many fresh seafood entrées. ~ 0309 Southwest Montgomery Street, Portland; 503-220-1865.

Located just west of Portland is the historic **Cornelius Pass Roadhouse and Brewery**, which was built in 1866 as the Imbrie Farm and still has the original octagonal barn on the grounds. Beers are brewed daily and you can always enjoy the large selection inside or out in the beer garden. Burgers, including a vegetarian version, and skin-on fries are the best bet for grub. ~ 4045 Northwest Cornelius Pass Road, Hillsboro; 503-640-6174, fax 503-640-2930.

tive carpeted rooms with potted plants, desks, fully equipped kitchenettes and posturepedic beds. The upper-story rooms have great views of downtown Portland, Mount Hood and Mount St. Helens. ~ 809 Southwest King Avenue; 503-226-6288, 800-532-9543, fax 503-274-0038; www.parklanesuites.com, e-mail de brah@parklanesuites.com. MODERATE TO DELUXE.

Just south of Portland in Beaverton, the **Shilo Inn Hotel** is a good choice for families and long-stay visitors. Each of the resort's 142 rooms features a queen- or king-sized bed, private bath and free high-speed internet access. Dad can smoke a cigar in the on-site sports bar while mom makes use of the 24-hour fitness center and junior splashes around in the seasonal outdoor pool. There's a picture-perfect gazebo and pond with geyser fountains in the courtyard. ~ 9900 Southwest Canyon Road, Beaverton; 503-297-2551, 800-222-2244, fax 503-297-7708; www.shiloinns.com, e-mail beaverton@shiloinns.com. MODERATE.

HIDDEN ►

Located southwest of Portland off Route 5, the **Sweetbrier Inn & Suites** resides in a park-like stand of fir. King-size beds, comfortable sitting areas, a garden pool, a children's play area and a nearby jogging track make this 99-room inn a winner. An adjacent building has 32 two-bedroom suites with workstations for businesspeople. A restaurant, jazz bar and lounge are here, too. ~ 7125 Southwest Nyberg Road, Tualatin; 503-692-5800, 800-551-9167, fax 503-691-2894; www.sweetbrier.com, e-mail reservations@sweetbrier.com. MODERATE.

DINING

Inventive Continental/Mediterranean cuisine and a chic, post-modern setting draw a well-dressed crowd to **Bluehour**. Suspended draperies divide the converted warehouse space (with 20-foot floor-to-ceiling windows) into more intimate spaces. Savory starters may include salmon *tartare* and bacon-wrapped scallops; main dishes might feature Muscovy duck with chanterelle mushrooms or roasted suckling pig with polenta. Finish the meal off

AUTHOR FAVORITE

For great views of the Willamette, head for **Ram Restaurant & Brewery**. The downstairs dining area, with its cherry-wood paneling, offers American fare in the form of steaks, chicken, pasta, burgers, salads and daily specials. The appetizers are especially popular. Alfresco seating is an option in the summer. Upstairs is a 21-and-over game room with pool tables, virtual-reality video games, a wall of TVs broadcasting sporting events and a dancefloor with occasional live music on Friday and Saturday nights in summer. ~ 320 Oswego Pointe Drive, Lake Oswego; 503-697-8818; www.theram.com. MODERATE TO DELUXE.

on a sweet note with chocolate truffle cake. Diners without reservations can drop by the casual café/bar. Sunday brunch. ~ 250 Northwest 13th Avenue; 503-226-3394, fax 503-221-3005; www.bluehouronline.com, e-mail info@bluehouronline.com. ULTRA-DELUXE.

Wildwood Restaurant and Bar draws from local Northwest ingredients to create a distinctive Oregon flavor just as it displays regional artwork to enhance its decor. You'll find such dishes as warm fingerling potato and olive salad, apple cider–glazed duck, and wild mushroom, kale and gruyère lasagna. The menu changes weekly to accommodate seasonal produce; a chalkboard details the day's specials. No lunch on Sunday. ~ 1221 Northwest 21st Street; 503-248-9663, fax 503-225-0030; www.wildwoodrestaurant.com. DELUXE.

Hurley's is an intimately elegant French restaurant furnished with oak furniture and white linen tablecloths. In the heart of Nob Hill, the restaurant presents entrées like duck with juniper-smoked sauce, ribeye bordelaise with pinot noir reduction and wild mushroom flan. There's an excellent wine list. Highly recommended. Dinner only. Closed Sunday and Monday. ~ 1987 Northwest Kearney Street; 503-295-6487; www.hurleys-restaurant.com, e-mail main@hurleys-restaurant.com. MODERATE TO DELUXE.

If sushi is what you crave, join the locals at **Mio Sushi**. You may have to huddle outside with the crowd that's arrived before you, but your tastebuds will thank you for your patience. The *maki* rolls are superb and include unique options like the Oregon roll, a succulent combo of avocado, fresh crab, asparagus and salmon. Non-fishy fare such as noodles and teriyaki is also available. Closed Sunday. ~ 2271 Northwest Johnson Street; 503-221-1469. BUDGET TO MODERATE.

High-tech Mex design is the hallmark of **Macheezmo Mouse**, where the burritos, tacos, salads and other entrées are all listed with their calorie content. There's no deep frying here, and many of the entrées come with brown rice and black beans. The bright decor attracts a budget-minded crowd that's become dependent on this quality fast food. ~ 9615 Southwest Washington Square Road; 503-639-2379. BUDGET.

SHOPPING

"Escape from the ordinary" is the motto at **Norm Thompson**, where you can find fine-quality clothing in a variety of materials. Enjoy a glass of Oregon wine as you check out the men's and women's apparel, foods and gifts. Closed Monday and Tuesday. ~ 1805 Northwest Thurman Street; 503-221-0764, fax 503-223-3426.

Pulliam Deffenbaugh Gallery specializes in contemporary Northwest art but includes work from other regions. Closed Sunday and Monday. ~ Northwest 9th Avenue at Northwest Flanders Street; 503-228-6665, fax 503-464-9650.

Another excellent place to look for fine local art is the **Laura Russo Gallery**. Paintings, original prints, drawings, watercolors and sculptures in a variety of media are all shown here. Closed Sunday and Monday. ~ 805 Northwest 21st Avenue; 503-226-2754.

We were impressed by the breadth of the offerings at **Contemporary Crafts Museum & Gallery**, a nonprofit organization showcasing everything from ceramic pins and medallions to metal sculpture. Highlighting crafts of the five disciplines (clay, glass, wood, fiber and metal), this eclectic gallery is a great place to shop for a gift. Closed Monday. ~ 3934 Southwest Corbett Avenue; 503-223-2654, fax 503-223-0190.

NIGHTLIFE

Classical-music buffs will enjoy the **Portland Baroque Orchestra**. Make it a point to hear this group if they're performing during your visit (October through April). ~ First Baptist Church, 909 Southwest 11th Avenue; Kaul Auditorium at Reed College; 503-222-6000, fax 503-226-6635; www.pbo.org.

Mission Theater is a historic movie theater that now doubles as a pub, with seating at tables and couches where you can dine and watch second-run films. There's also traditional theater seating on the balcony level. ~ 1624 Northwest Glisan Street; 503-223-4527, fax 503-294-0837.

PARKS

MACLEAY PARK This natural 104-acre park offers several excellent trails, a pond, creek and viewing windows overlooking a bird-feeding area. In addition, Pittock Mansion provides stunning views of the city and Mt. St. Helens. There's a good chance you'll spot deer and other wildlife on your walk. Hiking trails lead down to Lower Macleay Park, which is a gateway to 5000-acre Forest Park. The Portland Audubon Society's headquarters, bookstore and wildlife care center are adjacent to the park. Facilities include restrooms and a playground. ~ Take Lovejoy Street west to Northwest Cornell Road and continue to the park; 503-823-2223, fax 503-823-5297.

The trails that lead through orchards and gardens on Sauvie Island are ideal for leisurely exploration on foot.

COUNCIL CREST PARK Atop a Tualatin Mountain peak, this forested 45-acre park is a great way to see the Cascades and the Coast Range. Make your way through stands of fir and maple via Marquam Hill Trail. There's also a sculptured fountain of a mother and child. Facilities include picnic tables. ~ Southwest Council Crest Drive near Fairmount Boulevard; 503-823-2223, fax 503-823-5297.

HIDDEN ►

SAUVIE ISLAND WILDLIFE AREA This 12,000-acre haven ten miles northwest of Portland is an ideal place to spot great blue heron, bald eagles, sandhill cranes (during March and April migration) and 230 other bird species. Featuring a sandy beach on the Columbia, the refuge is also home to 37 mammal species including black-tailed deer. Small craft explore the sloughs while oceangoing freighters cruise by on the Columbia. For fishing, try for catfish, perch and crappie from slough and pond banks. There are portable toilets and bird observation platforms. Some areas are open year-round; other areas are closed from October to mid-April. Day-use only; you must obtain a parking permit ($3.50 per day/$11 annually), available at the Cracker Barrel and the Redder Beach RV Park on the island or at any Fred Meyer department store or G.I. Joe's Sporting Goods throughout Portland. ~ Take Route 30 west from Portland toward Astoria. Four miles past St. John's Bridge, take the Sauvie Bridge turnoff to the Island; 503-621-3488, fax 503-621-3025.

ELK ROCK GARDEN Ever since 1957 this refuge, also known as the Garden of the Bishop's Close, has been a favorite of Portland's garden societies. And why not? A terraced 13-acre estate overlooking the Willamette River and Elk Rock Island, the garden is also home to the Episcopal Diocese of Oregon's main office. Formal gardens and native plants, including 77 magnolia varieties, make this a spot for Zen-like contemplation. Also here are lily ponds, a rock garden and a small spring. Self-guided tour information is available from the visitors center. ~ 11800 Southwest Military Lane; 503-636-5613, fax 503-636-5616.

◄ HIDDEN

TRYON CREEK STATE NATURAL AREA Set in a shallow, steep-walled canyon, this 645-acre suburban park is a hot spot for hiking, biking and horseback riding. Tryon is forested with fir, alder and maple and also has a grassy meadow. Look for beaver and pileated woodpeckers. There's a trillium festival in the spring. Facilities here are restrooms, an observation area and a nature center. ~ Located six miles southwest of downtown Portland. Take the Terwilliger exit off Route 5 and follow signs to the park; 503-636-9886, 800-551-6949, fax 503-636-5318.

MARY S. YOUNG PARK A popular day-use area forested in fir, maple, cottonwood and oak, the park sits on the Willamette River. With 133 acres, this leisurely spot is perfect for fishing from the riverbank, riding or walking. There are restrooms and picnic tables. ~ Located nine miles south of Portland on Route 43; 503-557-4700, fax 503-656-4106.

Outdoor Adventures

INLINE SKATING

Skating may not be big-thrills adventure, but it sure is fun. In Portland, rollerskating even takes on an old-fashioned aura when you've got an amusement-park organ playing the music. Skaters are welcome to use any hard surface in the city's parks. ~ Portland Parks Department; 503-823-2223; www.portlandparks.org.

Text continued on page 64.

Oregon City—The Trail's End

Wagons, ho! So you missed out on the 19th-century move west? (Well, at least we weren't around then.) To get a sense of what it must have been like, head to Oregon City. Just a half-hour south of Portland, this community built along the 40-foot-high Willamette River waterfalls is one of the best places in the Pacific Northwest to understand and appreciate manifest destiny. For this was the destination that launched the migration of over 300,000 Americans to a blank slate known as the promised land.

The center of human endeavor for more than 10,000 years, the Willamette Falls was an important place long before the first white immigrants arrived. But once they did show up, things moved quickly. In 1818, just five years after the British took control of the Northwest region from the Astorians, the Americans and British agreed to jointly occupy Oregon Country. In 1829, Dr. John McLoughlin, the shrewd operator of the Hudson's Bay Company base at Fort Vancouver, built three homes at the Willamette Falls. Although the American Indians responded by burning these buildings, McLoughlin forged ahead with a new sawmill and flour mill.

American settlers began trickling in, and by 1841 the first wagon trains started to arrive. Pouring in by boat and by land, the pioneers soon spread across the Willamette Valley in search of farmsteads. Thankfully, you don't have to retrace the entire trail to learn of this riveting history. Just head to Oregon City's museums, homes, farms and cemeteries.

The place to begin your visit is the **End of the Oregon Trail Interpretive Center and Historic Site**. The center offers guided shows featuring living history presentations, a multimedia presentation, a hands-on area and exhibits displaying notable artifacts, photographs and maps. You'll gain a well-rounded perspective on immigrant history. You can also pick up helpful walking and driving tour guides to the community. Admission. ~ 1726 Washington Street; 503-657-9336, fax 503-557-8590; www.endoftheoregontrail.org.

Among the major Oregon City highlights are the **McLoughlin House**, where the Hudson's Bay Company leader and "Father of Oregon" retired.

Although his employer was British, John McLoughlin generously aided the new settlers and helped lay the groundwork for Americanization. Regular tours show off this 1846 home, which was a social hub in pioneer days. Highlights include a Chilkat Indian ceremonial robe, banjo-shaped clock, Hudson's Bay Company sideboard and lots of original McLoughlin family and Fort Vancouver furnishings. The home is closed on Monday and Tuesday and during the month of January. Incidentally, you can learn the rest of the McLoughlin story by visiting Fort Vancouver across the Columbia River from Portland. ~ 713 Center Street; 503-656-5146.

Step into the **Frances Ermatinger House**, a Federal-style residence showcasing antiques and memorabilia for another peak into this area's past. Admission. ~ 6th and John Adams streets. The **Stevens-Crawford Heritage House**, a historically preserved turn-of-the-20th-century site, has a small collection of American Indian artifacts. Closed Monday and Tuesday, and the month of January. Call ahead for hours. Admission. ~ 603 6th Street; 503-655-2866.

Well worth your time is the **Rose Farm Museum** (also known as the William Holmes House), one of the state's oldest residences. The first territorial governor was inaugurated at this home surrounded by rose plantings. A two-tiered piazza and second-story ballroom are highlights of this restored residence, now on the National Register of Historic Places. Open Sunday afternoon from March to October. ~ 536 Holmes Lane, Oregon City; 503-656-5146.

The **Clackamas County Historical Society Museum of the Oregon Territory** explores the history of Clackamas County with exhibits covering geology, traders and trappers, immigration, government and religion. Admission. ~ 211 Tumwater Drive; 503-655-5574, fax 503-655-0035.

Also of special interest is the **Oregon City Municipal Elevator**. Founded in 1916, this ride was designed to make it easy for residents to journey from the riverfront to the upper part of town. One of only four municipal elevators in the world, the 90-foot ride is a great way to enjoy views of Willamette Falls, particularly at sunset. ~ 300 7th Street (at Main Street), Oregon City; 503-657-0891.

PORTLAND EAST Rollerblade or rollerskate to the strains of the mighty Wurlitzer at the early-20th-century **Oaks Amusement Park** on the east bank of the Willamette. Skate rentals are available. ~ East end of the Sellwood Bridge; 503-236-5722.

At **Skateworld**, you can rent skates, including inlines. Public skating sessions are held Tuesday through Sunday. ~ 4395 Southeast Witch Hazel Road, Hillsboro; 503-640-1333.

PORTLAND WEST City ordinance prohibits skaters (and skateboarders) from most city center streets. One happy exception is the esplanade in **Waterfront Park**. When the weather is particularly pleasant, the concrete pathway (it's about ten feet wide) can get congested with cyclists, runners, skaters, skateboarders and strollers. But the mood is always congenial. ~ Front Street, from Southwest Harrison Street to Northwest Glisan Street.

ICE SKATING

PORTLAND EAST At **Lloyd Center Ice Rink**, the music is recorded but the fun is genuine. Skate rentals are available here, too. ~ 953 Lloyd Center shopping mall, between Northeast Multnomah and Halsey streets and Northeast 9th and 15th avenues, Portland; 503-288-6073; www.lloydcenterice.com.

PORTLAND WEST The **Valley Ice Arena** hosts several public skating sessions a day. Skate rental is included in admission fee, and Friday and Saturday nights are half-price admission. Call for times. ~ 9250 Southwest Beaverton-Hillsdale Highway, Beaverton; 503-297-2521.

PARA-GLIDING

With today's lightweight equipment, it's possible for just about anyone to learn to paraglide. Even a one-day introduction gets beginners flying off gentle training slopes or soaring high in tandem with an experienced instructor. Summer flights are usually along the coast, fall flights at the Columbia Gorge and spring flights around the Mt. St. Helens crater. In the Portland area, contact the **Hang Gliding and Paragliding School of Oregon** to arrange a flying adventure within a two-hour drive of the city. Tandem flights are also offered. Their season runs from March through November. ~ 14185 Southwest Yearling Court, Beaverton; fax 503-223-7448.

FISHING

Imagine catching a 350-pound sturgeon, even if you've never fished before. You can haul in these babies, which can come in at seven to ten feet and weigh upward of 300 pounds, year-round, right out of the Columbia. Walleye is another year-round favorite found in the Willamette; Tillamook Bay, about 65 miles west on the coast, is well known for trophy-size fall chinook salmon.

PORTLAND **Page's Northwest Guide Service** can set up a one-day Tillamook Bay fishing trip on a 25-foot, all-weather boat, or arrange an outing on the Willamette, Clackamas, Columbia or Sandy rivers. ~ Portland; 503-760-3373, 866-760-3370.

PORTLAND EAST **Don Schneider's Reel Adventures** specializes in full-day fishing trips on the Columbia River but also provides trips on the Sandy and Willamette. Schneider can custom-tailor an outing in a drift boat. ~ 57206 East Marmot Road, Sandy; 503-622-5372, 877-544-7335.

RIVER RUNNING

About 90 minutes from downtown Portland is a whitewater thrill ride—the White Salmon River, just north of the Columbia, in Washington. Designated a Wild and Scenic River, it moves "fast and furious" through the forest canyon. Southeast of Portland is the Clackamas, another popular whitewater river, with some Class III and IV rapids. It's about an hour away. Most whitewater-rafting trips are done in paddleboats (*you* paddle!), holding six to eight people, plus a guide. The passive adventurer who'd like to photograph the gorgeous mountain scenery instead of paddle should ask about oar-powered raft trips.

From March through October, the Clackamas River runs with some Class III and IV rapids (the water is too low the rest of the year).

PORTLAND AREA About 35 miles southeast of Portland, the Clackamas River is the best bet for a one-day whitewater adventure. **River Drifters,** one of the only outfitters operating in the spring on the Clackamas, can arrange a complete full-day trip on several rivers, including the Deschutes and White Salmon rivers. They also offer a whitewater and wine trip on the White Salmon, stopping for lunch or dinner at a local winery. ~ 405 Deschutes Avenue, Maupin; 800-972-0430.

GOLF

PORTLAND EAST **Eastmoreland Golf Course** is an 18-hole regulation course rated by *Golf Digest* as one of the country's most affordable places to play. ~ 2425 Southeast Bybee Boulevard, Portland; 503-775-2900; www.eastmorelandgolfcourse.com. The two 18-hole courses at **Glendoveer Golf Course** are lined with fir trees. There's also a driving range. ~ 14015 Northeast Glisan Street, Portland; 503-253-7507. Across the state border you can tee off on the par-72, 18-hole **The Cedars on Salmon Creek.** ~ 15001 Northeast 181st Street, Brush Prairie, WA; 503-285-7686.

PORTLAND WEST Just 30 minutes from downtown Portland, the four nine-hole greens at **Meriwether National Golf Club** are good walking courses. ~ 5200 Southwest Rood Bridge Road, Hillsboro; 503-648-4143; www.meriwethergolfclub.com. **King City Golf Club** is a challenging, nine-hole, semiprivate course that, says a local golf pro, is "harder than it looks." ~ 15355 Southwest Royalty Parkway, Tigard; 503-639-7986.

TENNIS

Among the numerous public clubs is **Portland Tennis Center,** which has four hardtop indoor (hourly per-person charge) and eight lighted outdoor courts (free). They also maintain a list of other public tennis courts throughout the city. ~ 324 Northeast 12th Street; 503-823-3189.

BIKING

To say that the Portland area is bicycle friendly is like saying New York has a lot of tall buildings—so what else is new? There are 260 miles of bike lanes in the metropolitan area (plus 83 miles of multi-use lanes), and city buses all have bike racks. *Bicycling* magazine has picked Portland as the country's top bicycle city. Morning, afternoon or entire-day bicycling in the area presents a variety of options, from a mountain-bike ride in a city park to a long-distance excursion along the Columbia River.

Visitors interested in bicycling in the Portland metropolitan area will find the going easier by first contacting one or more of these resources. The **Portland Bicycle Program** publishes a small map of the city's bikeway system; an accompanying brochure explains how to take your bike along on a bus. The map and brochure are free and available at the program's office and in some bike shops. ~ 1120 Southwest 5th Avenue, Room 800; 503-823-2925, fax 503-823-7576.

Multnomah County also puts out a map, but it just covers the east county area. ~ 1220 Southeast 190th Avenue; 503-248-5050.

The best resource is *Bike There*, a detailed bicycle map and safety guide for the metropolitan area. Bike and multi-use lanes are color coded to a use-suitability scale (off-street, low-traffic, etc.). *Bike There* is put out by Metro (an elected regional government). You can pick one up at Powell's Bookstore, most bike shops or at Metro headquarters at 600 Northeast Grand Street in Portland.

Just as the riders using them come in a variety of shapes and sizes, bike routes in the area are of varying lengths and distances. Beginners and intermediate riders would do well to contact **The Bike Gallery**, which sponsors weekend group rides that are open to the public. Two rides are usually offered: a road ride one day, a mountain ride the next. ~ 12345 Southwest Canyon Road, Beaverton; 503-641-2580.

City riders will find the northeast and southeast portions of the city more suitable. The terrain is relatively flat, and marked bike routes follow low- or medium-traffic streets.

AUTHOR FAVORITE

An excellent cycling getaway in the area is **Sauvie Island**, located ten miles northwest of Portland. Light traffic makes it a pleasure to pedal through this wildlife sanctuary. You can drive or take a Tri-Met bus out to the island.

PORTLAND EAST The **Springwater Corridor** follows an old railroad route along the southern flank of the city. The 16-mile trail extends from Southeast McLoughlin Boulevard east through Powell Butte Nature Park and Gresham to the city of Boring in Clackamas County. Most of this multi-use trail is unpaved.

PORTLAND WEST Mountain bikers will like **Forest Park,** which comprises 5000 acres west of downtown. The park has some rather hilly terrain, perfect for mountain biking, and one multi-use trail, Leif Erickson, is especially popular.

More experienced riders, of course, have the option of longer rides, perhaps west to the **vineyards** around Hillsboro. The Bike Gallery in Beaverton is a good source for information on suggested routes, distances and length of trips.

Bike Rentals For rentals of mountain bikes and trail maps, try **Fat Tire Farm.** ~ 2714 Northwest Thurman Street; 508-222-3276.

HIKING

A hiker's paradise, the Portland region has beautiful riverfront walks, urban trails and wilderness loops perfect for a brief interlude or an all-day excursion. Trail information is available from the Portland Oregon Information Center or the **Bureau of Parks and Recreation.** ~ 1120 Southwest 5th Avenue; 503-823-2223, fax 503-823-5297. All distances listed for hiking trails are one way unless otherwise noted.

CENTRAL PORTLAND Named for a former governor, **Tom McCall Waterfront Park** offers a 2-mile-long path along the Willamette River. This is an ideal way to get an overview of the downtown area.

PORTLAND EAST The **Springwater Corridor** (16.5 miles) begins at Tideman-Johnson Park and heads to Gresham and south to Boring, shadowing Johnson Creek. This multipurpose trail is a converted railway line that's part of the Rails to Trails project.

You don't have to go all the way to Mt. St. Helens to hike a volcano. Just take the **Mt. Tabor Perimeter Loop** (2.7 miles). Your hike on Southeast 60th Avenue, Southeast Yamhill Street, Southeast 71st Avenue and Southeast Harrison Drive (which becomes Southeast Lincoln Street) provides a pleasant overview of this landmark.

PORTLAND WEST Sauvie Island is ideal for short or long strolls. One of our favorite walks in the region is the hike from parking lot #5 in Crane Unit around **Willow Hole to Domeyer Lake** (1.5 miles). Another good bet is the hike from Walton Beach along the Columbia to **Warrior Rock Lighthouse** (3 miles).

With more than 5000 acres, Forest Park offers over 50 miles of connecting trails. Many of the routes are spurs off **Wildwood Trail** (27 miles), the primary route traversing this vast urban refuge. Depending on your time and mood, hike as much of this trail as you want, connecting easily to other convenient routes. Your starting point for Wildwood is Hoyt Arboretum's Vietnam Memorial. If you're feeling more ambitious, try **Marquam Nature Trail** (5 miles), leading from Hines Park to Washington Park via Terwilliger Boulevard and Council Crest Park.

Two mile-long walks will add to your enjoyment of Hoyt Arboretum. The **Conifer Tour** leads through a forest thick with spruce, fir and redwood. Also well worth your time is the **Oak Tour**.

Outfitters **Oregon Peak Adventures** offers guided hikes in Portland (Washington and Forest parks) along the Columbia River Gorge and on the Oregon coast. More challenging climbing and backpacking excursions are also available. ~ P.O. Box 25576, Portland, OR 97298; 503-297-5100, 877-965-5100; www.oregonpeakadventures.com.

Transportation

CAR

Most visitors to Portland arrive on one of three primary highways. **Route 5** bisects the city and provides access from the north via Vancouver, Washington. This same highway also is the main line from points south like the Willamette Valley and California. From points east, **Route 84** along the Columbia River is the preferred way to enter Portland. From the west, **Route 26** is a major highway into town. Secondary routes include **Route 30** from the west and **Route 99** from the south. For road conditions, call 503-222-6721.

AIR

Portland International Airport is the major gateway. Located ten miles northeast of downtown, it is served by Alaska Airlines, America West Airlines, American Airlines, Delta Air Lines, Hawaiian Airlines, Horizon Air, Northwest Airlines, Southwest Airlines and United Airlines. ~ www.portlandairportpdx.com.

Limousines, vans and buses take visitors to downtown locations, including **Raz Transportation** (503-684-3322) and **Prestige Limousines** (503-282-5009; www.limo-res.com).

BUS

Greyhound Bus Lines offers bus service to Portland from across the nation. The main downtown terminal is at 550 Northwest 6th Avenue. ~ 800-231-2222; www.greyhound.com.

Also consider the **Green Tortoise**, a New Age company with a fleet of funky buses. Each is equipped with sleeping platforms allowing travelers to rest as they cross the country. The buses stop at interesting sightseeing points en route. The Green Tortoise, an endangered species from the '60s, travels to and from the East Coast, Portland, Seattle, Los Angeles and elsewhere. It provides a mode of transportation as well as an experience in group living. ~ 494 Broadway, San Francisco, CA 94133; 415-956-7500, 800-867-8647; www.greentortoise.com.

TRAIN

Amtrak provides service from Washington and California via the "Coast Starlight." There is also a northerly connection to Spokane on the "Empire Builder." ~ 800 Northwest 6th Avenue; 800-872-7245; www.amtrak.com.

CAR RENTALS

At the Portland International Airport try **Avis Rent A Car** (800-331-1212), **Budget Rent A Car** (800-527-0700), **Dollar Rent A Car** (800-800-4000) or **Hertz Rent A Car** (800-654-3131). Cars are also available from **Bee Rent A Car** (503-233-7368) and **Enterprise Rent A Car** (800-736-8222).

PUBLIC TRANSIT

Tri-Met Buses/MAX Light Rail serve the Portland region. Buses blanket the city, while the MAX blue line extends east from downtown to the Gateway transit center and then on to Gresham. The red line provides direct service from downtown to the airport. There is free bus service downtown and in the Lloyd District in the "Fareless Square" region spanning 300 blocks. ~ 503-238-7433; www.tri-met.org.

TAXIS

Broadway Cab (503-227-1234), **Radio Cab** (503-227-1212) and **Yellow Cab** (503-253-2277) all provide convenient local service. In Hood River, call **Hood River Taxi and Transportation** (541-386-2255).

THREE

Columbia River Gorge

The Columbia River cuts an 80-mile swath through the Cascade Mountains on its way to the Pacific, leaving in its wake a magnificent landscape of towering basalt cliffs, waterfalls and forested bluffs known as the Columbia River Gorge. Because it forms a natural border between Oregon and Washington, exploring the Gorge is a two-state proposition, with a lot to see and do on both sides of the river.

Since long before the two states existed, the Gorge has both fascinated and terrified travelers. For centuries this part of the river was a major trading ground for American Indians who came from as far away as Northern California and British Columbia to meet, talk and barter. Lewis and Clark marveled at the Gorge as they journeyed down the Columbia on the last stretch of their westward trek. Less captivated were the Oregon Trail immigrants of the 1840s who had to detour south around Mt. Hood or else mount their wagons on homemade rafts for a treacherous ride through the rocks and rapids west of The Dalles.

Today, visitors have it a lot easier. On the Oregon side, Route 84 parallels the Columbia River from Portland through such prime Gorge sightseeing areas as Cascade Locks and The Dalles. On the Washington side, Route 14 follows a mostly water-level route through the Gorge on the north bank, providing good views of the Oregon shore and such river traffic as tugboats pushing grain-laden barges downstream. Frequently sighted at the eastern edge of the Gorge, particularly near Hood River, are the bright sails of windsurfers attracted to some of the best conditions for their sport in North America. Although it's possible to tour the Gorge in a loop drive, taking Route 14 one way and Route 84 the other, we recommend crisscrossing it at various points in between. Declared a national scenic area by Congress in 1986, the Columbia Gorge, less than an hour east of Portland, has been a busy area for tourism development during the past several years. Although most hotels and restaurants are still concentrated on the Oregon side, it is the Washington side around Stevenson, with its interpretive center and deluxe resort, where the most recent activity has taken place. Fortunately, the Gorge is still largely unspoiled and provides much to keep waterfall lovers, windsurfers, kayakers, hikers and history buffs enthralled for days.

SIGHTS

Although it's only half an hour from downtown Portland and the logical starting point for touring the Columbia Gorge region, many visitors to the region miss **Fort Vancouver**. What a pity. Located across the Columbia River from Portland, this National Historic Site is a cornerstone of Pacific Northwest history. Organized by the Hudson's Bay Company in 1825, the fort was originally a British fur-trading post and focal point for the commercial development of an area extending from British Columbia to Oregon and from Montana west to the Hawaiian Islands.

Ten structures have been reconstructed on their original fort locations. Collectively, they give a feel for life during the arrival of the first white settlers. One of the best ways to start your tour is at the visitors center with the introductory video. On your tour you'll see the re-created **Chief Factor's House**, once home to Dr. John McLoughlin, the British agent who befriended American settlers and is remembered as the "Father of Oregon." The phenomenal ability of the British to instantly gentrify the wilderness is reflected in the fine china, copper kettles and elegant furniture of this white clapboard home wrapped with a spacious veranda. You may be surprised to learn that the male officers dined without their wives.

The **Fur Warehouse** interprets how furs were collected and prepared for shipment to England. Also worth a visit are the **Blacksmith Shop, Bake House, Kitchen, Wash House, Palisade, Bastion, Jail** and a **Carpenter Workshop**. At the **Indian Trade Shop and Dispensary**, you'll learn how American Indians skillfully bartered their collected furs for British-made goods. Because most of the items were imported, there was a two-year hiatus between ordering goods and receiving them. Fort Vancouver: Admission May 1 to September 30. ~ 1501 East Evergreen Boulevard, Vancouver, WA; 360-696-7655, fax 360-696-7657; www.nps.gov/fova.

On nearby **Officer's Row**, you'll see 21 grand homes built for American Army leaders who served here during the latter half of the 19th and the early 20th centuries. These charming Victorians are the focus of a rehabilitation program combining interpretive and commercial use. Among the residences you can tour is the **Grant House**, which currently houses a restaurant serving classic Northwestern food. ~ 360-906-1101. The **George C. Marshall House**, an imposing Queen Anne structure, also offers tours every day. Call for weekend hours; tours are available Saturday and Sunday except during weddings or other event rentals. ~ 360-693-3103.

HIDDEN ► Next to Fort Vancouver is **Pearson Air Museum**. The field, opened in 1905, is the oldest operating airfield in the United States. Exhibits feature a display on the world's first nonstop transpolar flight (Moscow to Vancouver) in 1937—the Soviet aviators were greeted by General George Marshall, who hosted them at his residence—as well as the last remaining artifact from the *Hindenburg*. The airpark exhibit features flyable vintage aircraft, an aviation theater, a hands-on activity room and the nation's oldest wooden hangar. Closed Monday. Admission. ~ 1115 East 5th Street, Vancouver, WA; 360-694-7026, fax 360-694-0824; www.pearsonairmuseum.org, e-mail pearson@pacifier.com.

Originally constructed in 1909 as a Carnegie Library, **Clark County Historical Museum** has a better than good regional collection—from the American Indian artifacts and handicrafts to the historical doctor's office and general store. Not to be missed is the downstairs train room with a Pullman unit, railway telegram office, dining car china, a model train layout and photos of noteworthy local derailments. Closed Sunday and Monday. ~ 1511 Main Street, Vancouver, WA; 360-993-5679, fax 360-993-5683; www.chmuseum.org, e-mail cchm@pacifier.com.

To see more of Vancouver stop by the **Greater Vancouver Chamber of Commerce** and pick up the handy downtown walking tour brochure. ~ 1101 Broadway, Suite 120, Vancouver, WA; 360-694-2588, fax 503-693-8279; www.vancouverusa.com, e-mail yourchamber@vancouverusa.com.

Returning to the Oregon side of the river take Route 84 east up the Gorge to the **Historic Columbia River Highway** (see "Scenic Drive").

The taming of the Columbia River to provide low-cost power is one of the most controversial issues associated with the river. You'll get the pro side of the picture at **Bonneville Lock and Dam**, including the **Bradford Island Visitors Center**. You can also witness salmon swimming up underwater fish ladders. Extensive interpretive displays and an informational film provide an overview of the dam's operation and history. ~ Route 84, Exit 40, three miles west of Cascade Locks, OR; 541-374-8820, fax 541-374-4516.

On the Washington side of the Gorge, you can also learn how the dam operates, enjoy underwater views of fish ladders and visit the **Fort Cascades National Historic Site**. To get there, cross the Columbia River on the **Bridge of the Gods** (named for a bridge in a local Indian legend) and head west two miles on Route 14. The 59-acre historic site includes a one-mile self-guided trail featuring the sites of the old Portage Railroad, a one-time Chinook Indian village and a pre–Civil War military fort. ~ 541-427-4281, fax 541-374-4516.

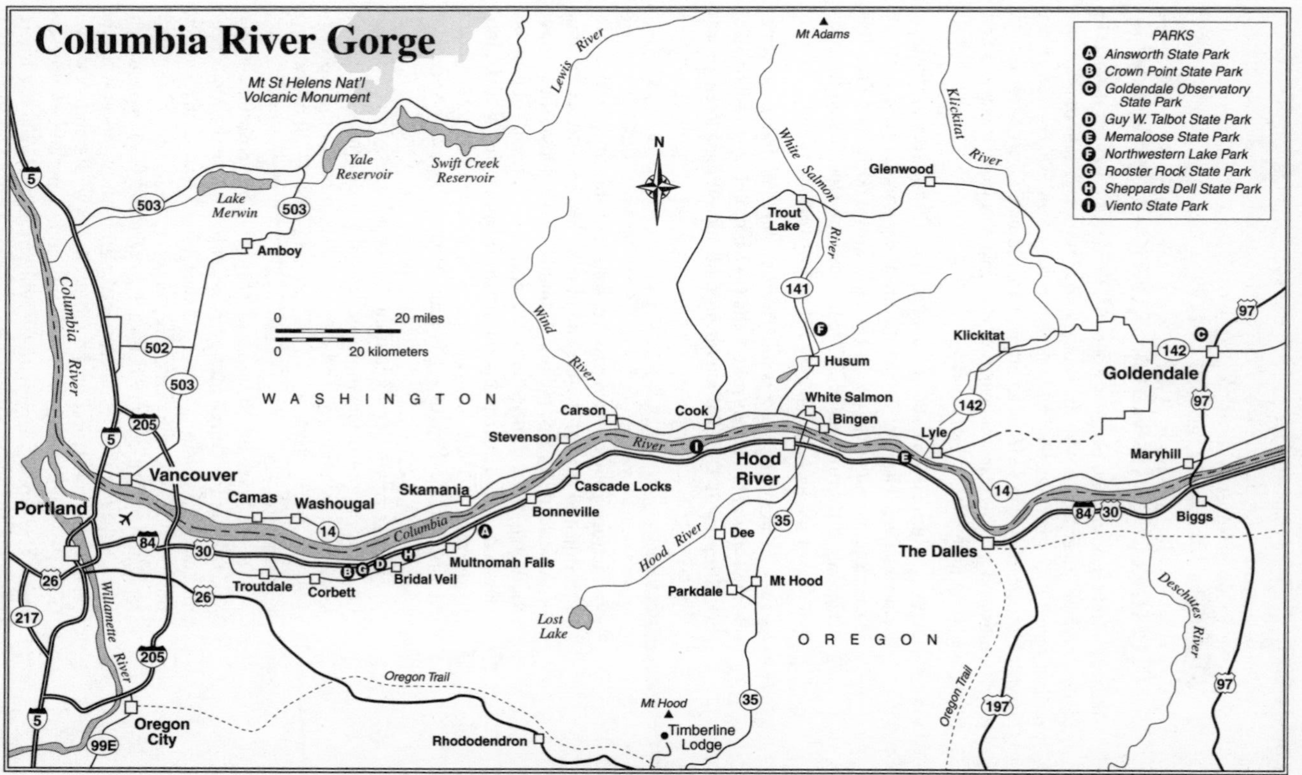
Columbia River Gorge
Mt St Helens Nat'l Volcanic Monument
PARKS
A Ainsworth State Park
B Crown Point State Park
C Goldendale Observatory State Park
D Guy W. Talbot State Park
E Memaloose State Park
F Northwestern Lake Park
G Rooster Rock State Park
H Sheppards Dell State Park
I Viento State Park
0 20 miles
0 20 kilometers
WASHINGTON
OREGON
Mt Adams
Mt Hood
Timberline Lodge
Yale Reservoir
Swift Creek Reservoir
Lake Merwin
Lost Lake
Columbia River
Willamette River
Lewis River
Wind River
White Salmon River
Klickitat River
Hood River
Deschutes River
Oregon Trail
Amboy
Glenwood
Trout Lake
Husum
Klickitat
Goldendale
Maryhill
Biggs
Lyle
The Dalles
White Salmon
Bingen
Hood River
Cook
Carson
Stevenson
Cascade Locks
Bonneville
Multnomah Falls
Skamania
Bridal Veil
Corbett
Washougal
Camas
Troutdale
Vancouver
Portland
Oregon City
Rhododendron
Dee
Parkdale
Mt Hood
N
5
205
84
30
26
217
99E
14
141
142
97
197
35
502
503

SCENIC DRIVE

Historic Columbia River Highway

This magnificent scenic route parallels Route 84, skirting the foot of sheer cliffs of the Columbia River Gorge with its wonderland of waterfalls, side canyons and verdant forest. The road was built by concrete tycoon Sam Hill, creator of the Maryhill Museum of Art, in 1916 as an attempt to convince Oregon legislatures to let him extend a highway up the length of the Columbia River. It was the first rural paved road in the Pacific Northwest.

VISTA HOUSE Turn off Route 84 at Troutdale (Exit 17) to reach the Historic Columbia River Highway. At the mouth of the gorge, a road turns off to the right and winds up to Vista House in Crown Point State Park. This octagonal structure, perched 733 feet above the river, has an information desk, a gift shop, an espresso bar and an awesome view.

WATERFALLS Among the major waterfalls that plunge into the gorge alongside the highway are **Latourelle Falls** (249 feet) in Guy W. Talbot State Park, **Sheppards Dell Falls** (two tiers, 50 and 60 feet) in Sheppards

Retrace your route across the Bridge of the Gods to the Oregon side and stop at the **Cascade Locks Museum** to see exhibits on American Indians, the first Columbia River locks, the portage road, logging and fishwheels. Water-powered, these rotating devices scooped so many salmon from the river that they were banned by the state in 1926. Closed Labor Day through Memorial Day. ~ Marine Park, 1 Northwest Portage Road, Cascade Locks, OR; 541-374-8535.

The sternwheeler **Columbia Gorge** is docked in Cascade Locks year-round. The multidecked old paddlewheel steamboat leads daytime and weekend dinner cruises through the Gorge. ~ 541-374-8619, 800-643-1354, fax 541-374-8428; www.sternwheeler.com.

On the Washington side of the bridge in Stevenson is the spacious **Columbia Gorge Interpretive Center**, where the focus is on the cultural and natural history of the Gorge. Located on a ten-acre site overlooking the river, the center includes a 37-foot-high replica of a 19th-century fishwheel, a restored Corliss Steam Engine, a theater with a nine-projector slide show re-creating the cataclysmic formation of the Gorge and several exhibits drawn from the oral histories of local American Indians and pioneer settlers. The world's largest rosary collection is also housed here. Admission. ~ 990 Southwest Rock Creek Drive, Stevenson, WA;

Dell State Park, **Bridal Veil Falls** (two tiers, 100 and 60 feet) and **Wahkeena Falls** (242 feet), where a mile-long trail leads to **Fairy Falls**, a magical 30-foot fan-shaped fall.

MULTNOMAH FALLS The most popular tourist attraction in Oregon, this cascade plunges 620 feet, making it the second-tallest waterfall in the United States. Walk up the paved trail to the observation bridge between the upper and lower falls, where you'll get a misty view of the entire falls. In 1995, a 400-ton rock the size of a Greyhound bus fell from the top of the falls to the upper pool as a result of the ongoing erosion that originally formed the gorge. It caused about 20 minor injuries from flying debris, reminding us that the amazing geology here is still transforming on a grand scale.

STILL MORE FALLS Two and a half miles beyond Multnomah Falls is **Horsetail Falls** (176 feet). Nearby, a trail leads almost two miles through the lush greenery of Oneonta Gorge to **Triple Falls**, a 135-foot segmented fall. The historic highway rejoins the interstate at Ainsworth State Park—unbelievably a mere 18 miles from where it began.

509-427-8211, 800-991-2338, fax 509-427-7429; www.columbiagorge.org, e-mail info@columbiagorge.org.

Farther east on Route 14 is **Carson Hot Springs Resort.** On the Wind River, this resort is well-known by weary travelers for its mineral baths and massages, and can provide a restful stop for those who have been hiking all day on its beautiful hiking trails; there's also an 18-hole golf course. From here you can drive east along Route 14 to Route 141, which leads north along the White Salmon River Valley to Trout Lake, then return to Route 14 and the town of White Salmon. ~ 372 St. Martin's Spring Road, Carson, WA; 509-427-8292, 800-607-3678, fax 509-427-7242.

If Carson Hot Mineral Springs starts to feel too hectic, head to the secluded **Wind River Hot Springs** nearby for a calmer alternative. Well off the beaten path, you can relax and float in these steamy hidden pools reached by a rough half-mile trail that runs alongside the river. Parking fee, $10 per car and two passengers, $2 per additional passenger. ~ Continue east on Route 14, past Carson, and cross the Wind River bridge. Turn left on Berge Road, continue for a mile, then left on Indian Cabin Road to the registration stand and parking lot.

◄ HIDDEN

Just east of White Salmon in the small town of Bingen, Washington, is the **Gorge Heritage Museum**, where you can view historic photographs and American Indian artifacts, including tools, arrow points and beadwork. Closed Monday through Wednesday, and October through May. ~ 202 East Humboldt Street, Bingen, WA; 509-493-3228; e-mail ghm@gorge.net.

Your next stop should be on the Oregon side at **Hood River,** which has become a windsurfing capital thanks to the strong breezes here. Stop at the **Hood River County Visitors Center** for information on this scenic hub. Closed weekends from mid-October to mid-April. ~ 405 Portway Avenue, Hood River, OR; 541-386-2000, 800-336-3530, fax 541-386-2057; www.hoodriver.org, e-mail info@hoodriver.org.

The **Hood River County Historical Museum** features exhibits on American Indian culture, the westward migration, pioneer farming, logging and the Columbia River. Also found here is a collection of period furniture and early-20th-century artifacts. Closed November through March. ~ 300 East Port Marina Park, Hood River, OR; phone/fax 541-386-6772.

If you're in town from mid-May to mid-October, visit the **Hood River Saturday Market,** which features local foods, crafts and artwork. ~ 616 State Street, next to Asbury Church; 541-387-8349.

HIDDEN ►

One of the prettiest drives in Oregon is the 20-mile trip from Hood River to **Lost Lake** (elevation 3140 feet). At the lake you'll have a stunning angle on Mt. Hood—have your camera ready—and can rent a canoe or paddleboat (motorized boats are banned on the lake). In addition to fishing for rainbow trout, visitors like to walk the three-mile Lakeshore Trail that circles the lake. To reach the idyllic retreat, take Route 281 south to Dee and then follow the signs west to the lake. Do keep an eye out for logging trucks en route.

Although many visitors miss it, we strongly recommend a visit to **The Dalles,** on the Oregon side of the Gorge. The end of the Oregon Trail, where immigrants boarded vessels to float down the Columbia (the Barlow Trail later made it possible to complete the

sights

AUTHOR FAVORITE

You'll enjoy panoramic views of the Cascades from the restored coaches of the scenic **Mt. Hood Railroad.** This 44-mile roundtrip journey links the Gorge with Mt. Hood along a route pioneered in 1906. The trip climbs up the Hood River Valley through steep canyons, orchards and forests. Special fall foliage trips are well worth your while as are murder-mystery and four-course dinner rides. The railroad runs April through October, with selected holiday trips between Thanksgiving and Christmas. ~ 110 Railroad Avenue, Hood River, OR; 541-386-3556, 800-872-4661; www.mthoodrr.com, e-mail mthoodrr@gorge.net.

overland journey), this city has a superb old-town walking tour. Pick up a copy of the route map at **The Dalles Area Chamber of Commerce.** Closed weekends from Labor Day to Memorial Day. ~ 404 West 2nd Street, The Dalles, OR; 541-296-2231, 800-255-3385, fax 541-296-1688; www.thedalleschamber.com, e-mail tdacc@gorge.net.

Highlights on this walk include the state's oldest bookstore, **Klindt's** (315 East 2nd Street), and the circa-1863 **Waldron Brothers Drugstore** nearby.

Visit the **Columbia Gorge Discovery Center** to learn about the volcanic eruptions and floods that formed the Gorge and the vegetation and wildlife that live there today. The Kids Explorer Room fills a windowed gallery with fun activities for youngsters to learn about the Lewis and Clark expedition. ~ 5000 Discovery Drive, The Dalles, OR; 541-296-8600, fax 541-298-8660; www.gorgediscovery.org.

The **Fort Dalles Museum** is a favorite stop. Only two fort buildings, the Surgeon's Quarters and the Garden Cottage, remain today. But the museum does preserve an excellent collection of pioneer artifacts, rifles, quilts and historic photographs. Closed December through February. Call for hours otherwise. Admission. ~ 15th and Garrison streets, The Dalles, OR; phone/fax 541-296-4547.

From here, take Route 30 east to Route 197 north. Cross the freeway to Bret Clodfelter Way and follow signs to **The Dalles Dam.** Perhaps the saddest part of this story focuses on the demise of the Gorge's best-known Indian fishing grounds. Wherever you go along this part of the Columbia River, in coffee shops and hotel lobbies, phone company offices and visitors centers, you're likely to see classic photographs of Indians dipping their nets into the river at heavenly Celilo Falls. To get the full picture, leaf through the scrapbook of Celilo Falls fishing pictures at the Fort Dalles Museum.

If you continue on Route 84 east of The Dalles for 12 miles you'll come to a small **Celilo Falls Marker**, which indicates where these bounteous fishing waters prospered before being destroyed by the dam in the late 1950s.

A few miles farther east, on the Washington side, is one of the most isolated museums in America. **Maryhill Museum of Art** was designed in 1914 as the mansion residence of eccentric millionaire Sam Hill, and was supposed to oversee a Quaker agricultural town. But the plan for a new town flopped and the house on the hill eventually became a museum. This eclectic assemblage was dedicated in 1926 by Queen Marie of Rumania, which helps explain the presence of treasures from that nation's royal collection. Also here are Russian icons, a large collection of Rodin sculptures, Charles M. Russell's *Indian Buffalo Hunt*,

◄ HIDDEN

French decorative arts, a good display of American Indian handicrafts and artifacts, and contemporary Pacific Northwest art, as well as one of the world's great chess collections. The museum also includes the world's only collection of post–World War II fashion mannequins. Views of the Columbia Gorge are spectacular, as are the sunsets. Closed mid-November to mid-March. Admission. ~ 35 Maryhill Museum Drive, Goldendale, WA; 509-773-3733, fax 509-773-6138; www.maryhillmuseum.org, e-mail maryhill@maryhillmuseum.org.

Three miles east of Maryhill Museum of Art is Stonehenge, Sam Hill's memorial to local soldiers who died in World War I.

Although most are built with public funds, astronomical observatories are seldom accessible to the general public. One exception is the **Goldendale Observatory State Park Interpretive Center**. Just 11 miles north of the Maryhill Museum and Columbia River, this gem was created by four amateur astronomers and later taken over by the state. Afternoon instructional tours feature an opportunity to gaze at occasional sunspots and the bright planet Venus. Depending on night sky conditions, interpretive specialist Stephen R. Stout may allow visitors to view moon craters, planets, binary stars, star clusters, nebulas and galaxies through a 24-inch telescope. April through September, closed Monday and Tuesday; closed Monday through Thursday the rest of the year. ~ 1602 Observatory Drive, Goldendale, WA; 509-773-3141, fax 509-773-6929; www.perr.com/gosp.html, e-mail goldendale.observatory@parks.wa.gov.

LODGING

The **Cedarplace Inn Bed and Breakfast**, a yellow two-story home built in 1907, offers one large guest room and two suites, decorated with antique furnishings including canopy beds and soft featherbeds with down pillows and comforters. All these attributes may sound fairly typical of Victorian-style luxury B&Bs everywhere, but the location of this one, at the mouth of the Columbia River Gorge Scenic Area, makes it an extra special spot for a romantic getaway. ~ 2611 South Troutdale Road, Troutdale, OR; phone/fax 503-465-1046. MODERATE TO DELUXE.

Located just above the Columbia Gorge Interpretive Center in Stevenson, Washington, is the **Dolce Skamania Lodge**, a modern resort built in the tradition of the grand mountain lodges of the late-18th century. Guests can congregate in the wood-paneled Gorge Room with its deep sofas and three-story river-rock fireplace. Public areas and the 254 guest rooms are handsomely decorated with mission-style furniture, Pendleton fabrics, petroglyph rubbings and American Indian–inspired rugs. The grounds include an 18-hole golf course, fitness center, whirlpools, swimming pool, and more. ~ 1131 Skamania Lodge Way, Stevenson, WA; 509-427-7700, 800-221-7117, fax 509-427-2547; www.skamanialodge.dolce.com, e-mail skamania@dolce.com. ULTRA-DELUXE.

With rooms often in short supply during the summer windsurfing season, visitors who arrive in the Hood River area without reservations may want to call the **Hood River Bed and Breakfast Association** room-finder hotline for information on what is available at local inns. ~ 541-386-6767; www.hoodriver roomfinder.com.

In Cascade Locks, 20 miles west of Hood River, **Bridge of the Gods Motel** provides affordable rustic rooms. All 17 units have queen-size beds; 11 of them offer kitchens. ~ 630 WaNaPa Street, Cascade Locks, OR; 541-374-8628. BUDGET.

The **Columbia Gorge Hotel** is a 40-room landmark where strains of Bach waft through the halls, sculptured carpets highlight the public areas and the fireplace is always roaring. This Mediterranean-style hotel tucks guests into wicker, brass, canopy or hand-carved antique beds. The dining room, home of a popular five-course farm breakfast, offers splendid riverfront dining. Relax in the Valentino Lounge, take a walk through the manicured gardens or enjoy a mineral wrap at the in-house spa. ~ 4000 Westcliff Drive, Hood River, OR; 541-386-5566, 800-345-1921, fax 541-386-9141; www.columbiagorgehotel.com, e-mail cghotel@ gorge.net. ULTRA-DELUXE.

The chandeliered **Hood River Hotel** is a restored brick landmark with 41 rooms and suites. Brightly painted rooms are appointed with oak furniture, four-poster beds, casablanca fans, wing chairs and antiques. Some offer views of the Columbia River. Comfortable sitting areas, a lobby offering jazz music and a cheery café are all part of the charm. Kitchenette suites are available. ~ 102 Oak Street, Hood River, OR; 541-386-1900, 800-386-1859, fax 541-386-6090; www.hoodriverhotel.com, e-mail hrho tel@gorge.net. DELUXE.

Situated in a restored 1909 historic downtown home, the charming **Oak Street Hotel** offers nine guest rooms (one of which is a suite). Queen-sized beds with intricate iron frames and handcrafted furnishings enliven the rooms, all of which have a private bath. There's a comfortable lounge downstairs with a fireplace. ~ 610 Oak Street, Hood River; 541-386-3845, 866-386-3845, fax 541-387-8696; www.oakstreethotel.com, e-mail reservations@oak streethotel.com.

Beautifully located overlooking the Columbia, **Vagabond Lodge** offers 42 spacious, carpeted rooms—some opening right onto the riverfront. All feature contemporary furniture, doubles or queens, microwaves, refrigerators and a secluded garden setting. Some suites have fireplaces, whirlpools and full kitchens. For the price, it's hard to beat this motel west of town. ~ 4070 Westcliff Drive, Hood River, OR; 541-386-2992, 877-386-2992, fax 541-386-3317; www.vagabondlodge.com, e-mail info@vaga bondlodge.com. BUDGET.

Located just five blocks from downtown Hood River is the 1908 Victorian **Inn at the Gorge Bed & Breakfast**. Three suites and two bedrooms have antique furnishings and private baths. Enjoy the surrounding gardens, nap in the hammock beneath the cedar tree or just laze the day away on the wraparound porch. Full breakfast included. ~ 1113 Eugene Street, Hood River, OR; phone/fax 541-386-4429; www.innatthegorge.com, e-mail stay@innatthegorge.com. MODERATE TO DELUXE.

The **Columbia Windrider Inn** is operated by an avid Columbia Gorge sailor and windsurfer who likes to play host to other sailboard afficionados. Situated on a quiet residential street, this historic 1921 home has maple wood floors and four large guest rooms, each with private bath, air conditioning and a queen- or king-size bed. Facilities include a swimming pool, a hot tub and a recreation room. ~ 200 West 4th Street, The Dalles, OR; 541-296-2607; www.windriderinn.com, e-mail chuck@windriderinn.com. BUDGET.

The family-run **Riverview Lodge** provides simple and reasonably priced motel accommodations as well as some two-room suites with kitchens and fireplaces year-round. You'll also find a heated indoor pool and hot tub. This place is great for families. ~ 1505 Oak Street, Hood River, OR; 541-386-8719, 800-789-9568; www.riverviewforyou.com. BUDGET TO DELUXE.

For contemporary motel accommodations try the **Cousins Country Inn**. The 93 fully carpeted rooms have oak tables and queen-size beds. Some have kitchenettes. Guests receive free use of the nearby health club. There's a pool on the premises, as well as Cousins, the only restaurant we know that has a John Deere tractor in the middle of the dining room. ~ 2114 West 6th Street, The Dalles, OR; 541-298-5161, 800-848-9378, fax 541-298-

AUTHOR FAVORITE

One of the frustrating facts of life on the road is the Sunday brunch. If you crave broccoli quiche, Italian sausages, artichoke frittatas, baklava, date tarts, fresh fruit and a dozen other treats, Monday to Saturday just won't do. Fortunately, the **Inn of the White Salmon** has solved this problem in an imaginative way. This lovely bed and breakfast offers brunch seven days a week. All you need do is check in to one of the inn's 16 countrified rooms featuring brass beds and antiques, and this splendid feast is yours. Across the Columbia from Hood River, this inn also features a comfortable parlor. ~ 172 West Jewett Boulevard, White Salmon, WA; 509-493-2335, 800-972-5226; www.innofthewhitesalmon.com, e-mail innkeeper@innofthewhitesalmon.com. MODERATE TO DELUXE.

6411; www.cousinscountryinn.com, e-mail info@cousinscountry inn.com. MODERATE.

DINING

Vancouver now boasts its own **Pizzicato Gourmet Pizza**, part of a popular Oregon chain known for sophisticated toppings and unique combinations. Try the *melanza*, with sweet red and yellow peppers, roasted eggplant, and fontina and goat cheese. Meat-eaters will love the *patate e prosciutto*, with rosemary red potatoes, prosciutto ham, smoked mozzarella and mushrooms. ~ 1900 Northeast 162nd Avenue, Vancouver, WA; 360-891-2081, fax 360-891-2057; www.pizzicatogourmetpizza.com. BUDGET.

In Stevenson, Washington, the **Cascade Room** at Dolce Skamania Lodge has a grand dining room with massive wooden ceiling beams and superb views of the Gorge. The specialties are Northwest-inspired dishes prepared in a wood-burning oven, including oak-crusted trout and roasted wild game, meats and seafood. ~ 1131 Skamania Lodge Way, Stevenson, WA; 509-427-7700, 800-221-7117, fax 509-427-2547; www.skamanialodge.dolce.com. DELUXE TO ULTRA-DELUXE.

The **Big River Grill** in downtown Stevenson is a convivial place with wooden booths and old photographs on the walls. Both locals and visitors come here to enjoy salmon chowder in bread bowls (Fridays only), pasta specials, salads topped with grilled meats and such vegetarian entrées as portobello ravioli and nutty garden burgers. ~ 192 Southwest 2nd Avenue, Stevenson, WA; 509-427-4888. MODERATE.

◄ HIDDEN

About 20 minutes north of the Gorge, and well worth the trip, is one of the Gorge's most intriguing restaurants, **The Logs**. You'll be impressed by the roasted chicken, hickory-smoked ribs, giant fries and huckleberry pie served in this log-cabin setting. The battered and deep-fried chicken gizzards and cheese sticks are a big hit with the regular clientele, who include locals, rafters, skiers and devotees of the rich mud pie. In business for six decades, this is the place where city slickers will come face to face with their first jackalope, safely mounted on the wall. ~ 1258 Route 141, White Salmon, WA; 509-493-1402; e-mail logsres@gorge.net. BUDGET.

◄ HIDDEN

Tucked away in the woods on the Oregon side is **Stonehedge Gardens**, an antique-filled home preparing Continental and Northwest dining at its finest. Set in a beautiful garden, this paneled restaurant has a tiny mahogany bar and a roaring fireplace. Among the dishes are scallop sauté, veal chanterelle, jumbo prawns and filet of salmon. Light entrées, such as a seafood platter, are also recommended. Dinner only. Closed Monday in winter. ~ 3405 Cascade Avenue, Hood River, OR; 541-386-3940. MODERATE TO DELUXE.

Locals enjoy **Sixth Street Bistro & Loft** for its casual dining and tasty cuisine. Pastas, salads and hamburgers are joined by more international items like *pad thai*, chicken satay or "Mexican stir-fry." The dinner menu includes steak, seafood and daily specials with a focus on local, organic ingredients. After dinner you can shoot pool or relax with a drink in the upstairs loft. ~ 509 Cascade Avenue, Hood River, OR; 541-386-5737. MODERATE.

It's hard to beat the breakfasts at **Bette's Place**, a small, mauve-toned café with floral curtains. Bette's bakes 14 kinds of muffins daily, including cinnamon, cranberry orange and Oregon blackberry, and also serves eggs Benedict, omelettes, strawberry waffles and pancakes topped with fresh fruit. Dinner served every first Friday of the month. ~ 416 Oak Street, in the Oak Mall, Hood River, OR; 541-386-1880; e-mail bettesr@gorge.net. BUDGET.

Pasquale's Ristorante has breezy indoor and sidewalk seating in the center of this resort town. The heart of the dining room is a handcrafted bar with an etched-glass mirror. Entrées include filet of salmon, gorgonzola ravioli and short ribs with mascarpone risotto. ~ In the Hood River Hotel, 102 Oak Street, Hood River, OR; 541-386-1900, 800-386-1859, fax 541-386-6090; www.hoodriverhotel.com, e-mail hrhotel@gorge.net. MODERATE TO DELUXE.

As its name suggests, **The Mesquitery Restaurant & Bar** is best known for its meat and seafood dishes cooked on a mesquite grill. Barbecue-glazed baby-back ribs and and garlic-and-parmesan-crusted salmon are among the highlights, as are heaping main-dish cobb and caesar salads. The inside dining area is filled with high-backed booths and rich wood paneling, while outside you'll find a two-level enclosed deck area with colorful planters. ~ 1219 12th Street, Hood River, OR; 541-386-2002, fax 541-386-2215. MODERATE.

An elegant dining room overlooking the Gorge, **Columbia River Gorge Dining Room** is a romantic place to dine on roast

AUTHOR FAVORITE

After a visit to Multnomah Falls it makes sense to dine at **Multnomah Falls Lodge**. The smoked-salmon-and-cheese platter and generous salads are recommended. The European-style lodge building with a big stone fireplace, scenic paintings of the surroundings and lovely views will add to your enjoyment of the Gorge. Buffet champagne brunch on Sunday ~ Off Route 84, Bridal Veil, WA; 503-695-2376, fax 503-695-2338; www.multnomahfallslodge.com, e-mail info@multnomahfalls lodge.com. MODERATE TO DELUXE.

pork tenderloin, fresh Oregon salmon, rack of lamb or Dungeness crab with lobster sauce and risotto. Done in an Early American design with oak furniture and candlelit tables, this establishment is well known for its lavish farm breakfast. ~ 4000 Westcliff Drive, Hood River, OR; 541-386-5566, fax 541-387-5414; www.columbiagorgehotel.com, e-mail cghotel@gorge.net. ULTRA-DELUXE.

Located in one of the most historic buildings in The Dalles, the **Baldwin Saloon** was built in 1876 and has an 18-foot-long mahogany back bar and turn-of-the-20th-century oil paintings on the brick walls. The restaurant is known for its seafood and oyster dishes (baked and on the half shell) and also serves thick sandwiches, burgers, soups and desserts. Breads and desserts are baked on the premises. Closed Sunday. ~ 1st and Court streets, The Dalles, OR; 541-296-5666. MODERATE TO DELUXE.

For heaping platters of chicken, steak or shrimp fajitas, the place to go is **Casa El Mirador**, a cozy family-run restaurant with murals of Mexico adorning the walls. Crabmeat burritos, chimichangas, tacos and other south-of-the-border staples also make good choices. ~ 1424 West 2nd Street, The Dalles, OR; 541-298-7388. BUDGET TO MODERATE.

For decades **Johnny's Café** has specialized in home-style breakfasts and lunches. Locals come here to feast on burgers, sandwiches and daily specials like caesar salad with grilled chicken and homemade pies. ~ 408 East 2nd Street, The Dalles, OR; 541-296-4565, fax 541-296-8759. BUDGET.

SHOPPING

Fort Vancouver Gift Shop is the place to go for books, maps and pamphlets on Pacific Northwest history. We recommend picking up a copy of *Outpost* by Dorothy Morris. ~ 1501 East Evergreen Boulevard, Vancouver, WA; 360-696-7655 ext. 16, fax 360-696-7657.

Aviation buffs will want to stop by the gift shop at **Pearson Air Museum.** The shop has an ace collection of memorabilia and souvenirs for adults and juniors alike. Closed Sunday through Tuesday. ~ 1115 East 5th Street, Vancouver, WA; 360-694-7026, fax 360-694-0824.

Pendleton Woolen Mills and Outlet Store offers big savings on irregulars. Tours of the mill, in operation since 1912, are available, but call first for schedule information. ~ #2 17th Street, Washougal, WA; 360-835-1118, fax 360-835-5451.

A good place to find books on the region is **Waucoma Bookstore**, which is also well stocked with fiction, children's books, cards, magazines, children's toys and handcrafted pottery. Closed Sunday in winter. ~ 212 Oak Street, Hood River, OR; 541-386-5353.

Text continued on page 86.

North of the Gorge

Since you've already dipped your toe into Washington while visiting the Columbia River Gorge, you may want to explore some of the treasures located in Southern Washington within 50 miles of the Oregon border. From an active volcano to forest-ringed lakes, the landscape provides plenty of opportunities for the outdoor enthusiast and for anyone who appreciates spectacular scenery. All of these attractions can be combined in a loop drive (during the summer only) that connects to the Gorge's eastern side.

At the southern end of the Washington Cascades an hour north of Portland and Vancouver, Mt. St. Helens might best be described as a cross between a geology lesson and a bombing range. On May 18, 1980, Mt. St. Helens, dormant for 123 years, blew some 1300 feet off its top and rendered 57 persons dead or missing, causing one of the largest natural disasters in recorded North American history. Today, access to this composite volcano remains limited because the eruption and resulting mudslides and floods erased the roads that formerly entered the area. In any event, Mt. St. Helens is an awe-inspiring and humbling experience—an absolute statement of nature's power and dominance.

Today **Mt. St. Helens National Volcanic Monument** covers 110,000 acres, created in 1982 to preserve and study the area that was devastated by the eruption. Interpretive sites and overlooks show the much-altered Spirit Lake, vast mud flows and the forests that were flattened by the blast. Trout and bass lure anglers to Silver Lake and the lakes behind dams on the Lewis River, northwest of the monument. Access to the monument is limited to a few Forest Service and county roads, most of which are closed in winter. Admission. ~ From Portland or the Gorge on Route 5, take Route 503 to Exit 21, up the Lewis River to the monument headquarters at Amboy and the southern flank of the monument; 360-247-3900. Visitors centers within the monument are open year-round; they're full-service centers with toilets, phones and staffed information desks.

A major sightseeing destination, **Mt. St. Helens National Volcanic Monument Visitors Center** is west of the volcano on Route 504 at Silver Lake, five miles east of Route 5. The center includes a walk-in model of the volcano's interior. A 22-minute film on the eruption plays on the hour, and a second 15-minute film plays every half hour. ~ Route 504; 360-274-2100. **Coldwater Ridge Visitors Center**, 38 miles farther east, is located in the area where the volcano erupted and offers guided walks from June to September. Interpretive exhibits focus on the biological story of the eruption. ~ Route 504; 360-274-2114, fax 360-274-2151.

The closest you can get to the volcano by car is **Johnston Ridge Observatory**, named for scientist David Johnston who was killed by the eruption. The observatory includes a theater, an exhibit hall, a bookstore and staff-guided lectures and walks. Call for winter hours. ~ Route 504, 52 miles east of the main visitors center; 360-274-2140, fax 360-274-2151

At **Windy Ridge** rangers give hourly talks in the amphitheater in summer. **Meta Lake Walk** is on the way to Windy Ridge, and rangers tell how plants and animals survived the eruption. A 30-minute talk is given in **Ape Cave** on the southern end of the monument. It includes a walk into the 1900-year-old lava tube that got its name from the outdoors adventure group, the St. Helens Apes, who discovered it in 1946. Windy Ridge is only accessible spring through fall. ~ South of the town of Randle, off Route 12.

Marked by the Mt. St. Helens National Volcanic Monument on the west and Mt. Adams on the east, the 1.4 million-acre **Gifford Pinchot National Forest** covers most of the southern Cascades to the Columbia River. Enclosing seven wilderness areas, the forest is accessed by a network of roads and trails. To get there, use Route 14 on the south, Route 503 extending east of Woodland, Route 504 on the west side of Mt. St. Helens and Route 12 on the north. ~ 360-891-5000, fax 360-891-5045.

The logging roads eventually lead to **Trout Lake**, a small town close to a naturally disintegrating lake of the same name with a Forest Service Ranger Station. Of interest are the **Big Lava Beds**, 14 miles west of Trout Lake, where unusual formations of basalt are found, and the **Ice Cave**, six miles southwest of Trout Lake, a lava tube where ice remains until late summer. There are picnic areas and restrooms, and over 50 campgrounds to choose from. Fishing is excellent in many of the area's frequently stocked lakes and in all rivers flowing out of the forest. In late summer, huckleberry-picking is very popular. The forest includes more than 40 campgrounds, some of which accept reservations (877-444-6777).

From Trout Lake, drive east 19 miles to the small cowboy town of **Glenwood**. There's not much more than a country tavern and post office, but at the Shade Tree Inn restaurant you can get directions to some of the more unusual sights in the area, such as a group of **quartz crystals** more than 200 feet in diameter and what is locally called "**volcano pits**," a series of small craters left behind by cinder cones.

From Glenwood, take the Glenwood–Goldendale Road to the junction with Route 142 and drive back southwest to Klickitat and the Columbia Gorge at Lyle. This takes you through the deep, winding **Klickitat River Canyon** with views of the river, a steelheaders' favorite. Mt. Adams often frames the scene. From Lyle, you're only about 15 minutes from both Hood River and The Dalles, back across on the Oregon side.

Columbia Art Gallery represents over 150 artists, primarily from the Columbia Gorge region. Featured are the works of photographers, printmakers, potters, glassblowers, jewelers, weavers, sculptors and painters. ~ 101 4th Street, Hood River, OR; 541-386-4512; www.columbiaartgallery.org.

On the Washington side of the Gorge, Stevenson's small, walkable downtown has some distinctive art galleries and gift shops.

The Dalles is home to Oregon's oldest bookstore, **Klindt's**, which dates from 1870 and still has an old-time ambience with high ceilings and glass-topped counters. Books on the Pacific Northwest, both new and used, are a specialty, as are rare and out-of-print books. ~ 315 East 2nd Street, The Dalles, OR; 541-296-3355.

The Dalles Art Center, located in the historic Carnegie Library, exhibits work by local and regional artists. Most of this fine art is available for purchase. The gallery showcases paintings, artists' greeting cards, pottery, jewelry, beadwork, glasswork, photography and baskets. ~ 220 East 4th Street, The Dalles, OR; 541-296-4759.

NIGHTLIFE A popular gay and lesbian nightspot in Vancouver, Washington, is **North Bank Bar & Grill**, which has a dancefloor and outdoor patio. Cover for drag shows. ~ 106 West 6th Street, Vancouver, WA; 360-695-3862.

The **Power Station Pub and Theater** is located in the former Multnomah County poor farm. The theater presents second-run movies in the farm's former power plant. The pub serves a full menu in the converted laundry building. Also on the premises is the **Edgefield Brewery** and a working winery and distillery. ~ 2126 Southwest Halsey Street, Troutdale, OR; 503-669-8610, 800-669-8610; www.mcmenamins.com, e-mail power@mcmenamins.com.

AUTHOR FAVORITE

Locally made jams, jellies, wine and other food products make terrific presents for the folks back home. **The Gift House** carries a variety of home-grown products, including wine and jams. ~ 204 Oak Street, Hood River, OR; 541-386-9234. Pick up a fine Oregon white or red at **The Wine Sellers**. ~ 514 State Street, Hood River, OR; 541-386-4647. **Rasmussen Farms** sells strawberries, Hood River apples, Comice pears and cherries. Apples and pears can be shipped as gift packs. ~ 3020 Thomsen Road off Route 35 south of Hood River, OR; 541-386-4622, 800-548-2243, fax 541-386-4702; www.rasmussenfarms.com, e-mail info@rasmussenfarms.com.

The **Skamania Lodge** has occasional live acoustic music or speakers before a woodburning fireplace in summer. ~ 1131 Skamania Lodge Way, Stevenson, WA; 509-427-2527, fax 509-427-2547.

Bungalow Bar & Grill has televised sports, two pool tables and dart boards. ~ 812 Wind River Highway, Carson, WA; 509-427-4523.

Full Sail Brewing Company offers tastings of their very popular hand-crafted beers, as well as a pub-style menu and deck seating with fine views of the Columbia. ~ 506 Columbia Avenue, Hood River, OR; 541-386-2247.

PARKS

ROOSTER ROCK STATE PARK Offering more than three miles of sandy Columbia River frontage, this 872-acre park is near the Gorge's west end. The rock, named for a towering promontory, is near a camping site chosen by Lewis and Clark in 1805. Well-known for swimming and beginner windsurfing, Rooster Rock also has excellent hiking trails, a small lake and a forested bluff. Anglers can fish for salmon. There are picnic tables and restrooms. Day-use fee, $3. ~ Located in Oregon 22 miles east of Portland on Route 84 at Exit 25; 503-695-2261, 800-551-6949, fax 503-695-2226.

VIENTO STATE PARK Originally a rest stop on the old Columbia River Highway, this 247-acre park includes a riverfront and Viento Creek forest section. Dramatic views of the Columbia River make this a popular camping and picnicking facility. It can get very windy, and be aware that trains pass through the gorge at night. Facilities include picnic tables, barbecue pits, showers and restrooms. Closed October through April. Day-use fee, $3. ~ Route 84 Exit 56, eight miles west of Hood River in Oregon; 541-374-8811, 800-551-6949.

▲ There are 18 tent sites ($10 to $14 per night) and 57 RV hookup sites ($12 to $16 per night).

AINSWORTH STATE PARK Ranking high among the treasures of the Columbia River Scenic Highway is this 156-acre park. Near the bottom of St. Peter's Dome, the forested park has a gorgeous hiking trail that connects with a network extending throughout the region. A serene getaway, the only sound of civilization you're likely to hear is that of passing trains. There are picnic tables, showers and restrooms. Closed November through March. ~ Route 30, the Columbia River Scenic Highway, 37 miles east of Portland on the Oregon side; 503-695-2301, fax 503-695-2226.

▲ There are 45 RV hookup sites; $12 to $16 per night. There are also five walk-in sites; $10 to $14 per night.

MEMALOOSE STATE PARK The park is named for an offshore Columbia River island that was an American Indian burial ground.

This 336-acre site spreads out along a two-mile stretch of riverfront and is forested with pine, oak and fir. Much of the park is steep and rocky. It can also be very windy. "Memaloose," in case you were wondering, is a Chinook word linked to the sacred burial ritual. There are horseshoes, a playground, interpretive programs in summer, showers and restrooms. Closed November through March. ~ Off Route 84, 11 miles west of The Dalles in Oregon. Take the Memaloose Rest Stop exit, then make a right into the park. Westbound access only; 541-478-3008, fax 541-478-2369.

▲ There are 63 tent sites ($12 to $16 per night) and 39 RV hookup sites ($16 to $20 per night). Reservations: 800-452-5687.

Outdoor Adventures

FISHING

This is a prime fishing area: salmon, steelhead, walleye and sturgeon are all found in the Columbia River area. For guides or charters in the Portland area, contact **Page's Northwest Guide Services.** ~ 14321 Southeast Bush Street, Portland, OR; 503-760-3373. For trips on the Columbia and Willamette rivers, try **Reel Adventures.** ~ 57206 East Marmot Road, Sandy, OR; 503-622-5372. In The Dalles, **Glenn Summers** offers fishing information. ~ P.O. Box 436, The Dalles, OR 97058; 541-296-5949. For both fishing and flyfishing information on steelhead, salmon and walleye in the Columbia and John Day rivers, contact **Fly by Nyte Guide Service.** ~ 2624 Old Dufur Road, The Dalles, OR; 541-298-2770. Also offering guided fishing trips in the Gorge area is **Northwest Guide Service.** ~ Woodard Creek Road, Skamania, WA; 509-427-4625.

The art of flyfishing abounds on rivers in the Gorge region. **The Gorge Fly Shop** arranges flyfishing excursions to such popular destinations as Deschutes. All levels of lessons are available. ~ 201 Oak Street, Hood River, OR; 541-386-6977; www.gorgeflyshop.com.

WIND-SURFING

Between the high cliff walls of the Columbia Gorge, east of Portland, winds on the river can hit 60 knots, so it's no wonder this is one of the world's best windsurfing areas, with Hood River its

AUTHOR FAVORITE

A little Washington gem on the White Salmon River north of the Columbia, **Northwestern Lake** is an ideal destination for a day trip where you can swim, fish, hike or just loaf. There are also summer cabins nearby for those who want to stay longer. ~ Head west from White Salmon on Route 14 to Route 141. Continue north five miles to the park.

capital. According to a local expert, "Once you learn the tricks and let the wind do the work for you, it's not as hard as it looks." And if you don't mind cool temperatures (50°F and lower) in winter, you can windsurf year-round.

Big Winds offers rentals and instruction for children and adults, and a full-service retail shop. Kitesurfing equipment is also available. ~ 207 Front Street, Hood River, OR; 541-386-6086, 888-509-4210; www.bigwinds.com.

If you're experienced and want to rent equipment, contact **Doug's Sports.** ~ 101 Oak Street, Hood River, OR; 541-386-5787, 800-211-8207; www.dougsports.com. **Hood River WaterPlay** offers lessons and equipment, and has a beginner beach area in front of the Hood River Inn. ~ Port Marina Park, Hood River, OR; 541-386-9463, 800-963-7873; www.hood riverwaterplay.com.

Swiss Swell also offers lessons in the Hood River area. Closed in winter. ~ 13 Oak Street, Hood River, OR; 541-490-7570; www.swiss-swell.com.

Hood River WaterPlay offers lessons and equipment, and has a beginner beach area in front of the Hood River Inn. ~ 100 Port Marina Way, Hood River, OR; 541-386-9463, 800-963-7873, www.hoodriverwaterplay.com

RIVER RUNNING

The White Salmon River north of the Columbia is a popular whitewater rafting spot.

There are some 30 Class II, III and IV rapids along the short course of the White Salmon River, a pool-and-drop mountain stream that is fed by rainfall and snowmelt from Mt. Adams, 30 miles distant. For a half or full-day guided whitewater adventure on the White Salmon and Klickitat rivers, call **Zoller's Outdoor Odyssey.** ~ 1248 Route 141, White Salmon, WA; 509-493-2641, 800-366-2004; www.zooraft.com. Also try **North Cascades River Expeditions.** ~ P.O. Box 116, Arlington, WA 98223; 800-634-8433; riverexpeditions.com.

River Drifters in Bend will outfit trips on the White Salmon, Deschutes and Owyhee rivers, among others. ~ P.O. Box 7962, Bend, OR 97708; 800-972-0430; www.riverdrifters.net.

Other often-rafted rivers in the Gorge are the Klickitat and the Wenatchee. An outfitter to contact is **River Recreation.** ~ P.O. Box 2124, Bothell, WA 98041; 800-464-5899. **Renegade River Rafters** offers two- to three-day trips on the Deschutes and half-day trips on the Klickitat. ~ P.O. Box 263, Stevenson, WA 98648; 509-427-7238.

In Washington, there's also **All Adventures Rafting,** which offers day trips to the Klickitat as well as three-day trips elsewhere. ~ P.O. Box 544, White Salmon, WA 98672; 509-493-3926, 800-743-5628; www.alladventures.net.

SKIING

With Hood River and the Columbia River Gorge practically at the foot of snowcapped Mt. Hood, it's possible to ski in the morning (even in July) and windsurf in the afternoon. **Mt. Hood Meadows** spreads across 2150 acres and offers 87 trails, most of which are intermediate and advanced level. In addition to alpine skiing, there are terrain parks and half pipes. Night skiing and 15 kilometers of cross-country trails are also available. ~ Take Route 84 Exit 64 in Hood River then follow Route 35 south to the Meadows entrance; 800-754-4663, 503-227-7669 (snowline); skihood.com.

GOLF

Hood River Golf and Country Club has 18 holes, full mountain views, pear orchards and a driving range. ~ 1850 Country Club Road, Hood River, OR; 541-386-3009. **Indian Creek Golf Course**, with its gentle rolling hills, is a dry, year-round 18-hole course. ~ 3605 Brookside Drive, Hood River, OR; 541-386-7770, 866-386-7770; www.indiancreekgolf.com. In Stevenson, Washington, there's the 18-hole **Dolce Skamania Lodge Golf Course**, with views of the Columbia River. ~ 1131 Skamania Lodge Way; 509-427-2541, 800-293-0418. In Carson, Washington, the **Hot Springs Golf Course** has 18 holes and is great for beginners. Currently closed for reconstruction. ~ Hot Springs Avenue and St. Martins Road; 509-427-5150. Located on Route 14 in Washington between Beacon Rock and North Bonneville is **Beacon Rock Public Golf Course.** There's nine holes near the Columbia with a sand trap and water hazards. ~ 509-427-5730.

A manmade tunnel passes behind the cascading water of Tunnel Falls.

RIDING STABLES

For equestrians, the Gorge area has limited options. **Northwestern Lake Riding Stables** provides guided trips on trails. ~ 126 Little Buck Creek Road, White Salmon; 509-493-4965, fax 509-493-8919; www.nwstables.com.

BIKING

The Columbia River Gorge along Route 84 is prime cycling territory, particularly along any portion of the 62-mile route from Portland to Hood River. The old Columbia River Highway, which parallels Route 84, is less trafficked, calmer, scenic and a wonderful way to experience the Gorge. The **Dalles Riverfront Trail**, a paved bike trail, extends from the west part of The Dalles to Dalles Dam.

The Oregon Department of Transportation (ODOT) publishes the **Columbia River Gorge Bike Map**, a free 15-page brochure of this scenic area's cycling opportunities. Look for the publication at Welcome Centers and bike shops, or contact the ODOT. ~ 123 Northwest Flanders Street, Portland; 503-731-8200.

Bike Rentals **Discover Bicycles** rents and sells mountain bikes, road bikes and tandems and can provide information about guided bike tours. ~ 116 Oak Street, Hood River, OR; 541-386-4820; www.discoverbicycles.com.

HIKING

All distances listed for hiking trails are one way unless otherwise noted.

Latourell Falls Trail (2.2 miles), on the Columbia River Highway three miles east of Crown Point, is a moderately difficult walk leading along a streambed to the base of the upper falls. To extend this walk another mile, take a loop trail beginning at the top of lower Latourell Falls and returning to the highway at Talbot Park.

Near the Bridal Veil exit off Route 84 is **#415 Angels Rest Trail** (4.5 miles), an easy hike leading to an overlook. This route can be extended another 15 miles to Bonneville Dam by taking the **#400 Gorge Trail**, an amazing path that passes many of the Gorge's stunning cascades, including Multnomah Falls, Triple Falls and Horsetail Falls.

Eagle Creek Campground at Exit 41 on Route 84 is the jumpoff point for the easy **#440 Eagle Creek Trail** to Punch Bowl Falls (2 miles) or Tunnel Falls (6 miles). You can continue to follow the wildflower-riddled path (part of the Pacific Crest Trail) through the Columbia Wilderness, up to Wahtum Lake (13 miles). Four campsites provide rest between Eagle Creek and the lake.

On the Washington side of the river west of Bonneville Dam is the one-mile trail leading to the top of **Beacon Rock**, an 800-foot monolith noted by Lewis and Clark. Ascended by a series of switchbacks guarded by railings, this trail offers numerous views of the Gorge.

East of Home Valley, Oregon, on Route 14 is the **Dog Mountain Trail** (6 miles), a difficult climb up 2900 feet for impressive views of Mt. Hood, Mt. St. Helens and Mt. Adams. During May and June, the surrounding hills are covered with wildflowers, making this an extraordinary time to hike the trail.

Transportation

CAR

Route 84 runs the length of the Columbia River Gorge on the Oregon side and just east of the town of Troutdale is paralleled by the **Historic Columbia River Highway**, a windy road that offers awesome views of the Gorge. **Route 14** travels along the river's Washington side. **Route 35** heads south from Hood River on the Oregon side toward Mt. Hood.

AIR

If you plan on flying to the Columbia River Gorge area, **Portland International Airport** is the closest airport. Alaska Airlines, America West Airlines, American Airlines, Delta Air Lines,

Hawaiian Airlines, Horizon Air, Northwest Airlines, Southwest Airlines and United Airlines all fly into Portland. ~ www.portlandairportpdx.com.

BUS

Greyhound Bus Lines (800-231-2222; www.greyhound.com) offers service four times daily to Hood River. The Hood River terminal is at 600 East Marina Way, Hood River, OR. ~ 541-386-1212. They also service The Dalles at 201 Federal Street, OR. ~ 541-296-2421.

TRAIN

Amtrak provides daily service to and from Portland. ~ 800-872-7245; www.amtrak.com.

CAR RENTAL

Your Rental and Party Center has one car they rent. 1113 Tucker Road, Hood River, OR; 541-386-2062. In The Dalles, contact **Enterprise Rent A Car.** ~ 100 East 2nd Street; 541-506-5007.

PUBLIC TRANSIT

Hood River is served by the **Columbia Area Transit.** Buses run to Parkdale, Odell and Cascade Locks. ~ 541-386-4202.

TAXIS

In Hood River, call **Hood River Taxi and Transportation.** ~ 541-386-2255. In The Dalles, try **The Dalles Taxi.** ~ 541-296-3965.

FOUR

Oregon Coast

As you take in the wonders of the Oregon Coast, do it with respect, for in a very real sense you are stepping into a paradise borrowed. In 1805, when Lewis and Clark arrived at the mouth of the Columbia River, only about 10,000 American Indians in such coast tribes as the Tillamook and Yaquina called this home. With roughly three square miles per inhabitant, these tribes were undisputed masters of their realm. The American Indians traveled almost entirely by water, were intensely spiritual and had, for the most part, a modest and self-sufficient lifestyle. Working hard during the spring and summer months, they harvested enough from the sea and forests to relax during the winter.

But their world began to change, indeed it was doomed, when distant entrepreneurs set sights on the region's vast resources. These men believed that the Northwest did not belong to its native populace but was instead destined to be claimed by a new master race of settlers thousands of miles away. Among them was John Jacob Astor, the richest man in America. Eager to monopolize the lucrative fur trade in the uncharted Northwest, he dispatched the ship *Tonquin* from New York in the fall of 1810. Then, in the spring of 1811, just about the time the *Tonquin* was sailing across the Columbia River Bar, a second overland group sponsored by Astor left St. Louis. They began by following the river route pioneered by Lewis and Clark but then forged a new trail across the Rockies, eventually reaching the Snake River, where they were turned back by impenetrable rapids. By early 1812, when the party limped into Astoria, the little settlement created by men from the *Tonquin*, it was clear that their patron's great vision remained distant. For one thing, most of the *Tonquin* group had headed north to Vancouver Island, where dictatorial captain Jonathan Thorn spurned the American Indians, triggering a massacre that destroyed almost everyone aboard. In a final insane act of revenge, a surviving crew member lured the American Indians back on the ship, went below and lit the ship's magazine, killing everyone aboard.

In September 1812, not long after they received news of this tragedy, the Astorians left behind at the little Columbia River settlement were visited by a party from the rival North West Fur Company. These newcomers announced that a British warship was en route to seize Fort Astoria. To make matters worse, they declared that the British had just won the War of 1812. Cut off from the news that would have exposed this lie, the Astorians decided to sell off their pelts and the first American settlement west of the Mississippi for pennies on the dollar. Then they began the long journey home.

While the British took over the fur trade, manifest destiny brought the Americans back on the Oregon Trail. In 1846, Oregon Country was returned to the Americans and new settlers gradually returned to the coast. Astoria and other settlements along the coast emerged as fishing, farming and logging centers. The arrival of the railroads spawned the development of resort towns like Newport and Seaside. Boardwalks, modeled after those found on the East Coast, soon sprang up to serve the growing clientele.

The coast may have been the magnet, but it didn't take the new arrivals long to discover that the lofty headlands, picturesque estuaries, rocky points, sand dunes and tidepools were only part of the attraction. Back behind the coastal rhododendron fields were rivers that offered legendary steelheading. Sunny valleys forested with fir, spruce, hemlock and cedar were perfect for camping. Stands of weird carnivorous plants, plunging waterfalls, myrtle groves and pristine lakes were all part of the draw. And the Indians, decimated by white man's diseases, were subjugated by the new settlers and ultimately forced onto reservations.

Having pushed the natives conveniently out of the way, the pioneers soon began reaping nature's bounty from the coastal region. Coos Bay became a major wood-processing center, and commercial fishing dominated the economies of communities like Port Orford. In other towns, such as Tillamook, the dairy trade flourished. And, of course, farming also began to emerge in the sunnier valleys east of the coast.

Today, thanks in part to a comprehensive network of state parks, the coast is equally appealing to motorists, bikers and hikers. While it's hard to improve on this landscape, humans have done their best to complement nature's handiwork. From bed and breakfasts heavy on chintz and lace to bargain oceanfront motels furnished from garage sales, accommodations serve every taste. Everywhere you turn, another executive chef weary of big-city life seems to be opening a pasta joint or a pita stand. Theater, classical music, jazz, pottery and sculpture galleries have all found a home in towns ranging from North Bend to Cannon Beach. A major aquarium in Newport, a world-class maritime museum in Astoria, a printing museum in Coos Bay, an antiquarian curio shop in Florence—these are just a few of the special places that are likely to capture your attention.

If you must go down to the sea again, and you must, rest assured that this coast offers the space all of us need. True, some of the northern beaches draw a crowd on weekends and holidays. But traffic is lighter on the South Coast, where beachcombing can be a lonely, at times solitary, experience. With vast national recreation areas, national forests and sloughs, it's easy to get lost in the region. Often foggy, the Oregon coast is hit by frequent storms in the winter months. But this

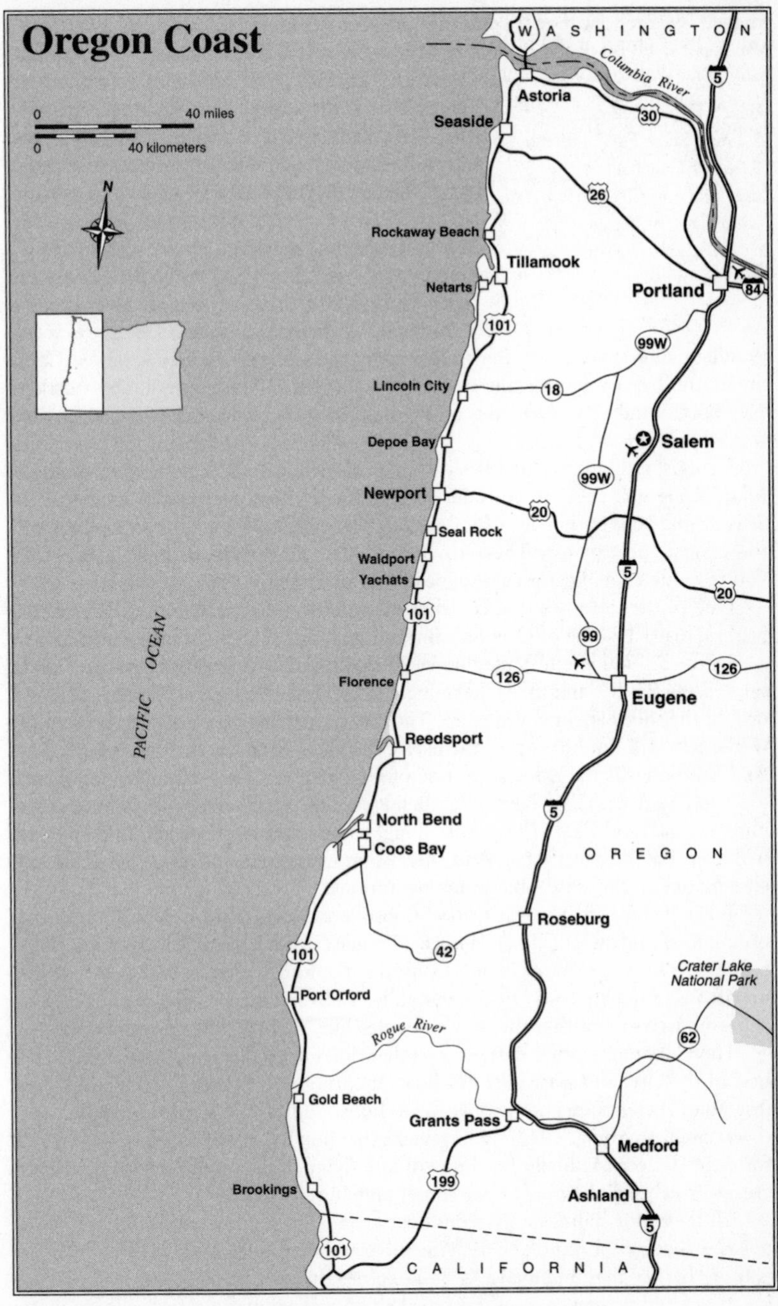
Oregon Coast
0 40 miles
0 40 kilometers
N
WASHINGTON
Columbia River
Astoria
Seaside
5
30
26
Rockaway Beach
Tillamook
Netarts
Portland
84
101
99W
Lincoln City
18
Depoe Bay
Salem
99W
Newport
20
Seal Rock
Waldport
Yachats
5
20
101
PACIFIC OCEAN
99
Florence
126
126
Eugene
Reedsport
5
North Bend
Coos Bay
OREGON
Roseburg
101
42
Crater Lake
National Park
Port Orford
Rogue River
62
Gold Beach
Grants Pass
Medford
Brookings
199
Ashland
5
101
CALIFORNIA

rugged weather is offset by mild periods in the summer or early fall. Even when the coast itself is socked in, inland valleys just a few miles away can be warm and sunny. The contrast continues: temperatures along the coast seldom fall below freezing, but the adjacent coastal peaks are frequently snowbound in the winter months. And while the surf is bracing, lakes adjacent to the coast feature warmer waters ideal for swimming and waterskiing.

Beach Drive, between Fort Stevens State Park and the town of Gearhart, is the only place in Oregon where you're allowed to drive your car on the beach.

To fully experience the coast, you're well advised to see it border to border, from Astoria to Brookings. But many travelers prefer to focus on one or two areas. If you're history minded, Astoria is a must. For pure scenic grandeur and small-town charm, it's hard to beat the Tillamook–Three Capes area. Another winner in this category is the Otter Rock community north of Newport. Windy Port Orford is a very special place, scenic, uncrowded and ideal for steelheading.

Groups with diverse interests such as surf fishing, arcade games and shopping for folk art will want to consider well-rounded resort towns like Lincoln City, Seaside and Newport. They offer sporting life, cultural attractions and all the cotton candy you can eat. These towns are also convenient to rural gems when you're ready to make a great escape.

One of the most alluring communities on the coast is Florence. A delightful historic district, some of Oregon's finest dunes, a good restaurant scene and easy access to the Willamette Valley make this community a popular getaway. In the same category is Bandon, a charming port with a commercial district that will delight the shoppers in your group. Those who are eager to take a jet boat to the wilderness will doubtless find themselves in Gold Beach, a major fishing center. And Brookings is the gateway to one of our favorites, the Chetco River country.

The Bay Area, Coos Bay/North Bend/Charleston, is an ideal choice for clamming on the tidal flats. The parks, sloughs and country roads south of the area will keep you busy for days. And there is an impressive variety of museums, including one of the state's finest art institutions.

When it comes to a trendy resort atmosphere with tasteful shopping malls, sign ordinances, café au lait, classical music, French cuisine and gallery openings, Cannon Beach is the coast's class act. Every day the tourist tide from the east washes in patrons of the arts and Oregon varietals. This town may set the record for merchant-punsters operating shops with names like "Sometimes a Great Lotion."

There are many other destinations that don't appear on any map. In fact, the best of the Oregon Coast may not be its incorporated cities or parklands. Think instead of rocky points home only to sea lions. Eddies so beautiful you don't care if you catch anything. Offshore haystacks that don't even have names. Dunes that form the perfect backdrop for a day of kite flying. Points that seem to have been created solely for the purpose of sunset watching.

All these possibilities may seem overwhelming. But we believe the following pages will put your mind at ease. An embarrassment of riches, the Oregon Coast is more byway than highway. As you explore the capes and coves, visit the sealion caves and sea-cut caverns, you're likely to make numerous finds of your own.

Those hidden places we're always talking about will tempt you to linger for hours, maybe even days. And however long you stay, give pause to remember that another people once lived here.

North Coast

Oregon's North Coast is one of the most heavily traveled tourist routes in the Pacific Northwest. From June to early October, you can expect to have plenty of company. While most travelers hug the shoreline, some of the best sightseeing is actually found a few miles inland. Less crowded and often sunnier, these hidden spots reward those willing to veer off Route 101.

A special tip for those who prefer to drive during off-peak times: Around 5 p.m. most of the logging trucks are berthed and the RVs are bedded down for the night. In the summer consider allocating a good part of your day for sightseeing. Then, at 5 p.m., when many of the museums and attractions close, take a couple of daylight hours to proceed to your next destination. Not only is the traffic lighter, the sunsets are remarkable. Plus, you'll be able to dine fashionably late.

SIGHTS

Why not follow the path of Lewis and Clark by taking Route 30 west from Portland along the Columbia River to **Astoria**, the first American settlement established west of the Rockies? Set on a hillside overlooking the Columbia River, Astoria is one of the Pacific Northwest's most historic cities. Grand Victorians, steep streets and skies that belong to the gulls and shorebirds make this river town a must. As you enter Astoria, stop at the **Uppertown Firefighters Museum**. The vintage collection includes a classic 1878 horse-drawn ladder wagon, antique motorized pumpers and fire-fighting memorabilia. Closed Monday and Tuesday. ~ 30th Street and Marine Drive, Astoria; 503-325-2203, fax 503-325-7727; www.clatsophistoricalsociety.org, e-mail cchs@seasurf.net.

Continue west to the **Columbia River Maritime Museum**. One of the nation's finest seafaring collections, this 40,000-square-foot building tells the story of the Northwest's mightiest river, discovered in 1792 by Captain Robert Gray and navigated by Lewis and Clark in 1805 on the final leg of their 4000-mile journey from St. Louis. Besides documenting shipwrecks, the museum offers exhibits on American Indian history, the Northwest fur trade, navigation and marine safety, fishing, canneries, whaling, sailing and steam and motor vessels. Interactive exhibits include a Coast Guard rescue mission, fishing on the Columbia River and taking the helm in a tugboat Wheelhouse. And that's not all. Docked outside is the *Columbia*, the last of numerous lightships that provided navigational aid along the Pacific Coast. Admission. ~ 1792 Marine Drive, Astoria; 503-325-2323, fax 503-325-2331; www.crmm.org.

Continue west along Marine Drive to Astoria, the city founded in 1812 by John Jacob Astor as a fur-trading post. Head to the **Astoria–Warrenton Area Chamber of Commerce** to pick up a helpful map and background. ~ 111 West Marine Drive, Astoria; 503-325-6311, 800-875-6807, fax 503-325-9767; www.oldoregon.com, e-mail oldoregon@charterinternet.com.

Among the many Astoria Victorians on the National Register of Historic Places is the **Flavel House**, a Queen Anne with Italianate columns and Eastlake-style woodwork around the doors and windows. Featuring six fireplaces, a library, music parlor and four-story octagonal tower, this home is one of the most visited residences on the Oregon coast. Admission. ~ 714 Exchange Street, Astoria; 503-325-2203, fax 503-325-7727; www.clatsophistoricalsociety.org, e-mail cchs@seasurf.net.

At the **Heritage Museum** you'll see artifacts from the *Peter Iredale*, a ship wrecked in 1906 that remains visible off the beach at nearby Fort Stevens State Park. Other highlights include displays on local logging camps, the land of Lewis and Clark, early town development and the "vice and virtue" exhibit, featuring a historic saloon. Admission. ~ 16th and Exchange streets, Astoria; 503-338-4849, fax 503-338-6265; www.clatsophistoricalsociety.org.

You'll also want to visit **Fort Astoria.** This small blockhouse replica was the home base for the Astorians when they settled here in the early 19th century. ~ 15th and Exchange streets, Astoria.

For a good overview, follow the signs up 16th Street to **Coxcomb Hill.** Pictorial friezes wrapping around the 125-foot-high Astoria Column, built in 1926, cover the region's heritage from its American Indian past to modern times. Unless you're prone to vertigo, climb the circular stairway to the top for a panoramic view of Astoria.

About eight miles west of Astoria in the town of Hammond is **Fort Stevens Historic Area and Military Museum.** On June 21, 1942, the fort became the first American continental military installation shelled since the War of 1812. Nine shots fired by a Japanese submarine hit the fort. Fortunately none caused any damage. (The same pilot also dropped a few ineffective bombs near Brookings on the southern Oregon coast.) While visiting, you can tour the fort in a two-and-a-half-ton Army truck or take an underground tour of Battery Mishler (fee; May through September). Don't miss the wreck of the *Peter Iredale*, now a rusty skeleton easily reached by following signs inside the park. Parking fee. Closed Monday and Tuesday October through April. ~ Fort Stevens State Park, Hammond; 503-861-2000, fax 503-861-0879; www.visitfortstevens.com.

During the rainy winter of 1805–1806, the 33-member Lewis and Clark party bivouacked at **Fort Clatsop National Memorial** for three months before returning east. Named in honor of the

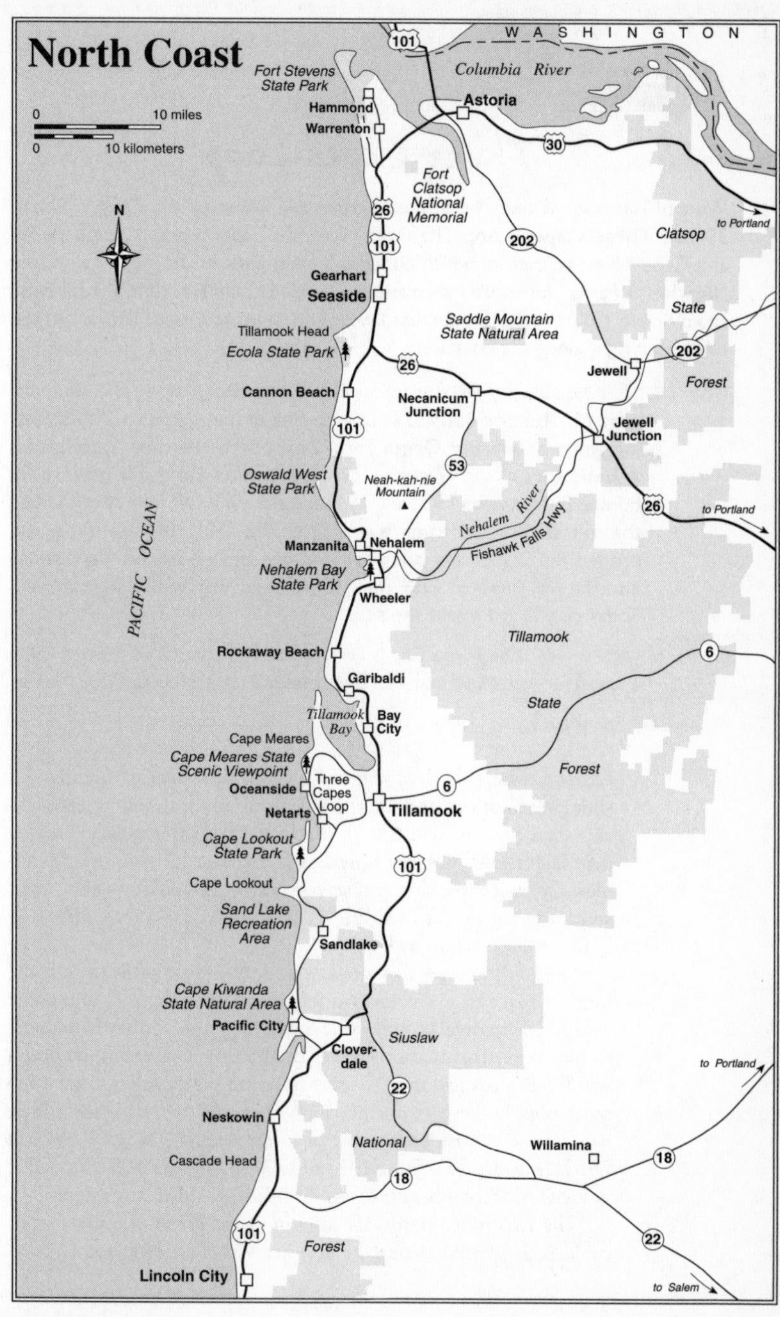
North Coast
0 10 miles
0 10 kilometers
N
WASHINGTON
Columbia River
Fort Stevens State Park
Hammond
Warrenton
Astoria
Fort Clatsop National Memorial
to Portland
Clatsop
Gearhart
Seaside
Saddle Mountain State Natural Area
State
Tillamook Head
Ecola State Park
Jewell
Forest
Cannon Beach
Necanicum Junction
Jewell Junction
Oswald West State Park
Neah-kah-nie Mountain
Nehalem River
Fishawk Falls Hwy
to Portland
PACIFIC OCEAN
Manzanita
Nehalem
Nehalem Bay State Park
Wheeler
Tillamook
Rockaway Beach
Garibaldi
State
Tillamook Bay
Bay City
Cape Meares
Cape Meares State Scenic Viewpoint
Oceanside
Three Capes Loop
Forest
Netarts
Tillamook
Cape Lookout State Park
Cape Lookout
Sand Lake Recreation Area
Sandlake
Cape Kiwanda State Natural Area
Pacific City
Cloverdale
Siuslaw
to Portland
Neskowin
National
Willamina
Cascade Head
Forest
Lincoln City
to Salem
101
30
26
202
53
6
22
18

SCENIC DRIVE

Three Capes Loop

West of Tillamook is one of the most picturesque drives on the Oregon Coast, 35-mile **Three Capes Loop**. The three capes are Cape Meares, Cape Lookout and Cape Kiwanda, each of which contains a state park of the same name (see "Beaches & Parks" for more information). The route starts in central Tillamook. From Route 101, take Bay Ocean Road west, and when you reach the fork in the road, bear right along the coast.

BAY OCEAN PARK As you follow Bay Ocean Road along the southern edge of Tillamook Bay, you'll come to one of the region's most fascinating ghost towns, Bay Ocean Park. Designed to become a pre-casino Atlantic City of the West, this 1912 subdivision eventually grew to 59 homes. But between 1932 and 1949 the sea cut a half-mile swath across the spit, turning it into an island. Over the next 20 years the ocean eroded the Bay Ocean landscape and one by one homes were swept into the sea. Finally, in 1959, the last five remaining houses were moved. Today only a sign marks the site.

CAPE MEARES The Three Capes Loop continues past Cape Meares Lake, a haven for waterfowl and shorebirds, before continuing to Cape Meares

Clatsop tribe, this reconstructed fort has introductory audiovisual slide presentations and interpretive displays. In the summer, buckskin-clad rangers armed with flintlock rifles offer muzzle-loading demonstrations or show how Lewis and Clark's team made candles, did woodworking and sewed hides. Admission. ~ Five miles south of Astoria off of Route 101; 503-861-2471, fax 503-861-2585; www.nps.gov/focl.

Oregon's answer to Coney Island, the town of **Seaside** is the kind of place to go when you long for saltwater taffy and game arcades, boardwalks and volleyball. Just head down Broadway to find the carnival atmosphere. By the time you reach the beach you'll feel a restless urge to start building sandcastles. One of the most popular resorts on the coast, it is easy to visit with a little help from the **Seaside Chamber of Commerce**. ~ 7 North Roosevelt Drive, Seaside; 503-738-6391, 800-444-6740, fax 503-738-5732; www.seasidechamber.com, e-mail info@seasidechamber.com.

The two-mile boardwalk known as the **Prom** offers a historical look at Seaside. Along the way are Victorian-style homes, arts-

State Scenic Viewpoint. While here you'll want to visit the **Octopus Tree**, a legendary Sitka spruce with six trunks extending horizontally for up to 30 feet before making a skyward turn. With just two more limbs this could have been the world's largest Hanukkah menorah. You can also take the short trail to the century-old Cape Meares lighthouse, surrounded by wild roses in the warm months.

THREE ARCH ROCKS Continue south to Oceanside and Three Arch Rocks Wildlife Refuge, home of Oregon's largest seabird colony. Half a mile offshore, these islands harbor 200,000 common murres as well as tufted puffins, pigeon guillemots, storm petrels, cormorants and gulls. You might spot a noisy sea-lion colony perched on the rocks below.

CAPE LOOKOUT At Cape Lookout State Park, nature trails and coast walks delight visitors. With 2000 acres of forested headlands abutting sandy dunes, Cape Lookout has some of the best walking trails on the coast. Dune buffs will enjoy visiting the **Sand Lake Recreation Area** seven miles south of Cape Lookout State Park. These 1000 acres of dunes attract the ATV crowd, who zoom up and over the dunes ceaselessly. **Pacific City**, on Cape Kiwanda, is famous for its dory fleet launched into the surf from the Cape Kiwanda beach.

The Three Capes Loop returns to Route 101 two miles east of Pacific City, two miles south of Cloverdale, and eight miles north of Neskowin.

and-crafts bungalows, Colonial revivals and English-style cottages. Another highlight is the Prom "Turnaround," marking the end of the Lewis and Clark Trail. At the south end is a reproduction of the cairn where the Lewis and Clark expedition boiled seawater during the winter of 1806 to make salt. More than three and a half bushels were produced for the return trip.

Of special interest is the **Seaside Museum.** Inside are American Indian artifacts (some dating back 2000 years), turn-of-the-20th-century photos of boardwalk hotels and bathhouses, a linotype printing press, and antique fire-fighting equipment. Admission includes a tour of the historic Butterfield Cottage. ~ 570 Necanicum Drive, Seaside; 503-738-7065, fax 503-738-0761; www.seasidemuseum.org, e-mail smhs@seasurf.net.

Also here in town is the **Seaside Aquarium,** where you can see marine mammals and feed local harbor seals. Kids love the hands-on interaction at the touch tank. Admission. ~ 200 North Promenade, Seaside; 503-738-6211, fax 503-717-0904; www.seasideaquarium.com.

Eighteen miles east of Seaside on Route 26 is the **Camp 18 Logging Museum**. Steam donkeys, cranes, train cabooses and other vintage equipment are among the exhibits. (There's a restaurant on the premises.) ~ Milepost 18, Route 26; 503-755-1818, 800-874-1810, fax 503-755-2815.

Follow Route 26 east to Jewell Junction and continue north on Fishawk Falls Highway toward Jewell. Just north of town is the **Jewell Meadows Wildlife Area**. Run by the Oregon Department of Fish and Wildlife, the sanctuary is a good place to spot Roosevelt elk, raptors, red-tailed hawks, songbirds and, in winter, bald eagles. ~ Route 202; 503-755-2264, fax 503-755-0706.

HIDDEN ►

Located south of Seaside is **Tillamook Head Trail**, a seven-mile route that extends to Cannon Beach's northern edge. Most of the route is within Ecola State Park. A highlight of this park is the tidepools of rocky Indian Beach. From the head you'll enjoy excellent views of the coast and the **Tillamook Rock Lighthouse.**

Cannon Beach, one of the most popular villages on the North Coast, is an artists' colony and home of photogenic **Haystack Rock**. Rising 235 feet ("the third-largest coastal monolith in the world") and accessible at low tide, this geologic wonder is a marine and bird sanctuary, and a good place to explore tidepools and look for puffins. With its resorts and condos, boutiques and small malls, Cannon Beach (it's named for a cannon that drifted ashore after a shipwreck) can be a busy place, especially in summer when the population increases fourfold. Gallery shows, the Stormy Weather Festival (early November's artist showcase), sandcastle contests and concerts in the park add to the fun.

How old is your Tillamook cheese? Medium cheddar is aged for 60 days, sharp cheddar for 9 months and extra sharp for nearly a year and a half!

Twelve miles south of Cannon Beach, **Oswald West State Park** offers a series of beautiful viewpoints. Just south of the park is **Neah-kah-nie Mountain**, a 1631-foot promontory surrounded by a 200-year-old American Indian legend. Indian lore holds that a wrecked Spanish galleon carrying gold and beeswax washed up on the beach and the surviving crew members tucked the treasure into a hole dug at the base of the mountain. But treasure hunters, using everything from backhoes to bare hands, have failed to strike it rich here.

A lovely spot on the North Coast is **Nehalem Bay**, separated from the ocean by a sandspit. The Nehalem River, a waterway filled with Chinook salmon, empties into the bay, making it one of the best fishing spots in the Pacific Northwest. You'll see boats crowding the bay during the prime fall fishing months.

Along the bay are three small resort towns. The northernmost, **Manzanita**, sits amidst trees at the foot of Neah-kah-nie Mountain. Many residents of Portland and Seattle make Manzanita a weekend retreat. In fact, more than 60 percent of the homes here are owned by people who are not residents year-round. A five-block-long strip of gift shops, restaurants and motels make this the bay's center for provisions. The historic **Nehalem** waterfront, located right where the river meets the bay, was a American Indian community before being replaced by canneries, lumber mills and dairy farms. Today, despite disastrous flooding in 1966, Nehalem continues to thrive, sporting an increasing number of clothing, gift and specialty shops. Nearby **Wheeler** is an increasingly popular town situated on the southern side of Nehalem Bay on a hill sloping down to the Pacific. Boutiques are beginning to sprout up in Wheeler, which is also the site of the **Nehalem Bay Visitors Center**. You can pick up information about Wheeler, Manzanita and the entire Nehalem Bay area here. Closed weekdays from November through April. ~ 425 Nehalem Boulevard, Wheeler; 503-368-5100, 877-368-5100; www.nehalembaychamber.com, e-mail nehalem@nehalemtel.net.

Heading south, Route 101 follows the curving shoreline around Tillamook Bay. On your way into **Tillamook** you'll probably want to stop to sample the familiar orange cheddar at **Tillamook Cheese**. A self-guided tour makes it easy to see the Pacific Northwest's largest cheese factory, Tillamook County Creamery Association, which produces 55 million pounds annually. An observation room offers a bird's-eye view of the cheddaring process. Free cheese samples. ~ 4175 North Route 101, Tillamook; 503-815-1300, 800-542-7290, fax 503-815-1305; www.tillamook cheese.com.

Next, stop by the **Tillamook Chamber of Commerce** to pick up helpful background information about this area. Closed Sunday. ~ 3705 North Route 101, Tillamook; 503-842-7525, fax 503-842-7526; www.tillamookchamber.org, e-mail tillcham ber@wcn.net.

Among the musts is the **Tillamook County Pioneer Museum**. Unlike many museums that display only a small portion of their holdings, this one is packed with 35,000 antiques, artifacts, dioramas, mounted animals, gems and gemstones and other items connected with the coast's pioneer life and natural history. Highlights include Tillamook basketry, pioneer implements, antique-clock section and fire-lookout cabin. You'll also learn that the giant hangars south of town berthed blimps that patrolled the West Coast for the Navy during World War II. Among the more recent additions to the military collection is a SCUD fragment retrieved during the 1991 Operation Desert Storm. Closed Monday. Admission. ~ 2106 2nd Street, Tillamook; phone/fax 503-842-4553; www.tcpm.org, e-mail clb@tcpm.org.

If you'd like to explore the world of dirigibles, head to the **Tillamook Naval Air Station Museum**, housed in a former blimp hangar that dates from 1943. It's the largest wooden clear-span structure in the world. The museum's collection features photographs, artifacts and 30 World War II and modern airplanes, as well as a vintage-aircraft restoration center. Admission. ~ 6030 Hangar Road, Tillamook; 503-842-1130, fax 503-842-3054; www.tillamookair.com, e-mail info@tillamookair.com.

From Tillamook, Route 101 runs inland for 26 miles, much of it through **Siuslaw National Forest**, before returning to the seashore six miles north of Neskowin.

HIDDEN ►

Seven miles south of town via Route 101, take the turnoff to 266-foot-high **Munson Creek Falls**, easily reached via a half-mile trail. This horsetail falls is the highest in the Coast Range, and is a popular spot for picnicking. The creek gorge is lovely.

South of Neskowin, Cascade Head Road leads to the **Cascade Head Scenic Research Area** and the **Cascade Head Experimental Forest**. These two areas, run as research facilities by the U.S. Forest Service, are full of colorful wildflowers and birds. The moderately difficult six-mile-long Cascade Head Trail follows the coast and provides plenty of opportunities to whale watch. Because these are special research areas, be sure to stay on the trails and not disturb any flora or fauna.

LODGING

A neoclassical revival with fir wainscotting, leaded glass, traditional American furnishings and a formal dining room, the **Rosebriar Hotel and Conference Center** offers 12 rooms in a renovated former convent. The rooms have wing-back chairs and mahogany furniture; some have fireplaces. One unit is located in a separate carriage house with a kitchenette and jacuzzi. A gourmet breakfast is included. ~ 636 14th Street, Astoria; 503-325-7427, 800-487-0224, fax 503-325-6937; www.rosebriar.net, e-mail rbhotel@pacifier.com. MODERATE TO ULTRA-DELUXE.

East of town, the **Crest Motel** sits on a grassy hilltop overlooking the Columbia River. This trim and tidy establishment has 40 modernized units with watercolor prints and writing desks, a jacuzzi and laundry facilities. Try for one of the quieter rear rooms. ~ 5366 Leif Erickson Drive, Astoria; phone/fax 503-325-3141, 800-421-3141; www.crest-motel.com, e-mail info@crest-motel.com. MODERATE.

Also on the Columbia River is **Best Western Lincoln Inn of Astoria**. The 75 motel units are spacious and comfortable, and most rooms have Columbia River or Young Bay views. The indoor pool, sauna and spa are open for guests' use; laundry facilities are a plus. Convenient to Astoria's historic district, this is an ideal spot to watch river traffic or fish. A full hot breakfast buffet is included, and freshly baked cookies are offered nightly. Pet-friendly. ~ 555 Hamburg Avenue, Astoria; 503-325-2205, 800-621-0641, fax 503-325-5550. MODERATE TO ULTRA-DELUXE.

Hillcrest Inn offers 26 attractive, pine-shaded units in a quiet garden setting close to this resort town's beach, shops, restaurants and nightlife. Choose between studios and one- and two-bedroom units with kitchens. Eclectic furniture ranges from fold-out sofas to wicker living-room sets. Some units have fireplaces, decks and spas. Barbecue facilities and picnic tables are provided for guest use. Adjacent to the inn is an ultra-deluxe five-bedroom beachhouse that sleeps up to 16 people; it rents weekly in the summer and requires a two-night minimum in the off-season. Family groups will find this establishment a good value. ~ 118 North Columbia Street, Seaside; 503-738-6273, 800-270-7659, fax 503-717-0266; www.seasidehillcrest.com, e-mail contact@seasidehillcrest.com. MODERATE.

The **Ocean Front Motel** is an older, 35-unit motel with two-room units on the beach. The carpeted rooms have wooden bed-frames, refrigerators and picture windows ideal for sunset watching. Kitchenettes are also available. Number 13, a one-bedroom cottage, is a bargain for the budget-minded. ~ 50 1st Avenue, Seaside; 503-738-5661; www.oceanfrontor.com. MODERATE.

Located right on the beach, the three-story **Seashore Resort Motel** has 54 spacious guest rooms with comfortable furniture, vanities, an enclosed pool, sauna and whirlpool. Within walking distance of Seaside's most popular attractions, it overlooks volleyball courts and the surf. ~ 60 North Promenade, Seaside; 503-738-6368, 888-738-6368, fax 503-738-8314; www.seashoreinn.com, e-mail info@seashoreinn.com. DELUXE.

A mix of sleeping rooms and one-bedroom units, the completely non-smoking **McBee Motel Cottages** are conveniently located on the south side of town, only one block from the beach. Some of the ten units in this older, motel-style complex offer kitchenettes and fireplaces. Some rooms are pet-friendly. ~ 888 South Hemlock Street, Cannon Beach; 503-436-2569, 866-262-

RADIO FREE ASTORIA

About 20 miles west of Portland you can tune in **KMUN** (91.9, 91.1 or 89.5 FM; www.kmun.org), one of the finest public-broadcasting stations in the Northwest. A kind of Radio Free Astoria, this listener-sponsored station features local kids reading their favorite fiction, opera buffs airing Bellini, and river pilots doing classical and variety shows.

2336, fax 503-436-9202; www.mcbeecottages.com, e-mail info@sandtrapinn.com. MODERATE.

Tucked between coastal pines and just up the street from a spectacular stretch of sandy coastline is the 13-room **Inn at Manzanita.** Split between four different buildings, each spacious room features a fireplace and bathroom with two-person jacuzzi tub; some rooms have alcove beds and balconies. Most rooms have wood-paneled walls, creating a comfortable cabin-like atmosphere. ~ 67 Laneda Avenue, Manzanita; 503-368-6754, fax 503-368-5941; www.innatmanzanita.com, e-mail info@innatmanzanita.com. DELUXE.

Set on a hill with commanding views of Nehalem Bay, the motel rooms at **Wheeler Village Inn** are small, clean and brightly painted. All six rooms have carpets and kitchenettes. Pull up a chair and enjoy the sunsets or relax outside in the landscaped garden. All rentals are done on a monthly basis only. ~ 2nd and Gregory streets, Wheeler; 503-368-5734; e-mail otoole@nehalemtel.net. BUDGET.

On Nehalem Bay, **Wheeler on the Bay Lodge and Marina** certainly is on the bay; it even has its own private docks. Ten motel-style units and suites, some with private decks, spas and kitchenettes, are furnished with fireplaces and VCRs. The lodge runs an on-site video store as well as canoe rentals. Rooms range from Victorian style to art deco; all are carpeted. There is an on-site video store, as well as kayak rentals and private bay cruises. It's convenient to fishing, crabbing, sailboarding, hiking and bird-watching. ~ 580 Marine Drive, Wheeler; 503-368-5858, 800-469-3204, fax 503-368-4204; www.wheeleronthebay.com, e-mail handy@nehalemtel.net. MODERATE.

Eclectic is surely the word for **Ocean Rogue Inn,** which features ten units overlooking Twin Rocks, a pair of giant rocks rising from the surf facing Rockaway Beach. Seven one-, two- and three-bedroom units have full kitchens and ocean views and two more-basic units offer beds, televisions, microwaves and refrigerators. Three units have gas fireplaces. Lawn furniture, a horseshoe pit, volleyball, barbecues, a fire pit, clam rakes and buckets make this family-oriented establishment appealing. ~ 19130 Alder Street, Rockaway Beach; 503-355-2093; www.oceanrogueinn.com, e-mail alandsyl@pacifier.com. MODERATE.

HIDDEN ►

SeaRose Bed & Breakfast promises a quiet, soothing stay just three minutes from the beach. The two guest rooms offer ocean views, queen-sized beds and private baths with clawfoot tubs and antique brass fixtures. From the dining room you can sometimes spot whales, sea lions or sea birds while enjoying your full breakfast. ~ 1685 Maxwell Mountain Road, Oceanside; 503-842-6126; www.searosebandb.com, e-mail judy@searosebandb.com. MODERATE.

On the Three Capes Scenic Loop, **Terimore Motel** has 26 units ranging from sleeping rooms to cottages. Located on the beach, these clean, modernized units are comfortably furnished. Some have lofts, sitting areas, kitchens and fireplaces. A quiet retreat, it's ideal for fishing, whale watching and agate collecting. ~ 5105 Crab Avenue, Netarts; 503-842-4623, 800-635-1821, fax 503-842-3743; www.oregoncoast.com/terimore, e-mail terimore@oregoncoast.com. MODERATE.

DINING

For fish-and-chips you'll have a hard time beating the **Ship Inn.** Huge portions of cod and halibut are served in the waterfront dining room along with chowder, generous salads and desserts. The full bar is one of the town's most crowded gathering places. Nautical decor gives diners the feeling they're out on the bounding main. ~ One 2nd Street, Astoria; 503-325-0033. BUDGET TO DELUXE.

A great spot for river watching, **Pier 11 Feedstore Restaurant & Lounge** is the place to go for seafood, prime rib, lobster tail and large salads. This renovated feed and grain building has picture windows with a wonderful view of the Columbia River. Done in a semi-nautical style, the dining room offers seating at oak tables with bowback captain's chairs. ~ Foot of 10th and 11th streets, Astoria; 503-325-0279, fax 503-325-6101. MODERATE TO DELUXE.

The **Columbian Café** is a small hole-in-the-wall place that locals love and visitors are charmed by. Intriguing knickknacks and framed pictures pepper the walls, and chiles dangle from the ceiling. Grab a seat in a booth or at the bar-top counter for crêpes or vegetarian fare, which the eatery specializes in. It's a great casual spot for lunch; the dinner menu offers several seafood specials and a wider selection of entrées. Everything is homemade, including the garlic jelly. ~ 1114 Marine Drive, Astoria; 503-325-2233. BUDGET TO DELUXE.

AUTHOR FAVORITE

One of the most beautiful dining rooms on the coast is found at **Café Uniontown**. An elegant, paneled setting with a mirrored bar, green tablecloths and marine view make this restaurant *the* place to go to enjoy rib-eye steak with shiitake mushroom, almond baked halibut, cioppino, steaks and pasta dishes. Located under the bridge in the historic Uniontown district, this is also a relaxing spot for a drink after a hard day of sightseeing. Dinner only. ~ 218 West Marine Drive, Astoria; 503-325-8708, fax 503-338-0130. MODERATE TO DELUXE.

Creekside Pizzeria overlooks a river that's home to gulls and ducks. Locals swarm this Italian eatery for its famous twice-baked Sicilian-crust pizza. Kids have a blast in the covered play area. ~ 2490 North Route 101, Seaside; 503-738-7763. MODERATE.

The **Pig 'N Pancake** can seat over 200 patrons at booths and tables to feast upon Swedish pancakes, crêpes suzettes and strawberry waffles. Lunch and dinner entrées include patty melts, garden sandwiches, seafood and steaks. ~ 323 Broadway, Seaside; 503-738-7243, fax 503-738-7014. MODERATE.

One of the most treacherous spots on the West Coast, the turbulent Columbia River Bar was a nautical grave-yard claiming scores of ships.

Convenient to the city's popular attractions, **Dooger's Seafood and Grill** serves crab legs, prawns, fish and chips, pasta dishes, burgers and steaks. The carpeted dining room sports oak furniture. Dessert specialties include marionberry cobbler. ~ 505 Broadway, Seaside; 503-738-3773. MODERATE.

Start your day with an omelette or gingerbread waffles at the **Lazy Susan Café**, a cut above your average café. Or try their seafood salad or seafood stew for lunch or dinner. The paneled dining room with bright-blue tablecloths and watercolor prints on the walls make the Lazy Susan a local favorite. Breakfast, lunch and dinner are served. Closed Tuesday. ~ 126 North Hemlock Street, Cannon Beach; 503-436-2816. BUDGET TO MODERATE.

With both take-out and in-house dining, **Pizza a fetta** is a good choice for a slice or an entire pie. In addition to regular toppings you can order sun-dried tomatoes, artichoke hearts, pancetta bacon or fruits. Cheeses include, Oregon blue, French feta, fontina and Montrachet chèvre. Closed Wednesday and Thursday during winter. ~ Village Center, 231 North Hemlock Street, Cannon Beach; 503-436-0333, fax 503-738-7104; www.pizza-a-fetta.com. BUDGET TO MODERATE.

For elegant Continental dining try the **Bistro Restaurant and Bar.** Set in a small house, this intimate dining room serves specialties such as sautéed oysters in a lemon-butter sauce, a hearty seafood stew, and six fresh seafood dishes nightly. Dishes change seasonally. Closed Tuesday from November through April. ~ 263 North Hemlock Street, Cannon Beach; 503-436-2661. MODERATE.

HIDDEN ►

Many museums have cafés in the basement or out on the patio. But **Artspace** is a rare find, a fine restaurant in an elegant gallery setting. You'll walk past contemporary paintings, prints, sculpture and jewelry by outstanding Northwest artists on the way to the dining area. Warm gold walls, a deep olive ceiling, and fun natural-paper tablecloths to draw on all add up to a cozy setting for homemade breads, soups and specialties like oysters Italia. Sunday brunch includes treats such as vegetarian eggs Benedict, eggs florentine and quiche. Open Friday, Saturday and Sunday.

Call for winter hours. ~ 9120 5th Street, Bay City; 503-377-2782, fax 503-377-2010. MODERATE.

If you're looking for good, honest deli fare with soup or salad on the side, head to the **Blue Heron French Cheese Company**. The deli counter in the midst of this jam-packed shop is stocked with goodies such as salami and provolone, smoked turkey and creamy brie or roast beef with cheddar cheese. ~ 2001 Blue Heron Drive, Tillamook; 503-842-8281, fax 503-842-8530; www.blueheronoregon.com. BUDGET.

Set in a shingled Craftsman house, **La Casa Medello** is the right place to go when you want south-of-the-border fare on the North Coast. The dark-wood interior featuring beautiful built-in cabinetry and casablanca fans is brightened by floral arrangements and plants. You can dine family-style at the big tables offering specialties like *chiles rellenos*, Spanish-rice salad, homemade tamales and generous burritos. If you're hungry try *la casa* fajita tostada with steak or chicken breast. ~ 1160 North Route 101, Tillamook; 503-842-5768. BUDGET TO MODERATE.

Nautical decor, pink walls and valances, ocean views and an oak counter make **Roseanna's Café** an inviting spot to enjoy Willapa Bay oysters, daily fish specials, vegetable penne, burgers and pesto salmon. This board-and-batten building is packed on the weekend with a loyal clientele that likes to toast those delicious moments when the sun finally burns through the fog. Closed Wednesday. ~ 1490 Pacific Street, Oceanside; 503-842-7351. MODERATE TO DELUXE.

A favorite coastal short-order joint is **Whiskey Creek Cafe**. ◄HIDDEN Locals and tourists flock to this carpeted, lodge-style building where the menu features gourmet burgers, fresh seafood specialties, chowders and lots of options for the kids. Picnic tables indoors and outside on the lawn attract a big beach crowd. Be sure to try the homemade pies for dessert. ~ 6060 Whiskey Creek Road, Netarts; 503-842-5117. BUDGET.

SHOPPING

M and N Workwear is where you can find flannel shirts, jeans, outerwear and casual menswear. Located beneath the bridge in the old Finnish Hall, this establishment is popular with fishermen, lumberjacks, farmers and tourists in the midst of shopping-mall deprogramming. Located in Astoria's historic Uniontown district, this is not a place for quiche eaters. ~ 248 West Marine Drive, Astoria; 503-325-7610, 877-272-5100; www.mnworkwear.com.

Caught in a downpour? Duck into **Let It Rain**, where you can find any imaginable accessory, from rain boots to water-proof purses, to keep you dry. Be sure to check out their gallery of fine art and unique umbrellas. ~1124 Commercial Street, Astoria; 800-998-0773; www.let-it-rain.com.

The **Wine Shack** offers a fine selection of rare, international and local wines. This funky little shack, with cozy wood-paneled walls and a stained-glass chandelier, shimmies every Saturday afternoon during its wine tasting. ~ 124 South Hemlock Street, Cannon Beach; 503-436-1100, 800-787-1765; www.beachwine.com, e-mail info@beachwine.com.

HIDDEN ► Our idea of a coastal gallery is **Artspace.** Contemporary Northwest sculpture and painting, jewelry and arts and crafts are all found in this intriguing showplace. WPA art from the '30s, '40s and '50s is also on display. There's a restaurant on the premises. ~ 9120 5th Street, Bay City; 503-377-2782, fax 503-377-2010.

Rainy Day Books focuses on new and used titles and has an excellent section on the Pacific Northwest as well as a large selection of greeting cards. This is also a good place to pick up inexpensive paperbacks that come in handy when you want to relax by the fireplace. Closed Sunday. ~ 2015 2nd Street, Tillamook; 503-842-7766; e-mail rdb@gorge.net.

NIGHTLIFE

Girtles presents rock bands every night except Monday, when locals show off with karaoke. Cover on Friday and Saturday. Closed Tuesday. ~ 311 Broadway Street, Seaside; 503-738-8417; www.girtles.com.

In Cannon Beach, the **Bistro Restaurant and Bar** has a guitarist on the weekends. Take a seat at the bar or order drinks and dessert at one of the adjacent tables. This romantic setting is the ideal way to wind up the evening. Closed Tuesday from November through April. ~ 263 North Hemlock Street, Cannon Beach; 503-436-2661.

For musicals and jazz piano, Broadway shows, murder mysteries, revivals, classical concerts, comedies and melodramas, check out the **Coaster Theatre Playhouse.** Closed in January. ~ 108 North Hemlock Street, Cannon Beach; 503-436-1242, fax 503-436-9653; www.coastertheater.com, e-mail info@coastertheater.com.

BEACHES & PARKS

FORT STEVENS STATE PARK This 3762-acre state park embraces a Civil War–era fort that defended the coast during World War II. The site of a rare coastal attack by a Japanese submarine in 1942, the park includes shallow lakes, dunes, sand flats and a pine forest. The paved bike trails are also good for skating. Of special interest are the oceanfront remains of a wrecked British ship, the *Peter Iredale*. A museum and guided tours offer historical perspective on the region. Fish the surf for perch. The razor clamming is excellent. There are picnic tables, showers, restrooms and a gift shop. Day-use fee, \$3. ~ Take Pacific Drive west from Hammond; 503-861-1671.

▲ There are 42 tent sites (\$17 per night), 174 RV hookup sites (\$19 to \$22 per night) and 15 yurts (\$29 per night). Hiker-

Let There Be Light

No matter where you are on the Oregon Coast, a powerful beacon may be sweeping the high seas and shoreline. Nine of these classic sentinels built since 1857 still stand. Five continue to operate as unmanned Coast Guard stations, and three inactive lighthouses are restored and open to the public. Those not open to the public attract visitors who come to admire the architecture.

Tillamook Rock Lighthouse, opened in 1881 and the state's only lighthouse that is actually offshore, was built and then ferried to the construction site by tender.

One of the best, located at **Cape Meares**, five miles south of Tillamook Bay, is a dormant beam that was built in 1890. Open year-round for a self-guided look-see, the lighthouse is part of Cape Meares State Scenic Viewpoint. ~ Off Route 101, ten miles west of Tillamook.

Off Route 101, just north of Yaquina Bay Bridge, is **Yaquina Bay Lighthouse**, built in 1871. Authentically restored with 19th-century furniture, Yaquina Bay features an interpretive exhibit. Newport's **Yaquina Head Lighthouse** was constructed in 1873. This automated light flashes every 20 seconds and is supplemented by a powerful radio beacon. You can catch one of the self-guided tours (fee). ~ Four miles north of Yaquina Bay.

One of the most photographed spots is **Heceta Head Lighthouse**, the brightest beacon on the coast. ~ Off Route 101, 13 miles north of Florence. Built in 1857, the **Umpqua Lighthouse** was the coast's first. Destroyed in an 1861 flood, it was replaced in 1894. The 65-foot tower emits a distinctive automated red-and-white flash and is adjacent to Umpqua Lighthouse State Park. Tours are offered Wednesday through Sunday from May through September. ~ Off Route 101, six miles south of Reedsport.

The 1866 **Cape Arago Lighthouse** is on a rocky island at the Coos Bay entrance. The unmanned Coast Guard beacon has an automated white light, fog signal and beacon. ~ Next to Sunset Bay State Park off Route 101.

The 1896 **Coquille River Lighthouse** was the last lighthouse built on the Oregon Coast. It serves as a public observatory with interpretive displays on the Coquille River region. ~ At the south end of Bullards Beach State Park, a mile north of Bandon.

In service since 1870, **Cape Blanco Lighthouse** is the westernmost navigational beacon in Oregon. It is also Oregon's oldest continuously operated light. This 300,000-candlepower light is near Cape Blanco State Park. Open Tuesday through Sunday from April to October for guided tours. Admission. ~ Nine miles north of Port Orford off Route 101.

biker sites ($4 per night) are available by request. Reservations: 800-452-5687.

ECOLA STATE PARK Forested with Sitka spruce and western hemlock, this 1303-acre park includes Ecola Point and the steep shoreline leading to Tillamook Head. The name Ecola comes from the Chinook word for whale, which was hunted in the waters offshore. You may see deer and elk during your visit. You can fish for perch. You'll find barbecue pits, picnic tables, group picnic shelter (available by reservation at 800-452-5687) and restrooms. Day-use fee, $3. ~ Off Route 101, two miles north of Cannon Beach; 503-436-2844.

SADDLE MOUNTAIN STATE NATURAL AREA A 3283-foot twin peak is the heart of this natural heritage site that features unusual plants and flowers. From the mountaintop you can see both the Columbia River's mouth and the Pacific Coast. Douglas fir, spruce, hemlock and alder shade the 2911-acre park. There are picnic tables and restrooms. Closed in winter from November through March, or until the snow melts. ~ Off Route 26, eight miles northeast of Necanicum Junction; 503-368-5943, fax 503-368-5090.

▲ There are 10 primitive sites; $10 to $15 per night.

OSWALD WEST STATE PARK With four miles of Pacific shoreline, this 2474-acre park provides great views of Nehalem Bay, as you walk only a half-mile from old growth forest to beach. Douglas fir, spruce and western red cedar dominate the rainforest in this park bounded on the south by legendary Neah-kah-nie Mountain. You'll want to visit the picturesque creeks, coves and scenic Arch Cape. Fishing is good at the beach for cod, perch and bass. You'll find picnic tables and restrooms. ~ Off Route 101, ten miles south of Cannon Beach; 503-368-3575.

▲ There are 30 primitive sites accessible by foot with wheelbarrows for walk-in campers; $10 to $14 per night. Closed November through February.

NEHALEM BAY STATE PARK Encompassing a three-mile-long sandspit at Nehalem Bay's mouth, this 889-acre park is a popular recreational area. The open, windswept landscape is ideal for kite flying. Nehalem Bay State Park is also a favorite for horseback riding, cycling and walking. There's good crabbing in the bay and, depending on the season, good fishing for steelhead, cutthroat trout, perch and chinook salmon. Facilities include picnic tables, restrooms, showers and an on-site airport. Day-use fee, $3. ~ Off Route 101, three miles south of Manzanita Junction; 503-368-5943, 800-551-6949.

▲ There are 267 RV hookup sites ($16 to $20 per night), 18 yurts ($27 per night), 17 horse camp sites ($12 to $14 per night) and hiker-biker sites ($4 per person per night). Reservations: 800-452-5687.

CAPE MEARES STATE SCENIC VIEWPOINT Named for an 18th-century British naval officer and trader, this 94-acre park and adjacent wildlife refuge encompass a spruce-hemlock forest and memorable ocean headlands. While the historic lighthouse no longer shines, the cape remains a landmark for tourists, who come to see the offshore national wildlife refuge and birds. Also here is the Octopus Tree, an exotic Sitka spruce that was once a meeting point for Tillamook American Indian medicine men. There are picnic tables and restrooms. ~ Off Route 101, ten miles west of Tillamook; 503-842-3182, 800-551-6949.

CAPE LOOKOUT STATE PARK With two miles of forested headlands, a rainforest, beaches and sand dunes on Netarts Bay, it's hard to resist this 2000-acre gem. It is also one of the highlights of the Three Capes Loop. There's excellent crabbing in Netarts Bay. You'll find picnic tables, restrooms and showers. Day-use fee, $3. ~ Off Route 101, about 12 miles southwest of Tillamook; 503-842-4981.

Thanks to an extensive trail network, Cape Lookout is an excellent place to observe sea lions and shorebirds.

▲ There are 176 tent sites ($12 to $16 per night), 39 RV hookup sites ($16 to $20 per night), 13 yurts ($27 per night), and a hiker-biker camp ($4 per person per night). Reservations: 800-452-5687.

CAPE KIWANDA STATE NATURAL AREA This 185-acre headland park has a beautiful, sheltered beach. On the road between Pacific City and Sand Lake, it has wave-sculptured sandstone cliffs, tidepools and dunes. Shore fishing is good. There are picnic tables and restrooms. ~ Off Route 101, one mile north of Pacific City; 503-842-4981, 800-551-6949.

Central Coast

Proceeding down the coast you'll appreciate an impressive state-park system protecting coastal beaches and bluffs, rivers and estuaries, wildlife refuges and forested promontories. With the Pacific to the west and the Siuslaw National Forest to the east, this section of the coast is sparsely populated but has more than its share of state parks and beaches. Anglers and hikers have plenty of options here, with many of the best spots only about 90 minutes away from Salem or Eugene.

SIGHTS

One of the largest communities on the coast, **Lincoln City** stretches along the shore for roughly ten miles. While the coastal sprawl may turn some visitors off, this region offers many fine parks, lakes and restaurants, and seven miles of clean, sandy (not rocky) beaches. Stop by the **Lincoln City Visitors and Convention Bureau** for helpful details on beachcombing, shopping for crafts and recreational activities. ~ 801 Southwest Route 101, Suite 1, Lincoln City; 541-996-1274, fax 541-994-2408; www.oregoncoast.org, e-mail info@oregoncoast.org.

Many visitors flock to **Devil's Lake**, a popular water sports and fishing area. But few of them realize that **D River**, located at the lake's mouth, is reputedly the world's shortest river, just under 120 feet long at low tide. This is also a terrific place to fly a kite.

HIDDEN ►

When it's foggy on the coast, it makes sense to head inland where the sun is often shining. One way to do this is to take Route 229 inland along the Siletz River. Six miles beyond the town of Kernville you'll come to **Medicine Rock**, a pioneer landmark. Indian legend held that presents left here would assure good fortune.

Proceed south to **Siletz**, named for one of the coast's better-known American Indian tribes. In 1856, at the end of the Rogue River Wars, the American Army created the Siletz Indian Agency, which became home for 2000 American Indians. Within a year, unspeakable conditions diminished their numbers to 600. The agency closed for good in 1925, and today the Siletz tribe gathers each August for its annual powwow featuring dancing and a salmon bake.

Continue on to visit the popular galleries and antique shops at **Toledo**. This small town operated one of the world's largest spruce mills during World War II.

From Toledo, follow Route 20 west to **Newport**. A harbor town with an array of tourist attractions, Newport is a busy place, especially during the summer. Like Seaside, Newport is filled with souvenir shops, saltwater-taffy stores and enough T-shirt shops to outfit the city of Portland. There are also fine museums, galleries and other sightseeing possibilities. Begin your visit to this popular vacation town with a stop at the **Greater Newport Chamber of Commerce**. Closed weekends from October through May. ~ 555 Southwest Coast Highway, Newport; 541-265-8801, 800-262-7844, fax 541-265-5589; www.newportchamber.org.

A short walk from the chamber is the **Oregon Coast History Center**. At the Log Cabin Museum and adjacent Burrows House you'll see Siletz basketry, maritime memorabilia, farming, logging and pioneer displays, patterned glass, Victorian-era household furnishings and clothing and many historic photographs. Closed Monday. ~ 545 Southwest 9th Street, Newport; 541-265-7509, fax 541-265-3992; www.newportnet.com/coasthistory, e-mail coasthistory@newportnet.com.

The most popular tourist area in Newport is **Bay Boulevard**, where canneries, restaurants, shops and attractions like **Undersea Gardens** peacefully coexist. Located on Yaquina Bay, this waterfront extravaganza gives you a chance to view more than 5000 species including octopus, eel, salmon and starfish. Scuba divers perform daily for the crowds in this bayfront setting. Admission. ~ 250 Southwest Bay Boulevard, Newport; 541-265-2206, fax 541-265-8195; www.marinersquare.com.

Across the street is one of the many **Ripley's Believe It or Not!** museums, a worldwide chain devoted to weird and mysterious objects. In this eclectic collection you'll find everything from

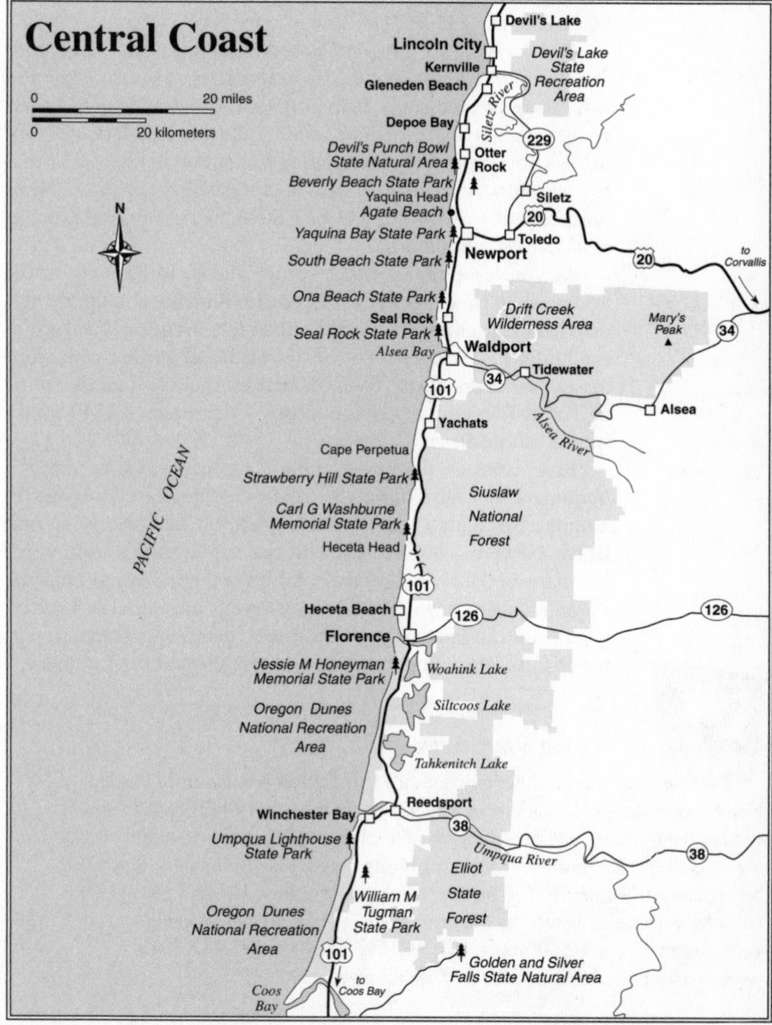

"working" fertility statues to contortionists and sword swallowers. In the same building **Wax Works** houses wax replicas of celebrities. Admission. ~ 250 Southwest Bay Boulevard, Newport; 541-265-2206, fax 541-265-8195; www.marinersquare.com.

The OSU **Mark O. Hatfield Marine Science Center** is the coast's premier aquarium, featuring a quarter-mile-long, wheelchair-accessible estuary loop. The center features hands-on displays, aquariums and exhibits interpreting the research being done at the center. ~ 2030 Southeast Marine Science Drive, Newport; 541-867-0100, fax 541-867-0138.

Next door is the **Oregon Coast Aquarium**, which has indoor and outdoor exhibits showcasing seabirds, marine mammals and fish in a re-created natural environment. Children love the interactive exhibits and the touch tank. A 200-foot underwater tunnel has you completely surrounded by sharks, halibut and other sea creatures. Admission. ~ 2820 Southeast Ferry Slip Road, Newport; 541-867-3474, fax 541-867-6846; www.aquarium.org, e-mail info@aquarium.org.

HIDDEN ►

As you leave the Hatfield Center and head back up to the bridge you'll pass **Zigzag Zoo/El Fincho Rancho**, a sculpture garden that deserves a place on the Oregon folk-art map. Wood sculptor Loren Finch has blanketed his yard and garden with ships masts, propellers, floats, fishnets, abalone shells and nicely carved figurines. The result is a kind of driftwood fantasia. ~ 2640 Southwest Abalone Street, Newport.

After crossing the bridge, follow the signs west to visit the **Yaquina Bay Lighthouse**, the tallest in Oregon at 93 feet, in Yaquina Bay State Park. Continue north on Mark Street to **Nye Beach**. Newport's historic beach district is more than a century old, but many of the early-day hotels, cabins and beach houses survive.

In Nye Beach you'll find the **Cloe–Niemela–Clarke Gallery**, where you can familiarize yourself with paintings, sculpture, pottery, handicrafts and photography by members of the Yaquina Art

sights

AUTHOR FAVORITE

It's pinniped heaven at **Sea Lion Caves**, just south of Heceta Head Lighthouse. Ride the elevator down to the two-story-high cave to see the resident stellar sea lions enjoying a life of leisure. The outside ledges are a rookery where these marine mammals breed and give birth in the spring and early summer. The bulls vigilantly protect their harem's territory. An overlook adjacent to the entrance is a great whale-watching spot. Admission. ~ 91560 Route 101; 541-547-3111, fax 541-547-3545; www.sealioncaves.com, e-mail info@sealioncaves.com.

Association. Closed weekdays in winter. ~ 839 Northwest Beach Drive, Nye Beach; 541-265-5133.

Drive north on Route 101 to **Agate Beach**, a great spot for rockhounds. Moonstones, jasper and tiger eyes are all found here. Continue north on Route 101 to the Otter Crest Loop. Begin by visiting **Devil's Punch Bowl State Natural Area**, near Otter Rock, named after a collapsed cavern flushed by high tides. There's a lovely beach here, and you can shop for a picnic or mask art in the tiny oceanfront hamlet of Otter Rock. Continue north past Cape Foulweather, named by Captain James Cook in 1778, to **Depoe Bay**, home to the smallest harbor in the world. This six-acre port is fun to explore on foot thanks to its seafood restaurants and shops.

While the harbor is the heart of this charming seaside village, you may also want to head across Route 101 to the coast, one of the best whale-watching spots in Oregon. A location for the movie *One Flew Over the Cuckoo's Nest*, Depoe Bay is also famous for **Spouting Horn**, where the surf surges above the oceanfront cliffs in stormy weather.

Return to Newport on Route 101 and continue southward ten miles to **Seal Rock State Park**. This wayside park has some of the best tidepools in the area and is a great place to watch the barking pinnipeds and hunt for agates.

Continue south on Route 101 to **Waldport** and **Alsea Bay**, one of the best clamming spots on the coast and easily accessed from numerous parks. Walport is a relatively peaceful alternative to the coast's busy tourist hubs.

Pick up Route 34 east along the Alsea River for nine miles to the **Kozy Kove Resort**. You can launch your boat here and explore this tributary bounded by the Siuslaw National Forest. You'll find a campground and a store that sells fishing and camping supplies. A great fishing spot, this section of the Alsea can be a sunny alternative to the foggy coast. ~ 9464 Alsea Highway, Tidewater; 541-528-3251; www.kozykove.com. ◄ HIDDEN

For a picturesque, albeit windy, drive, travel east 39 miles on Route 34 to the village of Alsea and follow the signs to **Alsea Falls**. The area around the 35-foot cascade makes a good spot for a picnic, and there's also three and a half miles of hiking trails through old-growth forest and Douglas firs. Along the way you may catch a glimpse of woodpeckers, beavers and white-tailed deer. ◄ HIDDEN

Return to Waldport and continue southward to **Yachats** (pronounced "Ya-HOTS"), a classy village with fine restaurants, inns and shops. This town is also home of the **Little Log Church**. Surrounded by a charming garden, this tiny house of worship has a handful of white pews for congregants warmed by a pioneer stove. ~ Located at 3rd and Pontiac streets; 541-547-3976.

To the south is Cape Perpetua, discovered by Captain James Cook in 1778. The 2700-acre **Cape Perpetua Scenic Area** has miles of trails ideal for beachcombing and exploring old-growth forests and tidepools. The **Cape Perpetua Visitors Center** is a good place to learn about the region's original inhabitants, the Alsi. Known for their woodworking, canoes and decorative, watertight basketry, the Alsi hunted in the Coast Range hills. The visitors center is closed November through April; call for seasonal hours. Admission. ~ Route 101, Cape Perpetua; 541-547-3289, fax 541-547-4616.

South of Reedsport is one of the most popular fishing ports in the dunes region, Salmon Harbor on Winchester Bay. The crabbing and rockfishing here are top-notch.

Two miles south of Cape Perpetua off Route 101 is **Strawberry Hill State Park.** The white blossoms of wild strawberries create a floral panorama in the spring months. This park is also a popular spot for seals that sunbathe on the shoreline's basalt rocks. A short path of steps will take you quite close to the seals. The tidepools shelter sea stars, anemones and bright-purple spin sea urchins. However, the pools are a protected reserve, so removal of anything is strictly forbidden. Down the road another two miles is the distinctive **Ziggurat**, a four-story pyramid-shaped bed and breakfast. ~ Ziggurat: 95330 Route 101, Yachats; 541-547-3925; www.newportnet.com/ziggurat.

As you continue on toward Florence, about six miles north of the city is **Darlingtonia Botanical Wayside**, a short path that takes you to see the bog where Darlingtonia, serpent-shaped plants also known as cobra lilies, trap insects with a sticky substance and devour them. They are in full bloom from May to mid-June.

In Florence, the **Chamber of Commerce** will quickly orient you to this Siuslaw River community. Closed most Sundays. ~ 290 Route 101, Florence; 541-997-3128, fax 541-997-4101; www.florencechamber.com, e-mail florence@oregonfest.net. Then, with the help of a chamber walking-tour guide, explore Florence's old town. A small artists' colony with a gazebo park overlooking the Siuslaw waterfront, **Florence** has a popular historic district centered around Bay Street. Here you can browse or sip an espresso.

Floating at the Old Town Docks is a beautifully restored, turn-of-the-20th-century sternwheeler, the **Westward Ho**. It operates from April through October and provides history and wildlife tours of the river during the day. Dinner cruises are offered on weekends. Closed Monday. ~ Bay Street, Florence; 541-997-9691, fax 541-997-8865; www.westward-ho.com, e-mail westho@harborside.com.

Florence is also the northern gateway to **Oregon Dunes National Recreation Area.** Miles of sandy beaches and forested bluffs laced by streams flowing down from the mountains make this region a favorite Oregon vacation spot. Woodlands and freshwater lakes provide a nice contrast to the windswept beaches. Numerous parks offer access to the dunes. Among them is **Oregon Dunes Overlook**, ten miles south of Florence. Admission. ~ 541-271-3611, fax 541-271-6019.

To gain perspective on the region's American Indian and pioneer history, visit the **Siuslaw Pioneer Museum**, a former Lutheran Church. Closed Monday and the month of December. Admission. ~ 85294 Route 101, one mile south of Florence; 541-997-7884; e-mail museum@winfinity.com.

Near Reedsport on Route 38 about four miles east of Route 101 is **Dean Creek Elk Viewing Area.** The herd of Roosevelt elk make for an unusual photo opportunity.

LODGING

The **Inn at Spanish Head** has 125 rooms and suites, many with kitchens. Furnished with wall-to-wall carpets, contemporary easy chairs, oak tables, nature prints and full ocean views, most of the units feature balconies. A pool, spa, recreation room, lounge and restaurant add to the resort atmosphere. ~ 4009 Southwest Route 101, Lincoln City; 541-996-2161, 800-452-8127, fax 541-996-4089; www.spanishhead.com, e-mail contact@spanishhead.com. ULTRA-DELUXE.

The **Salishan Lodge & Spa Resort** offers 205 units. In a forested setting above Siletz Bay, this lodge accommodates guests in two- and three-story, hillside buildings. Units all feature gas fireplaces, balconies, contemporary prints and carports. Golf, tennis, a fitness center, library and art gallery are just some of the amenities at this four-star resort. ~ 7760 North Route 101, Gleneden Beach; 541-764-2371, 800-452-2300, fax 541-764-3681; www.salishan.com, e-mail reservations@salishan.com. ULTRA-DELUXE.

One of the area's best deals is **Trollers Lodge.** Set on an ocean-view bluff, this 12-unit establishment has clean units with eclectic furniture, picture windows, TV and VCR, and kitchenettes. Picnic tables and benches are the ideal spots for watching the residential whale pod and migrating whales in season. One- and two-bedroom suites with full kitchens are also available, as are three deluxe- to ultra-deluxe-priced oceanfront homes. The location is good for deep-sea fishing trips. Pets are welcome in some units for an additional charge. ~ 355 Southwest Route 101, Depoe Bay; 541-765-2287, 800-472-9335; www.trollerslodge.com, e-mail trollers@newportnet.com. MODERATE.

Modeled after a 19th-century New England–style inn, the **Seahag Inn** overlooks the nation's smallest harbor. While the inn's 13 rooms and suites have a standard motel appearance, all the suites have a balcony or patio overlooking this picturesque harbor; some have bathtubs with whirlpool jets and fireplaces. There is also a parlor with comfortable sofas, and a library with a fireplace. All ground-level rooms are pet-friendly. Full breakfast is included. ~ 235 Southeast Bay View Avenue, Depoe Bay; 541-765-2322, 800-228-0448; www.seahaginn.com, e-mail stay@seahaginn.com. MODERATE TO DELUXE.

Don't be surprised if you find a couple sitting on an oceanview bench outside **Alpine Chalets**. They are probably coming back to remember a honeymoon spent at this oceanfront retreat adjacent to Devil's Punchbowl State Park. Blessed with its own private park and beach access, each one- and two-bedroom A-frame chalet here has a large, paneled sitting area furnished with contemporary fold-out sofas. All 11 units are fully carpeted and come with kitchens and casablanca fans. Pet-friendly units are available. ~ Otter Crest Loop, Otter Rock; 541-765-2572, 800-825-5768, fax 541-765-3135; www.oregonalpinechalets.com, e-mail info@oregonalpinechalets.com. MODERATE.

The Inn at Otter Crest offers 100 rooms including one- and two-bedroom suites with fireplaces, fully equipped kitchens and decks. The semiprivate cove boasts great tidepools; you can look for seals and, in season, migrating gray whales. Set in a fir forest, with duck ponds and wild rhododendron, the inn also sports a playground, a workout room, a pool, a hot tub and a sauna. There's also a restaurant and lounge on the premises. ~ Otter Crest Loop off Route 101, Otter Rock; 541-765-2111, 800-452-2101, fax 541-765-2047; www.innatottercrest.com, e-mail havefun@innatottercrest.com. MODERATE TO ULTRA-DELUXE.

The four-story **Sylvia Beach Hotel**, a honeymoon haven that had degenerated into a flophouse, was renovated and renamed for the proprietor of Shakespeare and Co. and first publisher of James Joyce's *Ulysses*. Her Paris bookstore and coffeehouse was a home away from home for writers like Joyce, Ernest Hemingway, T. S. Eliot and Samuel Beckett. Twenty rooms, each themed after an author, now accommodate guests. Our favorites are the ornate Oscar Wilde room featuring garish Victorian wallpaper (while dying in a Paris hotel room his last words were: "Either this wallpaper goes or I do"), the Dr. Seuss room (*The Cat in the Hat* is front and center), the Mark Twain room (fireplace, deck, antique school seat) and the Emily Dickinson room (marble dresser, green carpet, beautiful antique desk). While Henry Miller (*Tropic of Cancer*) didn't get his own quarters, this man of letters is appropriately commemorated in the basement restrooms. Incidentally, we'd love to see the owners add a James Joyce room in the years ahead. The hotel is completely nonsmoking and Aggie, the house cat, resides there. Breakfast is included. ~ 267

Northwest Cliff Street, Newport; 541-265-5428, 888-795-8422; www.sylviabeachhotel.com. MODERATE TO ULTRA-DELUXE.

The **Summer Wind Budget Motel** offers 33 fully carpeted rooms and kitchenettes with woodframe beds, sofas, pine coffee tables and stall showers. One of many Route 101 strip motels serving the Newport crowd, it's set back from the highway, and the rear rooms are relatively quiet. ~ 728 North Coast Highway, Newport; 541-265-8076; e-mail sands@pioneer.net. BUDGET TO MODERATE.

The **Cliff House** is a bed and breakfast on the ocean. It features a big fireplace in the living room and a gazebo in the front yard. Convenient to ten miles of walking beach, the inn also offers a jacuzzi, sauna and an on-call masseuse. Some of the four theme-decorated rooms have chandeliers and wall-to-wall carpeting. Full gourmet breakfast included. Reservations highly recommended. Gay-friendly. ~ 1450 Southwest Adahi Street, Waldport; 541-563-2506; www.cliffhouseoregon.com, e-mail innkeeper@cliffhouseoregon.com. MODERATE TO ULTRA-DELUXE.

Romantic, secluded accommodations on three-and-a-half forested acres above the ocean can be found at **The Oregon House**, an inn with cottages, guest rooms, suites and townhouse units, some with kitchens, fireplaces and marble bathrooms. One of the most charming is Oak Cabin, which has red-and-white-checked curtains, a red fireplace, a hot tub and a brass-and-iron bed. The grounds include a private beach, trails and a creek. Gay-friendly. ~ 94288 Route 101, Yachats; 541-547-3329, fax 541-547-3754; www.oregonhouse.com, e-mail metatoh@pioneer.net. MODERATE TO ULTRA-DELUXE.

The **Yachats Inn** has 35 pleasant motel accommodations, 16 of which are suites, with a rustic knotty-pine look and superb ocean views. Especially nice are the upstairs units, which include

AUTHOR FAVORITE

Turn up the Vivaldi and step right in to the circa-1914 **Edwin K Bed and Breakfast**, where the six rooms are named for six seasons (including Autumn and Indian Summer). As you might expect, Winter features a white Battenberg bedspread, while Fall has a flowered down comforter. A one-bedroom apartment, which sleeps up to six and is child-friendly, is also available. Furnished with oak armoires, chandeliers and white carpets, this elegant home has a backyard waterfall and Siuslaw River views. ~ 1155 Bay Street, Florence; 541-997-8360, 800-833-9465, fax 541-997-2423; www.edwink.com, e-mail info@edwink.com. DELUXE.

a glassed-in sunporch, great for watching a winter storm roll in. There is an indoor swimming pool and a lounge with stone fireplace, piano, books, games, puzzles and free coffee. Some suites feature decks or patios. Gay-friendly. ~ 331 South Coast Highway, Yachats; 541-547-3456, 888-270-3456, fax 541-547-4331; www.yachatsinn.com, e-mail geninfo@yachatsinn.com. BUDGET TO DELUXE.

HIDDEN ► Set in a sunny valley surrounded by the Siuslaw National Forest, a wildlife refuge and the Yachats River, **Serenity Bed and Breakfast** lives up to its name. Six miles from the coast, this resort is a verdant country retreat ideal for hiking, biking or birding. The Alt Heidelberg Room features an oak-frame double bed imported from a German castle; you can listen to a vintage collection of Bavarian music in the—what else—Bavarian room. Or perhaps you'd prefer to try one of this ten-acre bed and breakfast's other rooms featuring canopied beds, French-provincial furniture and an Italian writing desk. Three of the suites feature jacuzzis. The full gourmet German breakfast is accompanied by German music. ~ 5985 Yachats River Road, Yachats; 541-547-3813; e-mail serenitybnb@casco.net. MODERATE.

On a 40-foot cliff overlooking the Pacific six and a half miles south of Yachats, **See Vue** offers ten units. Each is individually named and themed. All have plants and antiques. Weekend reservations recommended well in advance. Pets are welcome. Gay-friendly. ~ 95590 Route 101, Yachats; 541-547-3227; www.seevue.com, e-mail seevue@seevue.com. BUDGET TO MODERATE.

An excellent bed and breakfast in the area is **Seaquest**, located six miles south of Yachats. Their two-and-a-half-acre bluff has grass lawns and private beach access. Five whimsical and eclectic rooms feature private baths with jacuzzi tubs and ocean views. A full gourmet breakfast is served. ~ 95354 Route 101, Yachats, between mile markers 171 and 172; 541-547-3782, 800-341-4878, fax 541-547-3719; www.seaq.com; e-mail seaquest@newportnet.com. DELUXE TO ULTRA-DELUXE.

On the Siuslaw River, the 40-unit **River House Motel** is a one-block walk from this popular town's historic shopping district. Many of the units have decks overlooking the river traffic and drawbridge. Rooms feature oak furniture and queens and kings with floral-print bedspreads. Some rooms have jacuzzis and overlook the waterfront. ~ 1202 Bay Street, Florence; 541-997-3933, 888-824-2750, fax 541-997-6263; www.riverhouseflorence.com, e-mail riverhouse@harborside.com. MODERATE.

If you're interested in cetaceans, consider checking in to **Driftwood Shores Resort & Conference Center**. An estimated 21,000 whales migrate south past this inn each winter and return northward in the spring. Overlooking Heceta Beach, the 127-unit establishment has rooms and kitchenette suites featuring nautical prints, stone fireplaces, picture windows, decks and contemporary furniture. An indoor pool, hot tub and restaurant are located on the premises. ~ 88416 1st Avenue, Florence; 541-997-8263, 800-422-5091, fax 541-997-5857; www.driftwoodshores.com, e-mail reservations@driftwoodshores.com. MODERATE TO ULTRA-DELUXE.

DINING

Kernville Steak and Seafood has a reputation for reasonably priced, hearty meals. Feast in the dining room beneath a vaulted ceiling with A-framed views of the river. Known for its steaks, prime rib, steamers and scallops, the restaurant also has an excellent vegetarian menu, seafood pasta salad and smaller appetizer portions for those who don't arrive famished. ~ 186 Siletz Highway, Lincoln City; 541-994-6200, fax 541-994-6208. MODERATE.

The Salishan Lodge & Spa Resort's casual **Cedar Tree** sunroom restaurant features a window view of the driving range and putting course. This lodge-style restaurant offers seafood specialties, pasta dishes, butter clams steamed in a broth of thyme, garlic and Rogue Golden Ale, sandwiches, seafood stew and Greek salad. Breakfast, lunch and dinner. ~ 7760 Route 101, Gleneden Beach; 541-764-2371, 800-452-2300, fax 541-764-3681; www.salishan.com, e-mail reservations@salishan.com. DELUXE TO ULTRA-DELUXE.

If you have binoculars on hand, you may want to use them at the Whale Cove Inn, a prime whale-watching spot.

For a step above in price, try the **Dining Room**, Salishan's romantic, tri-level gourmet restaurant with one of the biggest wine lists on the coast. Specialties include grilled duck breast with sweet potato polenta, peppered sturgeon chop and Chinook salmon. ~ 7760 Route 101, Gleneden Beach; 541-764-2371, fax 541-764-3681; www.salishan.com. DELUXE TO ULTRA-DELUXE.

If you've had it with minimalist nouvelle cuisine, head straight for the **Whale Cove Inn**. Half the customers leave with doggie bags, proof positive that few establishments offer more generous helpings of fresh salmon, cod or halibut. Also on the menu are vegetarian fettuccine dishes, steamed clams, clam chowder, beef marsala, scallops poached in white-wine sauce and a towering crab and shrimp Louie. Friday night you can find all-you-can-eat barbecue pork ribs. The dining room is a blend of semicircular booths and plastic tables with panoramic views. A prime choice for sunset dining. Breakfast, lunch and dinner. Closed for three weeks after Thanksgiving. ~ 2345 Southwest Route 101, one and a half miles south of Depoe Bay; 541-765-2255. MODERATE TO DELUXE.

Shrimp cocktail with ale sauce, a pizza crust made with stout, bangers with beer mustard, oysters with ale sauce—do we detect a trend here? The **Rogue Ales Public House** serves these specialties with its golden ales, stouts, lagers, award-winning Old Crustacean barley wine and gold medal–winning Rogue Smoke in a wood-paneled lounge. Tiffany-style lamps illuminate the booths, and the walls are decorated with classic advertising signs and pieces of the pub's history. The game room in the rear is good for a round of pool, or try your hand at blackjack in the card room. Specialties include sandwiches, salads and fish-and-chips. ~ 748 Southwest Bay Boulevard, Newport; 541-265-2537, fax 541-265-7528; www.rogue.com, e-mail press@rogue.com. BUDGET TO MODERATE.

Gino's Seafood and Deli offers crab and deli sandwiches, chowder and fish-and-chips. You can dine alfresco on picnic tables. A good bet for picnic fare. ~ 808 Southwest Bay Boulevard, Newport; 541-265-2424. BUDGET.

The Whale's Tale serves excellent breakfasts, vegetarian lasagna, cioppino, hamburgers, seafood poorboys and fish filets with mushrooms, lemon butter and wine. This dark-wood café has an open-beam ceiling, inlaid mahogany and oak tables and Tiffany-style lamps. A kayak frame, harpoon, whale's vertebrae and tail suspended from the ceiling complete the decor. Breakfast, lunch and dinner are served. Closed in January and on Wednesday from fall through spring. ~ 452 Southwest Bay Boulevard, Newport; 541-265-8660. MODERATE TO DELUXE.

Canyon Way Bookstore and Restaurant serves up a host of delectables in a contemporary setting. Choose between a main room with wood tables that has inlaid tiles, a garden room with view of the bayfront and, best of all, in the summer a handsome, enclosed brick patio with tables in a garden setting (lunch only). Dinner entrées change but may feature beef, seafood and chicken. Closed Sunday from Labor Day to July 4th. ~ 1216 Southwest Canyon Way, Newport; 541-265-8319. MODERATE TO DELUXE.

If you're looking for a sushi bar, try **Yuzen Japanese Cuisine**. Set in a former rathskeller with leaded glass windows and Tiffany-style lamps, the restaurant has been redecorated with red paper lanterns, paper screens and a wooden sushi bar. The menu includes tempura, sukiyaki, *katsu don*, bento dinners and sashimi. Closed Monday. ~ 10111 Northwest Route 101, Seal Rock; 541-563-

AUTHOR FAVORITE

The town of Toledo is home to one of the best galleries along the coast, **Michael Gibbons Gallery**. Located in the old vicarage of the city's Episcopal church, the gallery is both home and workspace for noted landscape painter Michael Gibbons. Closed Monday through Wednesday. ~ 140 Northeast Alder Street, Toledo; phone/fax 541-336-2797; www.michaelgibbons.net, e-mail gmg@newportnet.com.

4766; www.citydestinations.com/yuzen, e-mail takaya@yuzen.com. MODERATE TO ULTRA-DELUXE.

While some restaurants may be advertising "fresh crab" just flown in from Anchorage, **La Serre Restaurant Grill & Creperie** insists on truth in labeling. Only fresh local fish and crab off the boat are served in the contemporary dining room decorated with oak tables and chairs, oil lamps, potted plants and polished-hardwood floors. A bistro with a fireplace and full bar also provides a relaxed setting for drinks or dinner. La Serre specializes in seafood like razor clams and bay oysters, vegetarian entrées, chicken pot pies, steaks and fresh pastries, including crêpes made on an authentic French griddle. Dinner only. Closed Tuesday and the month of January. ~ 2nd and Beach streets, Yachats; 541-547-3420, fax 541-547-3042; www.laserreoregon.com. MODERATE TO DELUXE.

In Florence, the **Traveler's Cove Gourmet Café and Import Shop** provides a perfect lunch-and-shop stop. The open-air deck overlooks the Siuslaw River, and the kitchen turns out light seafood fare such as "crabby" caesar salad, Boston clam chowder and hot shrimp sandwiches. ~ 1362 Bay Street, Florence; 541-997-6845.

SHOPPING

There are good beachwear and swimwear departments at the **Oregon Surf Shop**, which also sells and rents surfboards, boogieboards, skimboards, wetsuits and kayaks for fun in and out of the water. ~ 4933 Southwest Route 101, Lincoln City; phone/fax 541-996-3957, 877-339-5672; www.oregonsurfshop.com.

The Wood Gallery shows the work of over 400 artists: beautiful wooden sculptures, myrtlewood bowls, cherry-wood cabinets and jewelry boxes. Also here are metal sculptures, elk antler knives, jewelry, ceramics, pottery and stained glass. Handmade children's toys, furniture and ceramic tables are all worth a look. ~ 818 Southwest Bay Boulevard, Newport; 541-265-6843, 800-359-1419, fax 541-265-7615; www.woodgalleryonline.com.

Oceanic Arts has innovative fountains as well as limited-edition prints, pottery, jewelry and decorative basketry. ~ 444 Southwest Bay Boulevard, Newport; 541-265-5963, fax 541-265-3946.

Forget your kite? For stunt, quad-line, box, delta, cellular, dragon and diamond kites try **Catch The Wind**. A full line of accessories, repairs and free advice are also available from the resident experts. ~ 1250 Southwest Bay Street, Florence; 541-994-9500, fax 541-997-6135.

Check out the original chainsaw wood carvings by artist Timothy Robins at his shop **Mystic Woods Wildlife Designs**. He specializes in caricature statues and bear carvings, but you'll also find intricately carved benches and nautical pieces. ~ 05890

Mercer Creek Drive, Florence; 541-997-9262; www.mysticwoods.net.

NIGHTLIFE To enjoy rock and jazz you can dance to, try the second-story lounge at **Salishan Lodge** on Thursday, Friday and Saturday. When you're tired of the dancefloor, take a table by the fireplace or at the bar. There is also a deck that overlooks the golf course. Contemporary painting completes the decorating scheme. ~ 7760 Route 101, Gleneden Beach; 541-764-2371, fax 541-764-3681.

The **Newport Performing Arts Center** presents concerts, dance programs and theatrical events in the Alice Silverman Theater and the Studio Theater. Both local groups and touring companies perform. ~ 777 West Olive Street, Newport; 541-265-9231; www.coastarts.org, e-mail occa@coastarts.org.

At **Rookie's Sportsbar** in the Best Western Agate Beach Inn, nine televisions project every sporting event imaginable. There's a pool table, sports memorabilia, darts and a relaxing view. ~ 3019 North Coast Highway, Newport; 541-265-9411, fax 541-265-5342.

BEACHES & PARKS **DEVIL'S LAKE STATE RECREATION AREA** Is there really a devil in the deep blue sea? That's what American Indian legend says right here in Lincoln City. Find out for yourself by visiting this 109-acre spot offering day-use and overnight facilities. The camping area is protected with a shore-pine windbreak. A day-use area is available at East Devil's Lake down the road. Fish for bass and trout. Facilities include picnic tables, rest-

sights

AUTHOR FAVORITE

Routes 42 and 33 between Coos Bay and Gold Beach are popularly known as the **Inland River Route**. Following the Coquille River south through the town of the same name, this route is the hidden Oregon of your dreams. You'll see farms, pastureland, orchards, birdlife and towering stands of fir. Twenty-three miles beyond the Route 101 turnoff is **Hoffman Memorial Wayside**, the first of two protected groves of the distinctive myrtlewood tree. Turning right onto Route 33 here, you'll come to the other grove in a few miles at **Coquille Myrtle Grove State Park** and soon enter **Siskiyou National Forest**. After traversing the east slope of 4075-foot **Iron Mountain**, you'll follow the **Rogue River** from the coastal mountains to the ocean, returning to Route 101 at Gold Beach. Allow at least half a day to drive this winding 123-mile route.

rooms, showers and a boat moorage. On Saturday an interpreter conducts kayak nature tours. ~ The West Devil's Lake section is at 1450 Northeast 6th Drive off Route 101. The day-use section is located two miles east of Route 101 on East Devil's Lake Road; 541-994-2002, 800-452-5687; www.oregonstateparks.org.

▲ There are 55 tent sites ($13 to $17 per night), 32 RV hookup sites ($18 to $21 per night) in the Devil's Lake section, and 10 yurts ($29 per night). Hiker-biker sites ($4 per person per night) are available.

DEVIL'S PUNCH BOWL STATE NATURAL AREA Don't miss this one. The forested, eight-acre park is named for a sea-washed cavern where breakers crash against the rocks with great special effects. Besides the thundering plumes, the adjacent beach has impressive tidepools. There are picnic tables, barbecue pits and restrooms in the Marine Gardens area. ~ Off Route 101, eight miles north of Newport; 800-551-6949.

BEVERLY BEACH STATE PARK Numerous coastal creeks make ideal hiking and camping areas. Among them is Spencer Creek, part of this 130-acre refuge. The windswept beach is reached via a highway underpass. Some of Oregon's best surf fishing is found here. You'll find picnic tables, restrooms and showers. ~ Route 101, seven miles north of Newport; 541-265-9278.

▲ There are 128 tent sites ($13 to $17 per night), 128 RV hookup sites ($17 to $21 per night) and 21 yurts ($29 per night). Hiker-biker sites ($4 per person per night) are also available. Reservations: 800-452-5687.

SOUTH BEACH STATE PARK South of Newport's Yaquina Bay Bridge, this 434-acre park includes a sandy beach and a forest with pine and spruce. Extremely popular in the summer months, the park includes rolling terrain and a portion of Yaquina Bay's south-jetty entrance. There is a paved bicycle trail. For anglers, try for striped perch in the south jetty area. You can also ride horses on the jetty. Boat ramps at the marina make it possible to boat in the bay. Facilities include picnic tables, restrooms and showers. ~ Route 101, two miles south of Newport; 541-867-4715.

▲ There are 228 RV hookup sites ($17 per night), 27 yurts ($29 per night), a hiker-biker camp ($4 per person per night) and 6 primitive sites ($9 per night). Reservations: 800-452-5687.

ONA BEACH STATE PARK Beaver Creek winds through this forested, parklike setting to the ocean. Picturesque bridges, broad lawns and an idyllic shoreline are the draws of this 237-acre gem. Good fishing can be found in the river for perch or trout in season, and from the shore. There are picnic tables and restrooms. ~ Route 101, eight miles south of Newport; 800-551-6949.

CARL G. WASHBURNE MEMORIAL STATE PARK A mile of sandy beach with forested, rolling terrain make this park yet another coastal gem. Elk are often sighted at 1089-acre Washburne Park. The south end of the park connects to Devil's Elbow State Park's Cape Creek drainage. There are six miles of hiking trails, including the spectacular Lighthouse Trail, which leads along dramatic coastline to the Heceta Head Lighthouse. Nearby fishing is excellent: there's tuna, bass and snapper in the sea, and several streams offer trout, salmon and steelhead. Clamming is also good. There are picnic tables, restrooms and showers. ~ Route 101, 14 miles north of Florence; 541-547-3416.

Several California gray whales have taken up summer residence along the Central Coast—one, at least, has returned to Depoe Bay since the 1970s and has been christened "Spot."

▲ There are 7 walk-in tent sites ($13 to $17 per night), 58 RV hookup sites ($17 to $22 per night), 2 yurts ($29 per night) and a hiker-biker camp ($4 per person per night).

SIUSLAW NATIONAL FOREST With two sections on the coast, this 630,000-acre region has more seacoast, 54 miles, than any other national forest in the continental United States. The terrain includes the Coast Range, Mt. Hebo and Mary's Peak. Oceanfront areas include the Cascade Head Scenic Area, Oregon Dunes National Recreation Area, Sand Lake Recreation Area and the Cape Perpetua Interpretive Center. While hiking some of the forest's 125 miles of trails, you may see deer, elk, otter, beaver, fox and bobcat. Northeast of Waldport, several trails lead into the old-growth forests at Cape Perpetua Scenic Area. Furthermore, there's boating and horseback riding in the summer. Incidentally, Siuslaw is taken from a Yakona Indian word meaning "far away waters." More than 200 species of fish including salmon, perch and trout can be caught in local streams and along the coast. Facilities include picnic areas, restrooms, showers and horseback corrals. ~ Route 101 passes through the Siuslaw in Tillamook, Lincoln and Lane counties; 541-750-7000, fax 541-750-7234; www.fs.fed.us/r6/siuslaw.

▲ There are 31 campgrounds, one with full hookups; $10 to $17 per night. Two of the best known are the Blackberry Campground between Corvallis and the coast on Route 34 (33 tent/RV sites at $10 per night; no hookups) and the Tillicum Beach site on the coast near Waldport (59 tent/RV sites at $17 per night; no hookups). The former is situated on the Alsea River near a boat landing and hiking trails; the latter is right beside a nice beach.

JESSIE M. HONEYMAN MEMORIAL STATE PARK This park is richly endowed with 500-foot-high sand dunes, forested lakes, rhododendron and huckleberry.

Bisected by Route 101, 522-acre Honeyman is ideal for water sports, dune walks and camping. As far as we know, it has the only bathhouse on the National Register of Historic Places. A stone-and-log structure at Cleawox Lake, the unit now serves as a store and boat rental. Anglers can find bass, trout, perch, bullhead and bluegill at Cleawox and Woahink Lake. Boating and waterskiing are allowed at Woahink. From October through April, off-road vehicles are allowed access to the dunes from the H-loop only. Picnic tables, restrooms, showers, a store and boat rentals are the facilities here. Day-use fee, $3. ~ Route 101, three miles south of Florence; 541-997-3641.

▲ There are 191 tent sites ($13 to $17 per night), 166 RV hookup sites ($17 to $21 per night), 10 yurts ($29 per night) and a hiker-biker camp ($4 per person per night). Reservations: 800-452-5687.

UMPQUA LIGHTHOUSE STATE PARK South of Winchester Bay, this park offers beautiful sand dunes and a popular hiking trail. Forested with spruce, western hemlock and shore pine, the 450-acre park is at its peak when the rhododendron bloom. Trout is the most common catch. Great views of the Umpqua River are available from the highway. The lighthouse (which belongs to neighboring Douglas County Park) was built to signal the river's entrance; catch a tour any day of the week. You'll find picnic tables, restrooms and showers. ~ Off Route 101, six miles south of Reedsport; 541-271-4631.

▲ Camping options include 24 tent sites ($12 to $16 per night), 20 RV hookup sites ($16 to $20 per night), 8 yurts ($27 to $65 per night) and 2 cabins ($35 per night). Reservations: 800-452-5687.

WILLIAM M. TUGMAN STATE PARK This 560-acre park includes Eel Lake, cleaned of logging debris and turned into a popular recreational area. An excellent day-use area, Tugman is ideal for swimming and boating. Restrooms and showers are available. ~ Route 101, eight miles south of Reedsport; 541-888-3778.

▲ There are 100 RV hookup sites ($12 to $17 per night), 13 yurts ($27 per night) and a hiker-biker camp ($4 per person per night).

GOLDEN AND SILVER FALLS STATE NATURAL AREA A pair of 100-foot-high waterfalls, old-growth forest including myrtlewood trees, and beautiful trails make this 157-acre park an excellent choice for a picnic. Cutthroat trout is a common catch here, as are crawdads. There are picnic tables, fire pits and restrooms. Bring your own water. ~ Off Route 101, 24 miles northeast of Coos Bay; 800-551-6949.

South Coast

The quietest part of the Oregon coastline, Oregon's South Coast offers miles of uncrowded beaches, beautiful dunes and excellent lakes for fishing or waterskiing. The smaller towns make an excellent base for the traveler who appreciates fine restaurants, museums, festivals and shopping. The Rogue and Chetco rivers offer rugged detours from the coast, ideal for the angler or rafter.

SIGHTS

A real sleeper, the **Coos Bay/North Bend/Charleston Bay area** is the coast's largest metropolitan area, a college town, fishing center and former logging center. Historic residential and commercial buildings, a grand harbor and a wide variety of outdoor adventure options lend character to this area. The **Bay Area Chamber of Commerce** is the ideal place to orient yourself. Closed Saturday and Sunday. ~ 50 Central Avenue, Coos Bay; 541-269-0215, 800-824-8486, fax 541-269-2861; www.oregonsbayareachamber.com, e-mail bacc@uci.net.

One of our favorite galleries in the Pacific Northwest is the **Coos Art Museum**, where 20th-century American graphic art and Northwest paintings, sculpture and prints form the heart of the collection. Special exhibits feature local and nationally known artists as well as occasional traveling international exhibitions. Closed Sunday and Monday. Admission. ~ 235 Anderson Avenue, Coos Bay; 541-267-3901, fax 541-267-4877; www.coosart.org, e-mail cam@presys.com.

The art museum is just one of 22 landmarks on the chamber of commerce's self-guided walking-tour brochure. This route includes Victorian homes, Greek Classic commercial buildings and the Myrtle Arms Apartments, a rare Oregon building done in the Mission/Pueblo style.

Worth a visit is the **Coos County Historical Society Museum,** where you'll see American Indian baskets, tools and dugout canoes. Pioneer logging and mining equipment and a homestead kitchen are also found here, along with a hands-on exhibit that gives you an opportunity to touch a variety of artifacts. You can learn about tidewater highways as well. Closed Sunday and Monday. Admission. ~ 1220 Sherman Avenue, North Bend; 541-756-6320; www.cooshistory.org, e-mail museum@uci.net.

A popular recreational region, the Bay Area offers watersports and fishing at **Tenmile Lakes**. The **Charleston Boat Basin** is ideal for sportfishing, clamming, crabbing, birdwatching and boating.

From Charleston, continue south four miles to **Shore Acres State Park**. Although the mansion of lumberman Louis Simpson burned down years ago, the grand, seven-acre botanical garden, including a 100-foot lily pond, is preserved. Admission. ~ 89814

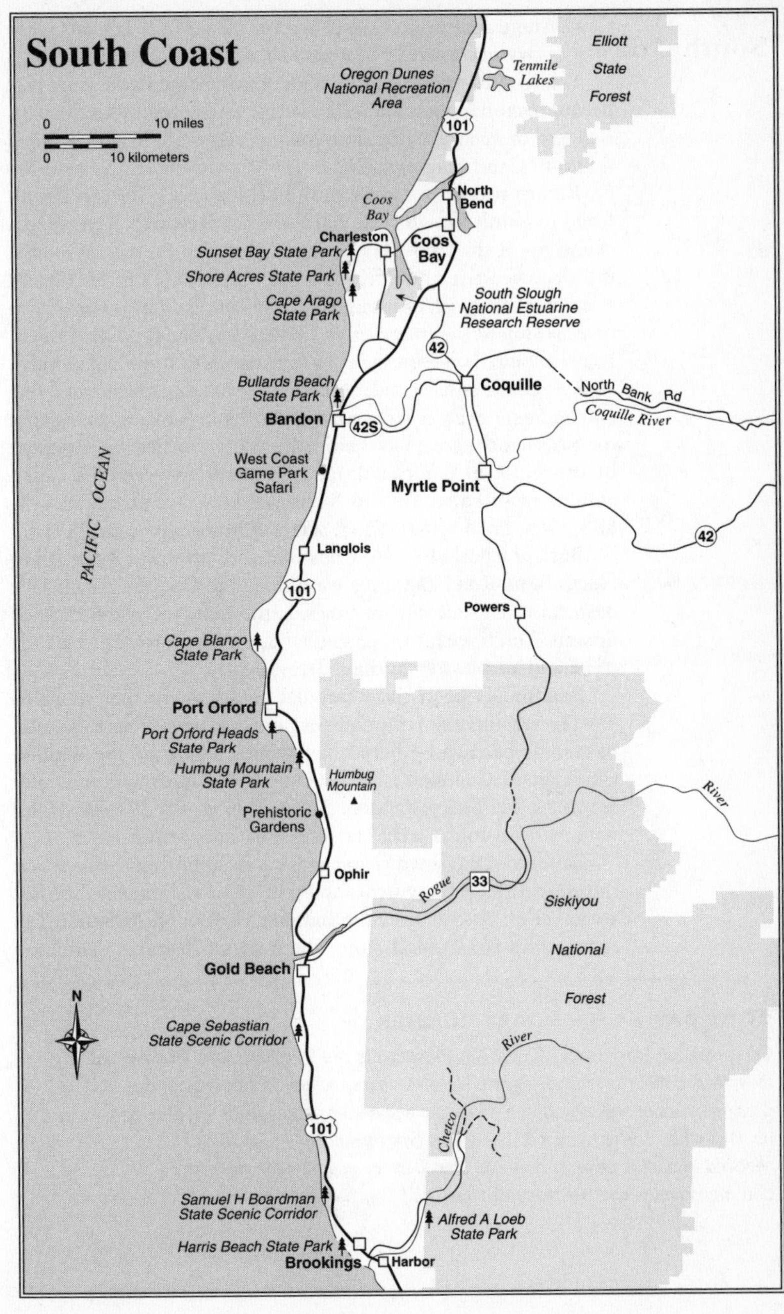
South Coast
0 10 miles
0 10 kilometers
Oregon Dunes National Recreation Area
Tenmile Lakes
Elliott State Forest
101
North Bend
Coos Bay
Charleston
Coos Bay
Sunset Bay State Park
Shore Acres State Park
Cape Arago State Park
South Slough National Estuarine Research Reserve
42
Coquille
North Bank Rd
Coquille River
Bullards Beach State Park
Bandon
42S
West Coast Game Park Safari
Myrtle Point
PACIFIC OCEAN
42
Langlois
101
Powers
Cape Blanco State Park
Port Orford
Port Orford Heads State Park
Humbug Mountain State Park
Humbug Mountain
Prehistoric Gardens
River
Ophir
Rogue
33
Siskiyou
National
Forest
Gold Beach
N
Cape Sebastian State Scenic Corridor
River
Chetco
101
Samuel H Boardman State Scenic Corridor
Alfred A Loeb State Park
Harris Beach State Park
Brookings
Harbor

Cape Arago Highway, Coos Bay; 541-888-3732, fax 541-888-5650; www.shoreacres.net, e-mail shore.acres@state.or.us.

From here, head south to **Cape Arago State Park**, your best bet for local tidepools and seal watching. The road into the park is closed to vehicle traffic, but you can still walk in, feet willing. ~ End of Cape Arago Highway.

Return toward Charleston and head south on Seven Devil's Road to **South Slough National Estuarine Research Reserve.** An extension of the Coos Bay Estuary, this splendid nature reserve is a drowned river mouth where saltwater tides and freshwater streams create a rich estuarine environment. Even if you only have time to stop at the Interpretive Center, don't miss South Slough. Easily explored on foot, thanks to a network of trails and wooden walkways, the estuary's tideflats, salt marshes, open water and forest communities are a living ecology textbook. A major resting spot for birds like the great blue heron, the slough can also be navigated by canoe. Open year-round, but the interpretive center is closed Sunday from Labor Day to Memorial Day. ~ Charleston; 541-888-5558, fax 541-888-5559; www.southsloughestuary.com.

HIDDEN ►

Back at Charleston and Coos Bay, pick up Route 42 south to **North Bank Road** and drive west along the Coquille River. This pastoral route, one lane at times, is the hidden Oregon of your dreams. You'll see farms, pastureland, orchards, towering stands of fir and an array of birdlife. Tread lightly.

Bandon is one of those popular resort towns that seems to have everything. From myrtlewood and cranberry bogs to salmon bakes, it's hard to be bored in Bandon. Swing by the **Bandon Chamber of Commerce** for brochures and information. ~ 300 Southeast 2nd Street, Bandon; 541-347-9616, fax 541-347-7006; www.bandon.com, e-mail bandoncc@harborside.com.

Bandon's **Old Town** is an engaging neighborhood where you can shop for cranberry treats and pottery or visit one of the local art galleries. Also here is the **Bandon Driftwood Museum.** Located in an old general store, the museum features driftwood

COOS BAY'S LEGENDARY RUNNER

Of special interest in the Coos Art Museum is the **Prefontaine Memorial Room**, a collection honoring the life and times of Steve Prefontaine, the distance runner who died in a 1975 car accident at the age of 24. During his short life Prefontaine set 11 United States indoor and outdoor records including several that still stand. Every year, a running event commemorates the memory of this Coos Bay native.

sculptures well worth a look. ~ 1st and Baltimore streets, Bandon; 541-347-3719.

One of the town highlights used to be **Tupper Rock**, a site sacred to the Coquille tribe and returned to them in 1990. Unfortunately, most of this blue-colored rock was removed many years ago to build the town jetty, and what was left of it now lies buried underneath a new rest home operated by the Coquille. South of town, **Beach Loop Road** leads past Bandon's scenic trio—Table Rock, Elephant Rock and legendary Face Rock. One of Oregon's most photographed spots, the offshore seastacks make an ideal backdrop at sunset.

West Coast Game Park Safari, located seven miles south of Bandon, gives visitors a chance to see more than 75 species including lions, tigers, snow leopards, bison, zebras and elk. On their walk through the park, children can pet cubs, pups and kits in the company of attendants. Many endangered species are found at this wooded, 21-acre site. In winter the park is only open weekends and holidays, weather permitting. Admission. ~ Route 101; 541-347-3106; www.gameparksafari.com, e-mail info@gamepark safari.com.

Port Orford, the first townsite on the Oregon Coast and westernmost town in the continental United States, is a major commercial and sportfishing center. Windsurfers flock to local Floras and Garrison lakes. The Sixes and Elk rivers are popular salmon and steelhead fishing spots.

Six miles south of Port Orford is **Humbug Mountain State Park**, where hiking trails offer majestic views of the South Coast. ~ 541-332-6774.

Continue another six miles to the **Prehistoric Gardens**. Filled with life-size replicas of dinosaurs and other prehistoric species, this touristy menagerie includes the parrot-beaked *Psittacosaurus*, an ancestral form of the horn-faced dinosaur. Open year-round, weather permitting; call for changing hours. Closed weekdays from November through February. Admission. ~ 36848 Route 101 between Port Orford and Gold Beach; 541-332-4463, fax 541-332-8403.

At **Gold Beach**, a settlement at the mouth of the Rogue River, you'll find yourself on the edge of one of the coast's great wilderness areas. Here you can arrange an ocean-fishing trip or a jet boat ride up the wild and scenic Rogue River. Along the way, you may see deer, bald eagle, bear or otter. Accessible only by water, some of the rustic Rogue lodges are perfect for an overnight getaway. It's also possible to drive along the Rogue to Agness. For more details, check with the **Gold Beach Visitor Center**. Closed Sunday in winter. ~ 94080 Shirley Lane, Gold Beach; 541-247-

2836, 800-525-2334, fax 541-247-0187; www.goldbeach.org, e-mail visit@goldbeach.org.

Fifteen miles south of Gold Beach is **Samuel H. Boardman State Scenic Corridor**, where you'll begin a 12-mile stretch that includes Arch Rock Point, Natural Bridges Cove, House Rock and Rainbow Rock. Many visitors and locals agree this is the prettiest stretch on the Oregon coastline.

Just when you thought it would never end, the Oregon Coast comes to a screeching halt. The end of the line is **Brookings**, the Chetco River port town that produces nearly 90 percent of the Easter lilies grown in America. They are complemented by exotic lilies and daffodils raised commercially in the area. **North Bank Chetco River Road** provides easy access to the fishing holes upstream. One of the most popular destinations is **Alfred A. Loeb State Park** ten miles east of Brookings. Redwood and myrtlewood groves are your reward. You can loop back to Brookings on South Bank Road. En route consider turning off on **Forest Service Road 1205** (Bombsite Trail) and take the trail to one of only two continental United States locations bombed by a Japanese pilot during World War II. The other location, bombed by the same raider, is farther up the Oregon coast at Fort Stevens. The raider, who used a plane built aboard an offshore submarine, returned years later to give the city a samurai sword as a peace offering.

The **Brookings/Harbor Chamber of Commerce** can provide additional information on visiting this region. ~ 16330 Lower Harbor Road, Brookings; 541-469-3181, 800-535-9469, fax 541-469-4094; www.brookingsor.com, e-mail chamber@wave.net.

Check out the world's largest Monterey cypress, found on the grounds of the Chetco Valley Historical Museum.

Shortly before reaching the California line, you'll see the Blake House, site of the **Chetco Valley Historical Society Museum** the oldest standing house in the region, visitors can check out a turn-of-the-20th-century kitchen, antique sewing machines, Lincoln rocker, patchwork quilts dating back to 1844 and American Indian artifacts. Once a trading post and way station, the old home is filled with period furniture. A new attachment contains old logging equipment and details the area's settlement days. Closed weekdays in winter; closed Sunday through Tuesday the rest of the year. ~ 15461 Museum Road, Brookings; 541-469-6651.

LODGING

A 1912 Colonial-style house, **Coos Bay Manor** has five rooms (three with private baths) themed in Victorian, regal and country-style. Also here are a Colonial room with four-poster or twin beds and a garden room furnished with white wicker furniture. A rhododendron garden, redwoods and a delicious breakfast add to the fun. The ten-minute walk to downtown Coos Bay and the boardwalk is a bonus. ~ 955 South 5th Street, Coos Bay; 541-269-1224, 800-269-1224; e-mail cbmanor@chanter.net. MODERATE.

If you're eager to crab or clam, consider unpretentious **Captain John's Motel**. On the small boat basin, this establishment is within walking distance of fishing and charter boats. Special facilities are available to cook and clean crabs. Forty-four rooms and kitchenettes are fully carpeted and feature contemporary motel furniture. Other accommodations include a two-bedroom apartment. ~ 63360 Kingfisher Drive, Charleston; 541-888-4041, fax 541-888-6563; www.captainjohnsmotel.com, e-mail info@captainjohnsmotel.com. BUDGET TO DELUXE.

One block from Bandon's old-town district, **Sea Star Guest House** offers four modern, carpeted units with brass or step-up beds, quilts and harbor views. Two are regular rooms and two are suites, with living rooms and lofts. ~ 375 2nd Street, Bandon; 541-347-9632; www.seastarbandon.com, e-mail seastarban@earthlink.net. BUDGET TO MODERATE.

In the same complex is the **Sea Star Youth Hostel**. The two dorms are sex-segregated and feature ten bunk beds. There are also five family/couple rooms that should be reserved in advance. No curfew. ~ 375 2nd Street, Bandon; 541-347-9632; e-mail seastar oregon@earthlink.com. BUDGET.

You can hear the foghorn from the **Bandon Beach Motel** where many of the 28 units have balconies overlooking the ocean. Nautical decor, wood paneling and vanities make these rooms appealing. There's also a pool and spa. Small pets are welcome in some rooms. ~ 1110 11th Street, Bandon; 541-347-4430, 541-347-9451. MODERATE.

The nearby **Gorman Motel**, perched atop a windy sea cliff, is just 30 feet from the rocky coast. All 18 sparsely furnished rooms offer ocean views, but you may prefer leaving your room to explore the surrounding walking trails. ~ 1090 Portland Avenue, Bandon; 541-347-9451. MODERATE.

American Indian legend tells us that Ewauna, the willful daughter of Chief Siskiyou, wandered too far out into the surf and was snatched up by Seatka, the evil spirit of the sea. Today, Bandon visitors learn that images of all the protagonists in this tragedy have been frozen in stone at Face Rock. That may be one of the reasons proprietors of **Best Western Inn at Face Rock** caution guests to be wary of the local surf. Adjacent to a public golf course, this 74-unit resort—including 20 suites with fireplaces and balconies—also has ocean views. Wallhangings and decks make the king- and queen-bedded rooms appealing. There's a restaurant on the premises. ~ 3225 Beach Loop Road, Bandon;

541-347-9441, 800-638-3092, fax 541-347-2532; www.facerock.net, e-mail contact@facerock.net. DELUXE TO ULTRA-DELUXE.

Castaway-by-the-Sea Motel offers rooms and suites overlooking one of the South Coast's most picturesque, albeit windblown, beaches. Kitchenettes, glassed-in decks, contemporary upholstered furniture, wall-to-wall carpeting and easy access to fishing make this 13-unit motel a popular place. ~ 545 West 5th Street, Port Orford; 541-332-4502, fax 541-332-9303; www.castawaybythesea.com, e-mail stay@castawaybythesea.com. MODERATE.

HIDDEN ►

Breathtaking views of the coast are found at **Home by the Sea**. Ceramic tile floors, myrtlewood beds with quilted spreads, a leather loveseat, a rocking chair, oriental carpets and stained glass add to the charm of these units. Rooms include private baths and mini-refrigerators; every room in this bed and breakfast comes with binoculars perfect for whale watching through the picture windows. Laundry and internet access are available. ~ 444 Jackson Street, Port Orford; 541-332-2855, 877-332-2855; www.homebythesea.com, e-mail reservations@homebythesea.com. MODERATE.

If you're an adventurer eager to deep-sea fish, raft the Rogue, boat, cycle or hike the coastal mountains, consider **Jot's Resort**. Jot's has 140 attractive, contemporary rooms, suites and condos with wall-to-wall carpet, oak furniture, vanities and decks featuring river views. Family units are available with two bedrooms, a kitchenette, and living and dining rooms. All deluxe rooms come with a microwave and refrigerator. Crabbing and clamming are great here. A full-service resort, there's a jacuzzi, sauna and two pools, an indoor and outdoor. ~ 94360 Wedderburn Loop, Gold Beach; 541-247-6676, 800-367-5687, fax 541-247-6716; www.jotsresort.com, e-mail jotsresort@harborside.com. MODERATE TO ULTRA-DELUXE.

On the Rogue River, **Tu Tu' Tun Lodge** can be a sunny alternative to the cloudy coast. Seven miles upriver from Gold Beach, this lodge offers 16 rooms with 12-foot-window walls, refrigerators, lounge chairs and decks or patios overlooking the water. Several have fireplaces and outdoor soaking tubs. There are also two houses for rent and two suites with kitchen facilities. Amenities here include hiking trails, horseshoes and, in the main lodge, a library and game tables. Outside you'll find a four-hole putt course and kayaks. ~ 96550 North Bank Rogue, Gold Beach; 541-247-6664, 800-864-6357, fax 541-247-0672; www.tututun.com, e-mail tututunlodge@charter.net. ULTRA-DELUXE.

Located in a Craftsman-style home designed in 1917 by Bernard Maybeck, **South Coast Inn Bed & Breakfast** is an inn with four rooms in the main house and a separate private cottage. Especially choice is the Rose Room, which has a large picture window framing the Pacific, a high-rise four-poster bed, and an old-fashioned clawfoot tub in the bathroom. A full breakfast is included (continental breakfast only in the cottage). ~ 516 Redwood Street, Brookings; 541-469-5557, 800-525-9273, fax 541-469-6615; www.southcoastinn.com, e-mail innkeeper@southcoast inn.com. MODERATE TO DELUXE.

At **Best Western Beachfront Inn**, 102 units, all with ocean views and some with kitchenettes, offer a quiet resting place. Furnished with contemporary oak dressers and tables, the king- and queen-bedded units come with microwaves, refrigerators, sofas and decks. Suites and some rooms have ocean-view jacuzzis. Inn amenities include a heated pool, an outdoor spa, sundeck and meeting rooms. ~ 16008 Boat Basin Road, Harbor; 541-469-7779, 800-468-4081, fax 541-469-0283; www.bestwesternoregon.com/c5.html, e-mail info@beachfrontinn.com. DELUXE TO ULTRA-DELUXE.

◀ HIDDEN

A one-lane road leads you to **Chetco River Inn Bed and Breakfast**, a get-away-from-it-all establishment on 40 wooded acres. An ideal retreat for fishing, swimming, hiking through myrtle groves or loafing on the riverbank, this contemporary solar-, propane- and battery-powered home is furnished with antiques and eclectic furniture. The inn has down comforters and large brass beds, casablanca fans and, by advance request, dinner. The cooking is innovative, and portions are generous. All five rooms have private baths. A private cottage is also available. Special discounts are offered for anglers who agree to catch and release their fish. ~ 21202 High Prairie Road, North Bank, 17.5 miles east of Brookings on the Chetco River; 541-251-0087, 800-327-2688, fax 541-469-4341; www.chetcoriverinn.com. DELUXE TO ULTRA-DELUXE.

DINING

For *chiles rellenos*, *chilaquiles*, chicken *mole* and *carne asada*, try **El Sol.** Spanish carvings, sombreros and photographs of Mexico give this popular little restaurant a festive feel. ~ 525 Newport Avenue, Coos Bay; 541-266-8212. BUDGET TO MODERATE.

AUTHOR FAVORITE

To get a big laugh at **Portside Restaurant and Lounge**, just ask if the fish is fresh. Grilled sole, deep-fried scallops, steamed clams, salmon and Coquille St. Jacques are among the specialties, as well as Maine lobster and Dungeness crab. I also recommend the cucumber boat, a salad with shrimp, crab and smoked salmon served with cucumber dressing and garlic toast. The contemporary dining room features photos of the fishing industry. ~ Charleston Bay Boat Basin, 8001 Kingfisher Road, Charleston; 541-888-5544; www.portsidebythebay.com. MODERATE TO DELUXE.

If you've been looking for Japanese or Chinese dishes, stop by **Kum-Yon's.** *Bulgoki*, *sushi*, *yakitori*, Mongolian beef, tempura *udon* and tofu dishes are just a few of the enticing specialties. Like the menu, the decor is pan-Asian with Japanese shell plaques, Korean wedding decorations and Chinese fans accenting the brick dining room. ~ 835 South Broadway, Coos Bay; 541-269-2662. BUDGET TO DELUXE.

Wheelhouse Seafood Grill and Lounge serves fresh seafood, pasta and steak in an upstairs lounge that overlooks the water. A lighter lunch menu offers tasty burgers and sandwiches. ~ 1st and Chicago streets, Bandon; 541-347-9331. MODERATE.

Paula's Bistro, where the dimly lit bar and knotty pine–paneled dining room are decorated with local art for sale, provides an interesting mixture of artsy bohemian culture. You'll find pasta, steak, seafood and chowder on the menu; the kitchen accepts special requests from guests who want something not found on the menu. A piano is available for your use. Dinner only. Closed Sunday and Monday. ~ 236 6th Street, Port Orford; 541-332-9378, fax 541-751-1999. MODERATE TO DELUXE.

For waterfront dining, try the **Nor'wester Seafood Restaurant.** Cedar woodwork, local artwork on the walls and a large fireplace create an inviting and cozy atmosphere. Sample the fresh fish, steaks, pasta or chicken. Dinner only. Closed December and January. ~ 10 Harbor Way, Gold Beach; 541-247-2333. DELUXE TO ULTRA-DELUXE.

Housed in a former seafood processing plant, the **Port Hole Café** is now a family restaurant serving scallops, oysters, veal cutlets and chicken-fried steak. Lighter fare is available for lunch, including salads and sandwiches. Breakfast, lunch and dinner. ~ 29975 Harbor Way, Gold Beach; 541-247-7411; www.portholecafe.com, e-mail portholecafe@gb.wave.net. MODERATE.

When the natives get restless for 4 a.m. breakfasts, fish and chips, burgers, clam chowder or shrimp cocktails, they head for the **Oceanside Diner**. This modest establishment seats customers at pine tables in the nautically themed dining room featuring fishing photos. ~ 16403 Lower Harbor Road, Brookings; phone/fax 541-469-7971. BUDGET.

A culinary time warp on the coast, **O'Holleran's Restaurant and Lounge** serves middle-of-the-road entrées in a modest dining room with wood tables and pictures on the wall. You'll find few bells or whistles on the traditional menu featuring steaks, prime rib and seafood. While you can't get blackberry catsup on the side, the food is well prepared. Dinner only. ~ 1210 Chetco Avenue, Brookings; 541-469-9907. MODERATE TO DELUXE.

You say Mexican food, we say **Rubio's.** A bright red-and-yellow bungalow decorated with piñatas and casablanca fans, this affordable stop also offers picnic-table seating outside beneath patio umbrellas. An extensive homemade menu features burritos, enchiladas verde, chicken fajitas and fresh fish. A brunch specialty is *huevos rancheros*. Burgers and sandwiches are also available for yankee appetites. Closed Sunday in winter. ~ 1136 Chetco Avenue, Brookings; 541-469-4919. MODERATE.

SHOPPING

Let's hear it for **Margaret Wichman, "The Bird Lady."** This folk artist, operating out of her garage, produces outstanding wind-powered whirlygigs perfect for your yard. You can choose between sprinklers, birds and other colorful Rube Goldberg-like contraptions. ~ 90910 Beacon Lane, Coos Bay; 541-888-3549.

Harbor seals and sea lions breed on offshore rocks near Port Orford, an area known as the "Thousand Island Coast."

For beaded earrings, silver and turquoise and other American Indian arts and crafts, visit **Klahowya!** The store also carries American Indian art originals, pottery, wildlife posters, ceramics and gifts celebrating the natural world. ~ 175 2nd Street, in the Continuum Center Plaza, Bandon; 541-347-5099.

If you're looking for smoked salmon, smoked albacore, crab or shrimp, head for **Bandon Pacific Seafood.** ~ 250 Southwest 1st Street, Bandon; 541-347-4454, fax 541-347-4313.

Zumwalt's Myrtlewood is the place to see the owner creating dinnerware, vases, sculptures, clocks and other popular souvenirs. ~ Route 101, six miles south of Bandon; 541-347-3654; www.zumwaltsmyrtlewood.com.

Jerry's Rogue River Museum and Gift Shop offers a broad selection of locally made arts and crafts. There is also an extensive collection of artifacts, photos and natural-history exhibits on the Rogue River area. ~ Port of Gold Beach; 541-247-4571, fax 541-247-7601; www.roguejets.com.

The Great American Smokehouse and Seafood Company produces gift packs with such delicacies as smoked salmon jerky, hand-packed tuna, sweet hot mustard and wild blackberry jam. ~ 15657 South Route 101, Brookings; 800-828-3474; www.smokehouse-salmon.com.

NIGHTLIFE

On Broadway Thespians presents contemporary drama, mysteries and musical theater in an intimate 90-seat auditorium. ~ 226 South Broadway, Coos Bay; 541-269-2501.

The bartenders at **Timber Inn Lounge** are cordial, and you can find some room out on the dancefloor. The ground-floor lounge features karaoke nightly. ~ 1001 North Bayshore Drive, Coos Bay; 541-267-4622, fax 541-267-5273.

For great sunsets, harbor views and music on the weekend, try the **Portside Lounge.** ~ Charleston Boat Basin, Charleston; 541-

888-5544, fax 541-888-9206; www.portsidebythebay.com, e-mail dine@portsidebythebay.com.

Lloyd's offers rock-and-roll bands on weekends year-round. There's a large dancefloor to let loose on. Occasional cover. ~ 119 2nd Street, Bandon; 541-347-4211.

Lord Bennett's offers jazz, country and pop in their antique-filled lounge on weekends throughout most of the year. Closed January. ~ 1695 Beach Loop Drive, Bandon; 541-347-3663, fax 541-347-3062; www.lordbennetts.com.

At **Rascals Lounge**, bands play occasionally to a dimly lit room with café seating and a full bar. If you don't want to dance, head on over to the low-stakes gaming tables and struggle against the odds. ~ Lower Harbor Road, Brookings; 541-469-5503, fax 541-469-7281.

BEACHES & PARKS

SUNSET BAY STATE PARK A splendid park on dramatic headlands, Sunset is forested with spruce and hemlock. Highlights include Big Creek, a popular stream flowing into the bay. As the name implies, this is the place to be when the sun sets. Swimming, canoeing, boating, clamming and crabbing are also popular activities. Picnic tables, restrooms and showers are the facilities here. ~ Off Route 101, 12 miles southwest of Coos Bay; 541-888-4902.

▲ There are 66 tent sites ($12 to $16 per night), 63 RV hookup sites ($16 to $20 per night), 8 yurts ($27 per night) and a hiker-biker camp ($4 per person per night). Reservations: 800-452-5687.

BULLARDS BEACH STATE PARK All good things come to an end, even the Coquille River. Fortunately, this 1289-acre park makes it possible to enjoy the tail end of the stream as it flows into the estuary and the Pacific opposite the city of Bandon. The Coquille River lighthouse is located in the park. A great recreation area, the park has fine dunes, beaches and forested lowlands. It's also ideal for crabbing and clamming. Fish for steelhead, silver and chinook salmon. Facilities include picnic tables, restrooms and showers. ~ Off Route 101, two miles north of Bandon; 541-347-2209, 800-551-6949.

▲ There are 185 RV hookup sites ($16 to $20 per night), 13 yurts ($27 per night), 8 primitive horse-camp sites ($12 to $16 per night) and a hiker-biker camp ($4 per person per night). Reservations: 800-452-5687.

CAPE BLANCO STATE PARK Settled by an Irish dairy farmer, these dramatic, pastured headlands include the westernmost lighthouse in Oregon. A windswept, 1894-acre retreat, Cape Blanco welcomes visitors to the Hughes House, built by a pioneer family in 1898. There's good surf fishing. You'll find picnic tables, restrooms and showers. ~ Off Route 101, nine miles north of Port Orford; 541-332-2973.

There are 53 RV hookup sites ($12 to $16 per night), 4 log cabins ($35 per night), 6 primitive horse-camp sites ($10 to $14 per night) and a hiker-biker camp ($4 per person per night).

PORT ORFORD HEADS STATE PARK You'll love this windblown and unforgettable 96-acre wayside. It encompasses the ocean bluff as well as Nellies Cove. The park protects marine gardens and prehistoric archaeological landmarks. There are picnic tables and restrooms. ~ Off Route 101, Port Orford; 800-551-6949.

HUMBUG MOUNTAIN STATE PARK A 1756-foot peak forested with fir, spruce, alder and cedar, Humbug is one of the coast's finest parks. Hiking trails, viewpoints, Brush Creek and ocean frontage make the 1842-acre sanctuary a great retreat. If you're feeling ambitious, why not take the three-mile hike up the wildflower-lined trail to the summit? You'll find picnic tables, restrooms and showers. ~ Off Route 101, six miles south of Port Orford; 541-332-6774.

There are 63 tent sites ($10 to $14 per night), 32 RV hookup sites ($12 to $16 per night) and a hiker-biker camp ($4 per person per night).

CAPE SEBASTIAN STATE SCENIC CORRIDOR This narrow park includes several miles of exceptional coastline. The centerpiece of the 1104-acre place is the cape, carpeted with wildflowers and rhododendron in the spring. Views are magnificent and whale watching is excellent. A spectacular one-and-a-half trail leads to the tip of the Cape. Old-growth Douglas fir and shore pine form a handsome backdrop. There is no drinking water here. ~ Off Route 101, seven miles south of Gold Beach;

sights

AUTHOR FAVORITE

Let's skip the superlatives and get to the point: Visit **Shore Acres State Park.** This 745-acre estate was once the site of a timber baron's mansion. Although the house burned down, the formal garden remains a showcase. Planted with azaleas, rhododendrons, irises, dahlias and roses, Shore Acres also offers trails on the forested bluffs. There are picnic tables, restrooms, an observation shelter and a gift shop. Day-use fee, $3. ~ Off Route 101, 13 miles southwest of Coos Bay; 541-888-3732.

800-551-6949. Not recommended for long RVs or vehicles towing trailers.

HARRIS BEACH STATE PARK Named for Scottish pioneer George Harris, this one-time sheep-and-cattle ranch is the southernmost state camping facility on the coast. The 172-acre park offers sandy beaches and great sunsets. The shoreline is punctuated with dramatic, surf-sculptured rocks, which make kayaking and surfing challenging. There's good fishing for salmon and perch. There are picnic tables, restrooms and showers. ~ 1655 North Route 101, Brookings; 541-469-2021.

▲ There are 63 tent sites ($13 to $16 per night), 86 RV hookup sites ($17 to $22 per night), 6 yurts ($29 per night) and a hiker-biker camp ($4 per person per night). Reservations: 800-452-5687.

HIDDEN ►

ALFRED A. LOEB STATE PARK On the Chetco River, this park can be a warm place when the coast is not. A one-mile trail leads to Loeb's redwood grove. There's also a myrtle grove here. A popular fishing region, particularly during the steelhead season, the Chetco is one of Oregon's special havens. With 320 acres, the park provides easy access to a prime stretch of this river canyon. Picnic tables, firepits, restrooms and showers are some of the facilities. ~ Located eight miles northeast of Brookings along the Chetco River; 541-469-2021.

▲ There are 48 RV hookup sites ($12 to $16 per night) and 3 log cabins ($35 per night). Reservations: 800-452-5687.

Outdoor Adventures

SPORT-FISHING

From mid-May or June through September or mid-October, charter companies and outfitters up and down the coast regularly run ocean fishing trips: from a half day of bottomfishing to longer reef-fishing outings. Tackle is usually provided, but a fishing license is required (you can purchase it through charter operators). And don't forget to bring lunch.

NORTH COAST **Charlton Deep Sea** accommodates up to 15 people, May through September, on trips for tuna, salmon, sturgeon and a variety of bottomfish. ~ 470 Northeast Skipanon Drive, Warrenton; 503-338-0569. **Garibaldi/D&D Charters** runs an annual trip each May for halibut; it's so popular, however, it's booked a year in advance. They offer several other trips, so you should have no trouble getting a spot on the salmon, light-tackle or deep-reef bottomfish trips. ~ 607 Garibaldi Avenue, Garibaldi; 503-322-0007, 800-900-4665; www.garibaldicharters.com.

CENTRAL COAST The oldest charter fishing company in the area, **Newport Tradewinds** has been running trips for halibut, salmon, tuna, bottomfish and clams since 1949. ~ 653 Southwest Bay Boulevard, Newport; 541-265-2101; www.newporttradewinds.com. **Depoe Bay Tradewinds** runs fishing trips year-round for tuna, halibut, salmon and clams, as well as bottomfish like sea bass and red snapper. ~ Depoe Bay; 541-765-2545, 800-445-8730. You can also arrange a guided fishing trip with **Dockside Charters.** ~ Depoe Bay; 541-765-2545; www.docksidedepoebay.com.

Well known for salmon, Oregon's coastal waters are also fished for ling cod, cabazon (a big, ugly bottom fish), sea bass, red snapper, albacore and halibut.

SOUTH COAST In Charleston, **Betty Kay Charters** has year-round half-day bottomfishing trips, as well as seasonal runs for tuna and halibut. ~ 7788 Albacore Street; 541-888-9021, 800-752-6303; www.bettykaycharters.com. Besides halibut fishing in May, **Bob's Sportfishing** offers several other trips, including a half-day bottomfishing excursion. ~ Charleston; 541-888-4241; www.bobssportfishing.com.

FISHING

You can rent a small boat and row out into a bay, such as Yaquina or Nehalem, for year-round recreational crabbing (always call first for tide information), as well as seasonal catches of perch, flounder, bass and salmon. Near Coos Bay, Ten Mile Lake is stocked with trout, crappie and catfish.

NORTH COAST **Jetty Fisheries** rents 16-foot aluminum Klamath boats. August through November, a run of salmon moves through the bay to spawn in the Nehalem River. Crabbing is good year-round. Crab-cooking and fish-cleaning facilities are provided. ~ Route 101 at Nehalem Bay, Rockaway Beach; 503-368-5746; e-mail jettyfishery@coastwipi.com.

CENTRAL COAST The **Newport Marina Charter and Store** rents 14-foot aluminum fishing boats and equipment for fishing and crabbing year-round. ~ 2122 Southeast Marine Science Drive, South Beach; 877-867-4470; www.nmscharters.com. On the Alsea River, **Kozy Kove Resort** rents fishing boats. Guides are available. ~ 9464 Alsea Highway, ten miles east of Waldport; 541-528-3251; www.kozykove.com. In Waldport try **McKinley's Marina**, which rents small boats that seat up to five. Boat rentals include bait. ~ Route 34; 541-563-4656. Near the Florence area try **Westlake Resort**, where you can rent 14- to 16-foot boats and try for perch, crappie and catfish. ~ Westlake; 541-997-3722; www.westlakeresort.com.

SOUTH COAST For a day of fishing for trout, crappie, bass, bluegill and catfish, rent an aluminum fishing boat at **Tenmile Marina, Inc.** The famous tall dunes separating the lake from the ocean are visible from the lake. Call for winter availability. ~ 7th and Park streets, Lakeside; 541-759-3137.

WHALE WATCHING The Oregon Coast provides a front-row seat to one of nature's magnificent shows: the annual migrations of the California gray whales. Although the southbound leg of the mammals' trip peaks in late December, it continues until February. Then, with calves in tow, the mammals begin the northbound journey in March. It continues through May. This is an excellent time to take a whale-watching tour: during this leg of the trip, the whales travel closer to shore and more slowly.

CENTRAL COAST Depoe Bay calls itself the whale-watching capital of the Oregon Coast. The mammals are probably attracted to the bay because of a unique environment that provides plenty for the whales to feed on. Whale watching here is almost a year-round activity.

Dockside Charters runs daily whale-watching tours. Once the boat reaches the migration route—usually about a mile or two offshore—it will stop and drift for a while so visitors can watch the whales feed. Owner Jim Tade will also take up to six people out in inflatable Zodiac boats for up-close looks at the mammals. ~ Depoe Bay; 541-765-2545; www.docksidedepoebay.com. **Depoe Bay Tradewinds** also operates daily one-hour whale-watching trips year-round. ~ Depoe Bay; 541-765-2345, 800-445-8730. **Newport Tradewinds** offers two-hour whale-watching trips all through the year. ~ 653 Southwest Bay Boulevard, Newport; 541-265-2101; www.newporttradewinds.com.

SURFING If you go surfing, keep in mind that you will be sharing the waves with cold water–loving great-white sharks so stick to common surfing areas. Surfing in Oregon hasn't reached the crescendo of activity that it has in California. Nevertheless, there are local contingents of surfers up and down the coast. Ecola State Park,

BEASTLY BEHAVIOR

Once you have spotted a whale, keep your eyes peeled for it to rise above the surface. Gray whales often "spyhop," thrusting their heads out of the water and balancing with their eyes exposed. Experts believe this is done to look around above the surface and possibly to orient themselves with reference to the shore or the sun. The most spectacular whale behavior, from a landlubber's viewpoint, is "breaching"—leaping completely out of the water, rolling sideways and falling slowly backward with an enormous splash. The reason for this is unknown. It could be to knock off barnacles or to signal other whales. It might be a courtship ritual, or then again, it might just be the giant beast's playful way of expressing the joy of life.

Indian Beach and Oswald West State Park are recommended North Coast surfing spots, and good for all skill levels. Along the Central Coast, Otter Rock, south of Newport, is good place for beginners. But only a few shops rent surfboards, wetsuits and various other "board" sports equipment.

NORTH COAST **Cleanline Surf Shop** in Seaside started out in 1980, renting wetsuits to diehard surfers ready to brave the cold winter waters. Now it rents just about everything, including wetsuits, surfboards and snowboards. ~ 719 1st Avenue, Seaside; 503-738-7888, fax 503-738-9793; www.cleanlinesurf.com.

CENTRAL COAST **Safari Town Surf Shop** rents wetsuits, surfboards, bodyboards and skimboards. The shop is about a half-hour's drive north of Otter Rock. Closed Monday and Tuesday in the winter. ~ 3026 Northeast Route 101, Lincoln City; 541-996-6335. Surfboards, boogieboards, skimboards and wet suits can be rented or purchased at the **Oregon Surf Shop.** ~ 4933 Southwest Route 101, Lincoln City; phone/fax 541-996-3957, 877-339-5672; www.oregonsurfshop.com.

WIND-SURFING & KAYAKING

Kayaking is popular on Coffenberry Lake at Fort Stevens State Park in Astoria. And in Langlois, on the South Coast, there's a windsurfing bed-and-breakfast inn, where you can take lessons after your continental breakfast.

NORTH COAST For kayak rentals, contact **Pacific Wave Limited.** The shop also offers kayaking lessons and guided kayak tours of the area's rivers, bays and estuaries. ~ 2021 Route 101, Warrenton; 503-861-0866, fax 503-861-4319; www.pacwave.net.

SOUTH COAST A sandspit separates the freshwater, spring-fed Floras Lake from the ocean. At the **Floras Lake House**, a bed and breakfast that sits just off the lake, the owners also operate a windsurfing school (equipment and wetsuit included for beginners). Mornings are best for lessons (steady northwest winds blow during the afternoon) on the lake, which is shallow and warm. Closed November to February; call for hours after Labor Day. ~ 92870 Boice Cope Road, Langlois; phone/fax 541-348-9912; www.floraslake.com, e-mail floraslk@harborside.com.

RIDING STABLES

Look no further than the Oregon Coast for impressive scenic backdrops to half-day guided rides through coastal mountain pine forest, open rides along beach dunes or mountain trail rides near the mouth of the Rogue River.

NORTH COAST Based out of Nehalem Bay State Park, **Northwest Equine Outfitters** offers early morning and sunset rides along the coast. Customized trips can be arranged. Open daily Memorial Day to Labor Day; by appointment only the rest of the year. ~ Nehalem Bay State Park; 503-801-7433.

CENTRAL COAST **C&M Stables** has guided rides through the dunes and along the beach or the mountains. Long (half-day) rides through the beaches and dunes can also be arranged. ~ 90241 Route 101, Florence; 541-997-7540; www.oregonhorsebackriding.com.

SOUTH COAST **Bandon Beach Riding Stables** specializes in open rides along the beach, and operates year-round. Maximum group of 16 people. Reservations recommended. ~ Beach Loop Drive, Bandon; 541-347-3423; www.bandonbeachridingstables.com.

GOLF

When rainfall along the coast can measure 60, 70, even 80 inches a year, good drainage is important for a golf course. The courses listed here all report good drainage, making them playable year-round. You can rent clubs and carts at the courses listed below.

NORTH COAST For a round of nine holes, try the public **Discount Dan's Golf Course.** It's a fun but challenging course, with ocean views from some holes. ~ 33377 Highland Lane, Gearhart; 503-738-5248; www.discountdans.com. At the 18-hole **Gearhart Golf Links,** ocean views are obscured by a condominium complex, but the terrain is relatively flat, making this public green quite walkable. ~ North Marion Street, Gearhart; 503-738-3538; www.gearhartgolflinks.com. Public facilities also include **Lakeside Golf Club,** which has a hilly, moderately challenging 18-hole course. ~ 3245 Northeast 50th Street, Lincoln City; 541-994-8442. In Gleneden Beach, try the 18-hole course at **Salishan Golf Links.** ~ Gleneden Beach; 541-764-3632; www.salishan.com.

CENTRAL COAST The scenic nine-hole, privately owned but publicly accessible **Agate Beach Golf Course** is fairly flat and walkable, with ocean views from some holes. This 3002-yard-long course has a driving range. ~ 4100 North Coast Highway (Route 101), Newport; 541-265-7331; www.agatebeachgolf.com. In Florence, **Sand Pines Golf Links** has an 18-hole course built on sand dunes, which provide excellent drainage and spectacular scenery. ~ 1201 35th Street; 541-997-1940; www.sandpines.com. There's a "wee bit o' Scotland" in Florence at the 18-hole, public **Ocean Dunes Golf Links,** an older, well-known, "true" links course, with high slope and difficulty ratings. ~ 3345 Munsel Lake Road; 541-997-3232. In Waldport, the nine-hole **Crestview Hills Golf Course** is flat and walkable, complete with a pro shop and a driving range. ~ 1680 Crestline Drive, Waldport; 541-563-3020; www.crestviewhillsgolf.com.

SOUTH COAST The John Zahler–designed **Sunset Bay Golf Course** is adjacent to Sunset Bay; it's public, nine holes, is walkable and is "about the only course in the area playable in the winter," according to a local pro. ~ 11001 Cape Arago Highway, Coos Bay; 541-888-9301. A little farther south is **Bandon Face Rock Golf Course.** Lessons are offered during the summer at this nine-hole executive course. ~ 3235 Beach Loop Road, Bandon; 541-347-3818; www.bandonbythesea.com. About 12 miles north of Gold Beach, the nine-hole, public **Cedar Bend Golf Course** is set in a valley with a creek winding through it. Alder, hemlock and fir trees add to the scenic beauty. Cedar Bend also has an 18-hole course. ~ 34391 Squaw Valley Road, Ophir; 541-247-6911.

TENNIS

Time for tennis? A good possibility is the court at **Goodspeed Park.** ~ 3rd Street and Goodspeed Place, Tillamook; 503-842-7525. On the coast, try **Bandon High School**'s two courts. ~ 11th and Franklin streets, Bandon; 541-347-9616. In Port Orford, play at **Buffington Park.** ~ 14th and Arizona streets, Port Orford; 541-332-8055. Additional public courts are at 2nd and Spruce streets in **Cannon Beach** (these courts are lighted), Northeast 4th and Benton streets in Newport (503-436-2623), and **Rolling Dunes Park** at Siano Loop and 35th Street in Florence (541-997-3436).

BIKING

Route 101 is the state's most popular biking trail. Every year, thousands of travelers do the coast, taking advantage of many side roads, hiker-bike camps and facilities that cater to the cycling crowd. Even to nonbicyclists, the 370-mile Oregon Coast Bike Route is well known. There are numerous sections that take in scenic and quiet county and city streets that have low volume traffic and slow traffic speeds. There are also backcountry sites set up for cyclists. If you're thinking about making the ride along the Oregon Coast Bike Route, get hold of the **Oregon Coast Bike Route Map.** It's free and published by the Oregon Department of Transportation. The department also publishes the **Oregon Bicycling Guide** that maps out bike routes throughout the state and provides information on various route conditions. It should be noted that Oregon Coast Bike Route is really for experienced cyclists. Besides the length of the trip (it takes about six or eight days to make the journey), the route rises and falls 16,000 feet along the way. ~ Oregon Department of Transportation Bikeway Program: 355 Capitol Street Northeast, Room 210, Transportation Building, Salem, OR 97310; 503-986-3400, fax 503-986-3407.

Bicycling along the spectacular Oregon Coast sounds like great fun, even for the weekend recreational cyclist. But you need your own bike—the farther south you travel, the harder it is to find rentals.

NORTH COAST An eight-mile paved route through **Fort Stevens State Park** passes through the park's historic section, then leads into a wooded area before crossing to parallel the ocean and looping back into the park. In Seaside you can ride along the two-mile boardwalk or head back into the Lewis and Clark area for rides along paved roads and some old logging roads.

The 83-mile **Seaside-Garibaldi Bike Tour** loops south along Route 101 and then takes Miami River Road back to Mohler where Routes 53 and 26 lead back to your starting point. You can shorten the trip to 52 miles by returning north at Nehalem.

Saddle Mountain State Natural Area's peak was originally called Swallahoost for a chief who, after being murdered, was said to have returned to life as an eagle.

The 40-mile **Three Capes Loop** route from Tillamook to Cape Kiwanda at Pacific City is scenic, steep and spectacular. Another gentler approach to Cape Kiwanda is Sandlake Road off Route 101 south of Tillamook.

CENTRAL COAST At the town of Toledo, whose art and antique galleries are worth a stop, follow Yaquina Bay Road west along the Yaquina River into Newport. It's a flat and scenic road that can easily be done as a loop.

Newport's **Ocean View Drive** is an excellent, four-mile alternative to Route 101. This route leads past the Agate Beach area and takes you through the historic Nye Beach community, one of Newport's earliest resorts. You'll wind up at Yaquina Bay State Park, home of the community's signature lighthouse.

HIDDEN ►

One of our favorite rides in Florence is **Rhododendron Drive** west from Route 101 to Spruce Point and then north to the Coast Guard Station. The roundtrip is eight miles.

The ten-mile roundtrip from **Charleston to Cape Arago** includes Shore Acres Botanical Gardens. **Seven Devil's Road** in Charleston leads to South Slough National Estuarine Research Reserve on a scenic 13-mile route that ends up at Route 101.

SOUTH COAST **Bandon Bypass** is a relatively easy trip that departs Route 101 at milepost 260.1 and follows Riverside Drive south through historic Old Town. It continues along Beach Loop Road before linking back up with the coast highway.

HIDDEN ►

Off Route 101 north of Bandon, **North Bank Road** winds for 16 miles along the Coquille River. This flat, scenic route is lightly trafficked (but watch out for logging trucks), lush and unforgettable. Then head south on Route 42 to Coquille and pick up South Route 42 back to Bandon. The roundtrip is 52 miles.

Bike Rentals In Seaside, **Prom Bike and Hobby Shop** is just three blocks from the beach. The shop rents three-speed cruisers, mountain bikes, kids' bikes, tandems and beach tricycles. Or you might try a surrey, rollerskates or inline skates. ~ 622 12th Avenue, Seaside; 503-738-8251. A few miles south, **Mike's Bike Shop** rents "fun-cycles"—big three-wheelers—for riding on the fairly level wide beach at low tide. Otherwise, you can rent mountain bikes to ride on nearby logging trails (they're private, however) or up to Ecola State Park, about a mile away. You may also rent beach cruisers. Closed Wednesday and Thursday in winter. ~ 248 North Spruce Street, Cannon Beach; 503-436-1266. In Newport, check out **The Bike Shop** for mountain, road and tandem bike rentals, as well as equipment and repairs. Closed Sunday. ~ 223 Northwest Nye Street, Newport; 541-265-2481. **Bicycles 101** in Florence rents mountain bikes and cruisers. Closed Sunday. ~ 1537 8th Street, Florence; 541- 997-5717.

HIKING

The Oregon Coast abounds with beautiful hiking opportunities within state parks and national forests. All distances listed for hiking trails are one way unless otherwise noted.

NORTH COAST **Fort Stevens State Park** has several easy trails, including the two trail, 1.8-mile stroll from Battery Russell to the wreck of the *Peter Iredale.*

Saddle Mountain Trail (2.5 miles) ascends the highest mountain on the coastal range. A difficult climb offering great views. It's located off Route 26 near Necanicum.

Tillamook Head Trail (7 miles) begins south of the town of Seaside and ascends to 1200 feet on the route to Escola State Park's Indian Beach. This is believed to be the route followed by Lewis and Clark when they journeyed to Ecola Creek.

Inland from Tillamook on Route 6 is the moderate-to-difficult **Kings Mountain Trail** (2.5 miles). This route takes you through the area of the famed Tillamook Burn, a series of 1933, 1939, 1945 and 1951 fires that took out enough lumber to build over one million homes. While the area, now the Tillamook State Forest, is covered with younger timber, some evidence of the old burn can still be seen. ◄ HIDDEN

Neah-kah-nie Mountain Trail (4 miles) is a challenging climb that begins 2.6 miles south of Oswald West State Park's Short Sands parking area. Great views of the coast.

CENTRAL COAST In the Siuslaw National Forest east of Pacific City, the **Pioneer Indian Trail** (8 miles) is highly recommended. This moderately difficult trail runs from Itebo Lake to South Lake through a fir forest and a meadow that has a wide array of wildflowers in the summer. ◄ HIDDEN

The **Estuary Trail** (.25 mile) at the Hatfield Marine Science Center is a great introduction to local marine life. This posted route is wheelchair accessible. ~ 2030 South Marine Science Drive, Newport; 541-867-0100.

Captain Cook's Trail (.6 mile) leads from the Cape Perpetua visitors center below Route 101 past American Indian shell middens to coastal tidepools. At high tide you'll see the spouting horn across Cook's Chasm. A bit more challenging is the **Cummins**

Creek Loop (10 miles) up Cook's Ridge to Cummins Creek Trail and back down to the visitors center. Enjoy the old-growth forests and meadows.

At the southern end of the Oregon Dunes National Recreation Area, **Bluebill Trail** (1 mile roundtrip), two and a half miles off Route 101 near Horsefall Beach Road, offers an easy and beautiful loop hike around the marshy area once known as Bluebill Lake. It includes an extensive boardwalk system.

SOUTH COAST The **Estuary Study Trail** at South Slough National Estuarine Research Reserve south of Coos Bay (1.5 miles) is one of the finest hikes on the Oregon Coast. Leading down through a coastal forest, you'll see a pioneer log landing, use a boardwalk to cross a skunkcabbage bog and visit a salt marsh.

HIDDEN ►

Shrader Old Growth Trail (1.5 miles) off Jerry's Flat Road, east of Gold Beach, is a pleasant loop where you'll see rhododendron, cedar, streams and riparian areas. The marked route identifies coastal species along the way.

HIDDEN ►

To really get away from it all, hike the **Lower Rogue River Trail** (12.2 miles) south from Agness. You'll pass American Indian landmarks, see picturesque bridges and spot wildlife as you hike this wild and scenic canyon.

Bandon to Fourmile Creek (8.5 miles) is one of the coast's most scenic walks. Begin at Bandon Harbor and head south past the Bandon Needles, dunes, ponds and lakes to the creek. Of course you can abbreviate this hike at any point. One easy possibility is to head south on Beach Loop Drive to the point where it swings east toward Route 101. Park here and take the short .2-mile walk through the woods and up over the dune to Bradley Lake, a good swimming hole.

Redwood Trail (1 mile) north of Alfred A. Loeb State Park, ten miles east of Brookings, is a beautiful streamside walk leading past rhododendron, myrtlewood and towering redwoods.

Transportation

CAR

From Northern California or Washington, the coast is easily reached via **Route 101**. Within Oregon, many roads link Portland and the Willamette Valley to resort destinations. **Routes 30** and **26** provide easy access to the North Coast communities of Astoria and Seaside, while **Route 6** connects with Tillamook. **Route 18** leads to Lincoln City, and **Routes 20** and **34** connect with the Central Coast region in the vicinity of Newport and Waldport. **Route 126** is the way to Florence. **Route 38** heads to Reedsport. To reach Bandon and the South Coast, take **Route 42**.

AIR

Horizon Air flies to **North Bend Municipal Airport**; www.coosbaynorthbendairport.com) and Harbor Airlines goes to **Astoria General Airport** (800-860-4093). The **Portland International Airport** (503-460-4234, 877-739-4636) and **Eugene Airport**

(541-682-5430), described in other chapters, also provide gateways to the coast.

BUS

Greyhound Bus Lines (800-231-2222; www.greyhound.com) serves many coast destinations. There is a highway stop in Lincoln City, along with stations in Newport at 956 Southwest 10th Street, 541-265-2253.

CAR RENTALS

Hertz Rent A Car has a location at North Bend Municipal Airport, as well as one at 1492 Duane Street in Astoria. ~ 800-654-3131.

PUBLIC TRANSIT

In Otis, Lincoln City, Newport, Waldport, Yachats, Toledo and Siletz, local service is provided by **Lincoln County Transit**. The same company provides service from Siletz and Yachats to Newport, and from Newport to Lincoln City. ~ 541-265-4900; co.lincoln.or.us/transit. Connections can be made from Bend, Corvallis, Salem and Albany through **Valley Retriever Bus Lines**. ~ 541-265-2253.

TAXIS

For service in Seaside, try **Seaside Yellow Cab**. ~ 503-738-5252. On the South Coast, **Yellow Cab** operates in Coos Bay/North Bend. ~ 541-267-3111.

FIVE

The Heart of Oregon

Drivers in a hurry barrel down Oregon's 280-mile Route 5 corridor in about five hours. Incredibly, that's the way many people see the region that lies at the end of the fabled Oregon Trail. Tempted by free land or the prospect of finding gold, the pioneers risked everything to get here. Today a new generation, rushing to reach Crater Lake, Mt. Hood or the Oregon Coast, speeds through, never knowing what they've missed.

That's progress. Fortunately, all it takes is a trip down a Route 5 offramp to get hooked on the Heart of Oregon, the 60-mile-wide region that extends from Salem to the California border. With the freeway left behind in the rearview mirror, you may understand why residents say God spent six days creating the Earth and on the seventh He went to Oregon.

Framed by the Klamath and Coast ranges on the west and the Cascades on the east, this is the place to find peaceful covered bridges and exciting rafting runs, the nation's oldest Shakespeare festival and a legislature that has made Oregon America's most environmentally conscious state. Home to two major universities, the center of Oregon agriculture and some of its most historic towns, the Heart of Oregon is where you'll find many of the state's best-known writers, poets, artists and artisans.

Just an hour from the state's famous mountain and seaside resorts, the Willamette Valley and the Ashland–Rogue River areas are the primary destinations in the Heart of Oregon. Fields of wildflowers, small towns with falsefront stores and gabled homes, businesses with names like "Wild and Scenic Trailer Park," pies made with fresh-picked marionberries—this is the Oregon found in the postcard rack. Soda fountains with mirrored backbars, jazz preservation societies, old river ferries, museums built out of railroad cars, music festivals and folk-art shrines—you'll find them all and even more here.

In many ways this area's heritage, touted by writers ranging from Washington Irving to Zane Grey, sums up the evolution of the West: American Indians followed by British fur traders, American explorers, missionaries, pioneer settlers, gold miners and the merchants who served them. The 19th-century nouveau riche tapped the hardwood forests to create Victorian mansions. As the mines were played out, lumber and agriculture became king. Strategically located on the main stage and rail lines to California and Washington, this corridor also became the principal gateway to most of Oregon's cities, as well as its emerging mountain retreats and coastal beaches.

But the Heart of Oregon story also has a special dimension, one told at local museums and historic sites. The fatal impact of American expansion on the American Indian culture began with the arrival of missionaries, who preached Christianity but left behind diseases that decimated their converts. In 1843 the promise of free land triggered a stampede as "Oregon or bust" pioneers sped west. Many became farmers who prospered in the California trade after gold was discovered in 1848 at Sutter's Mill. Three years later, after gold was found closer to home near Jacksonville, many settlers put down their plows and made a beeline for the mines. A new boom brought instant prosperity to this sleepy town as millions in gold dust poured through banks on California Street and miners dazzled their brides with mansions shipped in piecemeal from Tennessee.

Not sharing in this windfall were American Indians pushed from their ancestral lands by the settlers and miners. The Indians fought back in the Rogue River Wars between 1851 and 1856. But they were ultimately forced onto reservations, easing the path to statehood in 1859. Settled by Methodist missionaries in 1840, Salem was one of several towns that emerged as a regional supply center. Others included Eugene and Corvallis.

As the railroad improved access, businessmen discovered there was more to sell in Oregon than gold, lumber, dairy products and bountiful crops. Visitors began to explore the fishing streams, caves and forests. Chautauqua tents brought intellectuals and entertainers to Ashland, as Jacksonville offered a different kind of nightlife that gave preachers something to denounce on their pulpits. When Zane Grey showed up to fish the Rogue and the Umpqua rivers, the entire country read about it in his articles. As the good word spread, more visitors began arriving to raft these and other rivers, to see the waterfalls and photograph the vernacular architecture.

Although it was a long way from Middle America, tourists loved the Main Street look and unspoiled countryside of the Heart of Oregon. Culturally it became a hub for social experiments and alternative lifestyles, happily exported by local celebrities like Ken Kesey, who took his famous traffic-stopping bus on a national tour with the "Merry Pranksters" in the 1960s.

Although the Heart of Oregon can be overcast and wet during the winter months, summers tend to be sunny and hot, particularly in the Ashland–Rogue River area. While Route 5 is the mainline, Route 99 is a pleasant alternative. Because the Willamette Valley is flat, it's ideal terrain for cyclists. South of Eugene, the Klamath mountains frame picturesque valleys and towns such as Medford, Ashland and Jacksonville. At the bottom of the state the Siskiyous form the backdrop to the California border.

Because this is the state's primary transportation corridor, it's convenient to scores of popular attractions. Since you're only an hour from the beach or the Cascades, you can easily spend your days waterskiing or spelunking and your nights enjoying *King Lear*. Blessed with some of the state's finest resorts and restaurants, the Heart of Oregon also offers plenty of birdwatching thanks to several wildlife preserves found along the Willamette River. Here you're likely to spot great blue herons, red-tailed hawks, quails and woodpeckers. Deer, fox, opossums, coyotes and raccoons abound in the valley, while elk, bobcats, bear and flying squirrels are found in the southern mountains.

The region's highlands are pocketed by pristine lakes, hundreds of miles of remote hiking trails and resort lodges paneled in knotty pine. There's even downhill skiing on the highest peak here, 7533-foot Mt. Ashland. But there's little doubt that the signature attractions between Salem and Ashland are the river valleys. From the Willamette wetlands to the swimming holes of the Applegate River, it's hard to beat the streamside life. Rushing down from the Cascades, roaring through Hellgate Canyon, flowing through restaurants at the Oregon Caves, these tributaries define every area and delight every visitor.

One of the most attractive features is the proximity to the wilderness. You are seldom more than 15 or 20 minutes from the countryside, and even the bigger towns, such as Eugene and Salem, have major greenbelts within the city limits. Just north of Salem is Oregon's wine country. While the state capitol is the biggest draw, many historic homes and neighborhoods add to the charm of the central city.

Eugene's college-town status gives it the amenities you would expect in a larger community. Its central location makes the city an ideal base for visiting most of the state's popular destinations. And the city's Ecotopian fervor shows what can happen when environmentalists take control.

Jacksonville, a city that boomed during the rollicking gold rush days, is a delightful period piece, the kind of town where bed and breakfasts outnumber motels ten to one. The tree-lined streets, red-brick office blocks and dusty old bars make the town a favorite. Artists flock here and to Ashland, an Oregon mecca for the dramatic arts. Thoroughly gentrified, heavily booked and loaded with great restaurants, Ashland is the state's last temptation and a hard one to leave on the route south. No mere stepping stone to other parts of the state, the Heart of Oregon is an end in itself.

Salem Area

Although best known as Oregon's capital, Salem is a desirable place to spend a day for many other reasons. A short drive from Oregon's wine country, Salem is also close to several historic Willamette Valley ferries. Near the Willamette, the downtown area is rich with restored buildings, museums, churches and a pioneer cemetery.

SIGHTS

Most travelers from Portland drive down the Willamette Valley to Salem via Route 5. But a far more scenic approach is to exit Route 5 in southern Portland and pick up **Route 99 West** through Tigard. Here you can continue through Oregon's wine country on 99 West, head through McMinnville and then cut east to Salem at Rickreall. Even better, turn off Route 99 West at the town of Dayton and pick up **Route 221**, a beautiful backroad paralleling

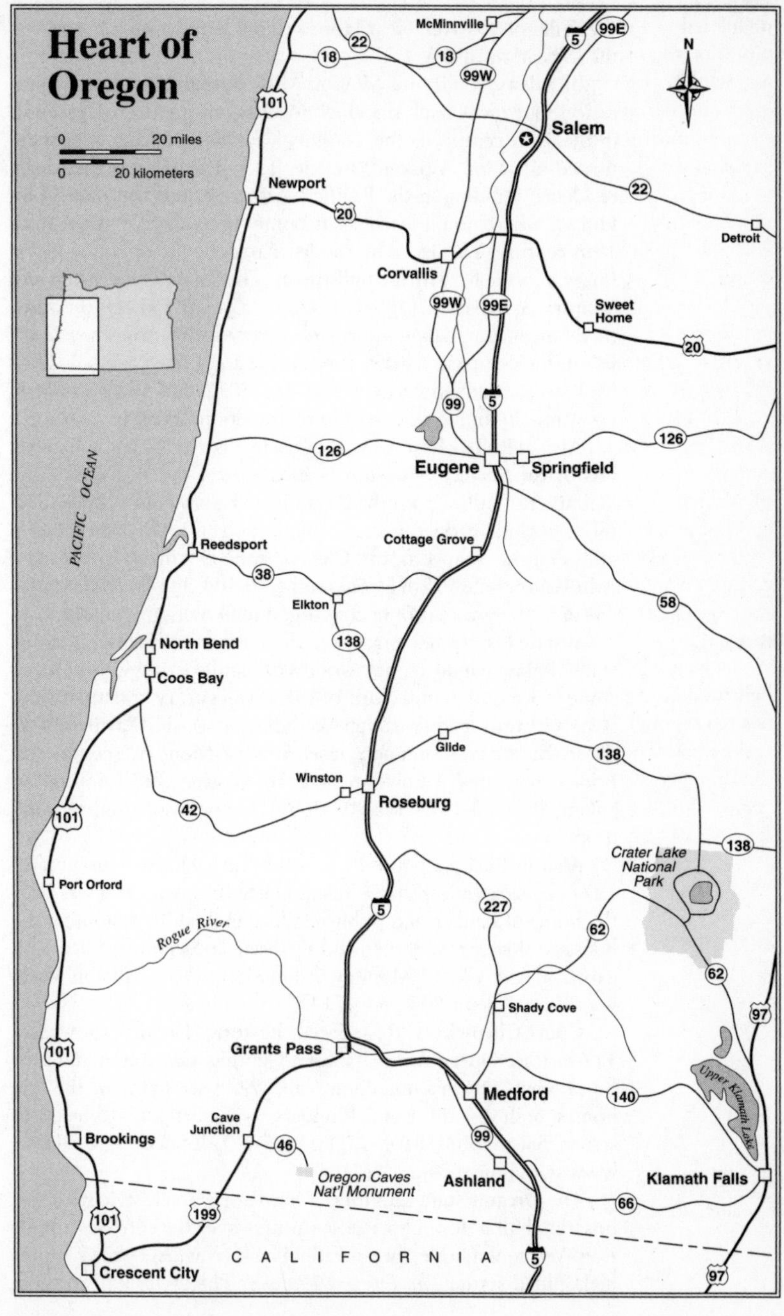

Heart of Oregon
0 20 miles
0 20 kilometers
PACIFIC OCEAN
McMinnville
Salem
Newport
Detroit
Corvallis
Sweet Home
Eugene
Springfield
Reedsport
Cottage Grove
Elkton
North Bend
Coos Bay
Glide
Winston
Roseburg
Crater Lake National Park
Port Orford
Rogue River
Shady Cove
Grants Pass
Medford
Upper Klamath Lake
Cave Junction
Brookings
Oregon Caves Nat'l Monument
Ashland
Klamath Falls
Crescent City
C A L I F O R N I A
N
5
99E
22
18
99W
101
20
99
126
38
138
58
42
227
62
97
140
46
199
66

the Willamette River. Near Hopewell it's fun to cross the river on the Wheatland Ferry.

In Salem, you'll find **Mission Mill Museum**, a historic restoration that turns back the clock to Oregon's pioneer days. Built in the 19th century is the Thomas Kay Woolen Mill, a factory-turned-museum. Adjacent are the Jason Lee House, the oldest residence standing in the Pacific Northwest, and the John Boon House, where you'll learn what family life was like in the mid-19th century. The 1841 Methodist Parsonage is open for tours. Enjoy a picnic here by the millstream. The **Salem Convention and Visitors Association** (503-581-4325, fax 503-581-4540; www.travelsalem.com, e-mail information@travelsalem.com) has an office in the complex. Closed Sunday. Fee for guided tours. ~ 1313 Mill Street Southeast, Salem; 503-585-7012, fax 503-588-9902; www.missionmill.org, e-mail info@missionmill.org.

Also within Mission Mill Museum is the **Marion County Historical Society Museum**, which traces the history of the Willamette Valley from the days of the Kalapuyan Indians. Exhibits include a dugout canoe made in 1860, blacksmith shop and pioneer schoolroom. Closed Sunday through Tuesday. Admission. ~ 260 12th Street Southeast; 503-364-2128, fax 503-391-5356; www.marionhistory.org, e-mail mchs@open.org.

Situated in formal gardens is the **Deepwood Estate**. With its stained-glass windows, oak woodwork and solarium, this Queen Anne is a monument to turn-of-the-20th-century craftsmanship. A nature trail leads through the adjacent Bush's Pasture Park. Closed Saturday in summer; closed Sunday, Monday, Tuesday and Friday in winter. Admission. ~ 1116 Mission Street Southeast, Salem; 503-363-1825, fax 503-363-3586; www.oregonlink.com/deepwood.

Also in Bush's Pasture Park is the **Bush House Museum**, an 1877 mansion with splendid Italian-marble fireplaces that was once the home of banker and publisher Asahel Bush II. Adjoining the house is a lovely rose garden and Victorian conservatory filled with exotic plants. Closed Monday. Admission. ~ 600 Mission Street Southeast, Salem; 503-363-4714.

Court-Chemeketa Residential Historic District showcases 117 historic Queen Anne, Italianate, gothic, Craftsman and saltbox homes. On this mile-long walk you'll see many of the fine homes built by the city's founders. ~ Court and Chemeketa streets, Salem; 503-581-4325, 800-874-7012, fax 503-581-4540; www.travelsalem.com.

The **Oregon State Capitol** is a four-story Greek-style structure boasting half a dozen bronze sculptures over the entrances. Built from Vermont marble, the state building is crowned by the 23-foot-high gilded statue *The Oregon Pioneer*. The tower and rotunda have reopened after repairs were made to fix damage caused by an 1993 earthquake (the quake measured 5.5 on the Richter scale). Tours up the 121 stairs of the tower run every hour in summer. Surrounding Wilson Park has a pretty fountain and gazebo. ~ 900 Court Street, Salem; 503-986-1387, fax 503-986-1131; www.leg.state.or.us.

Across from the capitol, **Willamette University** is the state's oldest institution of higher learning and the first university in the West (founded in 1842). On this shady campus you'll want to see the exhibit on the history of the school (which in many ways mirrors the history of Salem) at venerable **Waller Hall**. Cone Chapel (also in Waller Hall) is the place of worship for this one-time Methodist school. The campus is also home to an unusual formation of five giant sequoias known as the **Star Trees**; if you stand in the middle of them and look upwards, you'll see the shape of a star. The trees are near the **Sesquicentennial Rose Garden**, a blooming place for a walk across State Street from the capitol. ~ Willamette University: 900 State Street, Salem; 503-370-6300; www.willamette.edu.

Three Victorian houses on Salem's riverfront form **A.C. Gilbert's Discovery Village**, which is filled with hands-on exhibits pertaining to art, music, drama and science. Dedicated to magician

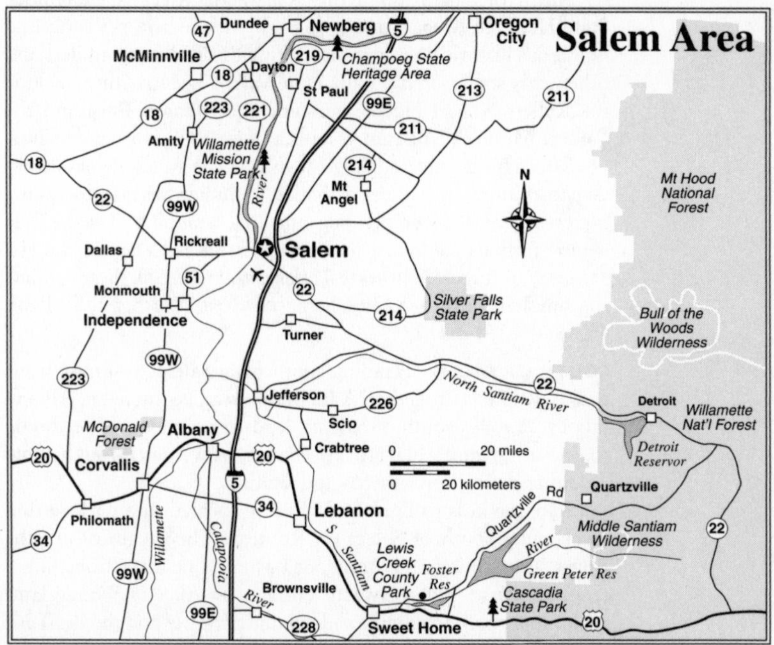

and inventor A. C. Gilbert, the museum allows young visitors to take part in everything from designing a greeting card to putting on a puppet show. Children can also enjoy the 20,000-square-foot outdoor play area. Admission. ~ 116 Marion Street Northeast, along the Riverfront at Front and Union streets, under the Marion Front Bridge, Salem; 503-371-3631, fax 503-316-3485; www.acgilbert.org, e-mail info@acgilbert.org.

NORTH OF SALEM The byways and secondary highways of the Willamette Valley north of Salem offer great possibilities for a day of sightseeing. Many of Oregon's best wineries are along Route 99 West—a rural and scenic alternative to Route 5. (See "Oregon's Wine Country" Scenic Drive.)

Mt. Angel Abbey is a 19th-century Benedictine monastic community 18 miles northeast of Salem. Visitors are welcome to take a walking tour of the Abbey, including the Romanesque church and retreat houses. A small museum focuses on the Russian Old Believer community, while another building emphasizes the natural history of the region. The beautiful library, designed by Alvar Aalto, features a display of rare books. Near the top of a 300-foot butte is the grotto of Our Lady of Lourdes. In July, the retreat hosts the Abbey Bach Festival. ~ 1 Abbey Drive, St. Benedict; 503-845-3025, fax 503-845-3027; www.mtangel.edu.

North of Salem along the Willamette River is **Champoeg State Heritage Area**, a 615-acre park with a visitors center and numerous historic buildings illustrating the lives of fur traders and other early settlers in the Willamette Valley. The structures include the **Robert Newell House Museum**, the **Manson Barn** and the **Pioneer Mother's Museum**, a replica of an 1840 pioneer dwelling. On Saturdays in July and August, visitors can watch living-history demonstrations of pioneer activities, including wheat processing, butter churning, cider pressing and blacksmithing. These single demonstrations culminate in Pioneer Farmstead Day on the last Saturday of August, a historical celebration where all these exhibits run simultaneously. ~ 8239 Champoeg Road Northeast, St. Paul; 503-678-1251 ext. 221.

SOUTH OF SALEM Heading south from Salem, you may want to skip Route 5 altogether. A fun loop drive, beginning in Albany (about 25 miles south of Salem), leads through Corvallis, home to one of Oregon's biggest universities, as well as through some accommodating rural towns and sights.

Take the kids to **Enchanted Forest**, located in a park setting seven miles south of Salem on Route 5. The dream of creator Roger Tofte, this family fun spot has fairytale attractions like a crooked house, Seven Dwarfs' cottage, an Alice in Wonderland rabbit hole, old-lady's-shoe slide, haunted house and the Big Timber log ride. Plays are performed in an outdoor theater. Closed

October to mid-March, and weekdays in September and April. Admission. ~ 8462 Enchanted Way Southeast, Turner; 503-363-3060; www.enchantedforest.com.

Heading southeast from Salem on Route 51, continue past the town of Independence and follow the signs seven miles south to the historic **Buena Vista Ferry,** which carries a handful of cars and cyclists across the Willamette in the time-honored manner. No trip to Oregon is complete without a ride on one of these old-timers. Closed Monday and Tuesday, and from November through April. ~ 503-588-7979.

Just west of Independence is the town of Monmouth, home to the **Jensen Arctic Museum.** This unique collection focuses exclusively on Arctic ecology and culture, boasting such artifacts as dog sleds, long boats, harpoons and kayaks. Children will appreciate the dramatic dioramas of Arctic foxes, caribou, polar bears and wolves. Closed Sunday through Tuesday. ~ Western Oregon University, 590 West Church Street, Monmouth; 503-838-8468.

Proceed south to Albany, where you can begin a circular drive of the area north of Eugene. South of Albany, Route 34 leads east to the town of Lebanon. Continue east to Sweet Home and one of the Northwest's better pioneer museums. In a 1905 woodframe church, the **East Linn Museum** collection is big on logging equipment, antique dolls, quilts, butter churns, linotypes and saddles. There's also a full blacksmith shop here. Closed December through January; closed Monday from June through September, and Monday through Wednesday from September through April. ~ 746 Long Street, Sweet Home; 541-367-4580.

The **Sweet Home Chamber of Commerce** provides information on this Cascades gateway. Closed Sunday. ~ 1575 Main Street, Sweet Home; 541-367-6186, fax 541-367-6150; www.sweethomechamber.org.

sights

AUTHOR FAVORITE

In the spring, don't miss **Schreiner's Gardens**, located five miles north of Salem. Although there are over 200 acres here, only 10 of them are open to the public, and that is only during the May-to-June blooming season. Still, a visit to this photographer's dream is a must during those months; the rest of the year, the gardens are closed while Schreiner's ships irises all over the world through its catalog business. ~ 3625 Quinaby Road Northeast; 503-393-3232, 800-525-2367, fax 503-393-5590; www.schreinersgardens.com, e-mail info@schreinersgardens.com.

SCENIC DRIVE

Oregon's Wine Country

Oregon's leading wine region, Yamhill County is an easy drive north from Salem or southwest from Portland. This area has more than 40 wineries and 100 vineyards, and is known for its exceptional pinot noir. Many wineries here also produce pinot gris, pinot blanc, chardonnay, riesling and champagne-process sparkling wines. Most wineries lie along pastoral Route 99W. The establishments listed here offer tours; call ahead to confirm visiting hours, which vary seasonally.

AMITY & MCMINNVILLE From Salem, follow Edgewater Street westbound. It becomes Route 22 as it takes you ten miles to the intersection with Route 99W. Turn north (right) and follow 99W for 20 miles to McMinnville, the Yamhill county seat. **Yamhill Valley Vineyards** is on a 150-acre estate. Try their pinot noir, pinot blanc and pinot gris wines in the elegant tasting room set in an oak grove. The cathedral ceiling and balcony overlooking the vineyard add to the charm. Closed Monday through Friday from mid-March to Memorial Day and Thanksgiving to mid-March. ~ 16250 Southwest Oldsville Road (off Route 18), McMinnville; 503-843-3100, 800-825-4845; www.yamhill.com, e-mail info@yamhill.com.

CARLTON From McMinnville, take Route 47 north to Carlton, a distance of seven miles. In the center of this historic town, **The Tasting Room** presents a selection of fine wines from around Oregon, with tastings each afternoon. Closed January through March. ~ Main and Pine streets, Carlton; 503-852-6733. Nearby, **Carlo & Julian** is known for innovative viticulture techniques including the use of frost for crop control and trained cats for gopher eradication. Producing less than 500 cases of handcrafted pinot noir, tempranillo and nebbiolo annually, the winery is open for tastings and sales over Memorial Day and Thanksgiving weekends and by appointment. ~ 1000 East Main Street, Carlton; 503-852-7432; e-mail carlo&julian@onlinemac.com. Half a mile farther down Route 47 is **Cuneo Cellars**. Taste their range of handcrafted varietals.

Perched in the foothills ten miles east of the town of Sweet Home are **Foster Reservoir** and the adjacent **Green Peter Reservoir** on Quartzville Road. Green Peter Reservoir offers the kind of views you'd expect to find in Switzerland.

Brownsville, west of Sweet Home on Route 228, is one of the valley's most charming small towns. You can pick up a walking-tour brochure that guides you to local museums, including the century-old **Moyer House**. Built from lumber milled in John

~ 750 Lincoln Street, Carlton; 503-852-0002; www.cuneocellars.com. Continue east on Main Street as it becomes Northeast Hendricks Road, then left on Northeast Kuehne Road to visit **Laurel Ridge Winery** and sample their pinot noir, riesling and gewürztraminer. Closed January. ~ 13301 Northeast Kuehne Road, Carlton; 503-852-7050.

NEWBERG Continue four miles farther north to Yamhill, then turn east (right) on Route 240. A drive of 12 rural miles brings you to Newberg, where **Rex Hill Vineyards** is a beautifully landscaped 25-acre winery with an inviting terraced picnic area. Furnished with antiques, the tasting room has a warm fireplace. ~ 30835 North Route 99W, Newberg; 503-538-0666; www.rexhill.com, e-mail info@rexhill.com.

DUNDEE & DAYTON At Newberg, turn southeast (right) and you'll find yourself back on Route 99W. Driving two miles south will bring you to Dundee, where **Sokol Blosser Winery**, established in 1971, was one of Oregon's first wineries. Here you'll enjoy great views of the Willamette Valley, along with a pleasant picnic area and contemporary tasting room offering not only the winery's fine pinot noir and pinot gris but also fruit preserves, gourmet mustards, salad dressings and candies. ~ 5000 Sokol Blosser Lane, Northeast Dayton; 503-864-2282; www.solkolblosser.com, e-mail info@solkolblosser.com. Established in 1987 by an Australian vintner in a one-time hazelnut processing plant, **Argyle** specializes in champagne-like sparkling wines and pinot noirs. The inviting tasting room is in a restored Victorian farmhouse. ~ 691 North Route 99W, Dundee; 503-538-8520. **Erath Winery** is set high above the Willamette Valley in the lovely Dundee Hills. You can sample the winery's wares in a rustic, wood-paneled tasting room. ~ 9409 Worden Hill Road, Dundee; 503-538-3318, 800-539-9463, fax 503-538-1074; www.erath.com. Four miles south of Dundee, **Wine Country Farm Cellars** makes rare varietals such as Muller-Thurgau in addition to pinot noir and riesling. You'll find a picnic area and a B&B, and visitors can get acquainted with the resident Arabian horses. ~ 6855 Breyman Orchards Road, Dayton; 503-864-3466, 800-261-3446, fax 503-864-3109; www.winecountryfarm.com, e-mail info@winecountryfarm.com. From here, it's a 20-mile drive back to Salem via Route 221.

Moyer's own sash and door factory, this Italianate home features 12-foot ceilings. Landscapes are painted on the walls and window transoms. ~ 204 Main Street at Kirk Avenue, Brownsville.

Howard Taylor and his wife, Faye, devoted 20 years to the creation of the folk-art capital of central Oregon, the **Living Rock Studios.** Howard created this memorial to his pioneer ancestors with 800 tons of rock. The circular stone building is inlaid with pioneer wagon-wheel rims, an American Indian mortar and pes- ◄HIDDEN tle, fool's gold, obsidian and coffee jars filled with crystals. A series of illuminated biblical pictures is displayed downstairs, while a circular staircase leads upstairs to a display of Taylor's carvings. Antiques and unique gifts are on display in the shop. Self-guided tours are available. Closed Sunday and Monday. ~ Route 228, west of Brownsville; 541-466-5814; www.pioneer.net/~mackey, e-mail mackey@pioneer.net.

A popular Oregon college town located on the west side of the valley at the edge of the coast range, **Corvallis** is also the seat of Benton County. A prominent landmark here is the **Benton County Courthouse**. The building, dating to 1887 and still in use, has an impressive clock tower. Closed weekends. ~ 120 Northwest 4th Street, Corvallis.

On the 500-acre **Oregon State University** campus in Corvallis, you'll find the OSU art department's **Fairbanks Gallery** in Fairbanks Hall (closed weekends; 541-737-4745) and **Giustina Gallery** at 26th and Western streets (541-737-6444), two small gallery spaces that usually feature rotating exhibits, often by the university's students. ~ OSU: Campus Way, Corvallis; 541-737-0123, fax 541-737-0625; www.oregonstate.edu/dept/arts.

For information on other local attractions, contact **Corvallis Tourism**. Closed weekends in fall and winter. ~ 553 Northwest Harrison Boulevard, Corvallis; 541-757-1544, 800-334-8118; fax 541-753-2664; www.visitcorvallis.com, e-mail info@visitcor vallis.com.

Located just six miles west of Corvallis on Route 20 is the **Benton County Historical Museum**. Situated in a former college dating from 1867, the museum has historical exhibits and a contemporary art gallery. Closed Sunday and Monday. ~ 1101 Main Street, Philomath; 541-929-6230, fax 541-929-6261; www.bentoncountymuseum.org, e-mail info@bentoncountymu seum.org.

East of Corvallis on Route 20 is **Albany**, where you'll find nearly 500 Victorian homes. One of the best is the **Monteith House**, which is a frame residence with period 19th-century furnishings. Dressed in Victorian costumes, docents lead intriguing tours. Closed Monday and Tuesday, and from mid-September to mid-June, except by appointment. ~ 518 Southwest 2nd Avenue, Albany; 541-967-8699, 800-526-2256. At the **Albany Regional Museum** are an old-time general store, a shoe-shine shop and an exhibit on Camp Adair, a World War II Army training site. Closed Sunday. ~ 136 Lyon Street Southwest, Albany; 541-967-7122.

To arrange tours of either location contact the **Albany Visitors Association**, where you can pick up a helpful walking-tour map. ~ 250 Broadalbin Street Southwest, Suite 110, Albany; 541-928-0911, 800-526-2256, fax 541-926-1500; www.albany visitors.com, e-mail info@albanyvisitors.com.

LODGING

Convenient to Route 5, the **Best Western Mill Creek Inn** has 109 units including junior suites with microwaves, refrigerators and wet bars. The large rooms have contemporary furniture and ample closet space. ~ 3125 Ryan Drive Southeast, Salem; 503-585-3332, 800-346-9659, fax 503-375-9618; e-mail bwmci@msn.com. MODERATE TO DELUXE.

George Washington never slept at **A Creekside Garden Inn**, but it looks as if he might have. Located just six blocks from the state capitol, this Mount Vernon colonial–style home has two-story columns and a veranda overlooking parklike grounds along Mill Creek. Each of the five antique-furnished rooms is decorated with a garden theme; three have private baths. Classic films are shown nightly with a "bottomless" popcorn bowl. A hearty full breakfast in the dining room or on the veranda is included in the room rate. ~ 333 Wyatt Court Northeast, Salem; 503-391-0837, 800-949-0837, fax 503-391-1713; www.salembandb.com, e-mail rickiemh@open.org. MODERATE.

During the 1850s, when U.S. currency was scarce in the Northwest, Oregon Territory minted its own "beaver money" —$5 and $10 gold coins stamped with a beaver image.

Only 15 minutes from downtown Salem, **Bethel Heights Farm Bed & Breakfast** still has a calm pastoral feel. Guest rooms have private baths and patios or balconies that look out over the farm's 20 acres and out to the Willamette Valley and Coast Range. Enjoy a game of croquet, read a book in the gazebo or stroll through the vineyards. Full breakfast included. ~ 6055 Northwest Bethel Heights Road, Salem; 503-364-7688. MODERATE.

Econolodge offers lodging just 50 yards from the Willamette River. Clean, air-conditioned rooms are furnished in modern decor. The price is right for this 61-room motel convenient to downtown. ~ 345 Northwest 2nd Street, Corvallis; 541-752-9601. BUDGET.

The **Sweet Home Inn Motel** has clean rooms with white and pink brick walls and contemporary furniture. A small garden is located at the inn, which is a block away from the museums and shops of this gateway to some of the valley's best boating and fishing. ~ 805 Long Street, Sweet Home; 541-367-5137, fax 541-367-8859. MODERATE.

DINING

Mushrooms are the key ingredient at the **Joel Palmer House Restaurant** and the lifelong passion of owners Jack and Heidi Czarnecki. The Czarneckis hand-gather wild mushrooms and use them in such delicacies as a three-mushroom tart, crabcakes with portobellos, and filet mignon with wild mushrooms. Each dish is carefully paired with a local Oregon wine and served in the elegant dining room of this stately 19th-century house. Dinner only. Closed Sunday and Monday. ~ 600 Ferry Street, Dayton; 503-864-2995; www.joelpalmerhouse.com, e-mail joelpalmerhouse@onlinemac.com. DELUXE TO ULTRA-DELUXE.

There's no MSG at **Kwan's**, a Chinese establishment with seating for more than 400 at comfortable booths and large tables ideal for the whole family. Specialties like imperial fried rice, curry lamb, Mongolian emu and mango chicken have won a loyal following. Entering this pagoda-style building, you'll find a 15-foot-tall redwood Buddha in the lobby. ~ 835 Commercial Street, Salem; 503-362-7711, fax 503-373-5818; www.kwanscuisine.com. MODERATE.

Michael's Landing serves prime rib and seafood salad in the restored Southern Pacific Station. One of the city's most popular restaurants, it has a great view of the Willamette. ~ 603 Northwest 2nd Street, Corvallis; 541-754-6141, fax 541-754-9578. MODERATE TO DELUXE.

For steaks, prime rib and fresh seafood, try **The Gables**. Portions are generous, and there's an extensive wine cellar. Dinner only. ~ 1121 Northwest 9th Street, Corvallis; 541-752-3364. MODERATE TO DELUXE.

HIDDEN ►

Located in a strip shopping center, **Amador's Alley** is one of the most popular Mexican restaurants in the area. Huge portions of *huevos con chorizo*, chile colorado and enchiladas rancheros are served up steaming. Diners are seated at plastic tables and chairs. Arrive early or be prepared to wait. Closed Sunday. ~ 870 North Main Street, Independence; 503-838-0170, fax 503-838-1710. BUDGET TO MODERATE.

Take one of the window booths at **The Point Restaurant** and enjoy a perfect waterfront view. Fresh fish, steak, prawns, lobster and generous salads are a few of the specialties. A fresh-baked loaf of bread comes with every meal. ~ 6305 Route 20, Sweet Home; 541-367-1560. MODERATE.

SHOPPING

The **Reed Opera House Mall** at Court and Liberty streets in Salem is a restored landmark that once presented old-time min-

AUTHOR FAVORITE

Just when you're about ready to give up on McMinnville as another franchise landscape, the chain stores of Route 99 give way to the town's well-preserved downtown. Tucked away in a storefront is **Nick's Italian Café**, where the kitchen prepares memorable dishes such as smoked salmon with pinenuts, veal parmesan and homemade lasagna with pesto, mushrooms and Oregon filberts. The prix-fixe menu is standard, but all items can be ordered à la carte. Don't despair if you can't get a reservation because there's nearly always seating available at the counter. Dinner only. Closed Monday. ~ 521 East 3rd Street, McMinnville; 503-434-4471, 888-456-2511; www.nicksitaliancafe.com, e-mail nickscafe@onlinemac.com. MODERATE TO ULTRA-DELUXE.

strel shows. Now the building is a prime shopping area. ~ 189 Northeast Liberty Street, Salem; 503-391-4481; www.reedopera house.com.

The Mission Mill Museum's **Mission Mill Store** (503-585-7012) sells the usual assortment of postcards, gifts and collectibles as well as blankets, clothes and hats. In the same complex, **Jacquelynn's Boutique** (503-371-0707) features women's clothing and fine linens. ~ 1313 Mill Street Southeast, Salem.

An excellent place for regional arts and crafts—pottery, sculpture, paintings, prints and jewelry, for example—is the **Bush Barn Art Center**. Closed Monday. ~ 600 Mission Street Southeast, Salem; 503-581-2228, fax 503-371-3342; www.salemart.org.

The **Albany Visitors Association** provides a handy map and guide to the many antique shops in the downtown area. ~ 250 Broadalbin Street Southwest, Suite 110, Albany; 541-928-0911, 800-526-2256. **The Book Bin** offers a selection of used books. ~ 415 West 1st Avenue; 541-926-6869.

NIGHTLIFE

The **Oregon Symphony Association** offers classical concerts as well as a pops series. ~ 707 13th Street Southeast, Salem; 503-364-0149, 800-992-8499 (tickets).

Pentacle Theatre is a well-established community theater with eight plays each season. ~ 324 52nd Avenue Northwest, Salem; 503-364-7121, 503-485-4300 (tickets); www.pentacle theatre.org.

For belly dancing, big band music, folk, reggae, rock or bluegrass, check out **McMenamin's Boon's Treasury**. This circa-1860 two-story brick building has live music Wednesday through Saturday nights. Artworks are frequently exhibited. ~ 888 Liberty Street Northeast, Salem; 503-399-9062, fax 503-399-0074.

For live bluegrass, try **Lenora's Ghost** every other Thursday. On Saturday night, a deejay will play CDs you bring in. Friday nights, there's karaoke. Occasional cover. ~ 114 Main Street, Independence; 503-838-2937.

PARKS

BUSH'S PASTURE PARK The Bush Collection of old garden roses is one of the highlights in this 89-acre park south of the capital. They were originally collected from pioneer homesteads to represent roses brought west on the Oregon Trail. Also here are natural wildflower gardens, a collection of flowering trees, the **Bush Barn Art Center**, featuring Northwestern artists, and the **Bush Conservatory**, the West's second-oldest greenhouse. Amenities include a picnic area, restrooms and tours of the Bush House Museum (fee), a playground and gardens. ~ 600 Mission Street, entry off High Street Southeast, Salem; 503-588-2410.

WILLAMETTE MISSION STATE PARK
Set in orchards and hop fields south of Wheatland's landing, this

1680-acre Willamette River park is the site of an 1830s Methodist Mission. A monument commemorates these early settlers. In the midst of the park are the historic Wheatland Ferry landings. This shady spot is a delightful retreat on a warm day. Fishing for bass and bluegill is popular with anglers. There are picnic tables, kitchen shelter areas, electricity, fire rings, restrooms, and bike and equestrian trails. Parking fee, $3. ~ Wheatland Road, 12 miles north of Salem; 503-393-1172, fax 503-393-8863.

Silver Falls State Park's South Falls Lodge, home to the visitors center, was built by the CCC, who used native stone and logs in its construction.

SILVER FALLS STATE PARK If you're addicted to waterfalls, look no further. Located in twin lava-rock gorges created by Silver Creek's north and south forks, the 8700-acre park has ten waterfalls. Also here are hiking, biking and equestrian trails leading through an old-growth fir forest with towering maples and quaking aspen ideal for fall-color buffs. South Falls, a seven-mile roundtrip hike from the highway, has the biggest drop, 177 feet, or 25 feet more than Niagara Falls. You'll find picnic tables, a snack bar, a playground, a swimming area, restrooms, rustic group lodging, a nature lodge, a jogging trail, bike trails and a horse camp. Parking fee, $3. ~ Route 214, 26 miles east of Salem; 503-873-8681, fax 503-873-8925.

▲ There are 46 tent sites ($12 to $16 per night), 47 RV hookup sites ($16 to $20 per night), 6 horse-camp sites ($16 to $48 per night) and 14 cabins ($35 per night). Reservations: 800-452-5687.

HIDDEN ►

McDOWELL CREEK FALLS COUNTY PARK This forested glen is a perfect refuge. An easy hike across the creek and up through a fir forest takes you to a pair of scenic falls. On a weekday you may have this park to yourself. There are picnic tables and vault toilets. ~ Located 12 miles southeast of Lebanon via Fairview Road and McDowell Creek Drive; 541-967-3917, fax 541-924-6915; www.co.linn.or.us/parks, e-mail parks@co.linn.or.us.

LEWIS CREEK COUNTY PARK On the north shore of Foster Reservoir, Lewis Creek Park is a good spot to swim and enjoy other water sports. Troll for bass and trout in the lake. This day-use park includes 20 acres of open space and 20 acres of brush and forest, as well as plenty of fine views of the Cascades. Picnic tables and a boat dock are the facilities here. Closed October through April. Parking fee, $3. ~ Four miles northeast of Sweet Home. Take Route 20 east to Foster Dam and turn left at Quartzville Road. At North River Road turn left to the park; 541-967-3917, fax 541-924-6915; www.co.linn.or.us/parks, e-mail parks@co.linn.or.us.

CASCADIA STATE PARK On the South Santiam River Canyon, this 253-acre park has a beautiful one-mile trail leading to a waterfall. Largely forested with Douglas fir, the park also has an open meadow on the north river bank. You can fish for trout in the river. Facilities include restrooms and picnic tables. ~ Route 20, 14 miles east of Sweet Home; 541-367-6021, fax 541-367-3757.

▲ There are 25 primitive sites ($14 per night).

HIDDEN

WHITCOMB CREEK COUNTY PARK With its stunning rainforest terrain on the shores of ten-mile-long Green Peter Reservoir, this 328-acre park in the foothills east of Sweet Home is a winner. It offers spectacular views of the Cascades and good trout fishing. The park is forested with fir and deciduous trees. You'll find picnic tables and restrooms. Boat ramps into the reservoir are located about a mile away. Closed October through April. ~ From Sweet Home take Route 20 east to Foster Dam and turn left at Quartzville Road. Continue north 15 miles to the park; 541-967-3917, fax 541-924-6915.

▲ There are 39 tent sites ($11 per night).

Eugene Area

College towns are often inviting and Eugene is no exception. Climb one of the town buttes and you'll find the city surrounded by rich farmland and beckoning lakes and streams. With the Cascades and the McKenzie River Valley to the east and the Coast Mountains to the west, Eugene has an ideal location. Eugene is at its best in the fall when maples, black walnuts, chestnuts and cottonwood brighten the landscape. The city, used for the filming of the movie *Animal House*, offers sidewalk cafés, malled streets and upscale shops.

SIGHTS

Pick up touring ideas at the **Convention and Visitors' Association of Lane County Oregon**. Closed Sunday in winter. ~ 754 Olive Street, Eugene; 541-484-5307, 800-547-5445, fax 541-343-6335; www.travellanecounty.com, e-mail info@cvalco.org.

Stop by the **University of Oregon**'s 250-acre campus. You'll find an arboretum with over 2000 varieties of trees; weekday tours for prospective students are offered from Oregon Hall at 13th and Agate streets. ~ 541-346-3111, 800-232-3825; www.uoregon.edu.

Among the campus highlights is the **Museum of Natural and Cultural History**. This collection is a good way to orient yourself to the state's geology, flora, fauna and anthropology. Permanent exhibits cover Oregon's fossil history and archaeology. Closed Monday and during university holidays. Admission. ~ 1680 East 15th Avenue, Eugene; 541-346-3024, fax 541-346-5334; natural-history.uoregon.edu, e-mail mnh@uoregon.edu.

Also recommended is the **Jordan Schnitzer Museum of Art** at the University of Oregon. The colonnaded sculpture court with pool adjacent to the entrance is one of the campus's architectural highlights. The collection, one of the best in the state, displays American, European and a wide range of Asian artworks. Call for hours. ~ Just east of 14th and Kincaid streets, Eugene; 541-346-3027, fax 541-346-0976; uoma.uoregon.edu.

Eugene is big on adaptive reuse of commercial buildings like the **5th Street Public Market**, home to over 40 shops, a five-star restaurant, 10 cafés, a gallery, a farmers' market, a video arcade and a courtyard that's a popular venue for local musicians and artists. ~ 296 East 5th Avenue, Eugene; 541-484-0383, fax 541-686-1220; www.5thstreetmarket.com.

Nestled on the grounds of Alton Baker Park, the **Science Factory Children's Museum & Planetarium** offers over 50 interactive hands-on exhibits, a planetarium and a chance to romp around and explore an indoor-outdoor environment. Other amusements include a computer lab, tot spot, puppet theater and traveling exhibits. The planetarium is closed during the week. Closed Monday and Tuesday. Admission. ~ 2300 Leo Harris Parkway, Eugene; 541-687-7888, fax 541-484-9027; www.sciencefactory.org, e-mail info@sciencefactory.org.

Flight enthusiasts should not miss the **Oregon Air & Space Museum**, located on the southwest side of the Eugene Airport. The museum showcases vintage aircraft as well as exhibits on early flying aces and the history of space exploration. Closed Monday and Tuesday. Admission. ~ 90377 Boeing Drive, Eugene; 541-461-1101; www.oasm.org.

The prime attraction in the neighboring town of Springfield is the **Springfield Museum**, which has a section detailing the history of this timber-industry town (the first mill opened in 1853) and a gallery with changing exhibits of artwork, antique collections and Americana. Closed Sunday and Monday. ~ 590 Main Street, Springfield; 541-726-2300, fax 541-726-3688; e-mail redmond@ci.springfield.or.us.

No trip to the Eugene area is complete without an excursion into the nearby countryside. You can head east on **Route 126** along the McKenzie River or southeast on **Route 58** to Lookout Point Reservoir, Oakridge and Salt Creek Falls. **Route 5** takes you south to Cottage Grove. Row River Road leads east past Dorena Reservoir and several covered bridges to the historic **Bohemia Mining District**. This mountainous region was the scene of a mid-19th-century gold rush that proved to be a bust. Today, tourists roam the district by car and four-wheel-drive vehicles to see lost mines, ghost towns like Bohemia City and covered bridges.

Before setting out for this national forest area be sure to check with the **Cottage Grove Ranger Station** (541-767-5000, fax 541-767-5075). Because there are active mining claims in the area, it is important not to trespass. The **Cottage Grove Museum** has a major exhibit on the Bohemia District, as well as displays on the *Titanic* and a covered bridge. The museum is open weekend afternoons in winter and Wednesday through Sunday afternoons in summer. ~ Birch and H avenues, Cottage Grove; 541-942-3963.

The **Willamette Valley Scenic Loop** is a 195-mile adventure. It begins and ends in Cottage Grove, looping through Corvallis, Salem and Albany. This backroad journey includes historical sites, museums, covered bridges, ferries, parks, gardens and wineries. A detailed brochure is available at the **Convention and Visitors' Association of Lane County Oregon.** ~ 754 Olive Street, Eugene; 541-484-5307, 800-547-5445, fax 541-343-6335; www.travellanecounty.com, e-mail cvalco@cvalco.org.

The **Roseburg Visitors Center and Chamber of Commerce** offers a handy city tour guide. Closed Sunday in winter. ~ 410 South east Spruce Street, Roseburg; 541-672-9731, 800-444-9584, fax

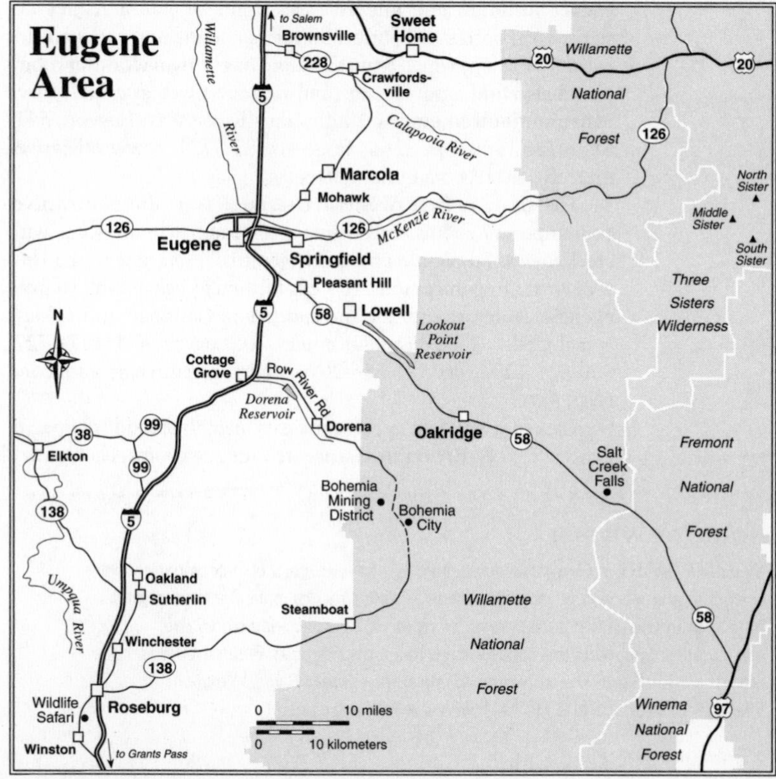

541-673-7868; www.visitroseburg.com, e-mail info@visitroseburg.com. Highlights include the **Roseburg Historic District** in the Mill Street/Pine Street neighborhood. You'll find many modest cottages built in the late 19th century. The **Floed-Lane House** is a Classic Revival featuring a full-length, two-tier veranda with half a dozen square columns supporting each level. It's open for tours on Sunday or by appointment. ~ 544 Southeast Douglas Street, Roseburg.

The **Douglas County Museum of History and Natural History** features American Indian and pioneer artifacts, a 19th-century railroad depot and natural history wildlife dioramas. Admission. ~ 123 Museum Drive, Roseburg; 541-957-7007, fax 541-957-7017; www.co.douglas.or.us/museum, e-mail museum@co.douglas.or.us.

LODGING

Valley River Inn enjoys an enviable view of the Willamette River. Adjacent to the 140-store Valley River Center, this 257-room hotel features Indian quilts hanging over the big lobby fireplace that faces a conversation pit. Large rooms, decorated with either wicker furniture and impressionist prints or Laura Ashley designs, open onto small patios. Bicycling and jogging paths are adjacent to the inn, which rents bikes and has its own workout room. You'll also find a pool, sauna and jacuzzi as well as a full-service restaurant and lounge. ~ 1000 Valley River Way, Eugene; 541-687-0123, 800-543-8266, fax 541-683-5121; www.valleyriverinn.com. DELUXE TO ULTRA-DELUXE.

The 65-unit **Best Western Greentree Inn** offers attractive, contemporary rooms with sitting areas and balconies, some with creek views. Some units have refrigerators. Adjacent to the University of Oregon campus, this establishment has a pool, jacuzzi, exercise center, restaurant and sports bar. Continental breakfast is included. ~ 1759 Franklin Boulevard, Eugene; 541-485-2727, 800-528-1234, fax 541-686-2094; e-mail greentreeinn@aol.com. MODERATE.

Tucked away in a quiet university neighborhood, the **Secret Garden Bed & Breakfast** features ten unique rooms, each with a

NONSTOP WILDLIFE

Wildlife Safari is Oregon's drive-through adventure, a 600-acre park where over 500 animals and birds roam freely. Visitors motor past Bactrian camels, hippopotamuses, lions, and scores of other species. In addition to the self-paced driving tour, the Safari Village has a petting zoo. Elephant rides are also available in the summer. Admission. ~ Safari Road, Winston; 541-679-6761, fax 541-679-9210; www.wildlifesafari.org.

different garden theme. The Scented Garden room is furnished in sumptuous colors and Indian and Tibetan antiques, while the Apiary is decorated in French country style. A striking mural in the upstairs sitting room depicts the mythical Daphne in the middle of her metamorphosis into a tree. Naturally, the landscaped grounds are meticulous and lovely. Full breakfast included. ~ 1910 University Street, Eugene; 541-484-6755, fax 541-431-1699; www.secretgardenbbinn.com, e-mail innkeeper@secretgardenbbinn.com. DELUXE TO ULTRA-DELUXE.

Pick your favorite musician at the **Excelsior Inn,** where classical composers such as Beethoven, Strauss and Verdi lend their names to guest accommodations. Each of the 14 musical rooms is distinctly decorated in dark cherry furniture, with elegant touches like writing desks, armoires, sleigh beds, arched windows and vaulted ceilings. Full breakfast from the inn's fine restaurant included. ~ 754 East 13th Street, Eugene; 541-342-6963, 800-321-6963; www.excelsiorinn.com, e-mail info@excelsiorinn.com. MODERATE TO ULTRA-DELUXE.

Business travelers will appreciate **The Oval Door Bed & Breakfast** for its corporate rates, high-speed internet connection, fax machines and in-room data ports. For tourists, though, there are plenty of other things to be excited about, including the gourmet breakfast prepared each morning by the owners/chefs. Relax away from the office with complimentary wine, tea and cookies. Within walking distance of downtown, the inn offers five rooms with private baths and floral decor. ~ 988 Lawrence Street, Eugene; 541-683-3160, 800-882-3160, fax 541-485-0260; www.ovaldoor.com, e-mail ovaldoor@ovaldoor.com. MODERATE TO ULTRA-DELUXE.

Overlooking Eugene, **The Campbell House** offers peaceful and elegant accommodations within walking distance to both city center and outdoor pursuits. The 18 rooms are individually decorated; all have a Victorian flavor with modern amenities. Some have fireplaces and jacuzzis. You'll also find a comfortable parlor and library. Full breakfast is served. ~ 252 Pearl Street, Eugene; 541-343-1119, 800-264-2519, fax 541-343-2258; www.campbellhouse.com, e-mail campbellhouse@campbellhouse.com. MODERATE TO ULTRA-DELUXE.

DINING

The emphasis at **Sweetwaters** is on Oregon cuisine featuring locally grown veal, lamb, lettuce, herbs, mushrooms and fruits. Seafood entrées include grilled salmon, Dungeness crab chowder and fresh swordfish. This contemporary dining room overlooking the Willamette River is complemented by a deck ideal for drinks before or after dinner. ~ Valley River Inn, 1000 Valley River Way, Eugene; 541-341-3462, fax 541-687-0289; www.valleyriverinn.com. MODERATE TO ULTRA-DELUXE.

Ambrosia prepares Italian specialties in a red-brick building distinguished by leaded glass, a mirrored oak and mahogany backbar, Tiffany-style lamps and a tintype ceiling. You'll find pizzas and calzones made with a plum tomato sauce, pasta and entrées like grilled fresh lamb and fresh seafood. There are 325 vintages on the wine list, including 30 ports. Outdoor dining is available. No lunch on Saturday and Sunday. ~ 174 East Broadway, Eugene; 541-342-4141, fax 541-345-6965. MODERATE TO DELUXE.

For pasta dishes, fresh salmon, lamb, steaks and generous salads, the **Excelsior Inn and Ristorante Italiano** is a good choice. Located in a Victorian near the university, this pleasing restaurant also has an excellent Oregon and Italian wine list and a generous brunch on Sunday. Ask for a table on the terrace. Open for breakfast, lunch and dinner; but no lunch on Saturday. ~ 754 East 13th Avenue, Eugene; 541-342-6963, 800-321-6963, fax 541-342-1417; www.excelsiorinn.com, e-mail info@excelsiorinn.com. MODERATE TO DELUXE.

HIDDEN ►

Café Zenon, an elegant, yuppified establishment with slate floor, marble tables, white tile and outdoor seating, has an eclectic menu that changes daily. Some of the more popular items are oysters Bienville, fettuccine rustica and Tuscan roast rabbit. There are an extensive wine list and excellent desserts. Open for breakfast, lunch and dinner. ~ 898 Pearl Street, Eugene; 541-343-3005. DELUXE.

Mekala's Thai Cuisine serves authentic Thai recipes and boasts nearly 100 items, including traditional curries, noodle dishes, stir frys, soups and seafood. There is heated outdoor seating, and a full bar downstairs. ~ 1769 Franklin Avenue, Eugene; 541-342-4872. MODERATE.

Situated between downtown and the university area, the **High Street Brewery and Café** is an ideal place to check out the locals and one of the café's inventive microbrews—from fruit beers to

AUTHOR FAVORITE

For a lively night on the town, I head to the **Oregon Electric Station Restaurant and Lounge**, a historic building magnificently reborn as a club-like dining and entertainment venue with oak paneling, high-backed tapestry chairs and antique train cars serving as dining areas. On weekends, jazz and blues bands elevate the mood. Fresh grilled seafood and prime rib highlight the menu. No lunch on weekends. ~ 27 East 5th Avenue, Eugene; 541-485-4444, fax 541-484-6149; www.oesrestaurant.com. MODERATE TO DELUXE.

pale ales to stout. Decorated with music posters from the 1960s, the café also serves soups, salads and sandwiches. The wooden booths and tables are conducive to long afternoons or late evenings, and there is also a large covered deck out back. ~ 1243 High Street, Eugene; 541-345-4905. BUDGET.

Tolly's Soda Fountain is one of the most inviting lunch counters in Oregon. Located in a brick building, Tolly's is an architectural landmark with a mirrored backbar, varnished mahogany counters and stools, brass footrests and Tiffany lamps. Enjoy a soda, milkshake or banana split. Also available are breakfast potatoes and eggs, as well as Reuben sandwiches, croissants, lasagna and fresh strawberry pie. The budget-priced breakfasts and lunches are bargains; dinner brings a higher price tag. No dinner on Monday and Tuesday. ~ 115 Locust Street, Oakland; 541-459-3796, fax 541-459-1833. MODERATE TO DELUXE.

SHOPPING

The largest shopping mall between San Francisco and Portland is Eugene's **Valley River Center**, which has several large department stores and nearly 130 shops and restaurants. ~ 293 Valley River Drive, Eugene; 541-683-5513.

The 5th Street Public Market has an impressive collection of shops and galleries. Among the best is **New Twist** (541-342-8686). ~ 296 East 5th Street, Eugene; 541-484-0383.

Dozens of other arts-and-crafts galleries are found in the Eugene area. **Ruby Chasm** sells necklaces, books, ceramics and tribal art. ~ 152 West 5th Avenue, Eugene; 541-344-4074.

Eugene's **Saturday Market** is an open-air marketplace held weekly from April through November, with more than 150 vendors selling everything from handcrafted furniture to quilts to floral arrangements. There are also a farmer's market, an international food court and live music. Holiday Market is held at the Lane County Fairgrounds weekends from Thanksgiving week to Christmas eve. ~ 8th and Oak streets, Eugene; 541-686-8885, fax 541-338-4248; www.eugenesaturdaymarket.org, e-mail info@eugenesaturdaymarket.org.

The cooperative **Circle of Hands** gallery offers paintings, sculpture, ceramics, jewelry and clothing by artists and craftspeople from the Eugene area. ~ 1030 Willamette Avenue, Eugene; 541-342-4957.

If you're searching for rocks and minerals, American Indian art or books on Northwest natural history, head for the **University of Oregon Museum Store**. Open Wednesday through Sunday afternoons. ~ 1680 East 15th Avenue, Eugene; 541-346-3024.

One of the most comprehensive feminist women's bookstores in the Northwest is **Mother Kali's Books**. Closed Sunday. ~ 720 East 13th Avenue, Eugene; 541-343-4864.

Housed in a circular 1924 landmark is the **Round Tu-it Gift Shop**, which sells Oregon crafts and food items, antiques, collectibles and homemade fudge. ~ 945 Gateway Boulevard, Cottage Grove; 541-942-9023.

NIGHTLIFE

The **Hult Center for the Performing Arts** is the home of the summer Oregon Bach Festival, Oregon Mozart Players, Eugene Concert Choir, Eugene's symphony, opera and ballet, as well as visiting artists from around the world. Performances take place in Silva Hall or the smaller Soreng Theater. ~ Between 6th and 7th avenues and Willamette and Olive streets, Eugene; 541-682-5000, fax 541-682-2700; www.hultcenter.org.

Three theater companies make their home in Eugene. The **University Theater** stages full-scale productions in the Robinson Theater and smaller plays in the Arena Theater. ~ Villard Hall; 541-346-4191, fax 541-346-1978; theatre.uoregon.edu. The **Very Little Theater,** which stages five productions a year, is considered one of the best community theaters in the Eugene area. ~ 2450 Hilyard Street; 541-344-7751. The **Actors Cabaret/Mainstage Theater** presents Broadway and off-Broadway comedies, dramas and musicals. ~ 996 Willamette Street; 541-683-4368, fax 541-485-5503; www.actorscabaret.org, e-mail cabaret1@aol.com.

An old standby for live reggae, rock, and folk shows is **W.O.W. Hall**, a 400-person venue and beer garden. Shows here are sponsored by the Community Center for the Performing Arts. ~ 291 West 8th Avenue, Eugene; 541-687-2746.

Allann Brothers Coffee House hosts an array of live performances including zydeco, blues, salsa, jazz, folk and classical trios on some Friday and Saturday nights. ~ 152 West 5th Street, Eugene; 541-342-3378, 800-926-6886, fax 541-342-4255.

One of Eugene's premier brewpubs is **Steelhead Brewery & Café**, which has a handsome brick interior filled with large palms and ficus trees, marble tables and a mahogany bar. The pub offers cable sports stations, beers from the adjoining microbrewery and a casual menu. ~ 199 East 5th Avenue, Eugene; 541-686-2739, fax 541-342-5338.

For jazz, try **Jo Federigo's Café & Jazz Bar**. An intimate cellar setting with hanging plants, fans and modern art provides the background for some of the region's finest musicians. Cover Friday through Sunday. ~ 259 East 5th Avenue, Eugene; 541-343-8488; www.jofeds.com.

The Valley River Inn's **Sweetwaters** presents live entertainment in a fireplace lounge setting on Friday and Saturday nights. On warm nights the strains of rhythm-and-blues, rock and standards drift out to the big deck overlooking the Willamette. ~ 1000

Bridging the Past

Oregon takes pride in the fact that it has more covered bridges (53) than any other state west of the Mississippi. Most of these wooden spans are found in the Willamette Valley, although a handful are scattered along the coast, in the Cascades, the Ashland–Rogue River area and around Bend. Although some have been retired and now serve only pedestrians and cyclists, all these bridges are worth a special trip.

Originally the idea of covering a bridge was to protect its plank deck and trusses from the elements. But aesthetics eventually proved as important as engineering, and Oregon's beautiful hooded spans became one of the state's signature attractions.

Highly recommended is the Calapooia River's **Crawfordsville Bridge** (Route 228) east of Brownsville. Clustered around the nearby agricultural communities of Crabtree and Scio are many other "kissing bridges" such as **Shimanek**, **Larwood** and **Hannah**. To the south, Lane County is home to 18 covered bridges, all listed on the National Register of Historic Places. The Lowell area, on Route 58 southeast of Eugene, has four spans, including the **Lowell Bridge**, which crosses a river later flooded to create a lake. Other bridges are at **Pengra**, **Unity** and **Parvin**. A highlight in the Cottage Grove area is **Chambers Bridge**, the only "roofed" railroad bridge on the West Coast. In the same region, south of Dorena Reservoir, is **Dorena Bridge**. Other covered bridges in the same area are found at **Mosby Creek** and **Currin**.

Douglas County has a number of fine spans. One is **Mott Bridge**, 22 miles east of Glide. Constructed in the '30s, this on-deck wood-truss arch bridge may be the only bridge of this type in the country. The **Rochester Bridge** (County Road 10A) west of Sutherlin is also historic. After county highway workers burned down a bridge in the late 1950s, residents feared the beloved Rochester nearby was destined for the same fate. Armed with shotguns, they kept an all-night vigil and saved the span.

Take the time to visit **Weddle Bridge** in Sweet Home. In 1987, after 43 years of service, it was damaged but, thanks to strong protests, the county wisely decided to take the bridge apart piece by piece and put it in storage. Donations and promotions raised $190,000 to reassemble the bridge, originally built in 1937 for $8500.

Great guides include *Roofs over Rivers* (Oregon Sentinel Publishing) by Bill & Nick Cockrell and *Oregon Covered Bridges: An Oregon Documentary in Pictures* (Pacific Northwest Book Company) by Bert and Margie Webber. Or contact the **Covered Bridge Society of Oregon**. ~ 503-399-0436.

Valley River Way, Eugene; 541-341-3462, fax 541-683-5121; www.valleyriverinn.com.

Sam Bond's Garage really feels like your next-door neighbor's garage-turned-music-venue, complete with wooden rafters. The atmosphere, consequently, is laidback and comfortable, with a small stage and tables. The crowd is more alternative than trendy; you'll see more dreadlocks than tube tops. There's live music every night, featuring local bands as well as touring artists. ~ 407 Blair Boulevard, Eugene; 542-343-2635; www.sambonds.com.

PARKS

BROWNSVILLE PIONEER PARK The forested, 25-acre city park along the banks of the Calapooia River is a short walk from the center of a historic Willamette Valley community. There are big playfields, shady glens and a spacious picnic area with picnic tables and restrooms. ~ Take Route 5 north from Eugene 22 miles to Route 228 and continue east four miles. An alternative scenic loop heads north from Springfield via Mohawk, Marcola and Crawfordsville; 541-466-5666, fax 541-466-5118.

▲ Permitted, though there are no formal sites; $10 per night for tents, $15 per night for RVs. Campgrounds are closed mid-October to mid-April.

HENDRICKS PARK AND RHODODENDRON GARDEN A glorious springtime spot when over 3500 rhododendrons and azaleas brighten the landscape. The 78-acre park is shaded by Oregon white oaks and Douglas fir. There are picnic tables, restrooms, trails and occasional Sunday tours during bloom season (call ahead). ~ Located at the east end of Summit Avenue, Eugene; 541-682-5324, fax 541-682-6834.

Ashland–Rogue River Area

If your vision of a good vacation is river rafting by day and Shakespeare by night, look no further. With the Klamath-Siskiyou mountains providing a rugged backdrop, this section of southern Oregon supports an array of fun activities: river rafting, downhill skiing, and, yes, the West Coast's best Shakespeare festival. Home of the largest concentration of bed and breakfasts in Oregon, Ashland is also your gateway to backcountry famous for its hidden gems.

The wild and scenic Rogue River is one of Oregon's signature attractions. It is also convenient to wilderness areas, mountain lakes, thundering waterfalls, marble caves and popular resort communities.

SIGHTS

A good place to orient yourself is the **Grants Pass Visitors Center**. Closed weekends from September through May. ~ 1995 Northwest Vine Street at 6th Street, Grants Pass; 541-476-5510, fax 541-476-9574; www.visitgrantspass.org, e-mail vcb@visitgrantspass.org.

Wildlife Images is a fascinating animal rehabilitation center. Each year more than 1500 injured animals are nursed back to health by veterinary staff and volunteers. Among the creatures you can see being treated are owls, eagles, black bears and cougars. Highly recommended. Daily tours are offered by appointment. ~ 11845 Lower River Road, Grants Pass; 541-476-0222, fax 541-476-2444; www.wildlifeimages.org, e-mail wildima@cdsnet.net. ◄HIDDEN

Pottsville Powerland has a vintage collection of tractors, farm and logging equipment, antique cars and fire trucks. A fair on Father's Day weekend features music, food, arts and crafts. It's five miles north of Grants Pass. ~ Pleasant Valley Road west of Monument Drive, Pleasant Valley; 541-479-2981. ◄HIDDEN

Although it's far from the core of Oregon's wine country, **Bridgeview Vineyards** is attracting a loyal following. Situated on 74 acres in the Illinois Valley, this European-style winery offers tastings. Try the gewürztraminer, chardonnay, merlot, pinot gris, pinot noir or riesling. ~ 4210 Holland Loop Road, Cave Junction; 541-592-4688, 877-273-4843, fax 541-592-2127; www.bridgeview wine.com, e-mail bvw@bridgeviewwine.com.

The **Oregon Caves National Monument** is the Pacific Northwest's grandest spelunking adventure. Fifty miles southwest of

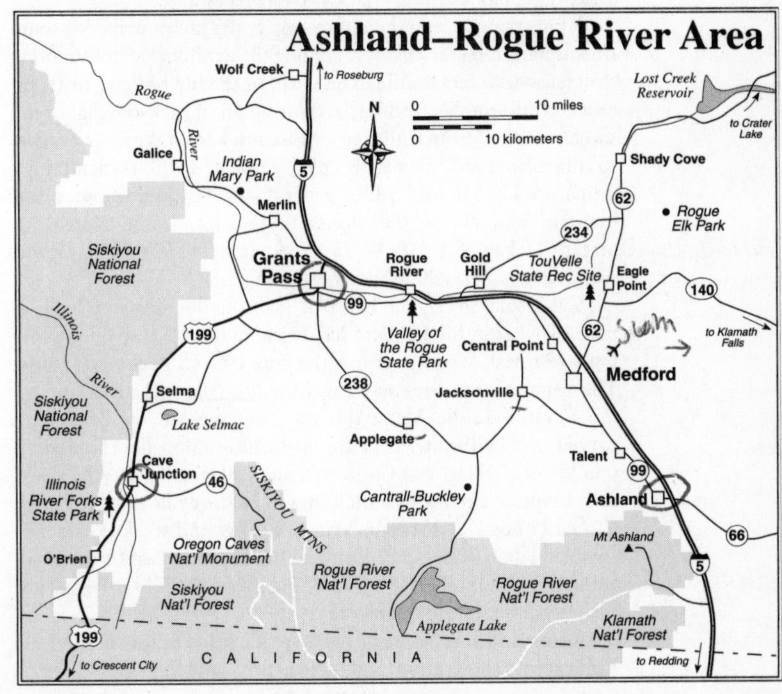

Grants Pass, it's reached by taking Route 199 to Cave Junction and then continuing east on Route 46. Five daily guided tours are led through the cave, which has over three miles of damp and dripping passageways lined with stalagmites, flowstone, translucent draperies and cave coral. Wear sturdy walking shoes that you don't mind getting muddy and a jacket—the caves are a constant 42°F. The tour is not recommended for those with respiratory or heart problems. Closed December through March. Admission. ~ 20000 Caves Highway, Cave Junction; 541-592-2100; www.nps.gov/orca.

> To avoid the summer crowds at Oregon Caves National Monument, arrive when the park opens at 9 a.m. If you can't make it before 11 a.m., your best bet is to visit after 4 p.m. for a late afternoon tour.

Southeast of Grants Pass is **Jacksonville**, a 19th-century mining town that has clung to its legendary frontier tradition. The entire town has been designated a National Historic Landmark with over 100 homes, stores and public buildings. Stop at the **Jacksonville Visitor's Center and Chamber of Commerce** to pick up a walking-tour map of the town's tree-lined streets. Closed Sunday in winter. ~ 185 North Oregon Street, Jacksonville; 541-899-8118, 800-727-7570, fax 541-899-4462; www.jacksonvilleoregon.org, e-mail chamber@jacksonvilleoregon.org.

Along the way you'll want to stop at the **Jacksonville Museum of Southern Oregon History**. Among the exhibits are gold-mining artifacts and a large-scale exhibit about the life of Peter Britt, pioneer photographer and Renaissance man of Jacksonville. In the same complex is the **Children's Museum**. Kids, take your parents to this former jail filled with "please touch" exhibits including a miniature kitchen and 1890s general store. Closed Monday and Tuesday, and during the month of January. ~ 206 North 5th Street, Jacksonville; 541-773-6536, fax 541-776-7994; www.sohs.org, e-mail publicrelations@sohs.org.

California Street, the heart of Jacksonville, is a step back in time. The graceful balustraded brick buildings have been lovingly restored. Worth a visit is the gothic **C. C. Beekman House.** The living history tour re-creates the lifestyle of the rich and famous, circa 1876. Along the way you see banker Beekman's carved oak bedframe, overstuffed furniture, lap desk and summer kitchen. Nearby at California and 3rd streets, visit the **Beekman Bank**, one of the first buildings in Jacksonville to be restored. Closed Labor Day through Memorial Day and weekdays in December. Admission. ~ 352 East California Street east of Beekman Square, Jacksonville; 541-773-6536, fax 541-776-7994; www.sohs.org, e-mail info@sohs.org.

Route 238 southwest of Jacksonville leads to the picturesque **Applegate Valley**, a two-mile-wide, fifty-mile-long canyon with memorable views and few tourists. After reaching the town of Applegate you can continue south on Applegate Road to the foot of the Siskiyous. Alternatively, Little Applegate and Anderson Creek roads loop back to Route 99.

Located about ten miles east of Jacksonville via Route 238, **Medford** is by far the largest city in the vicinity of Ashland and the Rogue River. A much-frequented stop in the area is **Harry and David's Original Country Village**, famous for the gift packs it ships nationwide. The store has a fruit stand, gourmet pantry and gift shop. Weekday tours of the packinghouse depart from the gift store. ~ 1314 Center Drive, Medford; 541-864-2277, 877-322-8000.

The **Medford Visitors & Convention Bureau** is an excellent source of information on southern Oregon. ~ 101 East 8th Street, Medford; 541-779-4847, fax 541-776-4808; www.visitmedford.org.

The nearby **Southern Oregon Historical Society's Historical Center** has an extensive collection of Jackson County artifacts as well as a large photography exhibit and research library. ~ 106 North Central Avenue, Medford; 541-773-6536, fax 541-776-7994; www.sohs.org, e-mail info@sohs.org.

Ten miles north of Medford off Route 62, **Butte Creek Mill** has been producing stone-ground products since 1872. Occasionally you may see the miller grinding wheat, rye and corn on giant white stones quarried in France, assembled in Illinois, shipped around the Horn to California and finally brought over the Siskiyous by wagon. Closed Sunday. ~ 402 Royal Avenue North, Eagle Point; 541-826-3531. ◄ HIDDEN

While **Ashland** is best known for the Oregon Shakespeare Festival, the play is not the only thing here. From shopping to restaurants to biking, this city offers plenty of diversions. Home to more bed and breakfasts than any other city in the state, Ashland has strict zoning controls that protect the architectural landscape.

To explore the possibilities, stop by the **Ashland Chamber of Commerce.** Closed weekends. ~ 110 East Main Street, Ashland; 541-482-3486, fax 541-482-2350; www.ashlandchamber.com, e-mail dana@ashlandchamber.com. A good place to begin your visit is the downtown plaza and verdant Lithia Park (see "Parks" below).

Across the street is the **Oregon Shakespeare Festival** and the fascinating **Backstage Theatre Tour**. This excellent behind-the-scenes program is a helpful introduction to stagecraft and the history of the OSF. Members of the theater company guide you through this 90-minute look at the dramatic arts. Closed November to mid-February. Admission. ~ 15 South Pioneer Street, Ashland; 541-482-4331, fax 541-482-8045; www.osfashland.org.

Most people come to Ashland for the plays, but the mountain lakes east of town are a tempting day trip. Take Route 5 north and pick up Route 140 east to Dead Indian Road. Turn south to the first and most picturesque of these retreats, **Lake of the Woods**, an ideal place for a picnic, swimming or sunbathing. Continue southeast to **Howard Prairie Reservoir** and **Hyatt Reservoir**, both popular for water sports and fishing. Return to Dead Indian Road for the cliffhanging descent back into Ashland, an entrance that rivals anything you're likely to see on the Elizabethan stage.

LODGING

An 1880s stage stop, **Wolf Creek Inn** now operates as a state historic property. The handsomely restored inn offers nine guest rooms with private baths. You'll find antiques, old photographs and brass beds in the medium-sized rooms. There's an on-site restaurant, and full breakfast is included in your stay. You can also see the room where Jack London stayed on his visit here. ~ 100 Front Street, Wolf Creek; 541-866-2474, fax 541-866-2692; www.wolfcreekinn.com, e-mail innkeeper@wolfcreekinn.com. MODERATE.

The **Pine Meadow Inn** is a relaxing bed-and-breakfast retreat surrounded by nine acres of meadows and woods. Four upstairs guest rooms are furnished with antiques and cozy comforts like fresh flowers, quilts and private baths. Enjoy the extensive library and the gardens, sit by the *koi* pond and waterfalls, or soak in the outdoor hot tub. Closed November through January. ~ 1000 Crow Road, Merlin; 541-471-6277, 800-554-0806, fax 541-471-6277; www.pinemeadowinn.com, e-mail pmi@pinemeadowinn.com. MODERATE TO DELUXE.

The **Riverside Inn** is the largest motel in town with an enviable location on the Rogue River across from Riverside Park. This 145-unit inn's large rooms and kitchenette suites are furnished with comfortable sofas and easy chairs. Most rooms have private balconies overlooking the river; some have whirlpool tubs and fireplaces. In some cases you can pick blackberries from your deck. There is a day spa, a beauty salon, and a full-service conference center, plus a swimming pool and spa. A Rogue jet-boat dock is next door, and there is some highway noise from the bridge traffic. ~ 971 Southeast 6th Street, Grants Pass; 541-476-6873, 800-334-4567, fax 541-474-9848; www.riverside-inn.com, e-mail info@riverside-inn.com. MODERATE TO DELUXE.

The Weasku Inn Resort features 17 units that include rooms in the main lodge, larger river suites that may be equipped with fireplaces, private decks and whirlpool tubs, and an A-frame cabin. Rooms have king- or queen-sized beds and are decorated in Pacific Northwest furnishings. Surrounded by fragrant pine trees, the riverfront setting offers great fishing and peaceful relaxation. Complimentary wine and cheese are served each evening, and an expanded continental breakfast is included in the rate. ~ 5560 Rogue River Highway, Grants Pass; 541-471-8000, 800-493-2758, fax 541-474-9848; www.weasku.com. ULTRA-DELUXE.

The **Oregon Caves Chateau**, in a wooded glen surrounded by waterfalls, is an ideal place to spend the night after a visit to the Oregon Caves National Monument. Faced with cedar shakes, this National Historic Landmark has two big marble fireplaces framed with fir timbers in the lobby. Moderate-sized rooms with 1930s furnishings and Pendleton bedspreads offer forest and pond views in this serene setting. Closed November through April. ~ 20000 Caves Highway, Cave Junction; 541-592-3400, fax 541-592-5021; www.oregoncavesoutfitters.com, e-mail caves@cavenet.com. MODERATE TO DELUXE.

The historic red-brick **Jacksonville Inn** offers eight nicely restored rooms with oak-frame beds, quilts, wall-to-wall carpets, antiques, gas-style lamps and floral-print wallpaper. The inn also has four honeymoon cottages, featuring king beds, fireplaces, jacuzzis and steam showers, located on a separate property. Full breakfast included. ~ 175 East California Street, Jacksonville; 541-899-1900, 800-321-9344, fax 541-899-1373; www.jacksonvilleinn.com, e-mail jvinn@mind.net. DELUXE TO ULTRA-DELUXE.

Rooms at the **Stage Lodge**, a faux-Victorian motel, are filled with cherry-wood furniture, armoires, ceiling fans and wall-to-wall carpets. Suites include wet bars, microwaves and double spas. There's some highway noise in the front units. ~ 830 North 5th Street, Jacksonville; 541-899-3953, 800-253-8254, fax 541-899-7556. DELUXE.

Convenient to downtown Jacksonville, the **McCully House Inn** is a charming 19th-century home where a grandfather clock sounds the hour and guests sip wine around the fireplace. This immaculate white house has hardwood floors, painted friezes on the

AUTHOR FAVORITE

Choose one of the Bard's works from the library and wander out to the lush gardens that surround the **Arden Forest Inn**. Nestle into a secluded spot and catch up on the play you're about to see at the Shakespeare Festival. The inn also has fine views of Mt. Ashland and Grizzly Peak. Two rooms in the main house and three in the carriage house feature tasteful, comfortable furnishings; some have mountain or garden views, others have private patios. The two-course gourmet breakfast is a delight. Gay-owned and gay-friendly. ~ 261 West Hersey Street, Ashland; 541-488-1496, 800-460-3912, fax 541-488-4071; www.afinn.com, e-mail aforest@afinn.com. DELUXE TO ULTRA-DELUXE.

walls and three rooms big on lace, walnut furniture and clawfoot tubs. The adjacent restaurant serves breakfast to all guests. ~ 240 East California Street, Jacksonville; 541-899-1942, 800-367-1942, fax 541-899-1560; www.mccullyhouseinn.com, e-mail mccully houseinn@charter.net. DELUXE.

Take an 1862 country estate, complete with a three-story barn, add a redwood deck, an English garden with 140 rose bushes and an orchard with hammocks and what do you get? **Under the Greenwood Tree Bed and Breakfast Inn**. Overfurnished with Persian rugs, Chippendale and chintz, this is the place for travelers who want to wind down with a full afternoon tea and pluck a truffle off their freshly ironed pillow before climbing into bed. Five rooms have queen beds and private baths. A regional three-course, farm-fresh breakfast prepared by a Cordon Bleu chef is included. ~ 3045 Bellinger Lane, Medford; 541-776-0000; www.greenwoodtree.com, e-mail utgtree@quest.net. DELUXE.

HIDDEN ►

Tour the world at the **Ashland Creek Inn**, where you can "visit" New Mexico, Marrakesh or Japan, depending on which internationally themed suite you choose. All seven suites include private entrances, baths, kitchenettes and decks. Full breakfast included. ~ 70 Water Street, Ashland; 541-482-3315; www.ash landcreekinn.com, e-mail reservations@ashlandcreekinn.com. DELUXE TO ULTRA-DELUXE.

Reached via a redwood staircase, the **Columbia Hotel** is a comfortable European-style inn. Rooms are furnished with brass beds, floral-print drapes, fans and wall-to-wall carpet. Some provide views of downtown and the surrounding mountains. Guests share a bathroom; suites with private baths are available ~ 262½ East Main Street, Ashland; 541-482-3726, 800-718-2530; www.columbiahotel.com. MODERATE.

The **Windmill Inn of Ashland** has 230 affordable and charming rooms with the amenities of a city hotel. Tennis courts, a heated outdoor pool and spa, and a fitness room on 14 acres add to the comfort of this country inn. ~ 2525 Ashland Street, Ashland; 541-482-8310, 800-547-4747, fax 541-488-1783; www.windmillinns.com. DELUXE.

Cedarwood Inn of Ashland is one of several modern motels found south of downtown. Choose between rooms with queens and courtyard family units with kitchens and decks. All 64 rooms have contemporary oak furniture. Pools, saunas and barbecue facilities are available. ~ 1801 Siskiyou Boulevard, Ashland; 541-488-2000, 800-547-4141, fax 541-482-2000; www.brodeur-inns.com/cedarwood. MODERATE TO DELUXE.

Set on 23 acres of oak-savannah hills just east of Ashland is the artists' retreat-like **A-Dome Studio**. A large wooden dome houses the two beautiful guest suites, each with pine interior and

HIDDEN ►

hardwood floors, a queen-size bed, a private bath and a spiraling staircase that leads to a loft with two twin beds. The ambience is homey yet elegant; patchwork quilts, stained-glass windows and country-western decor give the place a rugged charm. Other amenities include an open and sunny common space with a full kitchen, living room and natural stone fireplace. A pond on the property adds to the peaceful setting. ~ 8550 Dead Indian Memorial Road, Ashland; 541-482-1755, 541-488-8635; www.mind.net/adome, e-mail adome@mind.net. DELUXE.

Ashland is heavily booked during the Shakespeare season (mid-February to late October) when street vendors are out in force selling espresso.

For information on Ashland bed and breakfasts, and other inns across Oregon, check out **The Oregon Bed and Breakfast Guild.** ~ www.obbg.org. You may also contact **Ashland's Bed and Breakfast Network.** ~ 800-944-0329; www.abbnet.com.

DINING

Clam chowder is the staple at **The Laughing Clam.** Stop by for lunch or dinner and choose from sandwiches, large salads, fresh seafood and pasta (including the Seafood Mama—shrimp, scallops and clams in a cream sauce over lemon linguine), and steak. ~ 121 Southwest G Street, Grants Pass; 541-479-1110. MODERATE TO DELUXE.

Traversing a stream, the **Oregon Caves Chateau Restaurant** offers steaks, seafood, chicken and pasta dishes for dinner in the deluxe-priced formal dining room. There's also a 1930s-style budget-priced soda fountain. Scores of patrons seated on red stools enjoy sundaes, omelettes, french toast, salads, deli sandwiches and hamburgers. Don't miss this knotty-pine-paneled classic. Closed November through April. ~ 20000 Caves Highway, Cave Junction; 541-592-3400, fax 541-592-5021; www.oregoncaves outfitters.com, e-mail caves@cavenet.com. MODERATE TO ULTRA-DELUXE.

The **Jacksonville Inn** serves breakfast, lunch, dinner and Sunday brunch in the restored 19th-century Ryan and Morgan general-store building. The dimly lit, brick-walled dining room with red carpets and tablecloths creates a great setting for vast, seven-course dinners or à la carte dishes. A large menu features Oregon cuisine, including razor clams, scallops, prime rib and vegetarian dishes. The wine list is endless. No lunch on Monday. ~ 175 East California Street, Jacksonville; 541-899-1900; www.jacksonvilleinn.com, e-mail jvinn@mind.net. DELUXE TO ULTRA-DELUXE.

For patio dining, it's hard to beat the **McCully House Inn.** Entrées served outside or in one of the lovely dining rooms include mango-glazed salmon, tequila lime prawns and whiskey-peppered New York steak. You'll find Oregon wildflowers on every table. ~ 240 East California Street, Jacksonville; 541-899-1942, fax 541-

899-1560; www.mccullyhouseinn.com, e-mail mccullyhouse inn@charter.net. MODERATE TO ULTRA-DELUXE.

Outdoor seating with a creek running by is perfect for summer afternoons at **Back Porch Barb-B-Q.** Chow down on platters of barbecued chicken and ribs. ~ 605 North 5th Street, Jacksonville; 541-899-8821. MODERATE.

Phoenix-like, the **Bella Union** has risen from the ashes of one of Jacksonville's best-loved 19th-century saloons. Like its predecessor, this establishment is an important social center. On the menu you'll find pizza, seafood, pasta and sandwiches. You have your choice of several noisy dining rooms or the more serene heated patio out back. ~ 170 West California Street, Jacksonville; 541-899-1770, fax 541-899-3919; www.bellau.com, e-mail great food@bellau.com. MODERATE TO DELUXE.

Whether you choose a seat at the counter or one of the glass-paneled booths, you'll find the country-casual **Geppetto's** a comfortable place to enjoy Italian and Ashland cuisine like linguine, five-spice chicken, steak, prawns and snapper. Try the fresh fruit pies. Breakfast, lunch and dinner. ~ 345 East Main Street, Ashland; 541-482-1138; www.geppettosrestaurant.com, e-mail gep pettos@mricyberrom.com. MODERATE TO DELUXE.

The prime daytime gathering spot in town is the **Ashland Bakery & Cafe**, a sunny storefront eatery more commonly known as the "ABC." Menu offerings include buckwheat pancakes, deli sandwiches, salads, fruit muffins and other lunch/brunch fare; dinner in summer only. ~ 38 East Main Street, Ashland; 541-482-2117; www.ashlandbakery.com. BUDGET.

Looking for Asian cuisine served at a creekside setting? Consider **Thai Pepper**. Step into the romantic gray-walled dining room, take a seat on the wicker furniture and order such dishes as green chicken curry, yellow shrimp curry and crispy fish served with cold Singha beer. But your best bet, especially on a

AUTHOR FAVORITE

On a warm evening, the garden patio at the **Winchester Country Inn** is an ideal place to enjoy a rich, leisurely meal. Temptations here include Teng Dah beef, duck medallions, seafood cioppino, seasonal fish and lamb *du jour*. For dessert, try their award-winning bread pudding. This opulent Victorian, surrounded by a colorful garden, also has gazebo seating and a dining room decorated in burgundy tones with accents of blue. Dinner and Sunday brunch. ~ 35 South 2nd Street, Ashland; 541-488-1113, 800-972-4991; www.winchesterinn.com, e-mail ashland inn@aol.com. DELUXE.

warm evening, is a seat on the shady patio next to the creek. Dinner only. ~ 84 North Main Street, Ashland; 541-482-8058. BUDGET TO MODERATE.

A French bistro with stained-glass windows and dark wood-booths illuminated by Tiffany-style lamps, **Châteaulin Restaurant** prepares such dishes as *crêpe Mediterranées*, pan-roasted duck breast and filet mignon *au poivre verte*. Dinner only. Closed Monday from October through June. ~ 50 East Main Street, Ashland; 541-482-2264; www.chateaulin.com, e-mail doss@chateaulin.com. DELUXE TO ULTRA-DELUXE.

Alex's Plaza Restaurant has a good house pizza topped with pesto, pine nuts and cheese. Also on the menu are a vegetarian pasta with portobello mushrooms, seafood stew, New York steak and rack of lamb. Located in the first brick building built following the disastrous 1879 downtown fire, this second-story dining room still has its original fir floors. It's flanked by patios. No lunch on Monday. ~ 35 North Main Street, Ashland; 541-482-8818; www.mind.net/alexs, e-mail alexs@mind.net. MODERATE TO DELUXE.

Mediterranean, Italian and vegetarian fare served in a creek-side setting make the **Greenleaf Restaurant** worth a visit. Specialties may include breakfast dishes like mushroom frittatas and tofu scrambles. For lunch or dinner, try pasta primavera, fruit salad or red snapper. An excellent choice for to-go fare, they will also prepare picnic baskets. Closed Monday in winter and the month of January. ~ 49 North Main Street, Ashland; 541-482-2808; www.greenleafrestaurant.com, e-mail daniel@greenleaf restaurant.com. BUDGET TO MODERATE.

Brother's Restaurant and Delicatessen has an eclectic menu including shrimp omelettes, *huevos rancheros*, bagels and lox, and caesar and Greek salads. There's also a variety of vegetarian options. The carpeted, wood-paneled dining room with indoor balcony seating puts Brother's a cut above your average deli. Breakfast and lunch only. ~ 95 North Main Street, Ashland; 541-482-9671. BUDGET TO MODERATE.

SHOPPING

◄ HIDDEN

Fifteen miles northwest of Grants Pass is **Windy River Farms**, which has organic teas and culinary and medicinal herbs. ~ 348 Hussey Lane, Grants Pass; 541-476-8979.

Thread Hysteria stocks new name-brand clothing and accessories at discount prices. ~ 19 North Main Street, Ashland; 541-488-3982.

As befits a town dedicated to Shakespeare, Ashland's Main Street is lined with bookstores, including **Bloomsbury Books**, which is a good source for regional books and newspapers. Coffee and espresso drinks are served in an upstairs café. ~ 290 East Main Street, Ashland; 541-488-0029, fax 541-488-2942.

Tudor Guild Gift Shop, adjacent to the Elizabethan Theatre, sells all the Bard's works, as well as Oregon Shakespeare Festival merchandise, gifts, educational books, jewelry and toys with a dramatic flair. Closed Sunday from November through March. ~ 15 South Pioneer Street, Ashland; 541-482-0940, fax 541-488-4708; www.tudorguild.org, e-mail tudorguild@tudorguild.org.

After seeing a show in Ashland, pick up vintage and contemporary theater and dance posters, prints and lithographs at **Footlights**. Closed Monday. ~ 240 East Main Street, Ashland; phone/fax 541-488-5538; www.footlightsgallery.com.

Prior to evening shows at the Elizabethan, the Green Show Renaissance Musicians and Dancers offer free half-hour performances in the Oregon Shakespeare courtyard.

Picking up something great to wear to the theater is easy in Ashland, which boasts some highly individual boutiques. **Red's Threads** specializes in Indonesian batiks and lace cutwork. ~ 42 East Main Street; 541-488-2862. **Naturals of Ashland** offers contemporary women's clothing. ~ 110 Lithia Way; 541-488-3512.

Raw Elements combines metal, wood, stone, clay and plant fibers to create pieces of art that are both primitive and sophisticated. Look for garden decorations, mirrors, kitchen goods and wallhangings. ~ 77 Oak Street, Ashland; 541-482-7688.

The Northwest Nature Shop is a wonderful place to shop for birdhouses, minerals, wind chimes, hiking maps and nature and travel books. In a Craftsman-style house near downtown, this shop has a good selection of nature-oriented children's games. ~ 154 Oak Street, Ashland; 541-482-3241.

You can pick your own organically grown fruit at **Valley View Orchard** or shop at the farm store for cherries, apples, peaches, pears and more. Closed October to June. ~ 1800 Valley View Road, Ashland; 541-488-2840.

NIGHTLIFE

Rafters Bar & Grill at the Riverside Inn has an outdoor deck overlooking the Rogue River that's perfect for before-dinner drinks. ~ 971 Southeast 6th Street, Grants Pass; 541-476-7474; www.riverside-inn.com.

Britt Festivals offers classical, jazz, folk, dance, blues, bluegrass, world, pop and country music performances from mid-June to mid-September. Headliners such as Jewel, Brad Paisley and B.B. King, make this event a worthy companion to the nearby Oregon Shakespeare Festival. At this outdoor theater, you can choose between lawn and reserved seating in the natural setting of the historic Britt estate. ~ Britt Pavilion, Jacksonville; 541-773-6077, 800-882-7488; www.brittfest.org, e-mail info@brittfest.org.

The Oregon Shakespeare Festival is the nation's oldest and largest regional repertory theater, attracting more than 120,000 people each season. The most popular venue is the **Elizabethan Theatre**, which stages plays from June through October. The indoor **Angus Bowmer Theatre** also presents Shakespearian performances, as well as classics by Shaw and Wilder and contemporary playwrights. Both new and classic works are presented at the **New Theatre**. The season runs from mid-February to late October. Advance reservations are strongly recommended in peak season. ~ 15 South Pioneer Street, Ashland; 541-482-4331, fax 541-482-8045; www.osfashland.org.

The **Oregon Cabaret Theatre** holds professional productions including musicals, revues and comedies in a renovated church with table seating on the tiered main floor and in the balcony. Dinner theater also available. ~ 1st and Hargadine streets, Ashland; 541-488-2902, fax 541-488-8795; www.oregoncabaret.com.

Siskiyou Micro Pub features a deck overlooking Lithia Creek, 15 brews on tap and live entertainment. Bands of all kinds play on various nights. Occasional cover. ~ 31-B Water Street, Ashland; 541-482-7718.

The **Camelot Theater** is an off Broadway–style little theater group performing in Talent. ~ 101 Talent Avenue, Talent; 541-535-5250.

PARKS

VALLEY OF THE ROGUE STATE PARK This 316-acre park on the Rogue River is convenient to the Grants Pass Area. Near the interstate, it's central to many rafting operators. Trout, steelhead and chinook salmon are caught in the Rogue River. The grassy, mile-long riverfront park is shaded by madrone, black locust and oak. Facilities include picnic areas and restrooms. ~ Off Route 5, 12 miles east of Grants Pass; 541-582-1118, fax 541-582-1312.

▲ There are 21 tent sites ($12 to $16 per night), 146 RV hookup sites ($16 to $20 per night) and 6 yurts ($27 per night). Showers are available. Reservations: 800-452-5687.

BEN HUR LAMPMAN WAYSIDE On the south bank of the Rogue River opposite Gold Hill, the 23-acre wayside park is named for the late Ben Hur Lampman, a popular Oregon newspaper editor, fisherman and poet laureate. Emulate his fishing prowess by angling for trout and steelhead in the Rogue. Day-use only. ~ Off Route 5, 16 miles east of Grants Pass; 541-582-1118, fax 541-582-1312.

INDIAN MARY PARK This half-mile-long park on the Rogue River west of Merlin is another ideal retreat for the entire family. Kids can play on the sandy beach or enjoy themselves at the playground. If you're towing a boat or raft, you can launch it here. You can also fish from the beach. You'll find picnic areas, restrooms, playgrounds and a sand volleyball court. ~ From Grants Pass take Route 5 north to the Merlin exit. Continue west ten miles on Merlin-Galice Road; 541-474-5285, fax 541-474-5280.

▲ There are 34 tent sites ($13 to $15 per night), 57 RV hookup sites ($18 to $20 per night) and 2 yurts ($26 to $28 per night).

LAKE SELMAC A large Illinois Valley lake convenient to the Grants Pass area, this is a popular summer resort. The 160-acre lake near Selma is a good choice for fishing (trout, bass and crappie), canoeing and sailing. The waters here tend to be warmer than the nearby rivers. Facilities include a playground, picnic area, day-use park, disc golf course and horse corrals. ~ Located 2.3 miles east of Selma via Upper Deer Creek Road; 541-474-5285, fax 541-474-5280.

▲ There are 53 tent sites ($13 to $15 per night), 35 RV hookup sites ($18 to $20 per night) and 2 yurts ($26 to $28 per night).

ILLINOIS RIVER FORKS STATE PARK The largely undeveloped 511-acre day-use park at the junction of the east and west forks of the Illinois River is a secluded spot perfect for trout and steelhead fishing and birdlife and wildlife viewing. You'll find picnic tables and restrooms. ~ Route 199, one mile south of Cave Junction; 541-582-1118, 800-551-6949, fax 541-582-1312.

▲ Permitted in nearby U.S. Forest Service campgrounds in the Illinois Valley. Among them are Grayback and Cave Creek campgrounds (541-592-3311), respectively 12 and 17 miles east of Cave Junction on Oregon Caves Highway. Grayback has 38 tent sites ($16 per night); Cave Creek has 17 tent sites ($12 per night).

TOUVELLE STATE RECREATION SITE The 54-acre day-use facility is adjacent to Table Rock, an 1890-acre biologic, geologic and historic preserve forested with Pacific madrone, white oak and ponderosa pine. In the park you can swim or fish for salmon and trout. Facilities include picnic tables, restrooms and wildlife viewing platforms. Parking fee, $3. ~ Take Route 62 nine miles north of Medford to Table Rock Road; 541-582-1118, 800-551-6949, fax 541-582-1312.

CANTRALL-BUCKLEY PARK Just eight miles southwest of Jacksonville on a wooded hillside above the Applegate Valley, Cantrall-Buckley extends half a mile along the inviting Applegate River and offers beautiful views of this farming region. Swimmers head to the small cove, while anglers try for trout in the river. There are picnic areas, barbecue pits, showers and restrooms. Parking fee, $3. ~ Take Route 238 eight miles southwest from Jacksonville and turn right on Hamilton Road; 541-774-8183, fax 541-826-8360.

▲ There are 42 primitive sites ($10 per night).

ROGUE ELK PARK The nearly mile-long park on the Rogue includes a warm creek ideal for swimming, and the kids can swing out into the river Tarzan-style on a rope hanging from an oak limb. There's good rafting and fishing (steelhead and trout) in the Rogue. Shade trees make this park a good choice on warm days, and an ideal stopover en route to Crater Lake. You'll find picnic tables, restrooms and showers. Day-use fee, $3. ~ Route 62, eight miles north of Shady Cove; 541-776-7001, fax 541-826-8360; e-mail parks info@jacksoncounty.org.

The Rogue River's Hellgate Canyon—where sheer rock walls rise 250 feet—was the setting for the Meryl Streep film *The River Wild.*

▲ There are 22 tent sites ($16 per night) and 15 RV hookup sites ($18 per night). Closed mid-October to mid-April.

LITHIA PARK A beautiful place to walk or jog, Lithia Park was originally designed by John McLaren, the creator of Golden Gate Park in San Francisco. This 93-acre urban forest is filled with towering maples, black oaks, sycamore, sequoia, bamboo, European Beech, flowering Catalpa and the Chinese Tree of Heaven. Also here are a Japanese garden, rose garden and two duck ponds. Facilities include picnic tables, fire pits, a playground, a tennis court, a swimming hole, a band shell, a fountain and restrooms. ~ On the south side of the Ashland Plaza in Ashland; 541-488-5340, 800-735-2900, fax 541-488-5314; www.ashland.or.us.

Outdoor Adventures

FISHING

In a Northwest wonderland of sparkling lakes, rivers and mountain streams, it's no surprise that fishing is such a part of the scene. Even novice anglers should try casting a line; they're bound to catch something: fall salmon from coastal rivers and streams in October and November; winter steelhead, from December through March. Spring and summer bring trout (try Detroit Lake, or the McKenzie River for huge rainbow trout) and summer steelhead (the North and South Santiam rivers are the best spots).

SALEM AREA **Bill Kremers** arranges daily fishing trips on the west side of the Cascades, longer excursions on the Deschutes River. ~ 29606 Northeast Pheasant Street, Corvallis; 541-754-6411; www.oregonrivertrails.com. **White Water Warehouse** runs camping and rafting trips on the Rogue River from May to September; all levels of expertise are welcome. ~ 625 Northwest Starker Avenue, Corvallis; 541-758-3150, 800-214-0579; www.whitewaterwarehouse.com, e-mail fun@whitewaterwarehouse.com.

EUGENE RIVER AREA **Wilderness River Outfitters** runs one-day and overnight fishing trips locally on the Willamette, Umpqua and McKenzie rivers and throughout Oregon. They also have a fly-fishing school, offering a four-day course on the river. ~ 1567 Main Street, Springfield; 541-726-9471, fax 541-726-6474.

ASHLAND–ROGUE RIVER AREA For salmon and steelhead fishing, contact **Rogue Wilderness Inc.**, which has specialized in drift-boat fishing since 1975. Trips of one to four days can be arranged. ~ 325 Galice Road, Merlin; 541-479-9554, 800-336-1647; www.wildrogue.com. For a day trip to fish for salmon and steelhead on the Chetco near Brookings, on the Smith River, or in the Rogue estuary at Gold Beach, contact **Briggs Guide Service.** ~ 1815 Southwest Bridge Street, Grants Pass; 541-479-8058, 800-845-5091.

Kayakers should look for a copy of the book *Soggy Sneakers*, a regional guide to kayaking published by the Willamette Kayak and Canoe Club.

The Adventure Center will take you fishing on the Rogue from spring until fall. They'll also provide all gear including cots and boats with heated cabins. ~ 40 North Main Street, Ashland; 541-488-2819; www.raftingtours.com. Also contact **Howard Prairie Resort** for summer rental information. The resort provides boats and accommodations in an RV campground. ~ Hyatt Prairie Road, Ashland; 541-482-1979. In Klamath Falls, **Lake of the Woods Resort** provides fishing-boat rentals. ~ 950 Harriman Route, Klamath Falls; 541-949-8300.

RIVER RUNNING

A rafting or kayaking adventure can take you from the wild and scenic whitewater ruggedness of the Rogue River (where some of the rapids are Class III and IV) to an outing on the more gentle Willamette River or one of the local lakes. With dozens of rivers in the foothills surrounding Salem, Eugene and Ashland, you're never far from an enjoyable stretch of river. The North Santiam River near Salem is popular for both its rapids and views of the surrounding woods, while the McKenzie and Willamette near Salem lean more towards the serene than the adventurous. But by far the most popular area is around Ashland. Here the Rogue River offers everything from casual floats to spectacular rapids, like those in Hellgate Canyon.

One of the best regional resources for outdoor adventurers interested in fishing, hunting and rafting is the **Oregon Guides & Packers Association** in Eugene. The group publishes an extensive directory of guides and outfitters throughout the state. ~ 800-747-9552; www.ogpa.org.

SALEM AREA **White Water Warehouse** can set you up with hardshell kayaks, sea kayaks, canoes and rafts. Instruction in whitewater kayaking is also available. The company also runs overnight camp and float trips locally on the Rogue River from May to September. ~ 625 Northwest Starker Avenue, Corvallis; 541-758-3150, 800-214-0579; www.whitewaterwarehouse.com.

EUGENE AREA **Wilderness River Outfitters** runs a moonlit evening float along serene stretches of the Willamette. ~ 1567 Main Street, Springfield; 541-726-9471.

ASHLAND–ROGUE RIVER AREA Whether you paddle your own kayak or float with a guide, rafting is the ideal way to see the Rogue's wild and scenic sections. Choose between one-day trips and overnight trips. **Orange Torpedo Trips Inc./Grants Pass Float Co.** specializes in inflatable kayaking, with one-day and multi-day whitewater trips on the Rogue, Klamath, Salmon and North Umpqua rivers. ~ 210 Merlin Road, Merlin; 541-479-5061; www.orangetorpedo.com. **Rogue Wilderness Inc.** can set you up for a one-day, 13-mile scenic adventure in an inflatable kayak or an oar or paddle raft, and also arrange longer wilderness trips on the Rogue. ~ 325 Galice Road, Merlin; 541-479-9554, 800-336-1647; www.wildrogue.com. For a full- or half-day whitewater adventure led by a naturalist along the middle Rogue (water ratings range from Class I to IV) or the upper Klamath in a six-person paddleboat, contact **The Adventure Center**. Multiday rafting and camping trips are also available on nine rivers. Food, lodging and gear are included. ~ 40 North Main Street, Ashland; 541-488-2819; www.raftingtours.com.

Hellgate Jetboat Excursions will take you through the Rogue River's rugged Hellgate Canyon wilderness on one of several jetboat tours it operates. They also offer dinner and brunch trips. Closed Sunday from October through April. ~ 966 Southwest 6th Street, Grants Pass; 541-479-7204, 800-648-4874; www.hellgate.com, e-mail info@hellgate.com.

SKIING

ASHLAND–ROGUE RIVER AREA Although most of the Heart of Oregon lies in a valley between the Cascades and the Coast Range, the southern section of the Route 5 corridor passes through the Klamath-Siskiyou Mountains. Skiers in that area head for **Mt. Ashland**. At 7500 feet, it's the highest peak in the range and just 18 miles south of Ashland off Route 5. Facilities include a day lodge, rental shop, four lifts and 23 runs. You'll also find ungroomed cross-country trails here. ~ Route 5, Exit 6; 541-482-2897; www.mtashland.com.

BALLOON RIDES

SALEM AREA The quiet exhilaration of floating above it all—wine country, the river, rolling farmland—explains why ballooning is popular in the Salem area. From April to November, **Vista Balloon Adventures** operates one-hour flights over the wine country of Newburg (about 25 minutes north of Salem), followed by a catered breakfast. The company has seven balloons and can fly six to ten passengers in each. If you're the participatory type, you can put on some gloves and help inflate the balloon. Closed Tuesday. ~ Sherwood; 503-625-7385, 800-622-2309; www.vistaballoon.com, e-mail roger@vistaballoon.com.

RIDING STABLES

Along the western slopes of the Cascades, within a 30-mile drive of the Willamette Valley, lie some of the most pristine wilderness areas in the state, much of them U.S. Forest Service land. One of the best ways to explore these alpine meadows, old-growth forests and scenic mountain peaks is on a guided day-long or multiday trail ride from a local outfitter. Even if you only have a couple of hours, Mt. Pisgah just outside Eugene provides a good opportunity for a casual ride.

EUGENE AREA Three Sisters Wilderness, just east of Eugene in Willamette National Forest, takes its name from the North, Middle and South Sisters, three 10,000-foot-plus peaks that define the area. **Smart Ass Ranch** offers year-round trail rides in this wilderness area. Hunting, fishing and pack trips are also available. ~ Redmond; 541-280-9356; www.smartassranch.com.

GOLF

Public courses in the area offer a variety of landscapes, course lengths, and difficulty ratings.

SALEM AREA Built in 1928, **Salem Golf Club** is a lush, old-style Northwest course: 18 holes with meandering greens and big old fir trees. ~ 2025 Golf Course Road South, Salem; 503-363-6652. Near Stayton, the 18-hole **Santiam Golf Course** has lots of water and trees and is fairly flat. ~ 8724 Golf Club Road, Aumsville; 503-769-3485. In Corvallis, try the 18 holes at **Trysting Tree Golf Club.** ~ Route 34 and Northeast Electric Road, Corvallis; 541-752 3027. For a shorter match, visit **Marysville Golf Course**'s nine holes. ~ 2020 Southwest Allen Street, Corvallis; 541-753-3421.

EUGENE AREA The relatively flat 18-hole **Fiddler's Green** is famous for its pro shop. ~ 91292 Route 99 North, Eugene; 541-689-8464; www.fiddlersgreen.com. The circa-1920 nine-hole **Hidden Valley Golf Course** is tucked away in a picturesque little valley and lined with mature fir and oak trees. ~ 775 North River Road, Cottage Grove; 541-942-3046. In the Springfield area, tee off at the nine holes at **McKenzie River Golf Course.** ~ 41723 Madrone Street, Springfield; 541-896-3454.

ASHLAND–ROGUE RIVER AREA **Oak Knoll Golf Course**'s nine holes are regulation length and set on gently rolling greens. ~ 3070 Route 66, Ashland; 541-482-4311. The 18-hole, par-70 **Cedar Links Golf Course** is 6000 yards but an easy walk for the most part. ~ 3155 Cedar Links Drive, Ashland; 541-773-4373. You may also tee off at the nine-hole **Colonial Valley Golf Course.** ~ 75 Nelson Way, Grants Pass; 541-479-5568.

TENNIS

SALEM AREA The Salem Parks and Recreation Department operates plenty of free courts in the capital. At **Bush's Pasture Park** (Mission and High streets) there are four lighted courts; **Highland School Park** (Broadway and Highland Avenue Northeast) has two lighted courts; and there are four lighted courts at **Orchard Heights** (Orchard Heights Street and Parkway Drive). Courts are also available at **Hoover School/Park** (1104 Savage Road Northeast), **River Road Park** (3045 River Road) and **Woodmansee Park** (4629 Sunnyside Road Southeast). ~ 503-588-6261, fax 503-588-6305; www.cityofsalem.net/~parks.

EUGENE AREA Eugene Parks and Recreation operates four courts at **Churchill Courts** (1850 Bailey Hill Road), two lighted courts at **Washington Park** (2025 Washington Street) and four lighted courts at each of the following locations: **Amazon Courts** (Amazon Parkway and 24th Avenue), **Sheldon Courts** (2445 Willakenzie Road), **Echo Hollow Courts** (1655 Echo Hollow Road) and **West Mooreland Courts** (20th and Polk streets). ~ 541-682-4800.

For $20 per court (75 minutes), both indoor and outdoor courts are available to nonmembers at **Willow Creek Racquet Club.** ~ 4201 West 13th Avenue, Eugene; 541-484-7451.

ASHLAND–ROGUE RIVER AREA The Medford Parks Department operates four unlighted courts at **Fichtner Mainwaring Park** (Stewart Avenue and Holly Street), four lighted courts at **Bear Creek Park** (Siskiyou Boulevard and Highland Drive), ten courts (five lighted) at **North Medford High School** (Keene Way Drive and Crater Lake Road), and two unlighted courts at **Holmes Park** (185 South Modoc Avenue). ~ 541-774-2400.

BIKING

For recreational bicyclers, there are hundreds of miles of relatively flat, scenic bike trails that parallel beautiful rivers, parks and lakes throughout the valley. Experienced, active riders will enjoy the more challenging mountain trails or some of the longer loops in and around the region.

SALEM AREA The **Oregon Trans-America Trail** from the Dallas area near Salem heads south through the scenic wine country to Corvallis. Four miles of bike trails traverse **Willamette Mission State Park** (503-393-1172), which is surrounded by orchards and farm fields. **Silver Falls State Park** (503-873-8681), with its waterfalls and gorges carved out of lava, has a popular four-mile paved

AUTHOR FAVORITE

The best part about ascending **Mary's Peak**, about 15 miles south of Corvallis, is that you can cheat. The summit rises over 4000 feet—it's the highest in the Coast Range—but you can drive to a parking lot about three miles from the top. From there you can bike along the pavement to the summit, from which you'll get great views of the ocean and mountains to the east. When you're ready to descend, you can can follow one of several trails down.

bike trail. There is also a 27-mile perimeter trail. East of the city, there are trails "all over **Lyons and Detroit lakes**," according to one local enthusiast.

Near Corvallis, Oregon State University has its own gated research forest called **McDonald Forest** (541-737-4434). It's a hilly tract, but not steep, and its 15-mile trail system is very popular. From the top of Dimple Hill, which gains 800 feet in about four miles, you'll get a good view of the surrounding area. The university maintains several trails and outlines them in a map available at bike shops.

Bike trails can be found in state parks throughout the area, including **Holman** (four miles west of Salem).

The **Salem Bicycle Club** publishes a monthly newsletter that includes a two- or three-page "Ride Sheet," which lists club-sponsored rides and is usually posted in bike shops around town. Club rides vary from beginner (15 to 20 miles) to expert (100-mile loops to the coast). Weekend rides are held year-round; in the summer, evening and overnight rides are held during the week. ~ P.O. Box 2224, Salem, OR 97308; www.salembicycleclub.org.

A good time to visit the Fall Creek National Recreation Trail is spring when wildflowers abound.

EUGENE AREA Eugene is one of the nation's top biking cities: more than 8500 people commute to school and work on bikes, and there are 200 miles of bike paths. All this in a city with a population of only 120,000.

Eugene's **Willamette River Recreation Corridor** offers five bridges that connect the north and south bank bike trails. The flat 15-mile loop from Knickerbocker Bridge to Owosso Bridge takes you through or past parks and rose gardens, shops and restaurants in downtown Eugene, and the University of Oregon campus.

In summer 2005, the **Willamette Valley Scenic Bikeway** was inaugurated by the Oregon Parks and Recreation Department. This 136-mile route connects Eugene with Portland, taking in the beautiful scenery of this lush area.

Eight miles south of Eugene, the **Fox Swale Area** has eight miles of off-road trails ideal for mountain biking. Ride the Fox Hollow Road nine and a half miles over the summit and down into the valley to BLM Road 19-4-4. *Note:* The area gets muddy during the rainy season. Be sure to stay off private property in this area.

ASHLAND–ROGUE RIVER AREA From the town of Rogue River, east of Grants Pass on Route 5, head north eight miles along Evans Creek to Wimer and the glorious **Evans Valley**. It's a scenic, relatively easy four-mile ride out Pleasant Creek Road to the covered bridge. Look for elk in the meadows alongside the road.

If you'd like to join an escorted downhill bike tour on Mt. Ashland, contact **The Adventure Center**. Beside bike rentals (and insider tips about the more pleasant route past small rural farms and ranches for a two-hour loop to Emigrant Lake), this outfitter offers several different off-road bike tours, all guided, with extras like picnic brunch. ~ 40 North Main Street, Ashland; 541-488-2819, fax 541-482-5139; www.raftingtours.com.

Bike Rentals Bike rentals in Salem are hard to come by. Try **South Salem Cycleworks** for tandem, hybrid and road bikes. ~ 4071 Liberty Road, Salem; 503-399-9848.

Pick up mountain and cruise bikes at **Peak Sports**, the only rental shop in the city. The shop also still has a few three-speeds, which are perfect for an easy afternoon ride around town. ~ 129 Northwest 2nd Street, Corvallis; 541-754-6444.

Eugene Mountain Bicycle Resources Group publishes *Mountain Bike Ride Guide*, available at bike shops in the Eugene area. Of the more than 14 bike shops in Eugene, there are only two places to rent. **Hutch's** rents out city bikes and is attached to the Rack and Roll sales/repair shop. ~ 960 Charnelton Street, Eugene; 541-345-7521. **Blue Heron Bicycles** rents mountain and hybrid bikes in the spring and summer. ~ 877 East 13th Avenue, Eugene; 541-343-2488.

HIKING

Hiking does not necessarily mean huffing and puffing up steep mountain slopes. Several of the hikes mentioned here may be more aptly described as "walks." In any event, a hike or a walk along the river or through a park is a great way to get some exercise and to get to know the area. All distances listed for hiking trails are one way unless otherwise noted.

SALEM AREA **Riverfront Loop Trail** (4 miles) in Willamette Mission State Park offers a secluded stretch of river.

The Ten Falls Loop Trail (7 miles) at Silver Falls State Park reaches all ten waterfalls along Silver Creek Canyon. Shorter hikes (less than 2.5 miles) can also be taken from roadside trailheads to the individual falls.

Salem's **Rita Steiner Fry Nature Trail** (.3 mile) offers a pleasant stroll through Deepwood Park, adjacent to the historic Deepwood Estate.

On River Road South, a mile south of downtown, **Minto-Brown Island Park** has 15 miles of trails and paths.

◄ HIDDEN

EUGENE AREA Convenient to Eugene, the **Fall Creek National Recreation Trail** (13.7 miles) is ideal for day hikes and overnight trips in the hardwood and conifer Willamette National Forest. Pristine Fall Creek is visible from most of the trail, which begins west of the Dolly Varden Campground.

Eugene's **Mount Pisgah Arboretum** has more than seven miles of hiking trails. You can enjoy a lovely walk through oak savanna, a Douglas fir forest or along a seasonal marsh.

Pre's Trail is a Eugene memorial to legendary Oregon runner Steve Prefontaine. This all-weather trail through the woods and fields of Alton Baker Park offers parcourse-style routes ranging from .5 to 1.5 miles.

HIDDEN ► The **Kentucky Falls Recreation Trail** (8.5 miles) runs along Kentucky Creek through a forest of Douglas fir and western hemlock. Located 41 miles southwest of Eugene, it leads down 760 feet to the twin falls viewpoint.

ASHLAND–ROGUE RIVER AREA More than 30 trail systems are found in the **Illinois Valley Ranger District** surrounding the Cave Junction/Oregon Caves area. Trails run from half a mile to 15 miles. Possibilities include **Tin Cup Gulch**, the **Kalmiopsis Wilderness, Black Butte** and **Babyfoot Lake.**

Try Medford's **Bear Creek Greenway Trail** (5.5 miles), beginning at Bear Creek Park and running north through Medford to Pine Street in Central Point. The trail has three segments. One is near the Route 5 south interchange off Table Rock Road. A series of 18 interpretive stations points out more than 20 kinds of trees and berries as well as landmarks along the creek. The other trail segment (3.5 miles) is in the Talent area with the trailhead in Lynn Newbry Park. The trail runs south toward Ashland, passing wetland habitats and historical sites, with an interpretive guide available. ~ 541-774-8184.

Transportation

CAR

From Northern California, **Route 5** runs north over the border to Ashland and the Rogue River Valley. Route 5 also takes you southbound from Washington across the Columbia River into Portland. If you're arriving from the Northern California coast, pick up **Route 199**, which heads northeast through the Siskiyous into Southern Oregon and Grants Pass. Many other highways link the Willamette Valley with the Oregon Coast and central Oregon, including **Routes 126, 20** and **22.**

AIR

Two airports bring visitors to the Heart of Oregon: Eugene and Medford. In addition, the big **Portland International Airport** an hour north of Salem has convenient connections to all major cities and is serviced by Air Canada, Alaska Airlines, America West, American Airlines, Big Sky Airlines, Continental Airlines, Delta Air Lines, Frontier, Hawaiian Airlines, Horizon Air, JetBlue, Mexicana Airlines, Northwest Airlines, Southwest Airlines, United Airlines and United Express. ~ 877-739-4636; www.portlandairport.pdx.com.

Eugene Airport is served by America West Express, Delta Connection, Horizon Air, United Airlines and United Express.

In Medford, **Rogue Valley International–Medford Airport** is served by Horizon Airlines, United Airlines and United Express.

For ground transportation to and from the Eugene Airport call **Airport City Taxi & Limo.** ~ 541-484-4142.

In Medford, **Yellow Cab** serves the airport and links the Shakespeare capital with the Medford Airport. ~ 541-772-6288.

BUS

Greyhound Bus Lines (800-231-2222; www.greyhound.com) serves the Willamette Valley and Ashland–Rogue River area, with stations in Salem, Corvallis, Eugene, Grants Pass and Medford. ~ Salem: 450 Church Street Northeast; 503-362-2428. Corvallis: 153 Northwest 4th Street; 541-757-1797. Eugene: 987 Pearl Street; 541-344-6265. Grants Pass: 460 Northeast Agness Avenue; 541-476-4513. Medford: 212 North Bartlett Street; 541-779-2103.

TRAIN

Amtrak's "Coast Starlight" has daily service to the Willamette Valley, with stations in Eugene (433 Willamette Street), Albany (110 West 10th Street) and Salem (500 13th Street Southeast). ~ 800-872-7245; www.amtrak.com.

CAR RENTALS

You'll find many of the major agencies at the airports in Eugene and Medford. In Eugene, there are **Avis Rent A Car** (800-331-1212), **Budget Rent A Car** (800-527-0700) and **Hertz Rent A Car** (800-654-3131). In Medford, try **Avis Rent A Car** (800-331-1212), **Budget Rent A Car** (800-527-0700), **Hertz Rent A Car** (800-654-3131) and **National Car Rental** (800-328-4567).

PUBLIC TRANSIT

All the major Willamette Valley and Ashland–Rogue River cities have local public transit systems. While there are bus connections to many of the smaller towns, you'll need to rent a car to see many of the rural highlights.

The Salem area is served by **Cherriots** (503-588-2877). Contact the **Corvallis Transit System** (541-757-6998) in Corvallis. In Eugene, the **Lane Transit District** (541-687-5555) blankets the city. Medford, Jacksonville and Ashland are served by the **Rogue Valley Transportation District** (541-779-2877).

TAXIS

In Eugene, **Airport City Taxi** (541-484-4142) can take you downtown. In Medford, call **Yellow Cab** (541-772-6288).

SIX

Oregon Cascades

Some questions are impossible to answer. Here's one that came to mind while we traveled the highways and byways of the Oregon Cascades, swimming in crystal-clear pools, basking at alpine resorts, fishing pristine streams, dining on fresh salmon and cooling off beneath the spray of yet another waterfall: Why isn't this heavenly space positively jammed with people who want to get away from it all?

Except for a handful of places, such as Mt. Hood on a Saturday afternoon, Route 97 in the vicinity of Bend or Crater Lake's Rim Drive, it's often hard to find a crowd in this seemingly inexhaustible resort area. Sure, there's a fair number of timber rigs out on major highways. And the No Vacancy sign does pop up a good deal at popular resorts during the summer and weekends. But who cares when you can head down the road half a mile and check into a glorious streamside campground where the tab is rock-bottom and there's no extra charge for the nocturnal view of the Milky Way? The fact is that mile for mile, the Oregon Cascades offer some of the best wilderness and recreational opportunities in the Pacific Northwest.

To really get a feel for the area, you need a week or longer. But even if you only have time to buzz up to Mt. Hood for an afternoon, this is the best place we know to gain perspective on the volcanic history of the Pacific Northwest. A chain of peaks topped by 11,235-foot Mt. Hood, the Cascades have an average elevation of about 5000 feet. Heavily forested, these mountains are also the headwaters for many important rivers such as the Rogue, the Umpqua and the McKenzie. Klamath Falls is the principal southern gateway to the region, and Bend and Redmond provide easy access from the east. Within the mountains are a number of charming towns and villages such as Sisters, McKenzie Bridge and Camp Sherman. While the summer months can be mild and sunny, winter snowfalls blanket the western slopes with 300 to 500 inches of snow.

For some perspective on the Cascades, take a look at the area's good-old days. Begin with the evolution of one of the Northwest's signature attractions, Crater

Lake. Looking at this placid sea, it's hard to imagine what this region looked like 60 million years ago during the late Cretaceous period. As Lowell Williams has written: "At that time the Coast Ranges of Oregon . . . were submerged and the waves of the Pacific lapped against the foothills of the Sierra Nevada and the Blue Mountains of Oregon. Where the Cascade peaks now rise in lofty grandeur, water teemed with shellfish . . . giant marine lizards swam in the seas, and winged reptiles sailed above in search of prey."

Later, in the Eocene and Oligocene periods, roughly 25 million to 60 million years ago, the Crater Lake region became a low plain. Throughout this period and the late Miocene, volcanoes erupted. Finally, about one million to two million years ago, in the last great Ice Age, the Cascades were formed. The largest of these peaks became 12,000-foot Mt. Mazama. About 7000 years ago, this promontory literally blew its top, leaving behind the caldera that is now Crater Lake.

The American Indians, who viewed this area as a sacred and treacherous place, went out of their way to avoid Crater Lake. It was only after the white man arrived in the 19th century that it became a tourist attraction and eventually a national park. Today the lake is considered a unique national treasure.

Because they provided a tremendous challenge to settlers heading toward the Pacific Ocean on the Oregon Trail, the Cascades also gained an important place in the history of the West. Landmarks surrounding Mt. Hood tell the dramatic story of pioneers who blazed time-saving new routes to the promised land across this precipitous terrain. Of course, their arrival permanently altered American Indian life. Inevitably, efforts to colonize the Indians and turn them into farmers and Christians met with resistance. American Indian leader Captain Jack led perhaps the most famous tribal rebellion against the miseries of reservation life in the 1872–73 Modoc War. This fighting raged in an area that is now part of the Lava Beds National Monument across the border in California. Captain Jack and his fellow renegades were ultimately hanged at Fort Klamath.

While logging became the Cascades' leading industry, tourism emerged in the late 19th century. Summer resorts, typically primitive cabins built at the water's edge, were popular with the fishing crowd. Later, the arrival of resort lodges like the Timberline on the slopes of Mt. Hood drew a significant winter trade. But even as Oregon's best-known mountain range evolved into a major resort area, it was able to retain carefully guarded secrets. Little-known fishing spots, obscure trails, waterfalls absent from the maps—this high country became Oregon's private treasure.

Today, Oregon, one of the nation's most environmentally conscious states, is trying to find peaceful coexistence between the logging industry and environmentalists. The "spotted owl" controversy led to new logging restrictions in the fight to save old-growth forests for future generations. You'll be able to take a firsthand look at the subject in question on some of our recommended walks through old-growth preserves. Because logging has traditionally been such an important component of the local economy, many residents worry that further restrictions will threaten their livelihood.

A forest plan implemented in 1994 by the Forest Service under Bill Clinton, has remapped the Pacific Northwest, dividing it into sections of environmental reserve and areas open to logging. The protection of the riparian reserves (areas around rivers and streams) and late-successional reserves (sections of nearly old-growth forest) has caused the logging industry to shift some of its priorities. The plan, however, is not a law nor legally binding, and logging companies are waging persistent battles against it.

Although in many ways the lumber companies continue to practice business as usual, the rate of forest depletion has slowed. As you travel through the Cascades, realize that your economic contribution, in the form of tourist dollars, is helping local residents make the transition from a lumber economy to a diverse recreational region.

Walking into the Cascades backcountry, you can easily spend hours on a road or trail looking for company. This solitude is the area's greatest drawing card. Appreciate the fact that the only lines you'll have to bother with most of the time are the kind with a hook on the end.

Northern Cascades

Given their proximity to the state's major urban centers such as Portland and Eugene, the Northern Cascades are a popular destination, particularly on weekends and during the summer months. Most of the highlights, in fact, can be reached within a couple of hours. Pioneer history, American Indian culture and scenic wonders are just a few of the Cascades' treasures. And if you're looking for uncrowded, out-of-the-way places, relax. Those hidden spots are easily located, often just a mile or two off the most popular routes.

SIGHTS

Our visit to the **Mt. Hood** region begins on Route 26. Portions of this road parallel the time-saving trail first blazed in 1845 by pioneer Samuel Barlow. The following year he and a partner turned this discovery into a $5 toll road at the end of the Oregon Trail, the final tab for entry to the end of the rainbow. Today a series of small monuments commemorates the **Barlow Trail**. At Tollgate campground, a quarter-mile east of Rhododendron on the south side of Route 26, you'll want to visit a reproduction of the historic Barlow Tollgate. Continue five miles east of Rhododendron to the **Laurel Hill Chute** marker. You can take the short, steep hike to the infamous "chute" where wagon trains descended the perilous grade to Zigzag River Valley.

Two of the region's most popular fishing streams, the **Salmon River** and the **Sandy River** are convenient to old-growth forests, waterfalls and hiking trails. Continuing east, you'll reach Zigzag and **Lolo Pass Road**. This backcountry route on the west side of Mt. Hood leads to **Lost Lake**, a great escape (see Chapter Three for more on the lake).

After returning to Route 26, drive east to Government Camp and head uphill to Mt. Hood's **Timberline Lodge**, one of the Northwest's most important arts and crafts–style architectural landmarks. Massive is the word for this skiing hub framed with giant timber beams and warmed by a two-level, octagon-shaped stone

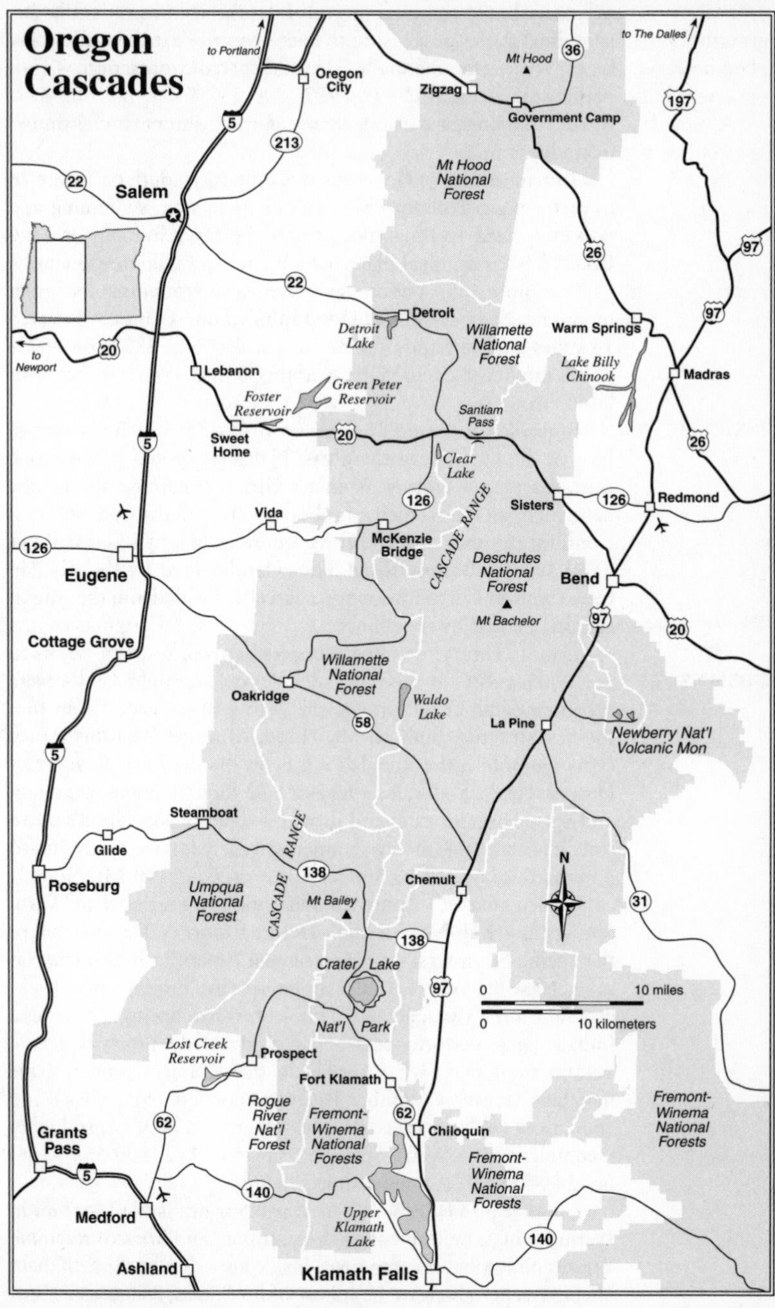
Oregon Cascades
to Portland
Oregon City
Zigzag
Mt Hood
36
to The Dalles
197
Government Camp
5
213
Mt Hood National Forest
22
Salem
26
97
22
Detroit
Detroit Lake
Willamette National Forest
Warm Springs
97
to Newport
20
Lake Billy Chinook
Madras
Lebanon
Green Peter Reservoir
Foster Reservoir
Santiam Pass
Sweet Home
20
5
26
Clear Lake
CASCADE RANGE
Sisters
126
Redmond
126
Vida
McKenzie Bridge
126
Eugene
Deschutes National Forest
Bend
Mt Bachelor
97
20
Cottage Grove
Willamette National Forest
Oakridge
Waldo Lake
58
La Pine
Newberry Nat'l Volcanic Mon
5
Steamboat
Glide
CASCADE RANGE
138
Roseburg
Umpqua National Forest
Chemult
N
Mt Bailey
31
138
Crater Lake Nat'l Park
97
0
10 miles
0
10 kilometers
Lost Creek Reservoir
Prospect
Fort Klamath
Rogue River Nat'l Forest
Fremont-Winema National Forests
62
Chiloquin
Fremont-Winema National Forests
62
Grants Pass
5
Fremont-Winema National Forests
140
Medford
Upper Klamath Lake
140
Ashland
Klamath Falls

fireplace. In the summer you can hike the wildflower trails surrounding the lodge. Be sure to check out the lower-level display on the lodge's fascinating history and current restoration. ~ Timberline Ski Area; 503-622-7979, 800-547-1406, fax 503-622-0710; www.timberlinelodge.com, e-mail information@timber linelodge.com.

Two miles east of Government Camp turn south on Route 26 to picturesque **Trillium Lake**, a popular fishing, swimming and non-motorized boating spot created by the damming of Mud Creek. This is an ideal place for a picnic and wildlife viewing.

For more information on the area surrounding the great mountain, contact the **Mt. Hood Information Center**. ~ Located 15 miles east of Sandy on Route 26; 503-622-4822, 888-622-4822, fax 503-622-7625; www.mthood.info, e-mail infoctr@mt hood.info.

Returning to Route 26, pick up Route 35 over Barlow Pass. East of the junction of these two highways, you'll pass a stone cairn marking a **Pioneer Women's Grave**. It commemorates the heroism of all the women who bravely crossed the Oregon Trail. Continue another one and three quarters miles to Forest Road 3530 and the **Barlow Road Sign**. Hand-carved by the Civilian Conservation Corps, this marker is a short walk from the wagon ruts left behind by the pioneers.

Half a century after the pioneers arrived, tourism began to put down roots on this Cascades Peak. Overnight guests were accommodated at the turn-of-the-20th-century **Cloud Cap Inn**, the first structure built on Mt. Hood. Although it no longer accepts the public, the shingled inn is on the National Register of Historic Places. Today, it serves as a base for a mountain-climbing-and-rescue organization and provides views of Mt. Hood's north side. It is accessible in late summer and early fall via a washboard dirt road. ~ Located 10.5 miles north of Route 35, Mt. Hood.

Return south to Route 26 and continue southeast to Warm Springs and **Kah-Nee-Ta High Desert Resort & Casino**, one of the Pacific Northwest's most intriguing American Indian reservations. Near the lodge entrance an interpretive display offers background on the Confederated Tribes of Warm Springs. American Indian dance performances and a traditional salmon bake are held at the lodge each Saturday in the summer months. Tribe members skewer Columbia River salmon on cedar sticks and cook it over alderwood coals. The hot springs pool is also highly recommended. ~ Warm Springs; 541-553-1112, 800-554-4786, fax 541-553-1071; www.kahneeta.com.

Another prime attraction in Warm Springs is the **Museum at Warm Springs**, built of native stone, timber and brick to resemble a traditional tribal encampment. Inside are exhibits, some of them interactive, pertaining to the culture of the Wasco, Paiute and Warm

Springs tribes. Included among the displays are art, artifacts, family heirlooms, trade items and historic photographs from the 1850s. The museum also offers a theater, a research library, tribal archives and craft demonstrations. Closed Monday and Tuesday from November through March. Admission. ~ 2189 Route 26, Warm Springs; 541-553-3331, fax 541-553-3338; www.warmsprings.com/museum.

Richardson's Recreational Ranch could also be called the world's largest pick-and-pay thunder-egg farm. Formed as gas bubbles in rhyolite flows and filled with silica, these colorful stones range from the size of a seed to 1760 pounds. You can pick up,

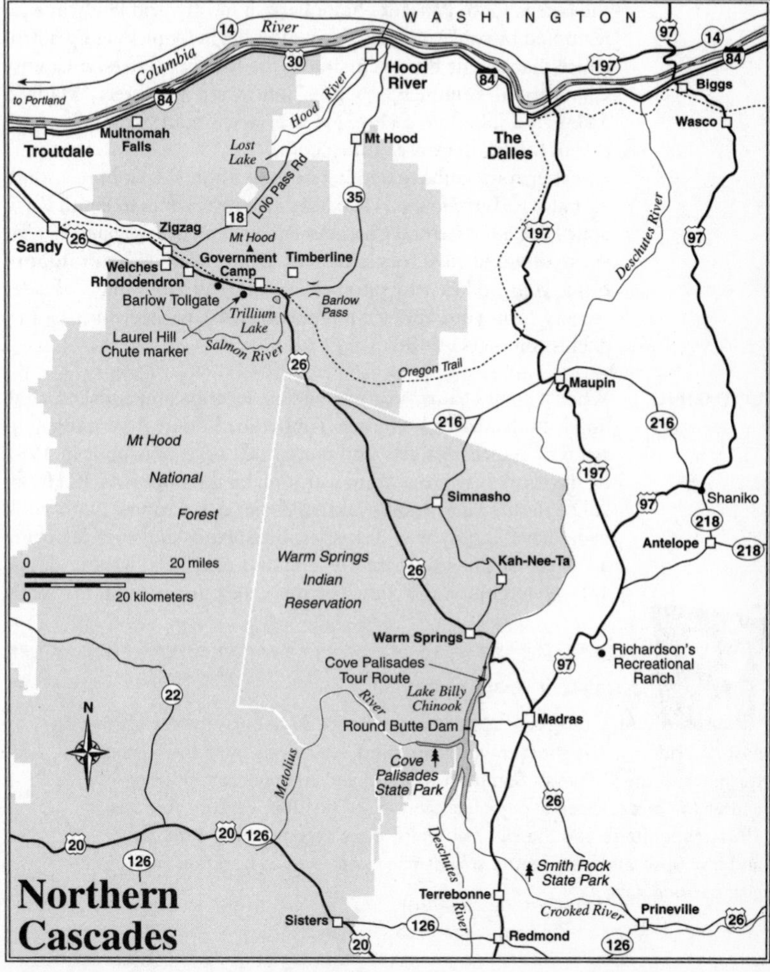

chisel or dig your thunder eggs out of 12 beds spread across this 4000-acre rock ranch. Closed mid-November to mid-April, depending on the weather. ~ Located 11 miles north of Madras on Route 97, at Milepost 81 turn right and continue southeast three miles; 541-475-2680, 800-433-2680, fax 541-475-4299.

The 31-mile **Cove Palisades Tour Route** off Route 97 is also a worthwhile excursion. Just southwest of Madras, the route circles Lake Billy Chinook, a popular place for recreational watersports. Three major rivers, the Deschutes, Crooked and Metolius, have cut canyons through this Oregon plain and merged at Lake Billy Chinook behind Round Butte Dam. Be sure to visit the observatory viewpoint on the lake's Metolius River arm. Adjoining the lake is **Cove Palisades State Park**, a mostly arid landscape interrupted by towering volcanic cones. Begin by picking up a brochure that details this excursion at the **Madras-Jefferson County Chamber of Commerce**. ~ 274 Southwest 4th Street, Madras; 541-475-2350, fax 541-475-4341; www.madraschamber.com, e-mail office@madraschamber.com.

After completing this tour, return to Route 97. Continue south 12 miles to Terrebonne. Then head east three miles to **Smith Rock State Park** (see "Central Cascades Parks" later in this chapter), a favorite of world-class rock climbers. Don't worry if you forgot to bring your spikes and pitons. You can still enjoy the Cascades scenery from your vantage point along the Crooked River Gorge. Admission. ~ 541-548-7501.

LODGING

When it comes to architecture, history, location and ambience, few hotels in the Cascades match **Timberline Lodge**. A veritable museum of Northwest arts and crafts, the lodge was built in 1937 by the Works Progress Administration on the slopes of Mt. Hood. All of the 70 guest rooms and 10 chalet dorm rooms (with bunk beds) have handwoven draperies, bedspreads and rugs featuring a variety of themes; there are iron-and-oak beds, writing desks, WPA watercolors and views of the valley and mountain. While

sights

AUTHOR FAVORITE

An interesting side trip along Route 97 about 41 miles northeast of Madras is the ghost town of **Shaniko**, which was once the bustling terminus of the Columbia Southern Railroad and an important shipping center for cattle, sheep and gold at the turn of the 20th century. Tour the 1901 schoolhouse and the city hall, which once accommodated the jail and firehouse, and imagine the streets filled with boys in buckskin and girls in bonnets.

the rooms are small, there is nothing modest about the public areas, which feature a two-level, octagon-shaped stone fireplace and banisters. It's perfectly situated for skiing, hiking or climbing. ~ Timberline; 503-622-7979, 800-547-1406, fax 503-622-0710; www.timberlinelodge.com, e-mail reservations@timberlinelodge.com. MODERATE TO ULTRA-DELUXE.

Relax at the **Mt. Hood Inn** after a day spent on the nearby ski slopes. Warm colors, pine furniture and mountain views characterize each of the 57 guest rooms and suites. There is a large indoor spa and fireplace in the common area; "king" suites offer their own in-room spas. Perfect for winter athletes, the inn also offers an on-site ski tuning room as well as ski lockers. Continental breakfast is included. ~ Route 26 at Government Camp Business Loop Road, Government Camp; 503-272- 3205, 800-443-7777, fax 503-272-3307; www.mthoodinn.com, e-mail info@mthoodinn.com. ULTRA-DELUXE.

If big resorts aren't your style, visit **Falcon's Crest Inn Bed & Breakfast**. Three intimate rooms and two suites, all with private baths, come decorated with family heirlooms and antiques. Wake up to a tray of coffee and pastry at your door, then head downstairs for a full breakfast in the dining room. A six-course, prix-fixe dinner is optional. Situated within minutes of SkiBowl, the inn also offers its own entertainment, everything from dinner theater to wine tastings to dances. ~ 87287 Government Camp Business Loop Road, Government Camp; 503-272-3403, 800-624- 7384, fax 503-272-3454; www.falconscrest.com, e-mail info@falconscrest.com. MODERATE TO DELUXE.

Huckleberry Inn offers 17 accommodations in varying price ranges. The units are spare and woodsy, and are popular with hikers scaling Mt. Hood. Standard rooms sleep small groups, while larger rooms with spiral staircases leading up to sleeping lofts accommodate more. Budget dorm rooms are sometimes available as well. The inn's 24-hour restaurant is also worth checking out for its wide selection of dishes using locally grown huckleberries. ~ Route 26 at Government Camp Business Loop, Government Camp; 503-272-3325, fax 503-272-3031; www.huckleberry-inn.com. MODERATE.

In the mid-1960s the federal government built the Dalles Dam on the Columbia River, submerging the ancestral fishing grounds of local Indians. The Confederated Tribes of Warm Springs used their compensation to pay for **Kah-Nee-Ta High Desert Resort**. Located in the midst of the 600,000-acre reservation, this resort offers visitors a variety of lodging choices. There are 139 rooms at the lodge, 30 guest rooms at the village, an RV park, and tepees with cement floors. Set in a red-rock canyon about an hour southeast of Mt. Hood, this resort offers kayaking, golfing, horseback riding, swimming pools, tennis, a water slide, bike rentals and gambling in a casino. ~ Warm Springs; 541-553-1112, 800-554-4786, fax 541-553-1071; www.kahneeta.com. MODERATE TO DELUXE.

HIDDEN ►

A thriving bed-and-breakfast inn in the midst of a ghost town is the **Shaniko Hotel**, a fine, two-story brick establishment with a wooden balcony dating from 1900 that has been restored by its current owners. The hotel provides 18 rooms decorated with historic photos from the town's early days and antique reproductions including nightstands that resemble old-fashioned iceboxes. Closed in winter. ~ 4th and E streets, Shaniko; 541-489-3441, fax 541-489-3444. MODERATE.

DINING

When the U.S. Olympic ski team is in town, they head to **Don Guido's Italian Cuisine** for a little carbo-loading. You don't have to be a world-class athlete, however, to enjoy the generous portions of pasta, veal, chicken and seafood that make the restaurant famous. After a long day of skiing, fill up on grilled eggplant, spaghetti carbonara, chicken *cacciatori* or clam linguine. There is also an extensive list of wines, ports, sherries and brandies. Dinner only, except breakfast served on Saturday and Sunday. Closed Monday through Wednesday during the winter. ~ 73330 East Route 26, Rhododendron; 503-622-5141. MODERATE TO DELUXE.

Hearty meals are always available at **Rendezvous Grill & Tap Room**, which features a changing menu with an emphasis on seasonal favorites. Start off with a savory appetizer (Swiss cheese melted over Yukon gold potatoes and winter squash or fried oysters), but save room for substantial entrées like rigatoni and alder-smoked chicken, *sake*-glazed salmon or beef filet with a chanterelle mushroom sauce. Lighter fare is served for lunch, but even chipotle–black bean burgers or New York steak sandwiches will leave you satisfied. Closed Monday and Tuesday from October through May. ~ 67149 East Route 26, Welches; 503-622-6837; www.rendezvousgrill.net, e-mail rndzvgrill@aol.com. DELUXE.

Convenient to the Timberline area is **Mt. Hood Brewing Company and Brew Pub**. Located in a three-story, stone-and-wood building, this establishment features a flyfishing motif with knotty-pine paneling, a red-quarry tile floor and a 43-foot-long copper bar. Through the large windows you can see the beer-brewing kettles. (Brewery tours are available on a limited basis.) The family-style menu offers gourmet pizza, pasta, steaks, salads and hamburgers. ~ Route 26 at Government Camp Business Loop Road, Government Camp; 503-622-0724, fax 503-622-0766; www.mthoodbrewing.com, e-mail pubinfo@mthoodbrewing.com. MODERATE.

At the Kah-Nee-Ta High Desert Resort, try the informal **Chinook Room** for a hearty buffet that may include anything from barbecued ribs to the lodge's famous Indian fry bread. The **Juniper Room** has specialties like venison steak, prawns, halibut, steamed clams blended in a seafood pot and birds in clay, a specialty that is cooked for three hours. ~ Warm Springs; 541-553-1112, fax 541-553-1071; www.kahneeta.com. MODERATE TO DELUXE.

◄ HIDDEN

Located in the historic Shaniko Hotel, the **Shaniko Cafe** is handsomely appointed with oak tables and chairs, as well as historic photographs and artifacts from the days when Shaniko was an important shipping center. Burgers, steaks and full breakfasts with biscuits and country gravy are among the home-style favorites. ~ 4th and E streets, Shaniko; 541-489-3415, fax 541-489-3444. BUDGET TO MODERATE.

SHOPPING

The Oregon Candy Farm is the place to shop for homemade hand-dipped chocolates. Even the nutmeats are roasted in-house. Part of the fun is watching the candy-making process (Monday through Friday) through big windows. Sugar-free chocolate is available. ~ 48620 Southeast Route 26, five and a half miles east of Sandy; 503-668-5066, fax 503-668-6830.

When it comes to shopping for American Indian arts and crafts, why not go to the source? At **Kah-Nee-Ta High Desert Resort**, both the Lodge and Village have gift shops offering beautiful basketry, handicrafts, blankets and jewelry. Many are made right on the reservation. ~ Warm Springs; 541-553-1112, fax 541-553-1071; www.kahneeta.com.

For limited-edition prints, posters, books, cards and other high-country souvenirs, visit the **Wy'East Store** adjacent to Timberline Lodge. A cross between a gift shop and a mountain outfitter, this is also a good place to find sportswear that will make you even more stylish on your way down the slopes. ~ Timberline; 503-272-3311 ext. 736, fax 503-272-3709.

AUTHOR FAVORITE

If you don't try the **Cascade Dining Room** in the Timberline Lodge, you'll be missing one of the best meals in the Pacific Northwest. Liveried waiters and waitresses preside over this arts-and-crafts establishment with a stone fireplace and views of the Cascade Mountains. On a frosty morning there's no better place to down fresh salmon hash or apple oat cakes from the breakfast buffet. Dinner entrées include rack of lamb, wild salmon, roast duckling and vegetarian specialties. ~ Timberline; 503-272-3311, fax 503-272-3710. DELUXE TO ULTRA-DELUXE.

Richardson's Recreational Ranch Gift Shop has a wide variety of polished spheres, as well as rocks from around the world. Choose from agates, jasper, marble, petrified wood, Moroccan fossils, novelty items and jewelry. ~ Located 11 miles north of Madras on Route 97, at Milepost 81 turn right and continue southeast three miles; 541-475-2680, fax 541-475-4299.

NIGHTLIFE

On Saturday, live bands play rhythm-and-blues at **Charlie's Mountain View**. This rustic mountain lodge offers booth and table seating. The walls and ceilings are appointed with old-time skis, boots, snowshoes, ski bibs and other high-country memorabilia. ~ Government Camp Loop off Route 26, Government Camp; 503-272-3333.

At the **Appaloosa Lounge** at Kah-Nee-Ta High Desert Resort, you can dance to live bands in a disco setting through the summer months. It's also fun to enjoy the music outside on the adjacent deck. When the stars are out this is a particularly romantic setting. ~ Warm Springs; 541-553-1112, 800-831-0100, fax 541-553-1071; www.kahneeta.com.

PARKS

MT. HOOD NATIONAL FOREST

This one-million-acre national forest is named for the 11,235-foot Cascades peak that dazzles newcomers and natives alike. Extending from the Columbia River Gorge south to the Willamette National Forest boundary, the resort region includes four major wilderness and roadless areas. Popular destinations include the Olallie scenic area, known for its beautiful lakes and wildflowers, and the Mt. Hood Loop, a 150-mile scenic drive circling Oregon's highest peak. Along the way, you'll see mountain meadows, waterfalls, scenic streams, major ski areas and the magical Columbia River Gorge. More than 4500 miles of rivers and streams and more than 160 lakes and reservoirs will delight anglers seeking trout, salmon or steelhead. Many trails are wheelchair accessible. There are picnic tables, visitors center and restrooms. Trailhead fee, $5 per vehicle for some trails, available at the visitors center. ~ Access is via Routes 84, 30, 35, 224 and 26; 503-668-1700; www.fs.fed.us/r6/mthood.

Thanks to dependable snowpack throughout the summer months, it is possible to spend the morning skiing on Mt. Hood and devote the afternoon to swimming in the warm waters of nearby Cascade Lake.

▲ Permitted in 106 campgrounds; $16 to $18 per night; RV sites without hookups are available. Three of the best sites for tent/RV camping are on Timothy Lake: the Gone Creek, Hood View and Oak Fork sites. Or try Trillium Lake, with 54 tent/RV sites close to boating and fishing. No hookups are available at any of the sites. Reservations: 877-444-6777 ($9 registration fee).

COVE PALISADES STATE PARK Located at the junction of the Crooked, Deschutes and Metolius rivers, this 4129-acre park encompasses two arms of Lake Billy Chinook. The cove is set beneath towering palisades and located on benchland punctuated by volcanic cones. Rich in petroglyphs and American Indian history, this region is a geological showcase. Fishing is excellent for smallmouth bass, trout and kokanee. Ten miles of hiking trails offer excellent panoramic views and opportunities to see wildlife. There is also a picnic area, restrooms, a marina, a playground, nature trails and concessions. Day-use fee, $3. ~ Off Route 97, 15 miles southwest of Madras; 541-546-3412, fax 541-546-2220.

▲ There are 94 tent sites ($13 to $17 per night), 174 RV hookup sites ($17 to $21 per night) and 3 cabins ($48 to $69 per night). Reservations: 800-452-5687.

Central Cascades

One of Oregon's top recreational areas, the Central Cascades include some of the state's finest museums and interpretive centers. A year-round getaway for hiking, fishing, climbing and skiing, this area is also famous for its volcanic scenery, mountain lakes and rafting. Within the national forests are some of the West's leading wilderness areas and great opportunities for wildlife viewing. The region is an ideal family resort and also boasts one of the best scenic drives in the Northwest, the Cascades Loop Highway.

Although none of the peaks have the name recognition of Mt. Hood, the Central Cascades are by no means inferior mountains. A trio known collectively as the Three Sisters rises above 10,000 feet, while relatively diminutive Mt. Bachelor (a mere 9065 feet) provides some of the Northwest's best alpine skiing. The topography is so daunting, in fact, that not many roads cross the Central Cascades, although a few open up in the summer to provide access to the area's voluminous mountain lakes and rivers. Still, plenty of destinations can be reached year-round, and there are enough outdoor activities to keep you busy for weeks.

SIGHTS

A good way to begin your visit is by heading west from Redmond 20 miles on Route 126 to **Sisters**. Gateway to some of the Cascades' most memorable scenery, this small town has a Wild West–style main street that delights tourists driving between the Willamette Valley and the Bend area.

After pausing to shop, dine or provision, head west nine miles on Route 20 and then turn north to the **Metolius River Recreation Area**. Here you can enjoy flyfishing and, in the winter, cross-country skiing. ~ 541-549-0251, fax 541-549-4253; www.sisterschamber.com, e-mail info@sisterschamber.com.

Nearby **Black Butte Ranch** is a resort area (see "Lodging" below) named for a towering volcanic cone. ~ Route 20, eight miles west of Sisters; 541-595-6211, fax 541-595-2077; www.blackbutteranch.com, e-mail info@blackbutteranch.com. To the west off Route 20, **Suttle Lake** is a resort destination as well, with easy access to the scenic treasures of the Mt. Washington Wilderness to the south. Continue west on Route 20 to Route 22 and **Detroit Lake**, a recreational area ideal for waterskiing.

HIDDEN ► This area is also home of the **Shady Cove Bridge**, an unusual, three-span, wooden-truss structure. The bridge, handcut and hand-assembled using hundreds of small interlocking pieces, links French Creek Road with Little North Santiam drainage.

From Detroit Lake, take Forest Road 46 northeast ten miles to **Breitenbush Hot Springs**, a New Age wilderness resort. Yoga, guided forest hikes, meditation, hot-springs pools, steam saunas and massage therapy are all part of the fun. The artesian hot springs boast 30 minerals said to have curative powers. ~ Forest Road 46, Milepost 10, Detroit; 503-854-3314, fax 503-854-3819; www.breitenbush.com, e-mail office@breitenbush.com.

HIDDEN ► Return to Route 22 and head southeast. Along this route is a major volcanic landmark, **Clear Lake**, the source of the McKenzie River. Created when lava blocked a canyon, this lake lives up to its name in every respect.

Continue south on Route 126 to **Sahalie Falls**, a wheelchair-accessible spot where the McKenzie River cascades 100 feet over lava cliffs. A short drive south is **Koosah Falls**, which plunges more than 80 feet. In the fall this waterfall divides into several sections. Southeast on Route 126 another 17.6 miles is the hamlet of **McKenzie Bridge**, gateway to many scenic highlights of the Central Cascades. The town proper consists of little more than the Log Cabin Inn and a small market.

Head east to the **McKenzie River Ranger District and Cascade Center** (541-822-3381) and pick up the **Aufderheide National Scenic Byway** audio tape. Following old logging roads, the byway winds through the Three Sisters Wilderness, passing mid-size peaks like Olallie Mountain (5708 feet) and Grasshopper Mountain (5651 feet). The byway parallels the south fork of the McKenzie River for much of the way. You can also begin this 60-mile tour from the south end at the **Westfir Lodge Bed and Breakfast Inn**. The same tape is available here. ~ Route 58, Westfir; 541-782-3103.

Before returning north to the McKenzie Bridge area, take a look around the Oakridge area. We liked the **Oakridge Pioneer Museum**, located three miles west of Westfir. Even if you're not into chainsaws—one of the Northwest's best collections is found here—you'll enjoy seeing the antique farming and logging implements, grocery displays, American Indian artifacts and vintage crockery. Parked just down the street are an antique logging truck, fire truck and caboose. The museum is open Saturday from 1 to 4 p.m., Tuesday and Thursday from 10 a.m. to noon, and with advance notice. ~ 76433 Pine Street, Oakridge; 541-782-2402.

Twenty miles east of Oakridge is pristine **Waldo Lake**. Clean enough to qualify as distilled water, the six-mile-long lake has astonishing visibility. Out on the water you can see down 100 feet to the bottom. While there are facilities, the lake, one of Oregon's largest, also has wilderness on the west and north shores. ~ Route 58. ◄HIDDEN

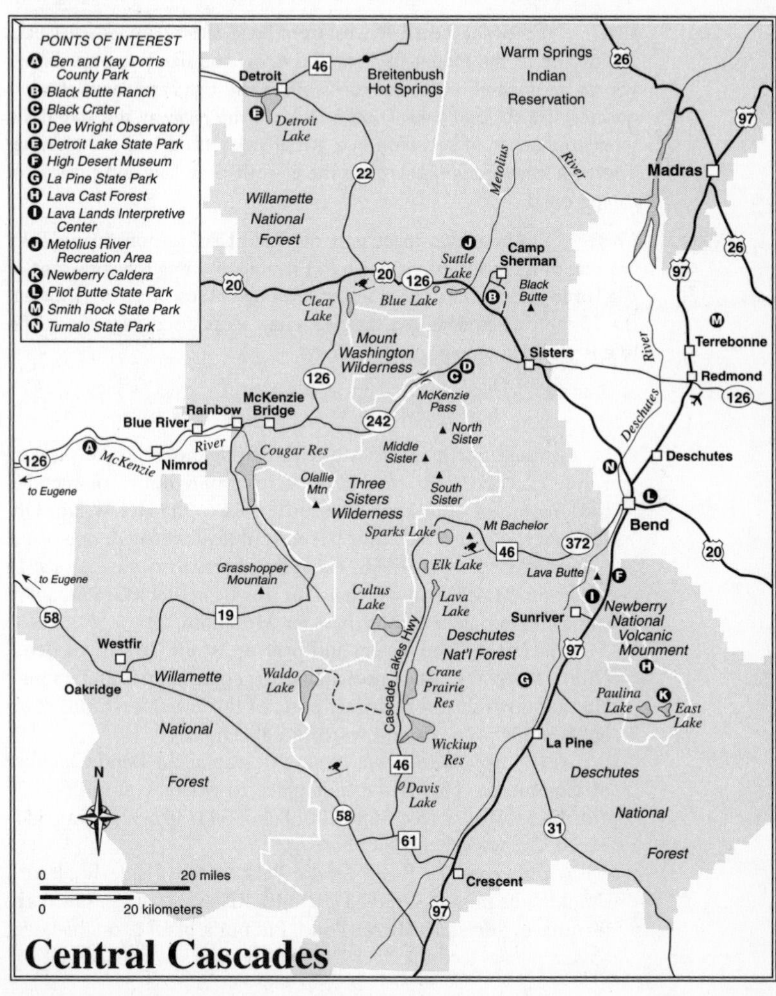

SCENIC DRIVE

Cascade Lakes Highway

This 87-mile mountain highway takes motorists close to Mount Bachelor and the Three Sisters Peaks on the Pacific Crest. Along the way are dozens of alpine lakes—large and small, natural and manmade—offering great fishing, camping, boating (mostly nonmotorized) and chilly swimming. From Bend, take Century Drive west. As it leaves town, it becomes Route 46, the Cascade Lakes Highway.

TODD LAKE Following Route 46 west from Bend, after 23 miles you'll pass the turnoff to the Mount Bachelor Ski Area. Another two miles brings you to an unpaved road that turns off to the right and leads about a quarter-mile to Todd Lake. Though close to the highway, this lake has a wonderful sense of seclusion in a glacial valley filled with wildflowers. There's a fishermen's trail around the 60-foot-deep lake and a primitive campground.

SPARKS LAKE About two miles past the Todd Lake turnoff, Sparks Lake has one of the prettiest views on this route, reflecting the snowcaps of the Three Sisters in its placid water. Although motorboats are allowed, the 10-mph speed limit and shallow water areas discourage them. The lake is ideal for canoeing and flyfishing.

Heading north to the McKenzie Bridge area again, pick up Route 126 east to Route 242 (a narrow route not recommended for long motor homes) up McKenzie Pass to the **Dee Wright Observatory**, where a half-mile paved trail leads through one of the Cascades' largest lava fields. From the observatory you can see 11 mountain peaks. Also worth a visit nearby is **Black Crater**, a volcanic summit close to North Sister Mountain.

Continue east to Sisters and pick up Route 20 east to **Bend**. One of Oregon's fastest-growing resort communities and a sunny alternative to the more drizzly parts of the Northwest, this town has become a year-round recreational center.

As you drive into town, be sure to stop at the **Bend Chamber of Commerce**. This is the best place to orient yourself. ~ 777 Northwest Wall Street, Suite 200, Bend; 541-382-3221, fax 541-385-9929; www.bendchamber.org.

In the center of Bend, **Drake Park** on Riverside Boulevard shouldn't be missed. On the Deschutes River, this urban sanctuary features picturesque **Mirror Pond**. Put out a blanket on the lawn, have a picnic, feed the ducks and study your own reflection.

DEVILS LAKE Four miles farther on, glacier-fed Devils Lake is one of the few lakes that can be seen from the highway and one of the high points of this drive. The crystalline turquoise water and 10-foot-deep white pumice bottom make it easy to see the trout that swim below, though catching them may be a challenge. There's a small campground, a hiking trail, and a trailhead for longer trails into the Three Sisters Wilderness.

HOSMER LAKE Five miles beyond Devils Lake is the turnoff to Hosmer Lake, a popular catch-and-release fishing lake that supports a landlocked salmon population. The tiny islands in the north part of the lake are home to otters and minks. Reeds and marshes make it hard to walk close to the water's edge, but hikers in the surrounding wildflower meadows and conifer forests may spot elk, deer and porcupines.

CRANE PRAIRIE RESERVOIR About 20 miles beyond the Hosmer Lake turnoff, manmade Crane Prairie Reservoir is one of the most popular destinations on the east slope of the Cascades for recreational motorboating. It's also a major habitat for ospreys, and visitors can watch as these big "fish eagles" dive at high speed to snag fish with their talons.

The Cascade Lakes Highway passes two other large manmade lakes, Wickiup Reservoir and Davis Lake, before returning to Route 97 at Crescent, midway between Bend (46 miles) and Crater Lake (51 miles). If you're planning to return to Bend, shortcut roads return due east to Route 97 from both Crane Prairie and Wickiup reservoirs.

Although strip development along Route 97 is changing Bend's small-town character, the past is well preserved at the **Deschutes Historical Center Museum.** Located in the Reid School building on the south end of downtown, the museum features exhibits on American Indian history, early-day trappers and explorers, pioneer trails and the lumber industry. Closed Sunday and Monday. Admission. ~ 129 Northwest Idaho Avenue, Bend; 541-389-1813, fax 541-317-9345; deschutes.historical.museum, e-mail info@deschutes.historical.museum.

Three miles south of Bend is the **High Desert Museum.** One of the finest collections in the Pacific Northwest, the indoor galleries are complemented by 20 acres of nature trails and outdoor exhibits. Permanent exhibits share the contemporary reservation experience of the Columbia Plateau Indians, as well as the natural history and settlement. A nice display here is a dawn-to-dusk "walk through time" that showcases the past. Along the way you can share in the cultural history of the Plateau Indians or check out the 19th-century heyday of the cowboy. After seeing Indian exhibits, crafts and quilting displays, visitors head outdoors to view the river-otter pool and a birds-of-prey show. Admission. ~ 59800 South Route 97; 541-382-4754, fax 541-382-5256; www.highdesertmuseum.org, e-mail info@highdesertmuseum.org.

Continue south on Route 97 to **Newberry National Volcanic Monument**, one of Oregon's geologic showcases and the product of more than 500,000 years of volcanic eruptions. Part of the Deschutes National Forest, the monument encompasses numerous volcanic landmarks. At the **Lava Lands Interpretive Center**, you'll find exhibits, dioramas, videos and interpretive staff who can suggest a variety of nature trails that lead through the lava flow. Call for spring and fall hours. Admission. ~ 58201 South Route 97; 541-593-2421, 541-383-4771 (winter), fax 541-383-4700; www.fs.fed.us/r6.

One piece of Devils Hill Flow volcanic rock was flown to the moon by Apollo astronaut James Irwin, who as an astronaut candidate trained in the area. The flow is located on Cascade Lakes Highway, between Devils and Sparks lakes.

Within this ten-square-mile lava flow are highlights like 6650-year-old **Lava Butte**, which changed the course of the Deschutes River. Reached by a paved road from the interpretive center, the butte offers a 360-degree view of the Cascades, the Lava Lands and the high desert to the east. You'll have to hike the final 100 yards to the summit. After enjoying the vista, you can continue west four miles from the interpretive center (follow the signs saying "Deschutes River Views") to reach **Benham Falls**, a popular picnic spot next to the Deschutes. To reach the falls, continue on the trail another quarter of a mile.

Much of the best sightseeing in the monument is found on the east side of Route 97. Two worthy spots in this fascinating region are **Lava River Cave** and **Lava Cast Forest.** The former, a lava tube, is great for spelunkers (fee). Flashlight in hand, you can walk a mile down this eerie tunnel (Oregon's longest uncollapsed lava tube), but bring warm clothing since it stays around 40° in the tube; it's closed in winter because of hibernating bats. The latter, explored via a mile-long, self-guided trail, is a unique piece of Oregon scenery. This unusual landscape was shaped when lava swept across a stand of pine 6000 years ago, creating molds of each tree.

The region's largest geologic feature is 500-square-mile **Newberry Volcano**, created by eruption from thousands of volcanos over the past half-million years in the area just south of Bend. **Paulina and East lakes,** two popular resort areas for anglers, are found in the 20-square-mile **Newberry Caldera**. Also worth a visit is the crater's shiny, black obsidian flow.

West of Bend is **Mt. Bachelor**, central Oregon's premier ski area (see "Outdoor Adventures" below). Continue up the **Cascade Lakes Highway** to tour one of the region's most idyllic resort regions. Todd, Sparks, Devils, Elk, Hosmer, Lava, Cultus and Davis lakes are a few of the popular spots for fishing, boating, swimming and camping. For those eager to head for the outback, there's easy access to high-country lakes, streams and creeks in the Three Sisters Wilderness.

Scenic highlights in this region include spots like **Devils Garden**, a beautiful meadow where you can spot pictographs left behind by Warm Springs Indians. ◄HIDDEN

LODGING

Sisters Motor Lodge offers comfortable bed-and-breakfast-style accommodations with funky, antique-decorated rooms. Four of the 11 rooms have kitchenettes; two-bedroom units are available. The full breakfast (available only during peak travel season; call ahead) includes fresh seasonal fruit, a hot entrée such as quiche or pancakes, juice and coffee. ~ 511 West Cascade Street, Sisters; 541-549-2551, fax 541-549-9399. MODERATE TO DELUXE.

When it comes to lodging, you really can get just about anything you want at **Black Butte Ranch**. This 1830-acre resort offers more than 100 condos, cabins and private homes. Chalet-style accommodations nestled in the pines have paneled walls and ceilings, decks, fireplaces and, in some condos, fully equipped kitchens. Choose between two golf courses, four swimming pools, 18 miles of bike and jogging trails and 23 tennis courts. There's canoeing in a spring-fed lake, as well as skiing, hiking, fishing, boating and horseback riding. ~ Route 20, eight miles west of Sisters; 541-595-6211, 800-452-7455, fax 541-595-2077; www.blackbutteranch.com, e-mail info@blackbutteranch.com. MODERATE TO ULTRA-DELUXE.

The **Metolius River Lodges** in Camp Sherman include 13 cabins with one, two or three bedrooms. Located about 15.5 miles northwest of Sisters, this wooded retreat is in an area ideal for mountain biking, cross-country skiing, flyfishing and water sports. The wood-paneled units have carpeting, fireplaces, kitchens, barbecues and rustic cabin furniture. ~ Five and a half miles north of Route 20, Camp Sherman; 541-595-6290, 800-595-6290; www.metoliusriverlodges.com, e-mail cabins@metoliusriverlodges.com. MODERATE TO ULTRA-DELUXE.

A small lake created by a dammed stream is just one of the attractions at Camp Sherman's **Lake Creek Lodge**. Eighteen one-, two- or three-bedroom knotty pine–paneled cabins feature Early American furniture, full kitchens, fireplaces and decks. Near the Metolius River, this 60-acre resort has tennis courts, a swimming pool, bike and hiking trails. In the summer they serve meals family style and offer special activities for children. ~ Forest Service Road, four miles north of Route 20, Camp Sherman; 541-595-6331, 800-797-6331, fax 541-595-1016; www.lakecreeklodge.com, e-mail stay@lakecreeklodge.com. DELUXE TO ULTRA-DELUXE.

As far as luxurious New Age facilities go, secluded **Breitenbush Hot Springs** has it all. Located in the western Cascades, this retreat provides everything from massage therapy to yoga to a spiritual/self-help workshop. Guests bring their own bedding and are housed in spartan, cedar-shake cabins paneled with fir; platform tents and campsites are available in summer. Geothermal heat and electricity from hydropower provide energy self-sufficiency. Guests can choose between hot tubs, *au naturel* hot springs overlooking the river and mountains and a hot natural-steam sauna complete with a cold-water tub. Vegetarian meals are included. Reservations required. ~ Forest Road 46, Milepost 10, Detroit; 503-854-3314, 503-854-3320 (day-of reservations), fax 503-854-3819; www.breitenbush.com. MODERATE.

Herbert Hoover, Clark Gable and Sean Penn have all stayed at the **Log Cabin Inn**. A 19th-century stagecoach stop, this three-story log building is on the National Historic Register and replaced the original building that burned down in a 1905 fire. Although the second-story bordello now serves only as a gift shop, many other traditions endure at the cedar-paneled dining room, bar and wraparound porch. Eight log cabins (two with kitchenettes) on this six-and-a-half-acre site face the McKenzie River. The units have period furniture, quilts, rockers, fireplaces, braided rugs and decks. ~ 56483 McKenzie Highway, McKenzie Bridge; 541-822-3432, 800-355-3432, fax 541-822-6173; www.logcabininn.com, e-mail lci@rio.com. MODERATE TO DELUXE.

Holiday Farm Resort has roomy cottages on the McKenzie River complete with fireplaces, decks and kitchenettes. The units make an ideal fishing retreat—you can cast for trout from your porch! This 90-acre resort has two private lakes and serves meals in a farmhouse that was once a stagecoach stop. ~ 54455 McKenzie River Drive, Blue River; 541-822-3715, 800-823-3715, fax 541-822-0346; www.holidayfarmresort.com, e-mail hfr@aol.com. DELUXE.

Just a few miles northeast of Oakridge, the **Westfir Lodge Bed and Breakfast Inn** is right across the street from Oregon's longest covered bridge. This hostelry offers eight rooms decorated in English country antiques with private baths. Evening dessert and a full breakfast are provided. ~ Across from the covered bridge, off Route 58, Westfir; phone/fax 541-782-3103. MODERATE.

The Riverhouse in Bend is one of over a dozen motels on the city's main drag. There are 220 rooms featuring contemporary furniture, floral-print bedspreads and sitting areas. In the evening you can relax in front of the fireplace or have a drink on your deck overlooking the Deschutes River. Deluxe-priced suites are available with kitchen facilities. An 18-hole golf course, jogging trail, two pools, two saunas and three whirlpools make this a good place to relax. ~ 3075 North Route 97, Bend; 541-389-3111, 800-547-3928, fax 541-389-0870; www.riverhouse.com, e-mail reservations@riverhouse.com. MODERATE TO ULTRA-DELUXE.

In the same part of Bend is the **Econo Lodge**, located directly beside the Bend Welcome Center and featuring 36 uniform motel rooms, a swimming pool and a hot tub. Continental breakfast served. ~ 3705 North Route 97, Bend; phone/fax 541-382-2211, 800-509-2211; www.econolodge.com. BUDGET.

The **Dunes Motel**, with 30 rooms, is close to downtown Bend. ~ 1515 Northeast 3rd Street, Bend; 541-382-6811, fax 541-389-7504. MODERATE.

Providing an extensive variety of children's programs during the summer, **Rock Springs Guest Ranch** is a family-oriented resort with comfortable, contemporary cabins in a forested setting. The pine-paneled cabins feature vaulted ceilings, light-pine furnishings, fireplaces, wet bars and sitting areas. On the grounds are horse stables, tennis courts, a pool, trout pond, a volleyball area and a hot tub. Rates include three meals daily. ~ 64201 Tyler Road, Bend; 541-382-1957, 800-225-3833, fax 541-382-7774; www.rocksprings.com, e-mail info@rocksprings.com. ULTRA-DELUXE.

Before the arrival of the white man, American Indians conducted rituals and ceremonies at Breitenbush Hot Springs.

Located across from Drake Park, **Lara House Bed and Breakfast** hosts guests in six big, carpeted rooms with easy chairs, antiques, colorful quilts and private baths, some with clawfoot tubs. You can take your full breakfast on the sun porch. This 1910 Craftsman also has a comfortable living room and an outdoor hot tub. ~ 640 Northwest Congress Street, Bend; phone/fax 541-388-4064, 800-766-4064; www.larahouse.com, e-mail larahousebnb@aol.com. MODERATE TO DELUXE.

The **Bend Riverside Motel** offers 193 rooms, studios and suites with park or river views. The studios and suites have fireplaces, kitchen facilities, saunas, hot tubs and tennis facilities. Convenient to downtown in a secluded setting. ~ 1565 Northwest Hill Street, Bend; phone/fax 541-389-2363, 800-284-2363; www.bendriversidemotel.com, e-mail bendrivers@aol.com. MODERATE TO DELUXE.

At the 3300-acre **Sunriver Lodge and Resort**, you can choose between 300 rooms and suites featuring pine furniture, fireplaces, wall-to-wall carpets and decks with views of the Cascades. Condos and homes are also available. All guests can take advantage of the pools, tennis courts, bicycles, canoes, skiing, golf, horseback riding and other facilities. ~ Route 97, 15 miles south of Bend, in Sunriver; 541-593-1221, 800-547-3922, fax 541-593-5458; www.sunriver-resort.com, e-mail info@sunriver-resort.com. ULTRA-DELUXE.

In the wooded Cascades foothills, **The Inn of the Seventh Mountain** is the only resort in Oregon with its own skating rink and waterslide. The 327 rooms, suites and apartments have kings, queens and Murphy beds, knotty-pine paneling, fireplaces and contemporary prints. Convenient to Mt. Bachelor, the inn is ideally located for horseback riding, whitewater rafting and mountain biking. ~ 18575 Southwest Century Drive, five miles west of Bend; 541-382-8711, 800-452-6810, fax 541-382-3517; www.seventhmountain.com, e-mail info@seventhmountain.com. MODERATE TO ULTRA-DELUXE.

HIDDEN ►

Built around a circa-1923 lodge, ten-unit **Elk Lake Resort** is a forested retreat ideal for fishing, canoeing, kayaking and loafing. The knotty-pine cabins, with two or three bedrooms, kitchens and small decks, are near wilderness hiking and Nordic skiing. For the adventurous, the resort is accessible only by cross-country skiing, snowcat and snowmobile in the winter months. ~ Cascade Lakes Highway, 30 miles west of Bend; 541-480-7228, fax 541-410-4917; www.elklakeresort.com, e-mail elkinfo@elklakeresort.com. DELUXE TO ULTRA-DELUXE.

DINING

In Sisters, **Ali's** provides a convenient solution for those who can't decide between a sandwich or a salad. Generous sandwiches served on an open-faced bagel or wrapped pita bread include curry chicken, dilly tuna, and lemon-ginger chicken. A wide variety of vegetarian sandwiches and smoked-turkey sandwiches are offered, as well as soups, pasta salads, bagels and ice cream. Lunch only. ~ Town Square, Sisters; 541-549-2547. BUDGET.

One of the most popular pizza parlors in these parts is **Papandrea's**. The modest board-and-batten establishment has indoor seating and patio service on picnic tables covered with green tablecloths. Antique farm implements decorate the dining room. All dough and sauces are homemade, and the tomatoes are fresh. ~ 442 East Hood Street, Sisters; 541-549-6081, fax 541-549-7407. MODERATE.

For dining in a contemporary setting, consider the **Restaurant at Black Butte Ranch**. This split-level establishment has cathedral ceilings, picture windows and early American furniture.

AUTHOR FAVORITE

A Bend tradition since 1936 and one of my state-wide top spots, **Pine Tavern** has an enviable location overlooking Mirror Pond. Built around late-18th-century ponderosa pines, the restaurant prides itself on home-cooked dishes like Marsala chicken, fresh salmon and their specialty, Oregon County prime rib using grain-fed beef. Don't miss the sourdough scones with honey butter. Seafood specials are offered each evening; there's also a children's menu. No lunch on Sunday. ~ Foot of Northwest Oregon Street, Bend; 541-382-5581, fax 541-382-5586; www.pinetavern.com, e-mail tavern@pinetavern.com. MODERATE TO DELUXE.

While enjoying the panoramic Cascades view, you can order prime rib, roast duck, oysters, halibut filet, pasta primavera with chicken or vegetables. Closed Monday through Wednesday in winter. ~ Route 20, eight miles west of Sisters; 541-595-1260, fax 541-595-1212; www.blackbutteranch.com, e-mail info@blackbutteranch.com. DELUXE.

Located in a shingled lodge-style building adjacent to the Metolius River, **Kokanee Café** is recommended for Pacific Northwest cuisine, including fresh, wild-caught seafood dishes, and organic meats and produce. The desserts are exceptional. Worth a special trip. Dinner only. Closed late October to April. Call for hours and reservations. ~ Camp Sherman; 541-595-6420. DELUXE. ◄ HIDDEN

Whether you choose one of the porch lunches served alfresco or head in to the paneled dining room for supper, the historic **Log Cabin Inn** offers fine dining in a traditional setting. This three-story log building, originally a stagecoach stop erected in 1886, was rebuilt in 1906 after a fire. Specialties include barbecued salmon, baby-back ribs, mesquite-barbecued prime rib, rainbow trout fresh from the McKenzie River and pioneer game stew. No dinner Monday and Tuesday in winter. ~ 56483 McKenzie Highway, McKenzie Bridge; 541-822-3432; www.logcabininn.com, e-mail info@logcabininn.com. DELUXE. ◄ HIDDEN

In a café-style dining room set in an old church, the family-run **Ernesto's Italian Restaurant** serves up rich, homemade lasagna, veal parmigiana and calzone. ~ 1203 Northeast 3rd Street, Bend; 541-389-7274, fax 541-389-1686. MODERATE.

For some different fare, head for **Deschutes Brewery and Public House.** This microbrewery, known for its Cascade Golden Ale and Black Butte Porter, homemade root beer and ginger ale, serves upscale pub fare like a pastrami Reuben, buffalo wings and vegetarian chili. ~ 1044 Northwest Bond Street, Bend; 541-382-9242, fax 541-385-8095; www.deschutesbrewery.com, e-mail info@deschutesbrewery.com. MODERATE TO DELUXE.

Located in a chalet-style building, **Marcello's Cucina Italiana** packs locals into its carpeted brick dining room nightly. Their reward is pasta, veal and chicken specialties, as well as calzones, seafood and, of course, a dozen varieties of pizza. Dinner only. ~ Beaver Drive and North Ponderosa Road, Sunriver; 541-593-8300, fax 541-593-5965; www.marcelloscucinaitaliana.com. MODERATE TO DELUXE. ◄ HIDDEN

For dining with a view of the Cascades, a good choice is **The Meadows.** The restaurant serves fresh seafood and Northwestern cuisine. In summer you can dine on the outdoor deck with its panoramic view. ~ Sunriver Lodge, Sunriver; 541-593-3740 or 541-593-1221, fax 541-593-4678; www.sunriver-resort.com, e-mail info@sunriver-resort.com. DELUXE TO ULTRA-DELUXE.

Text continued on page 222.

Gorges in the Mist

The land of falling waters, the Pacific Northwest is the place to go for plunging rivers. Thousands of waterfalls are found here, often convenient to major highways or trails. Reached via fern canyons, paths through old-growth forests and along pristine streams, waterfall hunting is great sport, even on a rainy day. And part of the fun is getting misted or sprayed by the raging waters.

In the Cascades, these falls are at their peak in late spring or early summer. But even if you come later in the summer or fall, there will still be plenty to see: deep, plunging streams, tiered falls that split into roaring ribbons before converging in swirling pools, horsetails that drop at a 90-degree angle while retaining contact with bedrock. And, of course, you can count on frequently spotting the distinctive waterfall that gives this region its name—the Cascades that drop down in a series of steps.

The Mt. Hood area offers some of the loveliest falls. Head east to Route 35 to the entrance of the Mt. Hood Meadows ski area. You'll see a sign marking the .2-mile trail to **Umbrella Falls**. Although these falls drop only about 60 feet, the verdant setting and fields of wildflowers make this an excellent choice, especially for families with small children. In early summer, the falls trail is reached via a hike through fields of wildflowers. Return to Route 35 and continue 1.4 miles east to **Switchback Falls**. At its peak, in the late spring, North Fork Iron Creeks drops 200 feet.

To the south, the McKenzie River has two highly recommended falls accessible via Route 126. Located 5 miles south of the Route 20 junction, the river drops more than 100 feet at **Sahalie Falls**. Continue south another .4 mile to **Koosah Falls**. A trail takes you down the river canyon to enjoy the view from a series of overlooks. Continue another 5.2 miles south to a road that heads to the McKenzie River Trailhead. After hiking upriver for 2 miles you'll discover that **Tamolitch Falls** have now run dry. Although the river has been diverted to a reservoir at this point, it remains a scenic spot. Thanks to local springs, the river begins anew at this location.

The Bend area is an excellent choice for waterfall lovers. **Tumalo Falls**, ten miles west of town, is reached via Galveston Avenue and Route 1828. The falls drop nearly 100 feet in an area badly damaged by a fire in 1979. South of town, off Route 97, is **Paulina Creek Falls**. Located in

Newberry Crater, this 100-foot drop is an easy walk from Paulina Creek Falls picnic ground. Accessible only in summer.

Century Drive, the beginning of the Cascade Lakes Highway west of Bend, provides easy access to **Lava Island Falls** on the Deschutes River. Take this road to Route 41 and drive south for .4 mile. Go left on Route 620 for .8 mile to reach the falls. If you take Route 41 south from Century Drive 3 miles and pick up Route 100 for .9 mile you'll reach Dillon Falls. Take Route 620 south about 3 miles from the intersection of Route 100 to see a 50-foot cataract called **Benham Falls**.

In the Umpqua River Valley, Route 138, nicknamed "The Highway of Waterfalls," provides access to 11 falls within a 50-mile stretch. Among them is **Susan Creek Falls**, located via a trail 7.5 miles east of Idleyld Park. You'll hike 1 mile north of the highway to reach the falls. Drive Steamboat Road northeast from Steamboat 4.2 miles to reach **Steamboat Falls**. Located at a forest-service campground, this small waterfall is circumvented by fish that use an adjacent ladder. Near mile marker 42 about 3 miles southeast of Steamboat are **Jack Creek** and tiered **Jack Falls**. These three falls are particularly rewarding for photo buffs.

Also popular are **Toketee Falls**. To see this 90-foot drop, take Route 138 to the Toketee Lake turnoff. Continue north .3 mile to the trail leading west .6 mile to the falls. East of Toketee Lake is Lemolo Lake, a popular resort destination. From here, Thorn Prairie Road leads to Lemolo Falls Road. Hike the Lemolo Falls Trail 1 mile west to this cataract.

Off Route 62, the main highway from Medford to Crater Lake, is one of the Cascades' grander waterfalls, 175-foot **Mill Creek Falls**. Accessible by Mill Creek Road, this scenic spot is an easy .3-mile hike from the Mill Creek Falls Scenic Area trailhead on the south side of Prospect. Also accessible on this hike are **Barr Creek Falls**, **Prospect Falls**, **Pearsoney Falls** and **Lower Red Blanket Falls**.

Within Crater Lake National Park, **Annie Falls** is off Route 62, 4.7 miles north of the park's southern entrance. Because this falls is located in an unstable canyon-rim area, visitors should approach it with extreme caution. Also in the park, close to Applegate Peak, is **Vidae Falls**.

To get a complete rundown on these watery delights, check with local park or ranger offices. Or pick up a copy of the definitive guide to this subject, *A Waterfall Lover's Guide to the Pacific Northwest* by Gregory A. Plumb (The Mountaineers).

Also at Sunriver Lodge is the more casual **Merchant Trader Café**, with outdoor patio seating. The breakfast menu includes homemade scones and granola. Baby back ribs, sandwiches, wraps and gourmet salads are offered for lunch and dinner. ~ Sunriver Lodge, Sunriver; 541-593-3790, fax 541-593-4678; www.sunriver-resort.com, e-mail info@sunriver-resort.com. BUDGET TO MODERATE.

HIDDEN ►

If you're looking for a hearty breakfast or coffee-shop lunch fare, try the counter at the rustic **Elk Lake Resort**. The dining area is a great place for bacon and eggs, pancakes or french toast. Burgers, salads and sandwiches fill the lunch menu. Although table service is available, we recommend taking a stool for the maximum waterfront view. Dinner specials served nightly. Call for spring and fall hours. ~ Cascade Lakes Highway, 30 miles west of Bend; 541-480-7228, fax 541-410-4917; www.elklakeresort.com, e-mail info@elklakeresort.com. MODERATE TO DELUXE.

SHOPPING

If you're in the market for jewelry, wood sculpture, pottery or basketry, try the **Folk Arts Gallery**. More than 120 Pacific Northwest artists are represented. ~ 222 West Hood Street, Sisters; 541-549-9556.

At **Out West Designs** you can buy ready-made jewelry or take home some unique beads and create some yourself. ~ 103 B Hood Street, Sisters; 541-549-1140, 888-768-8937.

HIDDEN ►

Stop by the **Blue Spruce Gallery & Pottery Studio**, which carries a beautiful collection of pottery, ceramic vases, custom-made lamps and dinnerware, paintings, jewelry and decorative art. ~ 550 Southwest Industrial Way #45, Bend; phone/fax 541-389-7745; www.theblueprucegallery.com.

Deschutes Gallery displays Northwest American Indian and Inuit art pieces, including masks, boxes, bowls, blankets, jewelry and dolls, as well as prints and paintings. ~ 521 Northwest Colorado Avenue, Bend; 888-981-8200.

NIGHTLIFE

For live Top-40 and classic-rock music nightly, head to the **Riverhouse**. This contemporary lounge has a roomy dancefloor, full bar and spacious deck overlooking the Deschutes. In warm

AUTHOR FAVORITE

Silver Sage Trading, the gift shop at the High Desert Museum, is a great place to browse for American Indian basketry, nature books, handmade jewelry, educational toys, beadwork, cultural items, cards and photos. ~ 59800 South Route 97, Bend; 541-382-4754; www.highdesertmuseum.org, e-mail sst@highdesertmuseum.org.

weather you can enjoy dining and drinks on the deck. ~ 3075 North Route 97, Bend; 541-389-3111, fax 541-389-0870; www.riverhouse.com.

Cascades Theatrical Company has presented musicals, dramas, comedies and Broadway hits since 1978. This theater produces six shows from late August to late June. ~ 148 Northwest Greenwood, Bend; 541-389-0803.

The **Obsidian Opera Company** performs a mix of classics and new productions November through March. ~ P.O. Box 182, Bend, OR 97709; 541-385-7055.

PARKS

DETROIT LAKE STATE PARK This 104-acre park is a popular day-use and overnight facility on the shore of one of the busier Cascade Lakes. A forested spot on the north shore of Detroit Reservoir, the park is divided into two units. The smaller Mongold is for day-use picnicking, boat launching and swimming. To the east is the Detroit Lake State Park campground, with a boat launch and boat slips. You can fish for trout and kokanee salmon. There are restrooms, showers, a visitors center and picnic areas. Closed December through February. Day-use fee, $3. ~ Route 22, two miles west of Detroit; 503-854-3406.

▲ There are 133 tent sites ($12 to $16 per night), 178 RV hookup sites ($16 to $20 per night). Reservations: 800-452-5687.

WILLAMETTE NATIONAL FOREST This 1.6-million-acre region (larger than the state of Connecticut!) covers from 10,495-foot Mt. Jefferson to the Calapooya Mountains northeast of Roseburg. Diverse terrain ranges from volcanic moonscapes to wooded slopes and cascading rivers. The National Forest recently annexed Opal Creek Wilderness; more than 400,000 acres of wilderness encompass seven major Cascade peaks. Home to more than 300 animal species, including deer, cougar, grouse and Roosevelt elk, this forest also boasts more than 600 varieties of rhododendron. There are over 1600 miles of hiking trails here, and mountain bikers cluster near the town of Oakridge to ride the foothills. In the winter months, heavy snowfall blankets the popular Nordic and alpine skiing areas at Willamette Pass and Hoodoo Ski Bowl. More than 1500 miles of rivers and streams, as well as 375 lakes, offer countless opportunities for fishing. You'll find picnic tables, interpretive centers and restrooms. Trailhead parking fee, $5. ~ Access via Routes 22, 20, 126, 242 and 58; 541-465-6521, fax 541-225-6220; www.fs.fed.us/r6/willamette.

▲ Permitted at over 80 campgrounds; free to $18 per night; RV sites available at most campgrounds. Some of the most popular sites are the Hoover Campground at Detroit Reservoir, and the Paradise and McKenzie Bridge campgrounds near the town of McKenzie Bridge along Route 126. One of the more secluded sites (Homestead Campground) can be accessed by Forest Service Road 19 near Blue River. For details, access the National Forest website (above). Reservations: 877-444-6777; www.reserveusa.com.

One of the world's purest bodies of water, Waldo Lake, is found in Willamette National Forest.

BEN AND KAY DORRIS COUNTY PARK A picturesque, 92-acre park at the head of Martin Rapids blending river frontage with an old orchard, this park is shaded by Douglas fir and big-leaf maple that add color to the region in the fall months. While a mile of river frontage is the park's leading attraction, the "Rock House," an outcropping that provided shelter for pioneers traveling the historic wagon road, is also worth a visit. This is one of Oregon's better places to catch trout. Facilities include picnic areas and restrooms. ~ Route 126, 31 miles east of Springfield; 541-682-2000, fax 541-682-2009; www.lanecounty.org/parks, e-mail laneparks@co.lane.or.us.

SMITH ROCK STATE PARK Along steep Crooked River Canyon, this day-use park is popular with climbers. They enjoy scaling striated Smith Rock, a formation rising several hundred feet above the tributary's north bank. Named for John Smith, a 19th-century pioneer, the park features decent fishing for rainbows and smallmouth bass. There are picnic areas and restrooms. The forest on the south bank suffered a fire in 1996, but the area has been replanted and is recovering. Day-use fee, $3. ~ Northeast Crooked River Drive, east of Route 97, nine miles northeast of Redmond; 541-548-7501, 800-551-6949.

▲ Permitted in the Bivouac Area for primitive hike-in camping. Space limited by parking; $4 per person per night.

TUMALO STATE PARK Convenient to the Bend area in Deschutes River Canyon, it is forested with juniper, ponderosa pine, willow and poplar. This 333-acre park has handsome basalt bluffs above the canyon. There's good trout fishing, too. Facilities include a picnic area, restrooms, showers, a playground and nature trails. Day-use fee, $3. ~ Located five miles northwest of Bend on O. B. Riley Road off Route 20; 541-382-3586, 800-551-6949.

▲ There are 58 tent sites ($13 to $17 per night), 23 RV hookup sites ($17 to $22 per night), 7 yurts ($29 per night) and a hiker-biker camp ($4 per person per night). Reservations: 800-452-5687.

DRAKE PARK This verdant, 13-acre park is along the Deschutes River and includes a riverfront strollway and footbridge across the river. Beloved by the local populace, the park is home to most of Bend's community events. Stroll alongside the river and be serenaded by geese and ducks. Adjacent to downtown

Bend, it includes picturesque Mirror Pond, actually just a part of the river that was widened and made into a peaceful place to sit beside. You'll find picnic areas and a playground (across the bridge at Harmon Park). ~ Take Franklin Avenue west from Route 97 into downtown Bend where it becomes Riverside Boulevard. Continue west to the park; 541-388-5435, fax 541-388-5429; www.bendparksandrec.org.

PILOT BUTTE STATE PARK A cinder cone that served as a landmark for Oregon pioneers is the heart of this 100-acre urban park. The 511-foot-high volcanic dome is located on the east side of Bend and is a very popular climb (it takes only about 15 minutes to scale). Ascend the spiral road to the top of this pine-covered butte to enjoy great views of the Cascades from Mt. St. Helens to the Three Sisters. Bring your own water. ~ Greenwood Avenue (Route 20), Bend; 800-551-6949.

LA PINE STATE PARK This rolling Deschutes River Valley park is shaded by pine and old-growth forest. Expect to spot mule deer as you explore this uncrowded 2333-acre getaway. It's ideal for boating and a good base for visiting the surrounding volcanic landmarks including Newberry Crater. Anglers can fly cast for rainbow and brown trout. There are restrooms, showers and picnic areas. ~ Located west of Route 97 on La Pine State Park Road, 27 miles southwest of Bend; 541-536-2071, 800-551-6949. ◄ HIDDEN

▲ There are 137 RV hookup sites ($13 to $17 per night), 5 rustic cabins ($38 per night) and 5 deluxe cabins ($19 to $70 per night). Reservations: 800-452-5687.

DESCHUTES NATIONAL FOREST Named for the popular river that descends the east slope of the Cascades, this 1.6-million-acre forest embraces Mt. Bachelor, the Three Sisters Wilderness, the Cascade Lakes region and Newberry National Volcanic Monument. Many popular resorts and five wilderness areas are found in the Deschutes forests, meadows and high country. Climbing from 3000 to 10,358 feet, the forest is dominated by ponderosa pine. You can explore the Three Sisters Wilderness via the South Sisters Climbing Trail from the Cascade Lakes Highway at Devils Lake Campground. The forest is known for its raftable rivers, spelunking and skiing. There are innumerable places to ski cross-country, including Dutchman Flat, Edison Butte and the Skyliner/Meissner area. Bend is the most convenient jump-off point. More than 240 miles of streams and 158 lakes and reservoirs make for ideal fishing. There are picnic tables, interpretive centers, marinas and restrooms. ~ Access via Routes 126, 242, 58, 97, 31, 20 and 46; 541-383-5300, fax 541-383-5531; www.fs.fed.us/r6/centraloregon.

▲ There are over 100 campgrounds for tents and RVs throughout the national forest; $5 to $17 per night; call for details. The best camping is found off the Cascade Lake Highway near one of the many lakes in the area. Paulina Lake in the Newberry National Volcanic Monument has 69 tent/RV sites ($10 to $12; no hookups). South of Elk Lake, the Hosmer campground has two campgrounds with lots of room for tent camping ($5; no hookups).

Southern Cascades

Blessed with several major wilderness areas that are great for viewing wildlife or birdwatching, the Southern Cascades are also the home of Oregon's only national park, Crater Lake. In addition to being drop-dead gorgeous—its chilly waters are an extraordinarily piercing shade of blue—the lake offers many recreational possibilities, from Nordic skiing to snowshoeing to hiking. The Southern Cascades also include a real sleeper, the Klamath Lake area.

SIGHTS

CRATER LAKE One of the world's most famous mountain lakes, tucked inside the caldera of a collapsed volcano, Crater Lake is known for its shimmering vistas and dark, cold depths. The best way to see this geologic wonder is to take **Rim Drive**, the 33-mile road circling Crater Lake. With more than 20 turnouts, it provides a thorough overview of this mountain-rimmed, deep-blue lake. Vertical lava flow patterns add to the majesty of the volcanic scenery. The drive is seasonal; contact the visitors center (541-594-3100; www.nps.gov/crla) to be sure the road is open.

While the crystal-clear waters are the prime attraction, the 1000- to 2000-foot-high rim walls create an excellent cutaway view of the remains of Mt. Mazama. Allow at least two hours for this trip around the 20-square-mile, 1000-foot-deep lake (the road itself is about 33 miles around). You'll want to begin your tour at the **Rim Village Visitors Center** (open June through September). A short walk below the visitors center is **Sinnott Memorial Overlook.** There's a small museum on this rock ledge where rangers present interpretative geology talks during the summer months. Drive clockwise around the lake to **Discovery Point,** where in 1853 explorer John Wesley Hillman became the first white man to spot this treasure. ~ Visitors Center: 541-594-3100; www.nps.gov/crla.

From here you'll want to go to major viewpoints. About three miles past Discovery Point is a turnout ideal for seeing one of the park's major volcanoes, **Union Peak.** Continue another seven-tenths of a mile to **Wizard Island Overlook.** It's named for the small Crater Lake island that is actually the top of a small volcano. For a panoramic view of the lake, perfect for photographs, pull off at **Steel Bay.** Rim Drive's highest viewpoint is **Cloudcap.** This is a great spot to see how part of Mt. Mazama was sliced away by the caldera's collapse. Also of special interest is **Pumice Castle,** an orange and pink landmark sculpted by the elements into a fortress-like formation.

The only access to the lakeshore is found at **Cleetwood Cove Trail.** This steep route takes you down to Cleetwood Boat Landing, where you can tour the lake by boat (admission). On this two-hour tour you'll be able to explore **Wizard Island,** a 700-foot-high cinder cone and see remnants of an older volcano called the **Phantom Ship.** ~ Boat tours: 541-594-2255.

Although America's deepest (1943 feet) lake is the centerpiece of this national park, other attractions are well worth your time. Southeast of Rim Village you'll find the **Steel Information Center** (open year-round), where you can see an 18-minute video on the lake, as well as interpretive exhibits. ~ 541-594-3100.

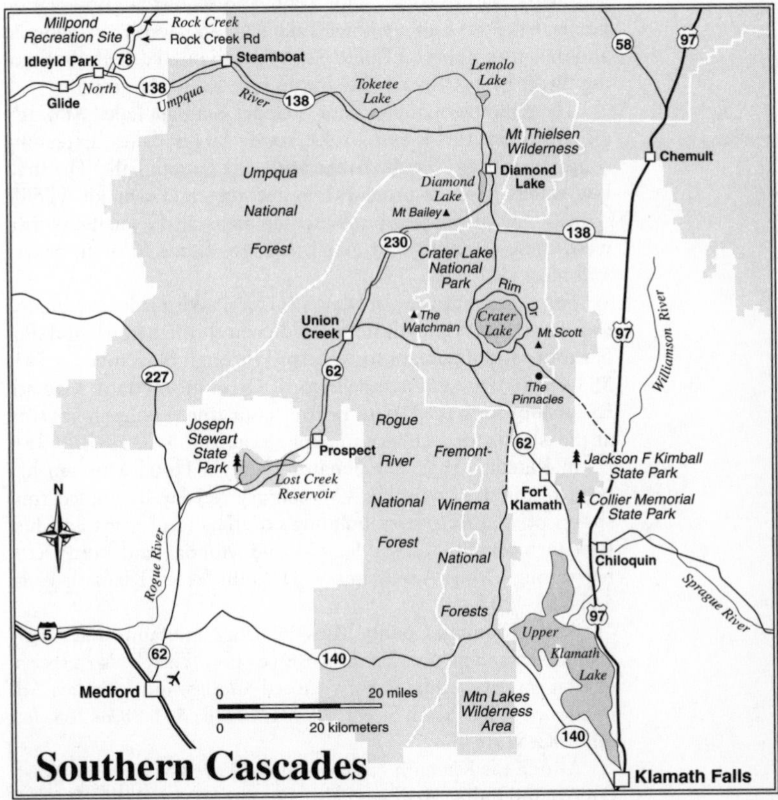

Southern Cascades

We also recommend visiting **The Pinnacles** area on the park's east side. Pumice and ash left behind by the Mt. Mazama collapse were gradually eroded by rain and snow. These formations evolved into rock pinnacles, further eroded by the elements into weird, hoodoo shapes. Today, hiking through these colorful canyons is one of the park's great pleasures.

Sixteen miles west of Crater Lake National Park in the vicinity of Union Creek is **Rogue River Gorge.** Here this mighty river is channeled into a beautiful little canyon easily accessed on foot. In the same area, a mile west of Union Creek, is **Natural Bridge** where the Rogue flows into a lava tube for a short distance before reappearing. The bridge is well worth a visit and is an easy walk.

KLAMATH LAKE REGION Although not in the mountains, its proximity to the high country makes the area around Upper Klamath Lake a favorite of travelers coming or going to them.

One of the best ways to explore the Klamath Lake area is via the **Upper Klamath Lake Tour Route.** Several state parks, botanical areas, nature sites, canoe trails and waterfowl observation points make this tour a winner. Take Route 97 south to Chiloquin and then turn north on Route 62 to Fort Klamath. (If you're coming direct from Crater Lake simply take Route 62 south.)

The centerpiece of your tour is **Upper Klamath Lake.** At nearly 64,000 acres, this is one of the state's largest lakes, extending south more than 25 miles to the town of Klamath Falls. The shallow waters here are prime fishing territory and a major wildlife refuge. One of the best birdwatching areas in the Pacific Northwest, these wetlands and marsh are also home to otter, beaver and muskrat.

For a different view of Klamath Lake, take a ride on a guided tour boat. The **Klamath Belle Paddlewheel** offers lunch and dinner tours and ice cream socials April through November. ~ 541-883-4622; www.klamathbelle.com. Or climb aboard **Klamath Excursions** for a one-, two- or four-hour tour. Longer tours stop at the islands for a chance to explore on foot. ~ 541-850- 6391.

In Klamath Falls, the **Senator Baldwin Hotel Museum** has been restored to its early-20th-century heyday. A guided tour shows off the four-story building's architectural gems and historic memorabilia. Closed Sunday and Monday and from October through May. Admission. ~ 31 Main Street, Klamath Falls; 541-883-4207.

At the **Klamath County Museum**, flora and fauna and American Indian and pioneer history are on display. There's also a special exhibit on geothermal energy. Closed Sunday and Monday. Admission. ~ 1451 Main Street, Klamath Falls; 541-883-4208, fax 541-883-5170.

Also in the Klamath Falls area is the **Favell Museum of Western Art and Indian Artifacts.** The contemporary building features

American Indian and Western art and artifacts, taxidermy and a vast collection of miniature firearms. You won't have trouble finding arrowheads because more than 60,000 are on display. Closed Sunday. Admission. ~ 125 West Main Street, Klamath Falls; 541-882-9996, fax 541-850-0125; www.favellmuseum.com.

LODGING

For cabins in a wooded setting, head for **Cultus Lake Resort**. Twenty-three spacious, pine-paneled units equipped with brick fireplaces, alcove kitchens and drop-beam ceilings are set in a forest glen. The lake is great for sailing, fishing, waterskiing and kayaking. There's also a beach for sunbathing and swimming. Be advised: some readers have had rude service from management. Units are rented by the week. Closed September 25 to mid-May. ~ Located 45 miles southwest of Bend off Cascade Lakes Highway; 541-408-1560, 800-616-3230; www.cultuslakeresort.com. MODERATE.

Twenty-five miles from Crater Lake in the small highway-side town of Chemult is the **Dawson House Lodge**, a 1929 train station boarding house that has been converted into a rustic yet cozy inn. Choose from five upstairs hotel rooms (all with private baths)

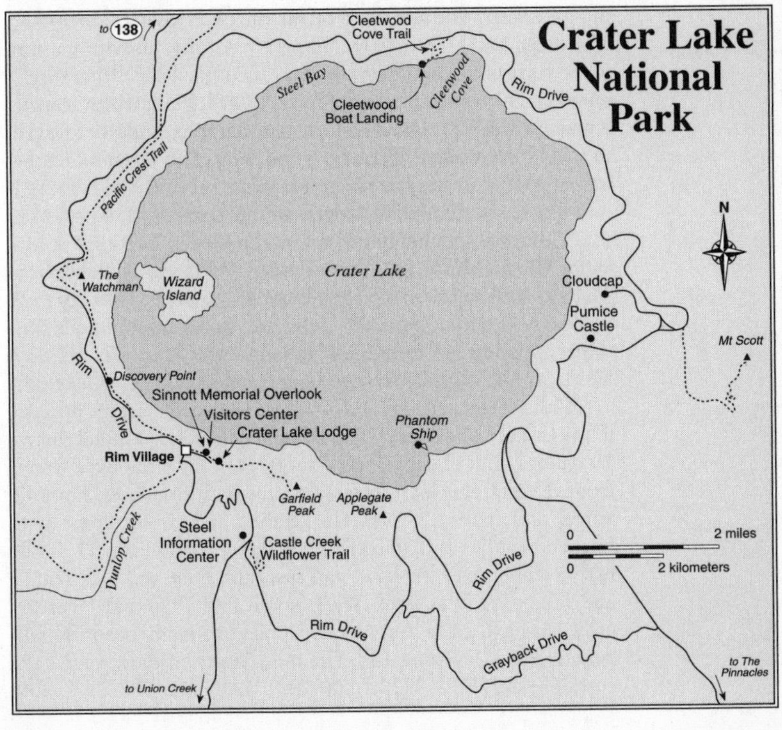

furnished with antiques, including one double unit featuring log-framed four-poster beds. The inn also offers three motel-style rooms, a studio-styled room, a loft and a second-story pine veranda. A continental breakfast awaits in the fireplace-warmed lobby each morning. ~ Route 97 at 1st Street, Chemult; 541-365-2232, 888-281-8375, fax 541-365-4451; www.dawsonhouse.net, e-mail dawson@presys.com. BUDGET TO MODERATE.

Zane Grey loved the north Umpqua River, and today a 31-mile stretch has been limited to "flyfishing only." In the heart of the river region 18 miles east of Idleyld Park is **Steamboat Inn**. An eclectic mix of streamside cabins, hideaway cottages, river suites and ranch-style homes, the inn serves meals family-style in the main lodge. Some of the 19 units are pine paneled; others offer river views, mini-kitchens, fireplaces, soaking tubs, quilted comforters and paintings by leading Northwest artists. Closed in January and February. ~ Route 138, Steamboat; 541-498-2230, 800-840-8825, fax 541-498-2411; www.thesteamboatinn.com, e-mail stmbtinn@rosenet.net. ULTRA-DELUXE.

Teddy Roosevelt and Zane Grey once stayed at Prospect Historical Hotel and Motel, a former stagecoach inn.

Crater Lake Lodge is a magnificent wood and stone structure built between 1909 and 1924 on the rim overlooking Crater Lake. The lodge has 71 rooms including a few lofts, all with natural-wood furnishings and many with views of the lake. Other superb views can be enjoyed from the lodge's Great Hall, which features a massive stone fireplace, historic photographs, and floor-to-ceiling windows framed in rustic wood bark. Closed mid-October to mid-May. ~ Crater Lake National Park; 541-830-8700, fax 541-830-8514; www.craterlakelodges.com. DELUXE TO ULTRA-DELUXE.

Additional lodging in the national park can be found at **Mazama Village Motor Inn**. Forty modern units are available from June to October. Board-and-batten exteriors, paneled interiors and wall-to-wall carpeting make these gray-toned accommodations rather appealing. ~ Crater Lake National Park, Route 62; 541-830-8700, fax 541-830-8514; www.craterlakelodges.com. MODERATE.

With 92 units, **Diamond Lake Resort** is the largest hostelry in the Crater Lake region. This complex includes 40 motel rooms, 10 studios and 42 cabins, all a short walk from the busy waterfront. Expect paneled, carpeted rooms with fireplaces, Franklin stoves and marine views. The studios and cabins come with kitchen facilities and, in some cases, private decks. An 11.5-mile biking trail circles the lake, and there are boat and bike rentals and hiking trails as well. While some find Diamond Lake too crowded for their tastes, it is convenient to many beautiful wilderness areas. ~ Route 138, five miles north of the Crater Lake entrance; 541-793-3333, 800-733-7593, fax 541-793-3309;

www.diamondlake.net, e-mail info@diamondlake.net. MODERATE TO ULTRA-DELUXE.

If you like the ambience of a historic inn but prefer the comfort of motel-style units, the **Prospect Historical Hotel and Motel** may be just the place. Located just a quarter mile off Route 62 and 28 miles from the south entrance to Crater Lake National Park, the white frame 1890 hotel has ten cozy rooms with Early American furniture, historical photos, quilts, vanities and access to a pleasant front porch. Once a stagecoach inn, it's now a National Historic Site. There are also 14 motel rooms. ~ 391 Mill Creek Drive, Prospect; 541-560-3664, 800-944-6490, fax 541-560-3825; www.prospecthotel.com, e-mail info@prospecthotel.com. MODERATE.

◄ HIDDEN

Motel-style units and cabins convenient to Upper Klamath Lake's Pelican Bay are found at **Rocky Point Resort**. Set in a fir forest frequented by elk and deer, this waterfront resort is a good place to photograph bald eagles, osprey and white pelican colonies. The five paneled rooms are clean and comfortable, and the four cabins offer kitchen facilities. Camping (33 RV hookups, 4 tent sites), boat rentals, moorage, fishing tackle and gift shop are all available on the premises. Closed November to April. ~ 28121 Rocky Point Road, Klamath Falls; 541-356-2287, fax 541-356-2222; www.rockypointoregon.com, e-mail rvoregon@aol.com. BUDGET TO MODERATE.

For inexpensive lodging try the **Maverick Motel**. Forty-nine carpeted guest rooms are brightly painted and furnished with darkwood furniture. There's an outdoor pool here. ~ 1220 Main Street, Klamath Falls; 541-882-6688, 800-404-6690, fax 541-885-4095. BUDGET.

DINING

With American Indian and pioneer decor, a menu featuring specialties like the buckaroo breakfast, and a parking lot filled with diesel rigs, station wagons and motorcycles, it's obvious that the **Wheel Cafe** cultivates an eclectic clientele. Take a seat at the counter and order turkey, swiss cheese, bacon and tomato on a sourdough roll or a chef's salad. ~ Route 97, Chemult; 541-365-2284, fax 541-365-2202; e-mail wagonwheel@presys.com. BUDGET TO MODERATE.

You'll have a hard time beating the **Steamboat Inn**. This establishment is famous for its fisherman's dinner. After enjoying hors d'oeuvres, wine and champagne in the library, guests head inside to the lodge where dinner is served family-style on gleaming wood tables illuminated by the glow of the fireplace. Appetizers are followed by salad, soup and homemade bread. One set dinner menu is served nightly. Entrées may include beef, fish, lamb or pork. Breakfasts here are also memorable. Don't miss the fruit rollups, an inn tradition. Dinner by reservation only. Closed January and February. ~ Route 138, Steamboat; 541-498-2230, 800-840-8825, fax 541-498-2411; www.thesteamboatinn.com, e-mail stmbtinn@rosenet.net. ULTRA-DELUXE.

For Mexican food, hamburgers, sandwiches and homemade soups, try **Munchies**. This full-service restaurant also serves fresh-baked pie. ~ 20142 Route 138, Glide; phone/fax 541-496-3112. BUDGET.

HIDDEN ►

An early American setting makes the carpeted **Prospect Historical Hotel and Motel Restaurant** a comfortable dining spot. From the prime rib to the pasta and chicken dishes, this establishment will challenge any dieter's willpower. There's also a selection of Northwest wines to complement your meal. The ambience is elegant. Dinner only. Closed October through April. ~ 391 Mill Creek Drive, Prospect; 541-560-3664, 800-944-6490, fax 541-560-3825; www.prospecthotel.com, e-mail info@prospecthotel.com. DELUXE.

With its beautiful setting overlooking Klamath Lake, rustic **Rocky Point Resort** is best known for its steaks and seafood. Open daily from Labor Day to Memorial Day; call for spring and fall hours. ~ 28121 Rocky Point Road, Klamath Falls; 541-356-2287, fax 541-356-2222; www.rockypointoregon.com, e-mail rvoregon@aol.com. MODERATE TO DELUXE.

SHOPPING

An excellent collection of limited-edition prints, American Indian and Western art, American Indian jewelry and arrowheads is found at the **Favell Museum Gift Shop**. Exhibited in an attractive, two-story shop, this store features many one-of-a-kind pieces on consignment from local and well-known artists, as well as a multitude of "made in Oregon" products like jams, syrups and candies. ~ 125 West Main Street, Klamath Falls; 541-882-9996, fax 541-850-0125; www.favellmuseum.com.

Over 150 artists and antique dealers at the Crafters Market sell wares including wood products, dolls, clocks, jewelry, quilts and toys. ~ 3040 Washburn Way, Klamath Falls; 541-882-5270.

For knives, cutlery, beads and beading supplies, American Indian earrings, arrowheads, buckskins and leather goods, visit **Oregon Trail Outfitters**. This board-and-batten building is extremely popular with visitors searching for a piece of the Old West. Closed Sunday. ~ 5728 South 6th Street, Klamath Falls; 541-883-1369, fax 541-883-8881.

NIGHTLIFE

Ross Ragland Theater hosts touring theater companies, country-and-western bands, jazz and blues and classical performers. The year-round calendar also includes special children's shows and, in the summer, locally produced musicals. ~ 218 North 7th Street, Klamath Falls; 541-884-5483, fax 541-884-8574; www.rrtheater.org.

The Linkville Playhouse offers a variety of plays and musicals from August through June. The local productions feature classics ranging from *The Secret Garden* to *You Can't Take It with You*. ~ 201 Main Street, Klamath Falls; 541-884-6782, 541-882-2586 (tickets).

PARKS

UMPQUA NATIONAL FOREST Named for the Umpqua Indians, this forest spans almost a million acres and embraces three wilderness areas, numerous waterfalls and high-country trails. Among the Umpqua landmarks are the world's tallest sugar pine, bedrock gorges and volcanic-rock formations. Within the Umpqua are volcanic ridges, pine benches, alpine forests and meadows laced by snow-fed streams. Major destinations include the scenic Umpqua River and Diamond, Lemolo and Toketee lakes. Most lakes allow swimming; only Lemolo Lake allows waterskiing. The forest is also convenient to Crater Lake. Kayaking and rafting are popular on the North Umpqua River. Mt. Bailey near Diamond Lake has downhill skiing, while the areas around Diamond and Lemolo lakes offer good cross-country trails. Hundreds of miles of streams and numerous lakes make this a great spot for angling, especially in the North Umpqua River. There are picnic tables, history programs, pack stations and restrooms. Trailhead parking fee, $5. ~ Access via Routes 138, 227, 1, 62 and 230; 541-672-6601, fax 541-957-3495; www.fs.fed.us/r6/umpqua.

◄ HIDDEN

▲ There are 54 campgrounds in the forest; $5 to $15 per night; RV sites without hookups are available. The Diamond Lake area is probably the most developed for camping, with three campgrounds around the lakeshore. Even better for those who want to be away from drive-in sites is the Twin Lakes campground (43 miles east of Glide), a walk-in (or bike-in) campground 10 miles from Route 138. You'll be camping in a primitive site under the stars amidst cold, clear high mountain lakes.

MILLPOND RECREATION SITE With half a mile of frontage on Rock Creek, this serene campground is a beautiful getaway near the community of Idleyld Park. It has a picturesque swimming hole and towering, moss-covered trees, and is the small Oregon park at its finest. You'll find picnic areas, a playground, a group campsite, a softball field and restrooms. Closed mid-October to early May. ~ From the town of Idleyld Park take Route 138 east to Route 78 (Rock Creek Road) and head north five miles; 541-440-4930, fax 541-440-4948.

◄ HIDDEN

▲ There are 12 tent/RV sites (no hookups); $8 per night.

CRATER LAKE NATIONAL PARK One of the unique geologic features of the Pacific Northwest, Crater Lake is irresistible. The 183,224-acre park offers 100 miles of hiking and cross-country skiing trails, a fascinating boat tour of this volcanic lake and opportunities for biking, fishing and backpacking. For anglers there's nothing to get excited about though there are rainbow trout and kokanee salmon off Wizard Island. There are picnic areas, restaurants, motel units and exhibits. Entrance fee (good for seven days), $10 per vehicle, $5 walk-in. ~ Route 62, 54 miles northwest of Klamath Falls; 541-594-3000, fax 541-594-3010; www.nps.gov/crla.

Crater Lake National Park rangers lead free snowshoe ecology walks on Saturday and Sunday (they provide the snowshoes).

▲ There are 200 tent/RV sites at Mazama Campground; $18 to $20 per night (without electrical hookups) or $23 per night (with electrical hookups). There are 16 tent sites at Lost Creek; $10 per night, no hookups. Backcountry camping by permit only. Campgrounds are closed in winter.

FREMONT-WINEMA NATIONAL FORESTS The Fremont-Winema National Forests lie on the eastern slopes of the Cascade Mountain Range in south central Oregon and expand east to "Oregon's outback" and the Warner Mountains. The 203-million-acre forests are famous for their fishing and waterfowl habitat, expansive views, dramatic cliffs and solitude. Although the forest elevation ranges from roughly 4100 to 9200 feet, much of the eastern portion of this semiarid region is high-plateau country. The Fremont-Winema are forested with pine and fir and have four designated wilderness areas, including the Mountain Lakes Wilderness Area. More than 200 bird species have been identified on this Pacific Flyway. In addition, antelope, elk, deer, bear, coyote, bobcat, beaver, otters and many other species live here. Dozens of lakes and rivers like the Sycan, Sprague and Williamson offer good opportunities to catch trout and mullet. Rock hounds can be happy here. You'll find picnic tables and restrooms. ~ Routes 97, 395, 31 and 140 all provide easy access; 541-883-6715, fax 541-883-6709; www.fs.fed.us/r6/frewin.

▲ Camping is permitted anywhere in the forest and there are 11 developed campgrounds with tent/RV sites; free to $13 per night.

HIDDEN ►

JACKSON F. KIMBALL STATE PARK This 19-acre Oregon state park is a scenic, forested spot on the headwaters of the Wood River. It's ideal for those seeking a quiet getaway. There's good fly-fishing for rainbow and brown trout. There is a picnic area. Closed November through March. ~ Route 232, three miles north of Fort Klamath; 541-783-2471, fax 541-783-2707.

▲ There are ten primitive sites; $5 to $9 per night.

COLLIER MEMORIAL STATE PARK Set in a ponderosa-pine forest at the junction of Spring Creek and Williamson River, this 655-acre park is a perfect place to spend the day or the night. The park is also a logging heritage site, filled with important mementos and lumberjack equipment. There's good trout fishing in the streams. You'll find picnic tables, restrooms, playground and a museum. ~ Route 97, 35 miles north of Klamath Falls; 541-783-2471, fax 541-783-2707.

▲ There are 18 tent sites ($11 to $15 per night) and 50 RV hookup sites ($13 to $17 per night). Closed November through March. Reservations: 800-452-5687.

JOSEPH STEWART STATE PARK A lush lawn leads down to Lost Creek Reservoir, making this park on the road to Crater Lake particularly inviting on a warm day. With 910 acres, there's room to spare for day and overnight use. Take a seat on a blanket beneath one of the pine groves and watch the waterskiers. Or toss in a line and wait for the big ones to nibble. With more than a mile of waterfront, this Rogue River Canyon park is a great place to take the kids. There's excellent fishing for bass, rainbow, brook or brown trout. Facilities include a picnic area, restrooms, showers and a marina. ~ Route 62, 35 miles northeast of Medford; 541-560-3334, fax 541-560-3855. ◄ HIDDEN

▲ There are 49 tent sites ($10 to $14 per night) and 148 RV hookup sites ($12 to $16 per night). Closed November through February.

Outdoor Adventures

FISHING

The Cascades are famous for rivers and lakes brimming with trout, salmon, bass and steelhead. Now that more and more people are trying to fish these waters, "We've got a shrinking resource," as one guide says; that's why you'll find him and others encouraging a catch-and-release policy for all fish caught. The point is that you can still wade out into the Deschutes to flyfish for wild trout or pull steelhead out of the Umpqua from aboard a drift boat and have the kind of experience immortalized in the fiction of Zane Grey.

NORTHERN CASCADES Whether you're an experienced fisher or a beginner, **Wy'East Expeditions** can arrange a day-long Deschutes River flyfishing trip for fall steelhead or, in the spring, wild rainbow trout. Overnight trips let you get out into areas that are a bit more remote. ~ 6700 Cooper Spur Road, Mt. Hood; 541-352-6457; e-mail bigcanoe@gorge.net.

So far, the national forest service has not issued permits to any guides or outfitters to take you fishing to mountain lakes in this part of the Cascades. You may, however, fish the lakes on your own. If you need gear, contact **Gorge Fly Shop** in Hood River. Besides renting gear and obtaining information, you can set up a guided trip on the Deschutes River, the John Day River, and other prime fishing spots in the area. ~ 201 Oak Street; 541-386-6977. In Maupin, **Michael McLucas** has been a fishing guide for over 25 years. He or his partner Mike Malefyt can take you out on the Deschutes for trout or steelhead fishing trips. ~ Oasis Resort; 541-395-2611; www.deschutesriveroasis.com.

CENTRAL CASCADES Although there's no commercial use permitted on the Metolius River (that is, no guided trips), it's a very popular flyfishing spot. **Fly Fisher's Place** can rent or sell you gear or arrange a guided trip on the McKenzie, the Deschutes or, near Prineville, on the Crooked River, where you can catch wild trout. ~ 151 West Main Street, Sisters; 541-549-3474. **High Desert Drifters, Guides, & Outfitters** specializes in flyfishing float trips for trout and steelhead on the Deschutes for either one day or several days. ~ 21030 Wilderness Way, Bend; 541-389-0607, 800-685-3474. **Sunriver Fly Shop,** also a guide service, offers fishing classes if you want to learn more. Some of its popular trips are to the Davis, Hosmer and Crane Prairie lakes, where you will catch a variety of trout between April and November. ~ 56805 Venture Lane, Sunriver; 541-593-8814; www.sunriverflyshop.com. Guided expeditions are also available through **A. Helfrich Outfitters,** who specialize in fly-fishing trips on the McKenzie River. Trips are led by a third-generation guide. ~ 2605 Harvest Street, Springfield; 541-726-5039, 800-328-7688; www.mckenzierafting.com.

SOUTHERN CASCADES Bill Conner of **North River Guide Service** primarily fishes the Umpqua, specializing in drift boat trips for two people per boat. Up to four couples may go at a time. Conner also leads flyfishing trips. ~ P.O. Box 575, Glide, OR 97443; 541-496-0309. In Klamath Falls, call **Roe Outfitters** for trips on the Williamson, Wood and Klamath rivers, all of which are popular for giant rainbow trout. ~ 9349 Route 97 South, Klamath Falls; 541-884-3825, 877-943-5700; www.roeoutfitters.com, e-mail guides@roeoutfitters.com.

RIVER RUNNING

The fun and excitement of a day of whitewater rafting is hard to beat, even with a crowd. Guided full-day trips usually include a riverside lunch stop along the way.

CENTRAL CASCADES **A. Helfrich Outfitters** lead full- and half-day rafting trips on the McKenzie River. ~ 2605 Harvest Street, Springfield; 541-726-5039, 800-328-7688; www.mckenzierafting.com. For a 17-mile run through Class III and IV rapids on the Deschutes, **Rapid River Rafters** puts in at Maupin, about 89 miles north. There are also whitewater trips down the McKenzie River (Class III). ~ 1151 Southeast Centennial Court #5, Bend; 541-382-1514, 800-962-3327; www.rapidriverrafters.com. **Sun Country Tours** rafts on the Class I to IV rapids; they run the Upper and Lower Deschutes, Upper McKenzie and North Umpqua from April through September. ~ 531 Southwest 13th Street, Bend; 541-382-6277, 800-770-2161; www.suncountrytours.com.

GOLF

In the Cascades, where resort courses comprise most of the golf options, forested mountain sides, emerald meadows, rivers coursing through fairways, elk lingering on the perimeters and wild geese flying overhead add a unique dimension to the experience.

NORTHERN CASCADES **Resort at the Mountain** has three nine-hole courses that are open to the public. The mountain setting makes all three scenic; the first nine is the longest, but fair and forgiving; the third nine, Fox Glove, is fairly narrow and the most challenging. ~ 68010 East Fairway Avenue, Welches; 503-622-3101; www.theresort.com. Located on an American Indian reservation, the championship 18-hole **Kah-Nee-Ta Golf Course** is a fairly flat course, set in a valley. This location is often sunny, so the course is open year-round. ~ Off Route 26, Warm Springs; 541-553-1112; www.kahneeta.com.

CENTRAL CASCADES The resort of **Black Butte Ranch** has two award-winning 18-hole courses: Big Meadow (flat and open) and Glaze Meadow (hilly and narrow). The courses are closed from late October to mid-March. ~ Route 20, eight miles west of Sisters; 800-399-2322 for tee times, 541-595-1500 for pro shop. At the semiprivate **Widgi Creek Golf Club**, an 18-hole championship course meanders beneath huge pine trees along the rim of the Deschutes River canyon. Closed November through March. ~ Century Drive, five miles south of Bend; 541-382-4449. Probably the most famous course in the Cascades and certainly one of the most picturesque in the Northwest, **Tokatee Golf Club** is set majestically in the McKenzie River Valley. "It's a walk with nature," says the pro. Tokatee, which is considered among the nation's top public courses, is closed December and January. Walk-ins are welcome. ~ 54947 McKenzie Highway, Blue River; 541-822-3220. South of Bend you will find three 18-hole courses at the **Sunriver Lodge and Resort**. ~ 1 Center Drive, Sunriver; 541-593-5300. Also try the 9-hole championship course at **Quail Run** (an expansion to 18 holes is planned for 2006). This scenic course has plenty of sandtraps, water and bunkers. Closed mid-November to mid-March. ~ Three miles west of entrance to Newberry National Monument; 541-536-1303.

The increasing popularity of white-water rafting in the Northwest means that a river like the Deschutes, where access is less restricted than on the North Umpqua and other rivers, can get pretty crowded—especially in the summer.

SOUTHERN CASCADES The **Circle Bar Golf Club** has a challenging public nine-hole course. ~ 48447 West Oak Road, Oakridge; 541-782-3541. The 18-hole public **Harbor Links Golf Course** isn't near a harbor, but it is near a lake. It's a short course, fairly flat and narrow, and has lots of water. This course is set in a more developed region. ~ 601 Harbor Isles Boulevard, Klamath Falls; 541-882-0609.

TENNIS

Many resorts in the Cascades have tennis courts available to guests; the public is permitted access sometimes as well.

CENTRAL CASCADES The **Kah-Nee-Ta High Desert Resort** has open courts. ~ Warm Springs; 541-553-1112. The **Sunriver Lodge and Resort** also rents four courts to the public. ~ Sunriver Junction at Route 97, 15 miles south of Bend; 541-593-1221.

The Bend Metro Park and Recreation District maintains a number of tennis courts in the city. None of them are night-lighted, but they're free and available on a first-come, first-served basis (access to the courts at schools, however, may be restricted due to school-related activities). There are four courts at **Juniper Park** (Franklin Avenue and Northwest 8th Street); two courts at **Summit Park** (Three Sisters Drive at Fairwell Drive, on the north side of Aubrey Butte); two courts at **Sylvan Park** (Summit and Promontory drives); and four each courts at **Bend High School** (230 Northeast 6th Street), **Mountain View High School** (2755 Northeast 27th Street) and **Central Oregon Community College** (2600 Northwest College Way). ~ Call 541-389-7275 for more information.

SOUTHERN CASCADES In Klamath Falls, four courts are available at **Moore Park.** ~ Lakeshore Drive; 541-883-5391. There are two indoor courts at **Harbor Isles Club.** ~ 541-884-3299. In Wiard Park, you can also play on one of the four courts at **Hilyard Park.** ~ Hilyard Avenue and Crest Street; 541-884-8816. If you time it right you may get on one of the four lighted courts at **Wiard Park.** ~ Wiard Street at Hilyard Avenue; 541-884-8816.

SKIING

Skiing in July? It's possible in Oregon's endless winter, and the Cascades offer a ton of alpine and Nordic opportunities.

NORTHERN CASCADES In the Northern Cascades, the best-known resorts are found on the slopes of Mt. Hood. They include the venerable **Timberline Lodge and Ski Area,** with six chairlifts serving an above-timberline snowfield and tree-lined runs. Three lifts operate on Friday and Saturday nights. From May to September, the resort offers a summer season at the 8500-foot level. ~ Timberline; 503-272-3311; www.timberlinelodge.com, e-mail info@timberlinelodge.com.

Another resort serving the same area is **Mt. Hood Skibowl,** with nearly 65 trails, 34 of which are lit for night skiing. ~ 503-272-3206, 503-222-2695 (snowphone); www.skibowl.com. **Mt. Hood Meadows** offers ten chairlifts serving 87 trails, rated 15 percent beginner, 50 percent intermediate and 35 percent expert. This resort offers runs for the physically challenged in conjunction with area organizations. ~ 503-337-2222, 503-287-5438, 800-754-4663.

CENTRAL CASCADES On Route 20's Santiam Pass west of Sisters, **Hoodoo Ski Area** is a good bet for families looking for alpine or Nordic skiing. ~ 541-822-3799; www.hoodoo.com. **Mt. Bachelor** west of Bend is Oregon's largest ski area, offering dry powder and a season extending to June. Ten chairs serve 3683 skiable acres, and there are 56 kilometers of groomed trails. ~ 800-829-2442; www.mtbachelor.com, e-mail info@mtbachelor.com. For full-service rental and repair of downhill skis and snowboards, try **Skjersaa's Sports Shop.** ~ 130 Southwest Century Drive, Bend; 541-382-2154. A full selection of skis, snowboards and snowshoes can be rented at **Eurosports.** ~ 182 East Hood Avenue, Sisters; 541-549-2471.

The Oregon Cascades boasts one of the longest ski seasons in the West.

SOUTHERN CASCADES **Crater Lake National Park** has extensive Nordic trails with views of the blue water beneath the snowcapped rim. ~ 541-594-2211. Diamond Lake Resort also has Nordic trails, as well as snowcat skiing on **Mt. Bailey**. The latter, limited to just 14 people per run (approximately 5 to 7 runs), transports skiers uphill to enjoy 6000 acres of deep-powder terrain. ~ 800-446-4555; www.mountbailey.com, e-mail skiqus@mountbailey.com.

RIDING STABLES

NORTHERN CASCADES From March to the end of September, guided hour-long rides wind through the hills or scenic red-rock country at **Kah-Nee-Ta High Desert Resort.** ~ Warm Springs; 541-553-1112; www.kahneeta.com.

CENTRAL CASCADES In the Sisters area, guided half-hour to all-day trail rides and overnight pack trips into the Cascades are operated by **Equine Management**, which operates stables at Black Butte Ranch. ~ Route 20, eight miles west of Sisters; 541-595-2061, 800-743-3035; www.oregoncowboy.com. **River Ridge Stables** takes up to ten riders into the forest and then back up the Deschutes River for an hour or more. There are also day-long rides, plus sleigh rides in winter. ~ Inn of the Seventh Mountain, 18575 Century Drive, Bend; 541-389-9458. **Sunriver Stables** at Sunriver Lodge and Resort also offers guided tours on horseback. One-hour tours survey the Sunriver area; four-hour rides go into Deschutes National Forest; full-day rides are also offered. ~ Sunriver Junction at Route 97, five miles south of Bend; 541-593-1221 or 541-593-6995.

SOUTHERN CASCADES Near Crater Lake, **Diamond Lake Corrals** is the place to go for one-hour, three-hour and all-day rides; there are also pack trips and chuckwagon rides. ~ 541-793-3337. **Equine Management** offers scenic trail rides out of Running Y Ranch Resort. ~ 5115 Running Y Road, Klamath Falls; 541-850-5691; www.oregoncowboy.com.

BIKING

From easy town rides to mountain biking on rugged backcountry trails, the Oregon Cascades offer thousands of miles of scenic cycling.

CENTRAL CASCADES In the Bend area, take **West Newport Avenue** for a six-mile trip to Shevlin Park or follow **O. B. Riley Road** five miles to Tumalo State Park. Another possibility is to take the road south 23 miles from Route 97 to **Newberry Volcano.**

At Black Butte Ranch, 18 miles of bike paths include the **Lodge Loop** (5 miles), the scenic **Glaze Meadow Loop** (4 miles) and the **Aspen Loop** (1.6 miles).

About ten miles from Sisters, **Suttle Lake**, with its "upsy-daisy" loop of about 13 miles, is a pleasant outing of moderate exertion for most people.

A popular **Cascades Loop** trail begins in Bend, heads west on Century Drive to Mt. Bachelor and then continues on Cascades Lakes Highway to Route 58. Allow several days to enjoy these demanding 74 miles.

SOUTHERN CASCADES One of the most popular biking trails in the Southern Cascades is the 11.5-mile **Diamond Lake Bike Path.** This level route is ideal for the whole family. The route takes cyclists from Thielsen View Campground to Silent Creek. Complete the loop on the highway returning to Thielsen View. A two-mile section of this route is wheelchair accessible.

The ultimate biking experience at Crater Lake is **Rim Drive**, offering the complete 33-mile overview of this volcanic landmark. Another excellent possibility is **Grayback Drive**, a scenic, unpaved route ideal for mountain bikes. In Klamath Falls, **Nevada Avenue** and **Lakeshore Drive** provide convenient bike-touring access to Upper Klamath Lake. This route continues west to Route 140 along the lake's west shore. **Kit Carson Way** also has a separated bike path.

Bike Rentals In Sisters, **Eurosports** rents mountain bikes in addition to children's bikes. The shop also has bike route maps as well as suggestions for rides in the area. Bikes are available in spring and summer. ~ 182 East Hood Avenue, Sisters; 541-549-2471. For mountain bike rentals in Bend, stop by **Pine Mountain Sports**. Summer only. ~ 255 Southwest Century Drive, Bend; 541-385-8080. **Summit Sports** rents front suspension bikes, tandems, hybrids and cruisers. ~ 7 Ponderosa Road, Sunriver; 541-593-5252, 800-871-8004; www.summitsportsonline.com.

In the Bend area, **Paulina Plunge**, as it's known, is a six-mile downhill waterfall mountain-bike tour that descends 3000 feet on groomed trails, with two stops along the way at several waterfalls and two waterslides in the Newberry Crater region. **Paulina Plunge Inc.** operates this activity, taking up to 15 people

Llamaland

One of the most singular sights you're likely to see while exploring the dry side of the Cascades is pastures full of llamas (pronounced "LA-mas"), those wooly long-necked South American cousins of camels. Llama ranching in the United States first appeared in central Oregon in the mid-1970s. The state now boasts about 170 llama ranches, of which more than half are located around Bend and the nearby towns of Sisters, Redmond and Prineville.

Llamas have been domesticated by the Inca people of the South American Andes for at least two thousand years. They have traditionally been raised there for wool and meat. Since they were imported to the United States, their main use has been as beasts of burden and companions, accompanying trekkers into mountain wilderness. Although a llama is not strong enough to carry a human rider, it can carry at least 40 pounds of backpacking and camping gear. Some outfitters rent llamas for independent hiking expeditions, while others organize guided trips. A growing number of outfitters use llamas to carry gear into the mountains in advance and await hikers with a fully set-up campsite.

Llamas also provide specialty wool, which is gathered by either frequent brushing or shearing. Llama wool has a higher warmth-to-weight ratio than sheep wool and comes in 22 natural shades of white, cream, beige, tan, brown, rust, gray and black. Although there is no organized commercial market for llama fiber, it is widely used by weavers and other craftspeople to make everything from scarves, ponchos, blankets and rugs to fishing flies. You'll find these products at galleries and arts-and-crafts shows throughout Oregon.

Perhaps the most unusual use of llamas is to guard livestock. Over the centuries they have developed instinctive behaviors for fighting off cougars and coyote-like Andean wild dogs. These behaviors, along with the Llama's larger size and almost impenetrable wool coat, make llamas more effective than dogs for protecting sheep flocks. They are also used to guard deer, cattle, and ducks and geese.

The economics of llama ranching is similar to horse ranching. Untrained llamas suitable as pets or guards sell for $250 to $1800. Llamas trained for trekking sell for up to $2000. Breeding males bring $2000 to $10,000 each, and breeding females $2000 to $12,000. For more information and to find out about llama ranch tours, contact the **Central Oregon Llama Association**. ~ P.O. Box 5334, Bend, OR 97708; 541-389-6855; www.centraloregonllamas.com.

per trip (guide ratio 15:1), May to late September. Call ahead for availability. ~ P.O. Box 8782, Bend, OR 97708; 541-389-0562, 800-296-0562.

HIKING

With hundreds of miles of trails, including many in wilderness areas, the Cascades are ideal for relaxed rambles or ambitious journeys. All distances listed for hiking trails are one way unless otherwise noted.

NORTHERN CASCADES Many of Mt. Hood National Forest's trailheads are rather tricky to find. Stop by the Clackamas County Regional Visitor Information Center on Route 26, just before the 39-mile marker (before Welche's), or at the Mt. Hood information center, 3 miles east of the Clackamas center, on the right.

Zigzag Trail (2 miles) takes you across the Hood River's east fork via a drawbridge (closed in winter). You'll continue up the canyon to Dog River Trail, which leads to a viewpoint overlooking Mt. Hood and the Upper Hood River Valley.

Tamanawas Falls Loop (5.5 miles) leads along the north bank of Mt. Hood National Forest's Cold Spring Creek. After hiking to scenic Tamanawas Falls, you'll return to the trailhead via Elk Meadows Trail.

Also in Mt. Hood National Forest is **Castle Canyon Trail** (.9 mile) climbing out of the rhododendron area to rocky pinnacles. Views of the scenic Zigzag Valley are your reward.

Another relatively easy possibility is **Bonney Meadow Trail**, reached by taking Route 35 to Bennett Pass and then following Routes 3550 and 4891 to Bonney Meadows Campground. Take trail #473 (3.5 miles) east along the ridge to enjoy the views of Boulder and Little Boulder lakes. Return to the campground by turning right on trail #472.

CENTRAL CASCADES Located 33.4 miles west of Sisters off Route 20 is the **Black Butte Trail** (2 miles), a steady, moderate climb to the top of a volcanic cone.

In the Detroit Lake area, you might want to try **Tumble Ridge Trail** (5.3 miles), which begins on Route 22. This demanding trek

AUTHOR FAVORITE

I can't resist the mountain-bike trails in the **Zigzag Ranger District**, with their scenic views of the Mt. Hood region. Among the best is the 12-mile Still Creek Road. This rarely traveled route connects Trillium Lake with the town of Rhododendron. You might also try the ten-mile Sherar Burn Road/Veda Lake trail which leads up to outstanding viewpoints.

heads up through second-growth forest, past Dome and Needle rocks to Tumble Lake.

Built along the Little North Santiam River, the **Little North Santiam Trail** (4.5 miles) crosses eight tributaries with stringer bridges. Fishing and swimming holes are easily reached from this trail leading through some old-growth forests. ◄ HIDDEN

Return east on Route 20 and turn south on Route 126. Continue for eight miles to Forest Service Road 2664 and go east 4.4 miles to **Robinson Lake Trail** (.3 mile). It's an easy family hike leading to a pleasant hideaway. ◄ HIDDEN

In the McKenzie Bridge area, the **Olallie Trail** (9.7 miles) is an all-day hike with memorable views of the Three Sisters, Mt. Washington, Mt. Jefferson and Bachelor Butte. Take this trail in summer and fall. The trailhead is three miles from Horse Creek Road.

For an easier hike off McKenzie Pass Highway (Route 242), take the **Lava River Trail** (.5 mile). This interpretive trail beginning near the Dee Wright Observatory leads through lava flows. Signs add to your understanding of this moonscape's volcanic past. Wheelchair accessible.

To the south, the Willamette National Forest's Middle Fork Ranger District offers many fine hikes including **Fisher Creek Trail** (6.5 miles). A great way to see a primitive-forest region, you'll get a closeup view of old-growth trees. The silence is deafening. The **Waldo Lake Trail** (21.8 miles) is a challenging route around this incredibly pure lake.

The **Lava River Cave Trail** (1.2 miles) is an easy, rather chilly trail through the state's largest lava tube. It's south of Bend off Route 97, one mile south of Lava Lands Interpretive Center, which is an excellent place to stop for some information on the area. Lanterns are available (seasonally) close to the parking lot.

Fourteen miles south of Bend off Route 97, **Lava Cast Forest Nature Trail** (.9 mile) takes you through one of the Pacific Northwest's weirdest landscape. You'll see tree molds created when molten lava destroyed a forest thousands of years ago.

SOUTHERN CASCADES Off Route 62, the road from Medford to Crater Lake, the **Upper Rogue River Trail** (6.5 miles) is an easy ramble. Begin at the Prospect Ranger Station in Rogue River National Forest and make your way through sugar pines, pausing along the way to cool off in the stream.

Toketee Lake Trail (.4 mile) runs parallel to this spot. Short spurs lead to the waterfront where you'll find otter, beaver, osprey and ducks complementing the scenery.

The **North Umpqua Trail** (79 miles) offers a wide variety of hiking opportunities. Skirting both the Boulder Creek and Mt. Thielsen wilderness areas, this route ranges from easy to difficult.

The last nine miles are in the Oregon Cascades Recreation Area and Mt. Thielsen Wilderness Area. Spur trails lead to waterfalls, fishing spots and campgrounds. Among the North Umpqua's most popular segments are **Panther Trail** (5 miles), beginning at Steamboat, and **Lemolo Trail** (6.3 miles), starting at Lemolo Lake.

Mt. Bailey Trail (5 miles) is a steep route located west of Diamond Lake. Your reward for climbing 3000 feet is a panoramic view of Diamond Lake, Mt. Thielsen and the Southern Cascades.

Running 2570 miles from Canada to Mexico, the **Pacific Crest Scenic Trail** is western America's back door to the wilderness, the kind of place John Muir lived for. Scenic, uncrowded, larger than life, it's worth a special trip. You can pick up a 30-mile segment at the North Crater Trailhead, a mile east of the Crater Lake National Park Trailhead on Route 138. Hike as much of this section as you care to. You can exit via the Tipsoo, Howlock Mountain, North Umpqua or Mt. Thielsen trails.

CRATER LAKE NATIONAL PARK **Watchman Peak Trail** (.7 mile) is a steep route up Watchman Peak. From the top you'll have a great view of Wizard Island.

It's ironic that most visitors to Crater Lake never actually reach the shore. Doing so requires a steep descent on **Cleetwood Cove Trail** (1.1 miles). This is the route that leads to boat tours of Crater Lake. Bring water and good shoes.

HIDDEN ► For a good workout, try the **Mount Scott Trail** (2.5 miles). Along the way you'll spot many small animals and birds. The gnarled whitebark pines make a good photographic backdrop. On top you'll have a 360-degree view of the park.

HIDDEN ► To see some of the national park's impressive pinnacles, take **Godfrey Glen Trail** (1-mile loop). This route leads through a hemlock and red-fir forest to a view of Sand Creek Canyon.

Located east of Crater Lake Lodge, **Garfield Peak Trail** (1.7 miles) is a fairly steep route offering views of the lake. Look for eagles and hawks along the way.

A short walk in the park is **Castle Crest Wildflower Trail** (.4-mile loop). This easy loop is the best way to sample Oregon wildflowers in mid-summer. An eden-like setting with small streams trickling down the hillside, the trail is one of Oregon's best-kept secrets.

Sevenmile Trail/Pacific Crest Trail (15 miles) west of Fort Klamath off Route 3334 West leads through the Sky Lakes Wilderness south of Crater Lake National Park. Sevenmile Trail hooks up with the Pacific Crest Trail for a 2.5-mile stretch and then cuts off to Seven Lakes Basin. You can also follow the Pacific Crest Trail to Devil's Pass and the steep ascent of Devil's Peak.

Transportation

CAR

The Cascades are a 50-to-100-mile-wide band extending almost the entire length of the state. They begin on the eastern edge of the Willamette Valley and Ashland-Rogue River area and extend to the high-desert region of central Oregon.

Route 26 travels east from Portland to the Mt. Hood area. You can also reach Mt. Hood by taking **Route 35** south from the Hood River area.

From Salem, take **Route 22** east to the Detroit Lakes and Santiam Pass area. **Route 20** east of Albany leads to the same destination, while **Route 126** is Eugene's mainline east to the McKenzie Bridge and McKenzie Pass area. **Route 58** southeast of Eugene is convenient to the Deschutes National Forest, and **Route 138** takes you from Roseburg to the Umpqua River Canyon.

All hiking trails in the Cascades are best tackled in the warmer seasons and not recommended to try in the winter months.

From Medford, take **Route 62** northeast to Crater Lake. An alternate route to Crater Lake is **Route 97** north of Klamath Falls. This same highway also provides access to the Bend area and the Central Cascades. If you're coming from the east, Routes 20 and 26 are the most convenient ways to reach the mountains.

AIR

Redmond Airport, 16 miles north of Bend, is served by Delta Air Lines, Horizon Airlines and United Express. **Klamath Falls Airport** is served by Horizon Airlines. The **Portland International Airport, Eugene Airport** and **Rogue Valley International–Medford Airport** are also convenient to the Cascades.

Redmond Airport Shuttle provides service from the Redmond Airport to Bend and Cascades destinations like Sunriver, Mt. Bachelor, Sisters and Black Butte Ranch. ~ 541-382-1687.

Luxury Accommodations offers limousine van service from the Portland airport to popular Northern Cascades recreation areas. ~ 503-668-7433.

BUS

Greyhound Bus Lines services Bend. ~ 1315 Northeast 3rd Street; 541-382-2151, 800-231-2222; www.greyhound.com.

TRAIN

Amtrak's "Coast Starlight" is a scenic and comfortable way to reach the Cascades. It serves stations in Klamath Falls, Chemult, Eugene, Salem, Albany and Portland, all convenient starting points for the mountain resorts. ~ 800-872-7245; www.amtrak.com.

CAR RENTALS

Arriving passengers at the Redmond Airport are served by **Budget Rent A Car** (800-527-0700), **Hertz Rent A Car** (800-654-3131), **Avis Rent A Car** (800-831-2847) and **Enterprise** (800-736-8222).

Car-rental agencies at the Klamath Falls Airport are **Enterprise** (800-736-8222), **Budget Rent A Car** (800-527-0700), and **Hertz Rent A Car** (800-654-3131).

In Bend, you can rent from **Hertz Rent A Car** (800-654-3131).

PUBLIC TRANSIT

Lane Transit District (541-687-5555) serves McKenzie Bridge. **Basin Transit Service** (541-883-2877) operates in the Klamath Falls area.

TAXIS

For taxi service, contact **Redmond Taxi** (541-548-1182) in Redmond. In Klamath Falls, call **Classic Taxi** (541-885-8294).

SEVEN

Eastern Oregon

By a quirk of geography, Eastern Oregon is where you'll find the truly rough and wild landscape and heritage of the Old West. In contrast to the fertile valleys and deep green forests of Western Oregon, the vast region east of the Cascades presents a much drier, wide-open landscape—ironically, the eastern section of the state is more "Western" than the part nearer the Pacific. Here is the ideal setting for a classic Western novel or movie: rolling sagebrush terrain, ruts carved into the earth by pioneer wagons, sites where American Indians fought in vain to keep their lands, and real-life cowboy towns where chaps and spurs are not an unusual sight on Main Street.

Some of the most interesting geology in North America can be found here due to its tortured creation by volcanoes. Throughout Eastern Oregon you will find vivid reminders of this creation process, particularly in the hundreds if not thousands of dead volcanoes and cinder cones, the lava flows that have not yet been covered by windblown soil, the brilliantly colored volcanic ash deposits and sheer canyons whose basalt walls were created by those lava flows.

In contrast to the sun-baked volcanic landscape are Northeastern Oregon's Wallowa Mountains, a spectacular alpine district of glacial lakes, pine forests and towering peaks that stands in total contrast to much of the region's sagebrush terrain. These are the ancestral lands of the Nez Perce Indians, who lived here peacefully until the inevitable clashes with white settlers in the mid-1800s. Chief Joseph, head of the Nez Perce tribe, tried valiantly to negotiate with the U.S. government during the Nez Perce War of 1877 to retain the tribe's lands, only to see his people scattered to reservations in Oklahoma, Idaho and Washington. Today the Wallowa Mountains are largely the domain of outdoor enthusiasts and artists, many of whom have opened galleries in Joseph.

Northeast of the Wallowas, straddling the Oregon–Idaho border, is yet another striking contrast of landscape, the Hells Canyon National Recreation Area. Nearly perpendicular cliffs soar up to 6000 feet above the Snake River to form the world's deepest river gorge. Hells Canyon can be explored from above, where winding roads give breathtaking views into the gorge below, or from the river itself, where a variety of raft and jet-boat excursions are available.

The path across Northeastern Oregon from the Idaho border to the Columbia River is Oregon Trail Country, the grueling last leg of the 2000-mile route from Missouri by which an estimated 300,000 immigrants made their way west during the 1840s and '50s. Several sites have been set aside that show ruts made by the wagons along the trail. You can see them at Vail, west of Ontario, and along the route near Baker City in Burnt River Canyon, Gold Hill, Durkee, Pleasant Valley and Baker Valley. Most of the settlers headed to the fertile lands of the Willamette Valley. Some of them stayed in Eastern Oregon, however, and their independent spirit has clearly helped forge the character of the region.

These pioneer roots are particularly evident in Northeastern Oregon's two major towns, Baker City and Pendleton, both of which are on the original Oregon Trail route now paralleled by Route 84. Baker City, once known as the Queen City of the Mines, was a boomtown during the late 19th century, a thriving center for gold mining, lumber and cattle and larger and far more prosperous than either Boise or Spokane. Today Baker City's quiet streets reflect a surprisingly elegant past, with dozens of gracious old Victorian homes and fine examples of stone masonry. By contrast, Pendleton *is* the Wild West—at least every September, when cowboys come from all over for the Pendleton Roundup, one of the nation's oldest and largest rodeo events. Even when it's not roundup time, however, Pendleton is still a place where you can buy a custom-made saddle and learn first-hand about the heritage of the Old West.

As rural as Northeastern Oregon is, it is downright citified compared to Oregon's southeast, one of the most sparsely inhabited regions in the continental United States. Truly where the deer and antelope play, this vast area of high desert sagebrush country is where preserves such as the Hart Mountain National Antelope Refuge and Malheur National Wildlife Refuge protect populations of antelope, bighorn sheep, mule deer, coyotes and other native species.

To travel Southeastern Oregon you need a sturdy, reliable car, a cooler for cold drinks and snacks, and it might not be a bad idea to take along camping equipment because hotels/motels are few and far between. Harney County is one the largest counties in the United States, larger in fact than many Northeastern states, but this part of the country is really wide open. The three counties that make up the southeastern corner cover 28,450 square miles with a population of only 12,400. Harney is the largest at 10,228 square miles and has the smallest population, just over 7600. One town, Wagontire on Route 395, has a population that hovers around seven. Some say it depends on how many children are home for the holidays.

Few roads run through this area: Route 395 from California and Route 95 from Nevada are the main north-south corridors. Route 20 goes across the center from Idaho to the Cascades, and Route 140 runs across the bottom from Northern Nevada through Lakeview to Klamath Falls. In Malheur County you will find evidence of a diverse culture since Basque shepherds, Mexican cowboys and laborers, Japanese-American laborers and various Europeans came through and left their marks.

Northeastern Oregon

For the most part, northeastern Oregon remains the parched land so inhospitable to settlers nearly two centuries ago. Nowadays, towns are still few and far between, leaving plenty of room for viewing the wagon ruts left by the original pioneers. Also a part of the northeastern Oregon experience are the vividly colored earthscapes at the John Day Fossil Beds National Monument and the whitewater rafting opportunities in the Snake River along the Idaho border. Capping it off in the state's northeastern corner is a surprisingly lush area surrounding the Wallowa Mountains that reminds many visitors of the Swiss Alps.

SIGHTS

At the Oregon–Washington border, Route 129 heading south from Clarkston, Washington, changes to Route 3 and runs along high

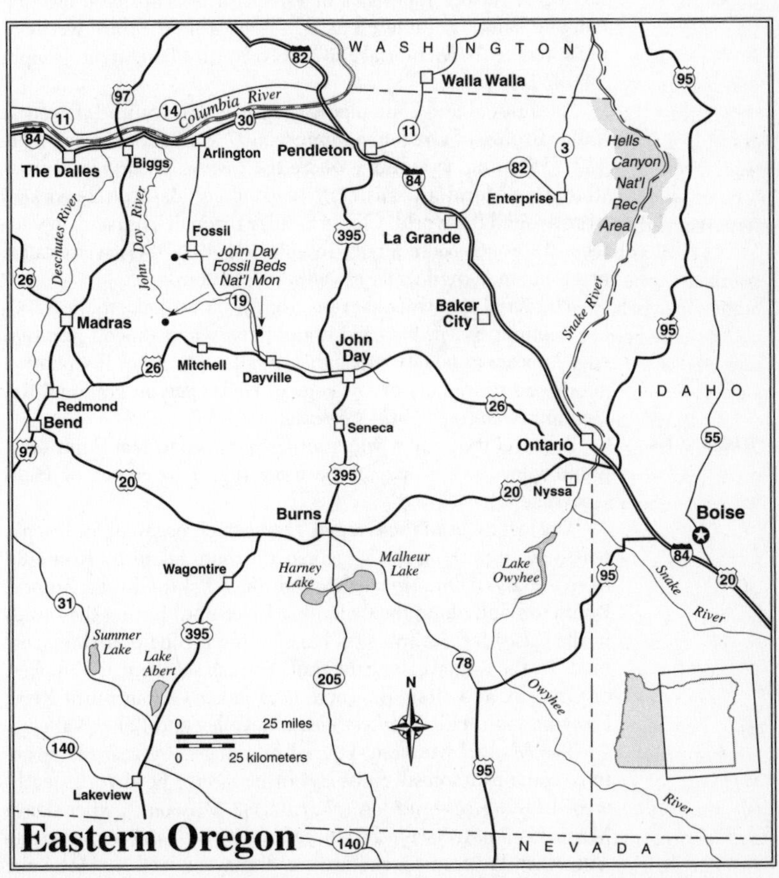

ridges and through ponderosa-pine forests until it enters the **Wallowa River Valley**. This valley is postcard-perfect with the jagged Wallowa Mountains providing an ideal backdrop to the broad valley with the lush farms and ranches, rail fences, ranch buildings and the small, winding Wallowa River. Once you've seen it you'll understand why it is becoming a haven for artists and writers.

The twin towns of **Enterprise** and **Joseph** can be used as a base for exploratory trips around Wallowa Lake and backpacking into the Eagle Cap Wilderness. Joseph is named after the revered Chief Joseph, head of the Nez Perce tribe last century. It is well worth exploring for its array of art galleries and for an introduction to the history of the region. Stop by first at the **Wallowa County Museum** to see exhibits depicting the worlds of the white pioneers and the Nez Perce Indians. The building, dating from 1888 and serving at various times as a newspaper office, hospital, meeting hall and bank, is of interest itself. Closed from the third weekend in September to Memorial Day. ~ 110 South Main Street, Joseph; 541-432-6095.

Traditional and contemporary bronzework can be viewed at **Valley Bronze of Oregon**, a foundry (307 West Alder Street; 541-432-7551) and showroom where the casting process is demonstrated and local artisans craft work alongside bronze workers from around the world. Closed Sunday through Thursday in winter. ~ 18 South Main Street, Joseph; 541-432-7445; www.valleybronze.com, e-mail gallery@valleybronze.com.

The **aerial tramway** that runs from Wallowa Lake to the 8200-foot summit of Mt. Howard is a popular way to spend part of a day. Another good day trip is the 30-mile drive from Joseph on a good road to Imnaha on the edge of **Hells Canyon National Recreation Area** (see "Parks" below).

HIDDEN ►

A gravel road takes you another 25 miles to **Hat Point** for a grand view across one of the most rugged stretches of Hells Canyon.

The last miles of the **Oregon Trail**, which began in St. Joseph, Missouri, run along the same general route taken by Route 84 from the city of Ontario northwest through Baker City, La Grande, Pendleton and along the Columbia River until hitting the rapids in the Cascades. Several sites have been set aside that show ruts made by the wagons along the trail. You can see them at Vail, west of Ontario, and along the route near Baker City in Burnt River Canyon, Gold Hill, Durkee, Pleasant Valley and Baker Valley.

The **Manuel Museum**, housed in a huge 200-year-old structure, contains impressive displays of Nez Perce beadwork, feathered headdresses and other artifacts. Museum owner Dave Manuel is a noted sculptor whose bronzes of Nez Perce warriors and other Western figures are on display as well. ~ Hot Lake

Springs, 66172 Route 203, La Grande; 541-963-4685; www.davidmanuel.com, e-mail manuel@eoni.com.

Heading in the opposite direction of the first Oregon Trail travelers—traveling southeast toward Idaho—the first major town you'll encounter is **Pendleton**. The region's Wild West heritage lives on in this city, particularly when the Pendleton Roundup, which includes an old-fashioned rodeo and night pageant of American Indian and pioneer culture, is in full swing in mid-September.

The **Heritage Station**, located in the city's 1909 train depot, houses a superb collection of historic photographs and such items as a one-room, turn-of-the-20th-century schoolhouse, a Union Pacific caboose and a railroad telegraph system. There are also changing exhibits that focus on the past through different lenses (transportation, communication, and so on). Closed Sunday and Monday. Admission. ~ 108 Southwest Frazier Street, Pendleton; 541-276-0012; www.umatillahistory.org, e-mail info@heritagestationmuseum.org.

SCENIC DRIVE

John Day Country

The fascinating fossils and fantastic scenery of John Day Fossil Beds National Monument are a long way from any populated area—and that's part of what makes this trip special. This trip is hard to complete in a single day, so plan to spend the night at a motel in John Day or Mitchell. From Portland, drive 108 fast miles east on Route 84 and turn south on Route 97 at Biggs, on the Columbia River just below John Day Dam. (Just about everything in this part of the state is named John Day, after an early explorer for John Jacob Astor's fur-trading company. Robbed by Indians and left afoot in this vast wasteland, Day eventually made it back to his base camp on the coast but never regained his sanity.)

SHANIKO AND ANTELOPE Driving 57 miles south on two-lane Route 97 will bring you to the semi-ghost town of Shaniko (page 204), where well-preserved wooden buildings and old wagons create an open-air museum. Another eight miles bring you to the equally sparsely populated ranch town of Antelope, which was overwhelmed in the 1980s when cult leader Bhagwan Shree Rajneesh and 500 followers established an ashram here (to the horror of the locals), and voted to change the town's name to Rajneesh. (Later, the guru left the country due to

Highlighting Pendleton's less savory past—the town once supported 32 saloons and 18 bordellos—is **Pendleton Underground Tours**, which explores a fascinating network of underground tunnels where some notorious businesses, including opium dens and honkytonk gambling rooms, once thrived beneath the streets. Reservations required. No children under six years old. Closed Sunday. ~ 37 Southwest Emigrant Avenue, Pendleton; 541-276-0730, 800-226-6398; www.pendletonundergroundtours.com.

A local business with a better reputation is **Pendleton Woolen Mills**, which has been producing fine clothes and American Indian–inspired shawls, robes and blankets since the early 1900s. The mills offer free tours and a showroom store. Closed for two weeks in August. ~ 1307 Southeast Court Place, Pendleton; 541-276-6911; www.pendleton-usa.com.

Located just east of Pendleton off Route 84 is the **Tamastslikt Cultural Institute**, where an interpretive center looks at the Oregon Trail migration from the perspective of the Cayuse, Umatilla and Walla Walla tribes, and details the way the settlers changed traditional Indian culture forever. ~ 541-966-9748;

IRS trouble, his followers moved away, and the 90 remaining residents changed the name back.)

CLARNO At Antelope, turn east on Route 218. A 22-mile drive through drab brown hills lead to the Clarno Unit of John Day Fossil Beds. The least colorful of the national monument's several units, it has a hillside trail among the petrified logs of a prehistoric forest and exhibits of fossilized seeds and nuts. Twenty more miles east lead to the tiny town of **Fossil**, where a homespun local museum displays not only fossils but also such oddities as an antique poker table and a two-headed calf.

SHEEP ROCK Sixty-five miles south of Fossil on Route 19, the highlight of the Sheep Rock Unit of John Day Fossil Beds is the **Basin Trail**, a colorful hike through blue and green painted desert with replica skeletons of prehistoric rhinoceroses and saber-tooth cats in the spots where the originals were found. The nearby visitors center has historical displays and a lab full of paleontologists at work.

PAINTED HILLS Turn west (left) on Route 26 and drive 32 miles, then take the well-marked three-mile access road to the national monument's Painted Hills Unit. Though the fossilized leaves found here may be of interest mainly to paleobotanists, the hike through the brilliant yellow, white and scarlet landscape is unforgettable. From here, the shortest route back to civilization is to continue west on Route 26, a distance of 194 miles back to Portland, traversing the south slope of Mt. Hood along the way.

www.tamastslikt.org. By contrast, white pioneer life is evoked by the well-preserved **Frazier Farmstead Museum**, a six-acre spread with a historic farmhouse and log cabin, antique farm implements and gardens. The 1890s home retains many of its original furnishings. Closed January through March and Sunday through Wednesday. ~ 1403 Chestnut Street, Milton-Freewater; 541-938-4636; www.museum.bmi.net, e-mail dbiggs@my180.net.

Don't miss the **National Historic Oregon Trail Interpretive Center** on top of Flagstaff Hill on Route 86 east of Baker City. The center has a permanent collection of artifacts found along the trail, a theater for stage productions and outdoor exhibits showing a wagon-train encampment and mine operation. ~ 541-523-1843; oregontrail.blm.gov.

You also can visit a number of **ghost towns**, all visible records of the boom-and-bust nature of the mining industry—with broken windmills, abandoned shacks and fireplaces surrounded by ashes from burned houses that bear witness to failed homesteads. Some of these towns are making a comeback. Neighboring Baker City are such falsefronted old-timers as Greenhorn, Sumpter, Gran-

Text continued on page 256.

North America's Deepest Gorge

The Snake River's colorful Hells Canyon, deeper by 2000 feet than Arizona's Grand Canyon, is the centerpiece of a 652,488-acre parcel, much of it wilderness. The gorge defines the border between Idaho on one side and Oregon and Washington on the other; although the largest section of wilderness surrounding the gorge lies in Oregon. The mile-and-a-half-deep abyss of North America's deepest gorge is surrounded by the **Hells Canyon National Recreation Area** and the Eagle Cap Wilderness. Upstream (south) on the Snake River, a series of hydroelectric dams have created three long, narrow reservoirs that delight boaters and anglers. There's also great hiking and horseback riding through the canyon. ~ Headquarters: 88401 Route 82, Enterprise; 541-426-4978.

The incredible scope of the gorge is apparent even to those who only see it from the surrounding hills. Visitors who continue farther into the canyon, either by water or by land, discover more than stark and spectacular scenery. In addition to petroglyphs and archaeological artifacts, the canyon is home to a plethora of unique botanical species and to a diverse wildlife that ranges from deer, elk, bighorn sheep and mountain goats to cougars, black bears, coyotes and a dazzling variety of bird life. The area around Wallowa Lake near Joseph has been dubbed "The Switzerland of America" for its gorgeous terrain of placid lakes and blooming meadows framed by craggy peaks. Physically speaking, Hells Canyon is worlds away from the parched landscape that constitutes the rest of Eastern Oregon.

Whitewater rafters, kayakers and drift boaters put in at the mouth of **Hells Canyon Creek**, just below Hells Canyon Dam, for trips downriver on the "national wild and scenic" portion of the Snake that extends north 32 miles to Pittsburg Landing, Idaho; 51 miles to Dug Bar, Oregon; and 79 miles to Grande Ronde, Washington. In the fall, steelhead fishing trips are extremely popular on the Snake. Remember that going on this part of the river during peak season (May 22 to September 10) requires a permit. If you're taking your trip independent of a licensed outfitter you need to call the "floatline" (509-758-1957). Permits are granted by a lottery system, but even if your name isn't chosen, you can still be put on a waiting list. ~ HCNRA, P.O. Box 699, Clarkston, WA 99403.

If you'd rather see this sensational area by foot, Hells Canyon has much wilderness to explore. With 900 miles of hiking trails, Hells Canyon offers plenty of challenges for hikers, especially backpackers, who can camp at the 19 campgrounds throughout the area. Many people hike down to the river via **Saddle Creek Trail 1776**, which begins where Forest Service Road 4230 meets Freezeout Creek, near the Imnaha River. This 11-mile path takes a direct, though very picturesque, route down to the river. From there you can gaze back up at the awesome green hills that surround you.

From the towns of Joseph and Enterprise, it's easy to enter the national recreation area. From June to October, the **Wallowa Mountain Loop Road** (Forest Service Road 39) is open, heading south from Joseph through the **Eagle Cap Wilderness**, an area that endured 23,000 burned acres after a 1989 lightning strike caused the enormous Canal Fire. This road connects with Route 86, which leads to Hells Canyon Dam, the major starting point for rafting trips down the Snake. You can also reach the dam by taking Route 86 directly from Baker City. You'll cross the Imnaha River, a major tributary of the Snake, and have an opportunity to make a very worthwhile detour to **Hat Point** (via Route 350 to Imnaha and Forest Service Road 4240), which has the most popular view of the Gorge from the Oregon side.

ite, Whitney, Bourne, Sparta and Cornucopia, which have colorful remains of the original towns and mining equipment standing among the summer homes that have taken root. Most of these towns are along Route 7 or on Forest Service roads leading off it.

Route 7 leads from Baker City southwest to Route 26, which you can stay on heading west to **John Day** and **Canyon City**, twin towns that look very much like the Old West. In fact, twice a year the main street of John Day is closed to vehicular traffic so that a local rancher can drive his cattle through town to and from their summer range.

The best-known museum in these parts was a store owned for decades by two Chinese immigrants, Ing Hay and Lung On. The **Kam Wah Chung & Co. Museum**, next to the city park in the center of John Day, began as a trading post on the military road that ran through the area. Then the Chinese laborers in the mines bought the building for a community center, general store and an herbal doctor's office. The museum has thousands of artifacts related to the building's history and more than a thousand herbs, some from China and others from the immediate area. Closed in winter. ~ Ing Hay Way, John Day; 541-575-0028; www.grantcounty.cc/business.php/181.

The **John Day Fossil Beds National Monument** is a three-part preserve that attracts serious and amateur photographers from all over the world to capture the vivid colors of the volcanic-ash deposits and the fossils of plants and animals. See "Scenic Drive" for more information. ~ 323651 Route 19, Kimberly; 541-987-2333, fax 541-987-2336; www.nps.gov/joda.

LODGING

Several of Pendleton's fine old homes are now B&B inns, providing elegant accommodations at reasonable rates. Among them is **A Place Apart**, a small bed and breakfast featuring two rooms with shared bath, queen-size beds and down comforters. The owners have preserved some of the building's unique colonial features, including the ornate front entrance staircase, original brass hardware, laundry and coal chutes and a pedestal bathtub. Antiques and collectibles add to the ambience. ~ 711 Southeast Byers Avenue, Pendleton; 541-276-0573, 888-441-8932; www.aplaceapartbnb.com, e-mail pkline@oregontrail.com. MODERATE.

Set on a hill overlooking downtown Pendleton is **Parker House**, a 1917 Italian Renaissance–style mansion with white columns and an interior still adorned with its original silk brocade wall coverings, oak paneling and crystal chandeliers. There are five guest rooms, including the pale-pink Gwendolyn Room, which has a fireplace and pleasant balcony. Breakfast is served in the formal dining room or, weather permitting, on a sunny porch. ~ 311 North

Main Street, Pendleton; 541-276-8581, 800-700-8581; www.parkerhousebnb.com. MODERATE.

One of the best hotels in Pendleton is the 170-room **Red Lion Hotel**, just off Route 84 on a hill above the city. Rooms have picture windows and balconies overlooking the wheat fields rolling off to the north and west. The hotel has a formal dining room with a window wall, a coffee shop, a lounge with weekend entertainment, a pool and a duck pond. ~ 304 Southeast Nye Avenue, Pendleton; 541-276-6111, 800-733-5466, fax 541-278-2413; www.redlion.com. BUDGET.

In the downtown area, the 36 rooms in the **Travelodge Pendleton** have most of the usual amenities. ~ 411 Southwest Dorion Avenue, Pendleton; 541-276-7531. MODERATE.

Most of the hotels in the Enterprise–Joseph area are in the moderate category. The lone exception is **Wallowa Lake Lodge**, a lodge under continual renovation located on the lakeshore with adjoining cabins (with kitchens) and rooms that are simply but pleasantly decorated. ~ 60060 Wallowa Lake Highway, Joseph; 541-432-9821, fax 541-432-4885; www.wallowalake.com, e-mail information@wallowalake.com. MODERATE TO DELUXE.

Another good place for country quiet in the Wallowas is century-old **White Tail Farm**. The farmhouse has two bedrooms, each with a private bath and furnished with high-backed antique beds, quilts and hooked rugs. Guests can fish in the river, watch for native nesting bald eagles or relax on a shaded lawn. Breakfast is included. ~ P.O. Box 1060, Joseph, OR 97846; 541-432-1630; www.whitetailfarm.com, e-mail vstewart@whitetailfarm.com. MODERATE.

The 11-acre White Tail Farm is home to a river nesting site for bald eagles.

An alpine look was adopted by builders of the **Chandler's Inn**, which has five simply furnished rooms. Three rooms at the top of a log staircase have private baths and the two downstairs share one-and-a-half baths off of a common sitting room and game room. ~ 700 South Main Street, Joseph; 541-432-9765; www.josephbedandbreakfast.com, e-mail cbbti700@eoni.com. MODERATE.

In Enterprise, the **Wilderness Inn** is a basic motel: clean and uncomplicated. ~ 301 West North Street; 541-426-4535. BUDGET TO MODERATE. Or try the **Country Inn**. ~ 402 West North Street, Enterprise; 541-426-4022. BUDGET.

It's worth making an overnight stop in La Grande just to stay at the **Stange Manor Inn**, a 1924 Colonial-style lumber baron's mansion that resembles the White House. Three of the four guest accommodations are suites, adorned with original tilework and cedar-lined closets. All guests rooms have private baths. Downstairs, guests can breakfast in a formal dining room and relax in a glassed-in sunroom overlooking the gardens. ~ 1612 Walnut Street, La Grande; 541-963-2400, 888-286-9463; www.stangemanor.com. MODERATE.

Baker City has about ten motels, most with the basic goodies of highway stopovers. For instance, the **Best Western Sunridge Inn**, just off Route 84, has 156 rooms, a pool, a dining room, a coffee shop and a lounge. ~ 1 Sunridge Lane, Baker City; 541-523-6444, 800-233-2368, fax 541-523-6446; www.bestwestern.com. MODERATE.

The selection is thin in the area of John Day Fossil Beds National Monument. The town of John Day has several motels in the low range. For instance, the **Best Western John Day Inn** has 39 units. ~ 315 Main Street, John Day; 541-575-1700, 800-243-2628, fax 541-575-1558; www.bestwestern.com. MODERATE. You can also try the similar but smaller **Budget Inn**. ~ 250 East Main Street, John Day; 541-575-2100, 866-575-2100. BUDGET.

One small motel is in Mitchell, the town nearest to the Painted Hills portion of the monument: the **Sky Hook Motel**, with only six units. ~ Route 26, Mitchell; 541-462-3569. BUDGET.

DINING

Red meat is almost required eating in cowboy towns, but in Pendleton you can find a wider variety at **Raphael's Restaurant and Catering**, a restaurant and cocktail lounge that displays the work of local American Indian artists. The menu has beef (of course), but monthly featured entrées may include crab, lobster or wild game. Closed Sunday and Monday. ~ 233 Southeast 4th Street, Pendleton; 541-276-8500; www.raphaelsrestaurant.com. DELUXE.

For a light breakfast or lunch, cup of espresso or glass of Oregon wine, try **Great Pacific Wine & Coffee Co.**, a convivial deli–espresso bar located in an 1887 brick building that was once a funeral parlor. Along with sandwiches, bagels and desserts, they offer coffee drinks and Northwest beers and wines. Closed Sunday. ~ 403 South Main Street, Pendleton; 541-276-1350. BUDGET.

AUTHOR FAVORITE

Good food is making inroads in the Wallowa Valley, and one of the first notable eateries was **Vali's Alpine Delicatessen and Restaurant**. German-Hungarian dishes such as goulash, chicken paprikas and wienerschnitzel are served, but for the nonadventurous there is also plain old American fare. The decor is also German-Hungarian. Open for continental breakfast (on Saturday and Sunday) and dinner only. Between Memorial Day and Labor Day, open every day except Monday and Tuesday; otherwise, open only Saturday and Sunday. ~ 59811 Wallowa Lake Highway, Joseph; 541-432-5691. MODERATE.

Another good choice in the Wallowas is **Russell's at the Lake,** a log structure with fine mountain views all around from your choice of indoor or outdoor seating. The best selections are the broiled steak, salmon, halibut and chicken dishes. Closed November to Memorial Day. ~ 59984 Wallowa Lake Highway, Joseph; 541-432-0591; e-mail russells@yahoo.com. BUDGET TO MODERATE.

In La Grande, the place to go for well-prepared Northwest cuisine is **10 Depot Street**, which offers fresh seafood and pasta dishes plus vegetarian items such as spinach lasagna and lentil-pecan patties. The prime rib has a reputation as the best in the Northwest. The house-made desserts are a standout, including $1.50 nightly specials that may include cheesecake, chocolate torte or fresh fruit crisps. Located in a vintage brick building that was once a hotel, the restaurant has a 1920s look with high booths, refinished tables and a turn-of-the-20th-century bar. Closed Sunday. ~ 10 Depot Street, La Grande; 541-963-8766. MODERATE TO DELUXE.

Of all the Western-style, steak-and-chops restaurants that abound in the region, **Haines Steak House** is the one not to miss. This log and timber landmark just north of Baker City sports a fine collection of pioneer Americana, including an authentic covered wagon (which holds the extensive salad bar). Charcoal-broiled steaks are the specialty, but there are fish, prime rib, chicken and other dishes as well. Closed Tuesday. Dinner and Sunday brunch only. ~ 910 Front Street, Haines; 541-856-3639. BUDGET TO DELUXE.

SHOPPING

Offering a fine selection of books on regional history and travel is **Armchair Books.** ~ 39 Southwest Dorion Street, Pendleton; 541-276-7323. Elsewhere in town, **Collectors Gallery** also highlights books of local interest and is a good source for Umatilla Indian artwork. Closed Sunday. ~ 223 Southeast Court Street, Pendleton; 541-276-6697.

Red's Clothing Company is the perfect place to find authentic cowboy gear, including boots, buckles, spurs, hats and saddles. Closed Sunday. ~ 233 South Main Street, Pendleton; 800-443-6928.

A great place to browse in Enterprise is the **Bookloft-Skylight Gallery**, which features local photographers and artists (and the occasional painting exhibit) and has a wide selection of books of regional history and general interest. Closed Sunday. ~ 107 East Main Street, Enterprise; 541-426-3351; www.bookloftoregon.com.

A few hours can happily be spent browsing in the art galleries and antique shops found along Joseph's Main Street. Works by local artists are on sale at **Valley Bronze of Oregon.** ~ 18 South Main Street, Joseph; 541-432-7445.

Billed the "Switzerland of Oregon," Wallowa Lake features the **Matterhorn Swiss Village**, which stocks mountain-themed souvenirs and gift items, as well as espresso and snacks. Closed October through May. ~ 59950 Wallowa Lake Highway, Joseph; 541-432-4071, 800-891-2551.

Baker City has become an antiques mecca. You'll find items dating back to the pioneer years of the town, including oak furniture bought at estate sales, glass, rock collections, kitchen utensils and tools. **Memory House Antiques** specializes in Depression glass and furniture. Closed Sunday and Monday in winter, Sunday in summer. ~ 1780 Main Street, Baker City; 541-523-6227.

NIGHTLIFE

Live music is hard to come by except on special occasions, such as rodeos and patriotic holidays. An exception is in Pendleton. **Crabby's Underground Saloon and Dance Hall** has deejay music on Thursday, Friday and Saturday night. It's located in a basement beneath several small shops, and in addition to the music and dancefloor has poker and pool tables. Closed Sunday. ~ 220 Southwest 1st Street, Pendleton; 541-276-8118.

Whether you are seeking a serious gallery exhibition or a fun-filled musical show, stop by the **Pendleton Center for the Arts.** Rotating exhibits and performances showcase local artists, dancers, comedians and musicians. Closed Sunday and Monday. Cover for shows. ~ 214 North Main Street, Pendleton; 541-278- 9201; www.pendletonarts.org.

Located on the Umatilla Indian Reservation, the **Wildhorse Resort and Casino** offers slot machines, card rooms, keno, off-track betting and high-stakes bingo. ~ Exit 216 off Route 84, Pendleton; 541-278-2274, 800-654-9453; www.wildhorseresort.com.

PARKS

WALLOWA LAKE STATE PARK On the southern end of the lake with large playground areas surrounded by trees, this park stretches from the lakeshore well back into the pine and spruce timber. Hiking trails are nearby. Good rainbow trout fishing can be found north of the park. There are day-use areas, a marina, a boat dock and a concessionaire. ~ Located at the southern end of Wallowa Lake on Route 82; 541-432-4185.

▲ There are 89 tent sites ($13 to $17 per night) and 121 RV hookup sites ($17 to $21 per night), two yurts ($29 per night) and one cabin ($58 to $80 per night).

HELLS CANYON NATIONAL RECREATION AREA This 652,488-acre monument protects the Snake River Gorge, a canyon that has an average depth of 6000 feet, the deepest river gorge in the world. It is one of the most popular whitewater-rafting trips in the United States. Rafts can be launched from Hells

Canyon Dam in Oregon and Pittsburg Landing on the Idaho side of the river. The Snake River is very swift, and swimming is allowed only in certain spots. There's fishing access from 18 sites; smallmouth bass, catfish and crappie are best. There is also sturgeon (catch-and-release only). Facilities include day-use picnic areas, scenic overlooks, a visitors center (closed Saturday and Sunday from Labor Day to Memorial Day) and restrooms. Higher elevations in the park are closed in winter. ~ You can reach the area two ways: by taking Route 86 from Baker City through Halfway to Forest Service Road 39; or by heading east on Route 350 from the town of Joseph south to Forest Service Road 39; 541-426-5546.

Hells Canyon was well known to prehistoric American Indians and early white settlers alike, as evidenced by 8000-year-old petroglyphs, artifacts from Chief Joseph's Nez Perce, remnants of 1860s gold mines and 1890s homesteads.

▲ There are numerous campgrounds. Indian Crossing (14 tent sites, $6 per night) is the starting point for some of the area's horseback riding and hiking trails, making it an ideal place to set up camp. Ollokot Campground (12 campsites, $8 per night) is also popular. Both campgrounds are only open in summer. There is also primitive camping along the river for rafters and backpackers.

UMATILLA NATIONAL WILDLIFE REFUGE Nestled along the banks of the Columbia River, this wildlife refuge covers 29,000 acres of marshes, sloughs, open water and nature trails. A prime nesting ground for waterfowl and other birdlife, this is the spot for thousands of mallards and Canada geese during the fall migration. Fishing is permitted in the Columbia River and is excellent for bass, walleye, steelhead and sturgeon. ~ From Pendleton, take Route 84 northwest for 35 miles to Route 730, and then head northeast. After five miles, turn left on Patterson Ferry Road to the refuge; 509-545-8588.

Southeastern Oregon

If you thought northeastern Oregon seemed lonely, you probably haven't yet experienced southeastern Oregon. To travel in this part of the state you need a sturdy, reliable car, a cooler for cold drinks and snacks, and it might not be a bad idea to take along camping equipment because hotels/motels are few and far between.

Harney County is the largest county in the United States, larger in fact than many northeastern states, but this part of the country is really wide open. Harney is the largest of the three counties in southeastern Oregon at 10,228 square miles and has the smallest population, just over 7500. One town, Wagontire on Route 395, has a population that hovers around seven. Some say it depends on how many children are home for the holidays.

Few roads run through this area: Route 395 from California and Route 95 from Nevada are the main north–south corridors. Route 20 goes across the center from Idaho to the Cascades, and Route 140 runs across the bottom from northern Nevada through Lakeview to Klamath Falls. In Malheur County you will find evidence of its diverse culture as Basque shepherds, Mexican cowboys and laborers, Japanese-American laborers and various Europeans came through and left their marks.

In Harney County are wildlife refuges around Malheur Lake and Steens Mountain. The only real population center is Burns. Crane, a tiny town southeast of Burns on Route 78, has the only public boarding school in the country.

SIGHTS

For helpful information and free maps of Oregon, Harney County, Steens Mountain and the Southeastern Oregon Auto Tour, visit the **Harney County Chamber of Commerce.** ~ 76 East Washington, Burns; 541-573-2636; www.harneycounty.com.

The region's wide-open terrain attracted cattle ranchers in the 19th century, spawning a generation of cattle barons such as Peter French, whose 100,000-acre spread was one of the biggest in the West. In the relatively thriving metropolis of Burns, the **Harney County Historical Museum** displays artifacts from the French ranch and other pioneer homesteads, everything from apple peelers to wagons to early photographs. Closed Sunday and Monday, and from October through March; call for hours in April. Admission. ~ 18 West D Street, Burns; 541-573-5618. Also illustrating the region's roots is **Oard's Museum,** which has an extensive collection of American Indian art and artifacts, including a costume worn by a Yakima chief in 1890. The museum also exhibits guns, spinning wheels, dolls and over 50 antique clocks. ~ 42456 Route 20 East, 23 miles east of Burns in Buchanan; 541-493-2535.

Farther east in Ontario, near the Idaho state line, is the **Four Rivers Cultural and Convention Center.** This unique museum traces the heritage of the four cultures that have lived in this remote area—Northern Paiute Indians, immigrant Basque sheepherders, Euro-Americans and Japanese Americans resettled from the West Coast during World War II. Particularly dramatic is the re-creation of living conditions in the Japanese internment camps. Closed Sunday. Admission. ~ 676 Southwest 5th Avenue, Ontario; 541-889-8191; www.4rcc.com.

Declared a migratory bird sanctuary in 1908, the **Malheur National Wildlife Refuge** has since been expanded to include more than 187,000 acres of lakes, ponds, flatlands and hills. The refuge provides a natural habitat to a diverse bird population comprising white pelicans, white-faced ibises, great egrets, whooping cranes and double-crested cormorants, to name a few. Malheur Lake is a major resting area for migratory birds on the Pacific Flyway. ~ Located 32 miles southeast of Burns on Route 205; 541-493-2612.

More traces of the early ranching era and some of the region's most interesting geology can be explored by driving 50 miles south from Burns on Route 205 to the town of Diamond. From there a marked side road leads to **Diamond Craters,** which holds some of the strangest volcanic craters and lava pits in the country. Just beyond the craters is the **Peter French Round Barn,** an architectural marvel the rancher used to break and exercise saddle horses. Constructed of native stone and measuring 100 feet in diameter, the barn is supported by soaring juniper trees and covered with a roof of 50,000 shingles.

Farther south off Route 205 near Frenchglen is the **Steens Mountain National Backcountry Byway,** a breathtaking 66-mile loop road that should be tackled only by high-clearance vehicles. The byway, the highest road in Oregon, climbs to over 9700 feet along the face of Steens Mountain for spectacular views of deep U-shaped gorges carved by glaciers and the Alvord Desert floor far below. Be on the lookout for golden eagles and wild mustangs.

Northeast of Lakeview on Route 395 is **Abert Rim,** at 30 miles the largest exposed fault in North America. The massive fault juts

up into the desert sky like a continuous cliff on the east side of Route 395, while on the west side of the highway is the talcum-white wasteland around **Lake Abert.**

Northwest of Lakeview just off Route 31 on county roads in Christmas Valley is **Hole in the Ground**, a 700-foot-deep crack caused by an earthquake. In the same area, **Fort Rock** is the remnant of a volcano crater and ocean shoreline that looks like one side of a destroyed fort. Indian sandals found there were carbon-dated and found to be 10,000 years old.

About 25 miles northeast of Christmas Valley is **Lost Forest**, a 9000-acre ponderosa-pine forest that has managed to survive in the middle of the harsh desert. The forest is surrounded by shifting sand dunes, which are popular with the all-terrain-vehicle set.

Oregon's longest lake, manmade **Lake Owyhee**, has miles of striking desert topography along its shores. It is reached by taking Route 201 south from Nyssa to the small town of Owyhee, then a county road that dead-ends at the lake. Farther down in the desert where the Owyhee River still runs free is some of the state's best whitewater for river runners.

LODGING

Sage Country Inn offers three rooms decorated with family antiques. This 1907 Georgian Colonial home is located in the heart of Burns but provides peaceful and secluded rest. ~ 351½ West Monroe Street, Burns; 541-573-7243; www.sagecountryinn.com, e-mail mchuseby@centurytel.net. MODERATE.

Down in the desert, Burns has four or five motels, including the **Days Inn Ponderosa Motel**. It has 52 ordinary but clean rooms that don't smell of disinfectant, and a swimming pool. ~ 577 West Monroe Street, Burns; 541-573-2047; www.daysinn.com. BUDGET.

The **Silver Spur Motel** offers 26 cozy and simple guest rooms with cable television, microwaves, refrigerators and coffee mak-

AUTHOR FAVORITE

For a real cowpoke experience, head to **Ponderosa Guest Ranch**, a 120,000-acre working cattle ranch that offers three-day and week-long vacations where visitors can ride, rope, drive cattle, brand calves, observe local elk and take part in other ranch activities. Accommodations are in rustic log cabins, each with private bathroom and a covered porch facing the sunset. There is also a main lodge with a lounge and jacuzzi. The rates include all meals and ranch activities. Three-day minimum stay. No guests under 18 years old. Closed mid-October through April. ~ Route 395, 35 miles north of Burns; 541-542-2403; www.ponderosaguestranch.com, e-mail ride@ponderosa-ranch.com. ULTRA-DELUXE.

ers. Pine furnishings, floral linens and wallpaper create a more pleasant, homey feel than the average motel. Guests have free access to a nearby health club and golf course. ~ 789 North Broadway Avenue, Burns; 541-573-2077, 800-400-2077, fax 541-573-3921; www.silverspurmotel.net. BUDGET.

◄ HIDDEN

Hotel Diamond is 54 miles southeast of Burns. Built in 1898 as a hotel, the wood structure serves as a point of departure for Malheur National Wildlife Refuge, Diamond Craters and the Pete French Round Barn Historical site. The hotel has five small, wood-trimmed rooms with shared baths and three rooms with private baths. Full breakfast included. ~ 10 Main Street, Diamond; 541-493-1898; www.central-oregon.com/hoteldiamond. MODERATE.

There are just a few places to stay in the area around Steens Mountain, Alvord Desert and Malheur and Harney lakes, so reservations are strongly recommended. A historic place is the 1924 **Frenchglen Hotel**, a classic ranch house with screened porch. Frenchglen has eight rooms decorated with rustic pine and patchwork quilts and has two shared baths. Breakfast, lunch and a family-style dinner are available. Closed mid-November to mid-March. ~ 39184 Route 205, Frenchglen; 541-493-2825; e-mail fghotel@centurytel.net. BUDGET.

Two miles north of Lakeview is **Hunter's Hot Springs Resort**, which owns one of Oregon's two geysers. Named Old Perpetual, it shoots water and steam 60 feet into the air every 90 seconds. The resort has a thermal pool, and the hot water is reputed to have healing powers. The 18 units are simply decorated in what the owner calls country style. The resort also offers a racquetball court. ~ Route 395 North, Lakeview; 541-947-4142, fax 541-947-2800. BUDGET.

DINING

Almost everyone's favorite place to eat in Burns is the **Pine Room Lounge** which specializes in steak and seafood. The family that owns this restaurant has a secret recipe for potato-dumpling soup, cuts all their own meat and makes their own bread. Closed Sunday and Monday. ~ 543 West Monroe Street, Burns; 541-573-2672. MODERATE TO ULTRA-DELUXE.

For a casual lunch or picnic fixings, a good bet is **Broadway Delicatessen Co.**, a bright, cheerful deli inside a historic quarried-rock storefront. The menu features made-to-order sandwiches on a choice of seven breads, pasta and potato salads, tossed green salads, a full espresso bar and daily soup specials. There are also house-made cheesecakes, bread pudding and other tempting desserts. Breakfast and lunch only. ~ 530 North Broadway, Burns; 541-573-7020. BUDGET.

SHOPPING

Unless you're a rockhound, souvenir shopping is likely to prove challenging in these parts. Perhaps your best bet is the gift shop at

Ontario's **Four Rivers Cultural Center**, where you'll find artworks and handmade gift items from the four cultures represented in the museum, as well as a large selection of adults' and children's books on Western history, American Indian and Japanese cultures, Japanese gardening and koi ponds. ~ 676 Southwest 5th Avenue, Ontario; 541-889-8191.

PARKS

MALHEUR NATIONAL WILDLIFE REFUGE At 187,000 acres, Malheur covers an interesting and diverse wildlife population and geological features. Malheur Lake is a major resting area for migratory birds on the Pacific Flyway. Fishing is permitted at Krumbo Reservoir. Malheur Field Station (541-493-2629) has dormitory and family housing and meals available. ~ Located 32 miles southeast of Burns on Route 205, then 6 miles on Princeton-Narrows Road; 541-493-2612.

HART MOUNTAIN NATIONAL ANTELOPE REFUGE This 275,000-acre refuge 65 miles northeast of Lakeview protects a large population of antelope, bighorn sheep, mule deer, coyotes, a variety of smaller animals and a bird population. Hart Mountain, the centerpiece of the refuge, rises to 8065 feet and has deep gorges, ridges and cliffs on the west side. The east side of the mountain climbs more gradually. For rockhounds, collections are limited to seven pounds per person. Fishing is permitted in Rock and Guano creeks depending on conditions. Restrooms and a visitors center are the only facilities. ~ Located 65 miles northeast of Lakeview on county roads off Routes 395 and 140; 541-947-3315; www.sheldon-hartmtn.fws.gov.

▲ Hot Springs Campground has 30 primitive sites (no fee).

Outdoor Adventures

RIVER RUNNING

In the Joseph area, **Cooley River Expeditions** provides raft and kayaking trips on the Deschutes, John Day, Owyhee and Klamath Rivers. ~ Joseph; 541-432-0461.

Some of the most challenging whitewater rapids anywhere can be found on the Owyhee River in southeastern Oregon's Malheur County. Among the outfitters offering raft and kayak trips on the Owyhee from April through May is **Oregon River Experiences.** ~ 18074 South Boone Court, Beavercreek; 503-632-6836, 800-827-1358; www.oregonriver.com. **Oregon Whitewater Adventures** offers five-day trips on the Owyhee. ~ 39620 Deerhorn Road, Springfield; 541-746-5422, 800-820-7238; www.oregonwhitewater.com.

For a list of other outfitters licensed to operate raft or float trips in Hells Canyon, write or call the **Wallawa Visitors Center.** ~ 88401 Route 82, Enterprise, OR 97828; 541-426-4978.

GOLF

Courses are scarce in eastern Oregon simply because there aren't that many people around. One of the few 18-hole golf courses in the northeastern region is the executive **Milton-Freewater Golf Course**, about 30 miles northeast of Pendleton. ~ 301 West Catherine Avenue, Milton-Freewater; 541-938-7284. The nine-hole **Echo Hills Golf Course** is par 36 and rather challenging, with hills and gullies. It's 23 miles northwest of Pendleton. ~ Take the Echo exit off Route 84; 541-376-8244. For18 holes, try the fairly flat but attractive course at **Pendleton Country Club.** ~ Route 395 between Pendleton and Pilot Rock; 541-443-4653.

South of Pendleton, the public, 18-hole **Baker City Golf Course** is a fairly easy course. ~ 2801 Indiana Avenue; 541-523-2358. Near Hells Canyon is the laidback, nine-hole **Alpine Meadows.** The par-72 course is surrounded by beautiful mountains. ~ 66098 Golf Course Road, Enterprise; 541-426-3246. Near the Idaho border is the 18-hole **Ontario Golf Course**, a 6700-yard course with six water holes. ~ Route 201, Ontario; 541-889-9022. **John Day Golf** is a challenging nine-hole course with hills and a sand-trap. ~ West Highway, John Day; 541-575-0170. The golf hub for Harney County in Southeastern Oregon is the nine-hole **Valley Golf Club.** ~ 345 Hines Boulevard/Route 20; 541-573-6251.

PACK TRIPS

The Eagle Cap Wilderness Area in the Wallowa Mountains is a popular location for horseback riding and overnight pack trips. **Eagle Cap Wilderness Pack Station** leads pack trips and shorter rides ranging from one hour to all day. ~ Route 1, Joseph; 541-432-4145. **Backcountry Outfitters** leads pack trips at a leisurely pace that leaves plenty of time for fishing, hunting or just relaxing. You can also arrange for special photography trips. Closed November through March. ~ P.O. Box 568, Union, OR 97883; 541-426-5908, 800-966-8080.

AUTHOR FAVORITE

Experience whitewater thrills on the Snake River in Northeastern Oregon, where the river cuts through walls of black basalt, forming Hells Canyon, the deepest gorge in the country. Spring is the best time to hit good whitewater, but be forewarned: classifications are arbitrary and the hard classes aren't necessarily the best. Watch water levels more closely than class. Operating from Memorial Day to mid-September, **Hells Canyon Adventures** offers wild whitewater-rafting adventures as well as gentle scenic trips through the canyon on a raft or jet boat. ~ Oxbow; 541-785-3352, 800-422-3568

Hurricane Creek Llama Treks arranges overnight pack trips with llamas through the Wallowas and Hells Canyon. ~ 63366 Pine Tree Road, Enterprise; 541-928-2850, 866-386-8735; www.hcltrek.com. **Wallowa Llamas** also provides llama pack trips here. ~ 36678 Allstead Lane, Halfway; 541-742-2961; www.wallowallamas.com. Several outfitters are licensed to lead overnight horse pack trips into the **Hells Canyon National Recreation Area** and **Eagle Cap Wilderness.** A few offer day rides and llama pack trips. For a list, contact park headquarters. ~ 88401 Route 82, Enterprise, OR 97828; 541-426-4978.

SKIING

Most of Eastern Oregon is too dry to offer good skiing, but there are a few exceptions, especially in the Wallowa Mountains. **Salt Creek Summit Winter Recreation Area** near Joseph offers downhill skiing at Ferguson Ridge as well as groomed cross-country ski trails and snowmobiling trails. ~ 541-426-5546.

Northwest of Baker City is **Ski Anthony Lakes**, which offers downhill skiing on an 8000-foot mountain plus cross-country trails, lessons, rentals and snowmobiling. ~ 541-856-3277; www.anthonylakes.com.

In Lake County off Route 31 near Lakeview is **Warner Canyon Ski Area**, which has uncrowded downhill and cross-country ski trails, a 35-mile snowmobile trail. Closed from March to mid-December, depending on the weather. ~ 541-947-6040.

BIKING

For the most part, automobile traffic is sparse in these regions, so bicyclists have little trouble finding long stretches of road that are practically deserted, and scenically beautiful. But they're also challenging and attract avid cross-country bicyclists, especially along Routes 3 and 86 in the Wallowa National Forest near Hells Canyon.

Routes have also been established along the Oregon Trail. One begins at Oxbow in Hells Canyon and follows Route 86 westward to **Halfway** and **Baker City**, then on Route 7 to Sumpter and through the **John Day** area before crossing the Cascades.

Bike Rentals Because of the remoteness of the trails here it's a good idea to bring your own gear. Otherwise, see if rentals are available at bicycle shops in cities and towns along your route.

HIKING

All distances listed for hiking trails are one way unless otherwise noted.

NORTHEASTERN OREGON The **Eagle Cap Wilderness** can be entered south of Enterprise and Joseph or from Lostine and has about a dozen major routes. One popular hike is from Wallowa Lake State Park (7.5 miles) to Ice Lake. The moderate trail is heavily used during the summer months.

The **Hells Canyon National Recreation Area** straddles the Snake River and offers some of the most rugged landscape in the canyon. About a dozen trails have been established here, with ratings from easy to difficult (although more of them tend to be difficult). The challenging **Western Rim Trail** (34 miles) gives great views of the canyon and has the advantage of going from the end of one Forest Service road to another. The **HC Reservoir Trail** (4.8 miles) runs along the river between Copper Creek and Leep Creek.

SOUTHEASTERN OREGON The **Sagehen Hill Nature Trail** is an informative microcosm of Southeastern Oregon's high-desert terrain. Located 16 miles west of Burns at the Sagehen Rest Stop on Route 20, the half-mile loop trail has interpretive stations identifying sagebrush, juniper, bitterbrush, buttercups, Mariposa lilies and other plant life. Along with great views of Steens Mountain to the southeast, the trail is a good place to see such birdlife as red-trailed hawks, sage grouse and golden eagles.

Transportation

CAR

Eastern Oregon is served by a network of roads that range from interstates to logging roads that have been paved by the Forest Service. **Route 97** serves as the north–south dividing line between the Cascade Mountains and the arid, rolling hills that undulate to the eastern boundary of the state.

Route 84 runs almost the entire length of the Columbia River Gorge in Oregon before swinging southeast at Hermiston and connecting Pendleton, La Grande and Baker City with Ontario on the Idaho border.

Another major highway is **Route 395**, starting south of the state border in California and connecting Lakeview, Burns, Penton and the Tri Cities, just across the Washington state line.

Route 26 is one of Oregon's loveliest drives. It runs from Astoria over the Coast Range to Portland, then over the Cascades at Mt. Hood into the desert at Prineville and through the John Day Fossil Beds National Monument to Ontario on the Snake River.

Certainly the loneliest major highway in the state is **Route 95**, which comes up from McDermitt, Nevada, to cross the Oregon desert for nearly 150 miles before arriving at the first town, Burns Junction. From there it heads northeast into Idaho.

AIR

The only scheduled air service here is at the **Eastern Oregon Regional Airport** at Pendleton, which is served by Horizon Air.

BUS

Eastern Oregon is served primarily by **Greyhound.** ~ 320 Southwest Court Street, Pendleton; 541-276-1551, 800-231-2222; www.greyhound.com. Also, **Amtrak** has a Boise-bound bus starting in Portland and calling on Pendleton, La Grande, Baker City and Ontario. ~ 800-872-7245; www.amtrak.com.

CAR RENTALS

The agencies at the Pendleton airport are **Budget Rent A Car** (800-527-0700) and **Hertz Rent A Car** (800-654-3131). Other, smaller airports served by scheduled airlines will have rental cars available, often by a local automobile dealer.

Index

Lodging Index

HOSTELS

LODGING SERVICES

Dining Index

HIDDEN GUIDES

Adventure travel or a relaxing vacation?—"Hidden" guidebooks are the only travel books in the business to provide detailed information on both. Aimed at environmentally aware travelers, our motto is "Where Vacations Meet Adventures." These books combine details on unique hotels, restaurants and sightseeing with information on camping, sports and hiking for the outdoor enthusiast.

PARADISE FAMILY GUIDES

Ideal for families traveling with kids of any age—toddlers to teenagers—Paradise Family Guides offer a blend of travel information unlike any other guides to the Hawaiian islands. With vacation ideas and tropical adventures that are sure to satisfy both action-hungry youngsters and relaxation-seeking parents, these guides meet the specific needs of each and every family member.

Ulysses Press books are available at bookstores everywhere. If any of the following titles are unavailable at your local bookstore, ask the bookseller to order them.

You can also order books directly from Ulysses Press
P.O. Box 3440, Berkeley, CA 94703
800-377-2542 or 510-601-8301
fax: 510-601-8307
www.ulyssespress.com
e-mail: ulysses@ulyssespress.com

HIDDEN GUIDEBOOKS

____ Hidden Arizona, $16.95
____ Hidden Bahamas, $14.95
____ Hidden Baja, $14.95
____ Hidden Belize, $15.95
____ Hidden Big Island of Hawaii, $13.95
____ Hidden Boston & Cape Cod, $14.95
____ Hidden British Columbia, $18.95
____ Hidden Cancún & the Yucatán, $16.95
____ Hidden Carolinas, $17.95
____ Hidden Coast of California, $18.95
____ Hidden Colorado, $15.95
____ Hidden Disneyland, $13.95
____ Hidden Florida, $18.95
____ Hidden Florida Keys & Everglades, $13.95
____ Hidden Georgia, $16.95
____ Hidden Guatemala, $16.95
____ Hidden Hawaii, $18.95
____ Hidden Idaho, $14.95
____ Hidden Kauai, $13.95
____ Hidden Los Angeles, $14.95
____ Hidden Maine, $15.95
____ Hidden Maui, $13.95
____ Hidden Miami, $14.95
____ Hidden Montana, $15.95
____ Hidden New England, $18.95
____ Hidden New Mexico, $15.95
____ Hidden New Orleans, $14.95
____ Hidden Oahu, $13.95
____ Hidden Oregon, $15.95
____ Hidden Pacific Northwest, $18.95
____ Hidden San Diego, $14.95
____ Hidden Salt Lake City, $14.95
____ Hidden San Francisco & Northern California, $18.95
____ Hidden Seattle, $13.95
____ Hidden Southern California, $18.95
____ Hidden Southwest, $19.95
____ Hidden Tahiti, $17.95
____ Hidden Tennessee, $16.95
____ Hidden Utah, $16.95
____ Hidden Walt Disney World, $13.95
____ Hidden Washington, $15.95
____ Hidden Wine Country, $13.95
____ Hidden Wyoming, $15.95

PARADISE FAMILY GUIDES

____ Paradise Family Guides: Kaua'i, $16.95
____ Paradise Family Guides: Maui, $16.95
____ Paradise Family Guides: Big Island of Hawai'i, $16.95

Mark the book(s) you're ordering and enter the total cost here ⇨ [ ]

California residents add 8.75% sales tax here ⇨ [ ]

Shipping, check box for your preferred method and enter cost here ⇨ [ ]

❑ BOOK RATE — FREE! FREE! FREE!
❑ PRIORITY MAIL/UPS GROUND — cost of postage
❑ UPS OVERNIGHT OR 2-DAY AIR — cost of postage

Billing, enter total amount due here and check method of payment ⇨ [ ]

❑ CHECK ❑ MONEY ORDER
❑ VISA/MASTERCARD ____________________ EXP. DATE ________

NAME ____________________ PHONE ____________

ADDRESS ________________________________

CITY ________________ STATE ______ ZIP ________

MONEY-BACK GUARANTEE ON DIRECT ORDERS PLACED THROUGH ULYSSES PRESS.

ABOUT THE AUTHOR

MARIA LENHART has been a freelance writer specializing in travel for two decades. She has contributed to *Travel/Holiday*, *Travel & Leisure*, *Odyssey*, *Business Travel News*, the *Christian Science Monitor* and many other publications.

ABOUT THE ILLUSTRATOR

MITTIE CUETARA graduated from The School of the Museum of Fine Arts in Boston. She lives in Oakland, California, and does freelance illustration, specializing in architectural and landscape drawing.